EU PROSPECTUS LAW

Pierre Schammo provides a detailed analysis of EU prospectus law (and the 2010 amendments to the Prospectus Directive) and assesses the new rules governing the European Securities and Markets Authority, including the case law on the delegation of powers to regulatory agencies. In a departure from previous work on securities regulation, the focus is on EU decision-making in the securities field. He examines the EU's approach to prospectus disclosure enforcement and its implementation at Member State level, and breaks new ground on regulatory competition in the securities field by providing a 'law in context' analysis of the Prospectus Directive and its negotiations.

DR PIERRE SCHAMMO is a lecturer in law at the University of Manchester. He was previously a research fellow in European financial and corporate law at the British Institute of International and Comparative Law.

INTERNATIONAL CORPORATE LAW AND FINANCIAL MARKET REGULATION

Recent years have seen an upsurge of change and reform in corporate law and financial market regulation internationally as the corporate and institutional investor sector increasingly turns to the international financial markets. This follows large-scale institutional and regulatory reform after a series of international corporate governance and financial disclosure scandals exemplified by the collapse of Enron in the US. There is now a great demand for analysis in this area from the academic, practitioner, regulatory and policy sectors.

The *International Corporate Law and Financial Market Regulation* series will respond to that demand by creating a critical mass of titles which will address the need for information and high quality analysis in this fast developing area.

EU PROSPECTUS LAW

New perspectives on regulatory competition in securities markets

PIERRE SCHAMMO

CAMBRIDGE
UNIVERSITY PRESS

CAMBRIDGE UNIVERSITY PRESS
Cambridge, New York, Melbourne, Madrid, Cape Town,
Singapore, São Paulo, Delhi, Tokyo, Mexico City

Cambridge University Press
The Edinburgh Building, Cambridge CB2 8RU, UK

Published in the United States of America by Cambridge University Press, New York

www.cambridge.org
Information on this title: www.cambridge.org/9780521517652

First published 2011

Printed in the United Kingdom at the University Press, Cambridge

A catalogue record for this publication is available from the British Library

Library of Congress Cataloguing in Publication data
Schammo, Pierre, 1976–
EU prospectus law : new perspectives on regulatory competition in securities
markets / Pierre Schammo.
p. cm. – (International corporate law and financial market regulation)
Includes bibliographical references and index.
ISBN 978-0-521-51765-2 (hardback)
1. Securities–European Union countries. 2. Disclosure of information–Law
and legislation–European Union countries. 3. Prospectus writing–Law
and legislation–European Union countries. I. Title.
KJE2247.S386 2011
346.24′0666–dc22
2011008026

ISBN 978-0-521-51765-2 Hardback

Fir meng Elteren

CONTENTS

PREFACE AND ACKNOWLEDGEMENTS

It is no exaggeration to say that EU securities regulation is one of the fastest growing fields in European law. Once relatively unexceptionable, it has moved to the forefront of internal market regulation. The establishment of a European System of Financial Supervision ('ESFS') testifies to both the EU's efforts and ambitions in this field. For those writing on securities regulation, the pace with which EU securities regulation develops and evolves has become something of a challenge. But it also presents an opportunity to work in a contemporary field and to witness and experience European decision-making and its interactions with national legal systems at first hand.

I finished the manuscript of this book shortly after agreement between Union institutions had been reached on a new ESFS. The fate of the Committee of European Securities Regulators (CESR) was sealed for good and the establishment of a new European Securities and Markets Authority (ESMA) was being awaited with great expectations. The year 2010 also saw a number of noteworthy reforms taking shape in the prospectus field. These reforms also offered new opportunities to map and examine these developments, but also to revisit earlier work on regulatory competition which I had completed as part of my D.Phil. thesis in Oxford and which is reflected in the final part of this book.

In writing this book, I have been fortunate to benefit from the comments and thoughts of many people. I owe a debt of gratitude to those practitioners, EU or national officials who agreed to be interviewed despite sometimes busy working schedules and who willingly shared views and thoughts on securities regulation. I would especially like to thank David Wright who has taught me an endless amount about the EU and how it works, and Hubert Grignon Dumoulin for his insight on financial markets and his invaluable comments on various draft chapters.

In the academic world, I am indebted to Stephen Weatherill, my former D.Phil supervisor in Oxford, for his endless encouragement and support. I am very grateful to Joseph McCahery for all his advice and support, and to Jeremy Richardson for challenging me to look 'beyond the law'. Niamh Moloney has given me much helpful advice over the years for which I would like to thank her as well. Thanks are also due to Eilís Ferran, Dora Kostakopoulou, Panos Koutrakos and my colleagues in Manchester.

My final words of gratitude are for the persons that are closest; my family and Ayaka for her patience, love and inspiration to bring this book to completion.

I have attempted to state the law as at 28 February 2011. Any error or mistakes are my responsibility.

Pierre Schammo
March 2011

ABBREVIATIONS

AMF	Autorité des marchés financiers
CARD	Consolidated Admissions and Reporting Directive (2001/34/EC)
CESR	Committee of European Securities Regulators
CJEU	Court of Justice of the European Union
Coreper	Comité des représentants permanents
EEA	European Economic Area
EP	European Parliament
ESA	European Supervisory Authority
ESC	European Securities Committee
ESFS	European System of Financial Supervision
ESMA	European Securities and Markets Authority
ESMAReg	ESMA Regulation (EU No. 1095/2010)
ESRB	European Systemic Risk Board
FESCO	Federation of European Securities Commissions
FSA	Financial Services Authority
FSAP	Financial Services Action Plan
FSA-LR	Listing Rules made by the FSA
FSA-PR	Prospectus Rules made by the FSA
GAAP	Generally Accepted Accounting Principles
ISA	Israel Securities Authority
LPD	Listing Particulars Directive (80/390/EEC) (repealed)
MAD	Market Abuse Directive (2003/06/EC)
MiFID	Markets in Financial Instruments Directive (2004/39/EC)
PAD	Prospectus Amending Directive (2010/73/EU)
PD	Prospectus Directive (2003/71/EC)
POD	Public Offers Directive (89/298/EEC) (repealed)
PR	Prospectus Regulation ((EC) No 809/2004)
RG	Règlement Général of the AMF
TD	Transparency Directive (2004/109/EC)
TEU	Treaty on European Union
TFEU	Treaty on the Functioning of the European Union
UKLA	UK Listing Authority

TABLE OF CASES

Opinions of the Court

TABLE OF LEGISLATION

Consolidated Version of the Treaty on European Union [2010] OJ C83/1

Consolidated Version of the Treaty on the Functioning of the European Union [2010] OJ C83/1

Council Directive (EEC) 80/390 coordinating the requirements for the drawing-up, scrutiny and distribution of the listing particulars to be published for the admission of securities to official stock exchange listing [1980] OJ L100/1 (repealed)

Council Directive (EEC) 89/298 of 17 April 1989 coordinating the requirements for the drawing-up, scrutiny and distribution of the prospectus to be published when transferable securities are offered to the public [1989] OJ L124/8 (repealed)

Directive (EC) 2001/34 of the European Parliament and of the Council of 28 May 2001 on the admission of securities to official stock exchange listing and on information to be published on those securities [2001] OJ L184/1

Regulation (EC) No 1606/2002 of the European Parliament and of the Council of 19 July 2002 on the application of international accounting standards [2002] OJ L243/1

Directive (EC) 2003/6 of the European Parliament and of the Council of 28 January 2003 on insider dealing and market manipulation [2003] OJ L96/16

Directive (EC) 2003/71 of the European Parliament and of the Council of 4 November 2003 on the prospectus to be published when securities are offered to the public or admitted to trading and amending Directive 2001/34/EC [2003] OJ L345/64 (as amended)

Directive (EC) 2004/39 of the European Parliament and of the Council of 21 April 2004 on markets in financial instruments amending Council Directives 85/611/EEC and 93/6/EEC and Directive 2000/12/EC of the European Parliament and of the Council and repealing Council Directive 93/22/EEC [2004] L145/1

Commission Regulation (EC) 809/2004 of 29 April 2004 implementing Directive 2003/71/EC of the European Parliament and of the Council as regards information contained in prospectuses as well as the format, incorporation by reference and publication of such prospectuses and dissemination of advertisements [2004] OJ L149/1

Directive (EC) 2004/109 of the European Parliament and of the Council of 15 December 2004 on the harmonisation of transparency requirements in relation to information about issuers whose securities are admitted to trading on a regulated market and amending Directive 2001/34/EC [2004] L390/38

Commission Regulation (EC) No 1569/2007 of 21 December 2007 establishing a mechanism for the determination of equivalence of accounting standards applied by third country issuers of securities pursuant to Directives 2003/71/EC and 2004/109/EC of the European Parliament and of the Council [2007] L340/66

Regulation (EC) 216/2008 of the European Parliament and of the Council of 20 February 2008 on common rules in the field of civil aviation and establishing a European Aviation Safety Agency (...) [2008] OJ L79/1

Commission Regulation (EC) No 1289/2008 of 12 December 2008 amending Commission Regulation (EC) No 809/2004 implementing Directive 2003/71/EC of the European Parliament and of the Council as regards elements related to prospectuses and advertisements [2008] OJ L340/17

Directive (EU) 2010/73 of the European Parliament and of the Council of 24 November 2010 amending Directives 2003/71/EC on the prospectus to be published when securities are offered to the public or admitted to trading and 2004/109/EC on the harmonisation of transparency requirements in relation to information about issuers whose securities are admitted to trading on a regulated market [2010] OJ L327/1

Regulation (EU) No 1095/2010 of the European Parliament and of the Council of 24 November 2010 establishing a European Supervisory Authority (European Securities and Markets Authority), amending Decision No 716/2009/EC and repealing Commission Decision 2009/77/EC [2010] OJ L331/84

FSA Prospectus Rules

FSA Listing Rules

FSA Enforcement Guide

France

Règlement Général

Code Monétaire et Financier

Introduction

Prospectus regulation is one of the core pillars of European securities regulation. The seeds of the prospectus regime, as we know it today, were sown by the Financial Services Action Plan and the Risk Capital Action Plan which foresaw many other measures that are nowadays pillars of the EU securities and financial markets framework.[1] In 2003, the call to modernise the 'Directives on prospectuses'[2] led to the adoption of a single directive, the Prospectus Directive ('PD'). As a Lamfalussy directive, it was given flesh by implementing legislation and, in time, by soft-law measures. Together, these measures put in place a more comprehensive regime of rules and disclosure requirements that apply to persons who wish to make a public offer or seek admission of securities to trading on a regulated market in the EU.

This book examines the prospectus disclosure regime and the institutional choices that underpin it. The PD was designed to succeed where earlier directives had failed. A new, improved, mutual recognition system – the so-called 'single passport' system – was fashioned to facilitate cross-border capital raising. A more aggressive form of 'maximum harmonisation' was supposed to bring about uniformity and, thereby, greater consolidation of rule-making competence at EU level. Since 2003, the regime and the institutional framework that governs it have developed. The directive was only recently amended in order to make it more effective and to ensure that the new European Securities and Markets Authority ('ESMA') has all the necessary powers to act in the prospectus field. The Lamfalussy framework, which deals with rulemaking, supervision and enforcement, has seen noteworthy changes as well. The Lisbon Treaty

[1] European Commission, 'Financial services: implementing the framework for financial markets: action plan' (COM(1999) 232, 11 May 1999) (the 'FSAP'), http://ec.europa.eu/internal_market/finances/docs/actionplan/index/action_en.pdf; European Commission, 'Risk capital: a key to job creation in the European Union' (April 1998) (the 'RCAP'), http://ec.europa.eu/internal_market/securities/docs/risk_capital/sec98_552_en.pdf.

[2] 'FSAP' 22. See also 'RCAP' 23.

replaced the old comitology system, which, *inter alia*, governed decision-making at Lamfalussy Level 2, by new rules on delegated and implementing acts. What is more, the worldwide financial crisis gave, after some initial hesitations, the necessary impetus to a new round of reforms which ultimately led to important institutional changes, including the establishment of a new European System of Financial Supervision ('ESFS'). ESMA replaced the Committee of European Securities Regulators ('CESR') in January 2011. In short, the EU has firmly established itself as the main actor shaping prospectus disclosure regulation while collective securities actors such as ESMA are the main force for bringing about consistency in the application of EU securities legislation.

It is against this background that the book pursues two lines of enquiry, tied together by a common interest in European decision-making in the securities field.[3] It first examines the substantive law on prospectus disclosure, including the framework that governs its creation, implementation and enforcement. Often presented as a 'maximum harmonisation' directive, the reality is more complex: first, the scope and boundaries of the maximum harmonisation regime are not necessarily obvious; second, maximum harmonisation is only one facet of a regime which uses a mixture of regulatory techniques, including a form of equivalence-based regulation; third, the lack of an autonomous enforcement apparatus[4] forces the EU to rely on the enforcement efforts of national actors and on collective securities actors such as ESMA to keep order among competent authorities. Thus, although the EU legislature is the main force shaping the regulatory regime,[5] Member State competence persists in important areas. One such area is the approval of prospectuses. One of the main messages of this book concerns this approval system. It fulfils, for better or worse, an enforcement function, but curiously, it currently also allows safeguarding decision-making powers elsewhere; for example, in the field of equivalence-based regulation.

The second theme of this book concerns regulatory competition. As a subject of study, its interest has been in sharp decline. Calls in favour of

[3] I have gained much insight on EU decision-making from Fritz Scharpf's work on policy-making (e.g., F. Scharpf, *Governing in Europe – Effective and Democratic?* (Oxford University Press, 1999); F. Scharpf, *Games Real Actors Play – Actor-Centered Institutionalism in Policy Research* (Westview Press, Boulder CO, 1997)).

[4] By 'enforcement', I mean mostly enforcement of EU rules and regulations against issuers and other market actors.

[5] For a more detailed analysis of the changes to the regulatory landscape in financial markets, see N. Moloney, *EC Securities Regulation* (Oxford University Press, 2008).

regulatory competition as an institutional arrangement in the securities markets field have mostly been silenced. The mainstream literature on securities regulation has mostly moved on, turning for inspiration and insights to new fields of interest such as law and finance, a scholarship that is more empirically grounded, but still controversial in its claims and conclusions.[6] And yet, the interest in regulatory competition is not exhausted. Indeed, the thesis of this book is that regulatory competition remains a subject of interest in the securities field. But there is a need to conceptualise it differently by engaging in a more meaningful manner with decision-making at European level. In the law and economics literature, which has dominated the study of regulatory competition and securities regulation, decision-making at EU level has mostly been outside the scope of enquiry. It has been treated as a 'black-box' and little time and effort has been invested in describing and examining 'what happens in the box, who acts and how'.[7] Deterministic assumptions about the behaviour of policy actors at EU level, with no further enquiry into the empirical reality of decision-making at this level, have left the securities literature with little useful insight. Likewise, harmonisation has been treated as an outcome or worse, a *fait accompli*, instead of being seen as a process involving actors with interests and ideas who are meant to find common agreement over sets of rules and arrangements. Law and finance scholarship has also been mostly unconcerned about the mechanics of European decision-making. Wide-scale empirical studies have admittedly shed new light on distinct legal systems and enforcement mechanisms, but here too decision-making at EU level has generally been sidestepped.[8]

Hence, there is a need for a more grounded approach which integrates European decision-making more closely into regulatory competition studies and pays due attention to the behaviour and decision-making of collective securities markets actors.[9] In short, the question is not whether regulatory competition is 'efficient', but how it affects EU decision-making

[6] See especially the work by La Porta, Lopez-de-Silanes, Shleifer and Vishny which I will discuss in Chapters 5 and 7.

[7] I borrow the phrase from C. Radaelli, 'The puzzle of regulatory competition' (2004) 24 *Journal of Public Policy* 1, 19.

[8] See Chapter 5 for details.

[9] In developing this perspective, I have, *inter alia*, benefited from Nicolaïdis's work on 'managed mutual recognition'. See e.g., K. Nicolaïdis, 'Regulatory cooperation and managed mutual recognition: elements of a strategic model' in G. Bermann, M. Herdegen and P. Lindseth (eds.), *Transatlantic Regulatory Cooperation – Legal Problems and Political Prospects* (Oxford University Press, 2000) 571.

and EU regulatory output in the prospectus field. The book attempts to work towards answers, sometimes in a descriptive manner, sometimes in a more analytical fashion, but at all times with the aim of gaining useful insights for the literature on securities regulation. In this process, old themes will be revisited (e.g., Hirschman's 'threat of exit' hypothesis)[10] and new themes will emerge, such as the discursive dimension of regulatory competition at EU level. The process of implementation of European rules, which in many respects represents the ultimate test of the effectiveness of EU law, will not be ignored either.

The various themes that the book pursues are developed in five parts and the next eleven chapters. Chapter 1 begins by introducing the different actors that participate in the creation, implementation and enforcement of EU prospectus law, and the formal institutional setting in which they act and interact. It sets the scene for the following parts that deal, in turn, with prospectus disclosure regulation, prospectus disclosure enforcement and regulatory competition. Chapter 2 is an introductory chapter on prospectus disclosure regulation. It discusses the main questions that prospectus disclosure has raised in the literature. Chapters 3 and 4 examine the two main disclosure models under the EU regime: first, an ordinary disclosure model based on 'maximum harmonisation' disclosure items; and second, a more illusive regime based on equivalence provisions. Chapter 5 is the first chapter that deals with enforcement. Its aim is to review the debate on enforcement and to present the issues that require attention. Chapter 6 continues the examination of enforcement by considering the EU's approach to prospectus disclosure enforcement and the arrangements that the EU legislature has adopted. Chapter 7 looks at the application and implementation of these arrangements at national level and, for that purpose, turns to prospectus disclosure enforcement in France and the UK. Chapter 8 introduces the part of the book on regulatory competition. It examines the debate on regulatory competition and its underpinnings. Chapter 9 defines the perspective on regulatory competition which this book seeks to explore. Chapter 10 is the empirical part of this study. In an effort to examine the propositions and suggestions of the previous chapter, it turns to the negotiations of the PD. The book ends with a conclusion in Chapter 11 which summarises earlier findings and makes a set of proposals for the future.

10 A. Hirschman, *Exit, Voice and Loyalty – Responses to Decline in Firms, Organizations, and States* (Harvard University Press, Cambridge MA, 1970).

PART I

Prospectus disclosure in a wider institutional context

1

Actors and institutions

I Introduction

This chapter introduces the different actors that participate in the creation, implementation and enforcement of EU prospectus law and the formal institutional setting in which they act and interact. Actors include policy- and rule-making actors such as the European Commission, the European Parliament ('EP') and the Council, but also committees such as the European Securities Committee ('ESC'); collective actors such as the former Committee of European Securities Regulators ('CESR') and its successor, the European Securities and Markets Authority ('ESMA'); and national actors – competent authorities, in EU jargon – such as the UK Financial Services Authority ('FSA') or the French *Autorité des marchés financiers* ('AMF').

The institutional framework is, meanwhile, made of rules, requirements and procedures that actors must observe when choosing between different regulatory, supervisory and enforcement arrangements. They mostly spring from the EU's founding Treaties, which were reshaped in 2009 as a result of the entry into force of the Lisbon Treaty, and from the European Court's interpretation of EU primary law – think of cases such as *Meroni* or *Romano*.[1] In the securities sector, it is common to identify the institutional framework with the Lamfalussy process[2] whose four-level approach not only addresses rule-making, but also deals with the implementation, application and enforcement of EU legislation. The Lamfalussy process did not require Treaty changes and its arrangements merely reflect what is, as a matter of law, permissible within the constitutional boundaries set

[1] Case 9/56 *Meroni v High Authority* [1958] ECR 133; Case 98/80 *Romano v Institut national d'assurance maladie-invalidité* [1981] ECR 1241.

[2] The Lamfalussy approach was the brainchild of the Lamfalussy Committee, a group of experts set up at the request of Ecofin Ministers in July 2000. See 'Final Report of the Committee of Wise Men on the Regulation of European Securities Markets' (Brussels 15 February 2001), http://ec.europa.eu/internal_market/securities/docs/lamfalussy/wise-men/final-report-wise-men_en.pdf (hereinafter, the 'Lamfalussy Report').

by the Treaties. As a result, the Treaties shape the Lamfalussy process; it changes and evolves in sync with them. It is also affected by institutional and regulatory reforms that take place within the EU's constitutional framework, such as, for instance, the recent reforms that established a European System of Financial Supervision ('ESFS') and new collective actors such as ESMA. As we will see later, the ESFS refashioned, *inter alia*, Lamfalussy Level 3, blurring, by the same token, the distinction between hitherto different levels of decision-making. What is more, as a procedural approach that has no constitutional status, the Lamfalussy approach is not a source of substantive power for actors. The competence and powers of competent authorities, for instance, the main actors involved in enforcing EU prospectus law, are defined by national legislation.

This chapter proceeds as follows. Section II begins with policy and rule-making actors and examines the arrangements governing their decision-making. Section III deals with collective securities markets actors, i.e., the (former) CESR and ESMA. Section IV, turns to national financial markets authorities – competent authorities – and especially to two of the most prominent authorities, the AMF and FSA. Section V concludes by drawing lessons with respect to the pattern of institutional change in the securities field.

II Policy- and rule-making actors

As mentioned in the introductory section, in examining which actors are involved in prospectus regulation and how policies and rules are made in the securities sector, the Lamfalussy four-level approach provides a starting point. Under the Lamfalussy process, as originally agreed, each of the four levels corresponds to a specific level of competence. Framework principles – that is 'core political principles, the essential elements of each [legislative] proposal'[3] – are adopted at Level 1 in the form of directives or regulations through a legislative procedure. At Level 2, these Level 1 principles are given flesh by detailed implementing measures. Level 3 seeks to ensure consistency in the implementation and application of EU rules. Level 4 focuses on the enforcement of EU rules against non-compliant Member States. The ESFS introduced noticeable changes to the Lamfalussy four-level approach. Thus, although policy- and rule-making continue being within the purview of levels 1 and 2, following the adoption of the ESFS, the point is somewhat in need of a reassessment.

[3] 'Lamfalussy Report' 22.

As we will see in section III, ESMA participates more vigorously in the creation of binding standards which are endorsed by the Commission as delegated or implementing acts.[4] But for now I will skip over ESMA's role and concentrate on the role of EU institutions at Lamfalussy Level 1 and Level 2. These levels are governed by distinct decision-making procedures and, as mentioned, involve different actors.

A *Level 1 decision-making*

At Level 1, rule-making is governed by the ordinary legislative procedure,[5] the former co-decision procedure under the EC Treaty. It is the standard legislative procedure for the adoption of internal market legislation under the Treaties and involves the European Commission, the Council (in one of its different configurations) and the EP. Under the ordinary legislative procedure, the decision-making process is effectively divided into different 'readings' and requires the Council and the EP to agree on a common text following a proposal by the European Commission.[6] This process can involve up to two readings and might be followed by conciliation and a third reading if the Council and the EP cannot reach agreement after the second reading.[7] Conciliation marks the final attempt to find agreement between the institutions. The conciliation committee will consist of Council members (or their representatives) and representatives of the EP.[8] The European Commission is meant to facilitate agreement. If the

[4] I will examine the role of ESMA separately hereinafter. But already worth noting is that ESMA cannot adopt these standards autonomously. To make them legally binding, the Commission must endorse them. These standards are conceptually different from 'ordinary' delegated and implementing acts that are adopted at Level 2, although they have, in fact, the same constitutional bases (TFEU Arts 290 and 291).

[5] TFEU Art 294.

[6] TFEU Art 289(1). Note that the Lisbon Treaty allows, in some specified cases, the ordinary legislative procedure to be launched following an initiative of a group of Member States or the EP, or following a recommendation from the European Central Bank, or following a request by the Court of Justice or the European Investment Bank (TFEU 289(4)).

[7] According to TFEU Art 294, conciliation is averted at second reading if the EP agrees with the Council's position (known as a 'common position'), or if the EP fails to take a decision, or finally if it rejects it outright. In the latter case, however, the outcome is different, as the proposal is deemed to be rejected. If the EP adopts amendments to the common position, the Council needs to approve them (in which case, the proposal is passed). If the Council does not approve them, conciliation ensues. Legislative proposals can, of course, already be adopted at first reading, but it presupposes that the Council agrees with the EP's position on the Commission's proposal (or agrees outright with the Commission's text in the case where the EP has left the Commission's proposal unchanged).

[8] TFEU Art 294(10).

committee is successful in hammering out an agreement, the agreed text will still require adoption by the Council and the EP. If conciliation fails, or if the Council or the EP does not adopt the agreed text, the legislation fails.

Like the co-decision procedure, the ordinary legislative procedure can be time-intensive, complex and cumbersome. It not only requires agreement between institutions, but also between Member States within the Council which may involve lengthy and intricate negotiations.[9] National interests play naturally an important part in this process. In order to facilitate decision-making, the Council relies on committees which operate beneath it and help it to deal with its work and decision-making load.[10] These committees include the Committee of Permanent Representatives or *Comité des représentants permanents* (Coreper) in which Member States are represented by senior Member State officials and which prepares the work of the Council.[11] They also include a whole network of working groups attended by Member State officials and experts (e.g., national regulators) who work on legislative proposals.[12] One of the advantages of this system is that, in practice, most matters can be resolved in advance of Council meetings. Resolved matters are known as 'A' points on the Council agenda, as opposed to 'B' points on which Council members will need to find agreement.[13]

The functioning of the EP depends similarly on delegation and work in committees. Committees consider legislative proposals, propose amendments by drafting reports and resolutions which are submitted to

[9] The voting rules are somewhat complex. Within the Council, Member States must vote by qualified majority (TEU Art 16(3)). But Council members must act unanimously at first reading where amendments to the Commission's text are tabled which the Commission decides not to endorse (TFEU Art 293(1)). Likewise, Council members must act unanimously at second reading where they vote on EP amendments that the Commission does not endorse (TFEU Art 294(9)). The EP meanwhile votes by simple majority at first reading. At second reading, the EP's plenary can only reject the Council's position (the common position) or adopt amendments to it, by a majority of its component members (Art 294(7)).

[10] T. Christiansen, 'The Council of Ministers: facilitating interaction and developing actorness in the EU' in J. Richardson (ed.), *European Union – Power and policy-making* (Routledge, Abingdon, 2006) 147, 161–2. See also F. Hayes-Renshaw and H. Wallace, *The Council of Ministers* (Palgrave Macmillan, Basingstoke, 2006) 68–100; A. Arnull *et al.*, *European Union Law* (Sweet & Maxwell, London, 2006) 34ff.

[11] TEU Art 16(7).

[12] Christiansen, 'The Council of Ministers: facilitating interaction and developing actorness in the EU' 161.

[13] *Ibid.*, 162.

the plenary session of the European Parliament in 'more or less a "take it or leave it" form'.[14] Within the committee itself, most of the work is entrusted to the designated *rapporteur* who, if politically and technically skilled, can be a powerful individual in the Parliament and during inter-institutional negotiations.[15] The latter often take place in 'trilogues',[16] i.e., informal contacts between designated representatives of the Council, the EP and the Commission that allow them to sound out the space for bargaining well in advance of reaching the conciliation stage.[17] Trilogues have proven to be an essential and effective means for the institutions to expedite decision-making and reach agreement. Indeed, the recent deal on the European System of Financial Supervision illustrates the point perfectly, as the institutions were able to reach agreement at first reading – a remarkable outcome given the size of the reforms – after having hammered out an inter-institutional agreement over the package of measures in a series of trilogues in September 2010.

Hence, delegation, i.e., work in committees and, especially, trilogues, contribute significantly to facilitating agreement within or among EU institutions, especially when there is political will and momentum to adopt reforms. But for reasons that will be discussed in more detail in Chapter 9, the capacity of EU decision-making processes to produce *effective* solutions cannot be taken as a given. The Lamfalussy Committee sought to address problems with decision-making under the co-decision procedure by calling for yet more delegation of decision-making. In other words, it recommended delegating decision-making to a subordinate level which it branded 'Level 2' of the Lamfalussy process.

[14] S. Hix, *The Political System of the European Union* (Palgrave Macmillan, Basingstoke, 2005) 93 noting further that '[a]mendments to the proposed committee resolutions can be made in the full plenary, but without the backing of a committee and the EP party support that goes along with this, amendments are less likely to be adopted by the parliament'.

[15] See on this G. Benedetto, 'Rapporteurs as legislative entrepreneurs: the dynamics of the codecision procedure in Europe's Parliament' (2005) 12 *Journal of European Public Policy* 67.

[16] See for details European Parliament, Council and Commission 'Joint Declaration on Practical Arrangements for the Codecision Procedure (Article 251 of the EC Treaty)' [2007] OJ C145/5.

[17] See J. Peterson and E. Bomberg, *Decision-making in the European Union* (Macmillan Press, Basingstoke, 1999) 35 ('[t]he difficulty of negotiating in formal conciliation committees puts a premium on such forums which facilitate informal bargaining').

B *Level 2 decision-making*

Before the entry into force of the Lisbon Treaty, decision-making at Level 2 was known as comitology decision-making.[18] The Commission, assisted by a comitology committee, the European Securities Committee, whose meetings were attended by 'high-level' Member State representatives and presided over by the European Commission,[19] adopted detailed rules and measures in order to give flesh to Level 1 rules.[20] The entry into force of the Lisbon Treaty introduced significant changes. Before examining the new rules, I will begin by discussing comitology decision-making prior to the entry into force of the Lisbon Treaty, as it bears witness to the inter-institutional issues involved with such delegated decision-making.

1 Comitology prior to the entry into force of the Lisbon Treaty

Comitology decision-making has long been a source of inter-institutional discord,[21] with each institution seeking to protect its interests (and Member States' interests, in the case of the Council). The EP has had the hardest feelings for comitology. Before the entry into force of the Lisbon Treaty, the power to entrust the Commission with the adoption of implementing measures flowed from Article 202 EC which allowed the Council to entrust the Commission with powers to implement the rules which it adopted. Because of the wording of Article 202, the EP's claim to be involved in comitology decision-making was left open to challenge by other institutions.[22] But as the EP, as an institution, grew stronger, it began increasingly to assert its position. It only agreed to support the

[18] The literature on comitology is impressive. See e.g., C. Joerges and E. Vos (eds.), *EU Committees: Social Regulation, Law and Politics* (Hart, Oxford, 1999); E. Vos, '50 years of European integration, 45 years of comitology' (Maastricht Faculty of Law Working Papers, 2009–3), http://papers.ssrn.com/sol3/papers.cfm?abstract_id=1345729; K. St Clair Bradley, 'Halfway house: the 2006 comitology reforms and the European Parliament' (2008) 31 *West European Politics* 837; C. Joerges and J. Neyer, 'From intergovernmental bargaining to deliberative political processes: the constitutionalisation of comitology' (1997) 3 *European Law Journal* 273; E. Vos, 'The rise of committees' (1997) 3 *European Law Journal* 210; NewGov (J. Almer), 'The reform of comitology and the parallel reform of the European financial services sector' (ref. 7/D07c, December 2006), www.eu-newgov.org.

[19] For details, see Commission Decision of 6 June 2001 establishing the European Securities Committee [2001] L191/45 (as amended), Art 3.

[20] For details, see 'Lamfalussy Report' 28–31.

[21] See generally on this Vos, '50 years of European Integration'; Bradley, 'Halfway House'; NewGov, 'The Reform of Comitology'.

[22] For a detailed analysis, see Bradley, 'Halfway House' 838–840.

Lamfalussy approach, for instance, after being given a number of high-level assurances by the Commission on, *inter alia*, the transparency of the comitology decision-making process, and after the Commission agreed to other measures such as a three-month period for the Parliament to provide an opinion on draft implementing measures and committed itself 'to take the utmost account of the Parliament's position'.[23] The EP used various other means to manage comitology. For example, it used its budgetary powers, by starting to hold back funding for comitology committees, in order to make progress on the adoption of a new comitology procedure, the so-called regulatory procedure with scrutiny or PRAC (*procédure de réglementation avec contrôle*).[24] It also used the co-decision procedure and its power to oppose legislation under co-decision as a means to pressure the Council into new comitology reforms.[25] But the Parliament's most targeted way of managing comitology was the use of so-called 'sunset clauses'. These clauses essentially set a time limit to the delegation of implementing powers to the Commission, thereby forcing the Commission to periodically ask the EU legislature to renew its implementing powers. Tensions between institutions were somewhat diffused in 2006 when finally the PRAC was adopted which became the main Level 2 decision-making procedure, as far as Lamfalussy legislation was concerned.[26] The procedure was somewhat tortuous.[27] Under the PRAC, the main actors involved in decision-making were the Commission and the ESC, as the relevant comitology committee in the securities field. But the Council and the Parliament also had rights. Indeed, the main feature of the PRAC was that it distributed powers more evenly between the Council and the EP. Essentially, if after the Commission had submitted its draft implementing measures to the comitology committee, the latter issued a positive opinion, the Council and the European Parliament were given equal (but limited) powers to oppose the draft measures. They could claim that

[23] Statement by Romano Prodi, www.europarl.europa.eu/comparl/econ/lamfalussy_process/ep_position/default.htm.

[24] See European Parliament, 'Report on the draft Council Decision amending Decision 1999/468/EC laying down the procedures for the exercise of implementing powers conferred on the Commission' (A6–0236/2006, 3 July 2006) 8.

[25] G. Schusterschitz and S. Kotz, 'The comitology reform of 2006' (2007) 3 *European Constitutional Law Review* 68, 76 (referring in this context to the Eight Company law Directive and the Capital Requirements Directive); Bradley, 'Halfway House' 844.

[26] Council Decision of 17 July 2006 amending Decision 1999/468/EC laying down the procedures for the exercise of implementing powers conferred on the Commission [2006] OJ L200/11.

[27] Art 5a Council Decision of 28 June 1999 [1999] OJ L 184/23 (as amended).

the Commission had gone beyond its implementing powers; that the draft was not compatible 'with the aim or the content of the basic instrument'; or that the principles of subsidiarity or proportionality had not been satisfied.[28] If the committee did not issue a positive opinion, or failed to issue an opinion altogether, the Commission had to submit a proposal regarding the measures to the Council who could decide to oppose or adopt it. If the Council contemplated doing the latter (or if it did not act within the prescribed time period), the EP had the final say: it had the right to oppose the proposed measures, but only on the grounds mentioned above.

The adoption of the PRAC represented a noteworthy achievement for the EP. It gave the EP greater powers over Lamfalussy Level 2 decision-making. As part of the deal, the EP agreed that it was best not to insist on sunset clauses.[29]

2 Delegated and implementing acts under the Lisbon Treaty

The replacement of former Article 202 EC with new provisions governing the adoption of delegated and implementing acts in the Lisbon Treaty represented final constitutional recognition of the EP's authority as co-legislator in this domain.[30] The Lisbon Treaty profoundly reshaped the comitology system.[31] For the first time it laid down a formal hierarchy of European norms by differentiating between, on the one hand, legislative acts and, on the other hand, delegated and implementing acts. Legislative acts are those adopted by legislative procedure.[32] Their adoption is a matter for the European legislature.

[28] Art 5a(3)(b).

[29] Statement by the European Parliament, the Council and the Commission concerning the Council Decision of 17 July 2006 amending Decision 1999/468/EC laying down the procedures for the exercise of implementing powers conferred on the Commission (2006/512/EC) [2006] C255/1, para. 3 ('PRAC Statement'). See also Bradley, 'Halfway House' 849 referring to the 'sunset clauses' as the 'real sticking point' for finding agreement between institutions. Bradley also notes that the practice of adding sunset clauses was not, therefore, necessarily ruled out (*ibid.*, 849).

[30] See Arts TFEU 290 and 291. The EP's powers under Art 291 are more limited for reasons that will become apparent hereunder.

[31] On the new provisions, see P. Ponzano, "'Executive' and 'delegated' acts: the situation after the Lisbon Treaty" in S. Griller and J. Ziller (eds.), *The Lisbon Treaty – EU Constitutionalism without a Constitutional Treaty?* (Springer, Vienna, 2008) 135; J-C. Piris, *The Lisbon Treaty – A Legal and Political Analysis* (Cambridge University Press, 2010) 102–4.

[32] TFEU Art 289(3).

Delegated acts Delegated acts are 'non-legislative acts of general application'.[33] They are adopted by the European Commission in order to 'supplement or amend certain non-essential elements of the legislative act'.[34] Consequently, a delegated act cannot be a substitute for a legislative act. Furthermore, the Commission must be authorised to adopt a delegated act by the legislative act whose non-essential elements the delegated act will amend or supplement.[35] The legislative act will structure the delegation by defining a framework within which the Commission is authorised to act and, in particular, by specifying 'the objectives, content, scope and duration of the delegation of power',[36] as well as the conditions of the delegation.[37] The TFEU itself envisages two conditions. First, the legislature can provide that the delegation may be withdrawn at the initiative of either the Council or the EP; second, it can state that a delegated act can only come into force if no objections are raised by the EP or the Council within a specified period of time.[38]

One of the most noteworthy features of delegated acts is that the Commission is not required, as a matter of law, to seek endorsement of its measures with committees made of Member State officials. Nevertheless, as a practical matter, the Commission has decided to continue consulting national experts.[39] Indeed, in the financial services field, a declaration to the Lisbon Treaty records explicitly the Commission's intention to maintain its existing practice of consulting Member State experts when preparing delegated acts in this field.[40] National experts appointed to the European Securities Committee will therefore continue playing a role at Level 2, although their role will no longer be tied to the PRAC decision-making procedure.

33 TFEU Art 290(1). 34 *Ibid.* 35 *Ibid.*

36 *Ibid.* 37 TFEU Art 290(2).

38 *Ibid.* Note that the TFEU pre-determines the necessary voting requirements for such measures to be taken. In Council, Member States vote by qualified majority. The EP votes by a majority of its component members.

39 Communication from the Commission to the European Parliament and the Council 'Implementation of Article 290 of the Treaty on the Functioning of the European Union' (COM(2009) 673 final, 9 December 2009) 7 (noting that national experts will have 'a consultative rather than an institutional role in the decision-making procedure'), (hereinafter, the 'Commission Communication on Article 290').

40 Declaration 39 on Article 290 of the Treaty on the Functioning of the European Union (annexed to the Final Act of the Intergovernmental Conference which adopted the Treaty of Lisbon, signed on 13 December 2007) [2010] OJ C83/350 (hereinafter, 'Declaration 39 on Article 290').

Delegated acts and the PD When the PD was revised in 2010, the text of the directive was also amended in order to introduce the new rules governing the delegation of powers.[41] As amended, various provisions of the directive now authorise the Commission to adopt delegated acts.[42] In order to manage this delegation, the legislature added a number of safeguards. As amended, the PD states that the EP or the Council can 'at any time' revoke a delegation of powers given under any of the specified articles of the directive.[43] The EP or Council are also empowered to oppose a delegated act during a three-month period that follows the date of notification of the delegated act[44] and thereby prevent the act from coming into force.[45] Third, the directive limits the duration of a delegation to four years.[46] This article is not a classic sunset clause, at least not if we define such a clause as one which automatically suspends or terminates the powers of the Commission and requires a positive action to be taken to renew such powers. The PD's original sunset clause had been removed in 2008 when the new rules on the PRAC were introduced.[47] This original sunset clause suspended the powers of the Commission and required it to seek a new authorisation from the Council and EP. The new clause evidently functions differently. Article 24a states that upon expiry of the four-year period, the delegation is renewed automatically for the same period of time, unless the EP or the Council decides to revoke the delegation. The most apparent difference with the old sunset clause is thus that the delegation is not automatically suspended at the end of the four-year period. The point is worth noting. The fact that the Council or Parliament must revoke a delegation of powers changes the dynamics between institutions. The Council and Parliament are no longer in a 'reactive mode'.[48] They must take a positive action to provoke the end of the delegation of powers; a subtle change, but significant nonetheless. To be sure, Article 24a also requires the Commission to produce a report on the delegation 'at the latest six months before the end of the four-year period'. But the text

[41] See, in particular, PD Arts 24a, 24b and 24c, as amended by Directive 2010/73/EU [2010] OJ L327/1.

[42] E.g., Arts 1(4), 4(1)(e), 7(1), 14(8). [43] Art 24b(1).

[44] This period can be prolonged by another three months (Art 24c(1)).

[45] Art 24c(1) and (3). [46] Art 24a.

[47] Directive 2008/11/EC of the European Parliament and of the Council of 11 March 2008 [2008] L76/37.

[48] I borrow the expression from A. Héritier, 'The accomodation of diversity in European policy-making' (1996) 3 *Journal of European Public Policy* 149, 150 who uses it in another context.

of Article 24a does not suggest that such a report is a precondition to the automatic renewal of the delegation.

Implementing acts The second type of act that the Commission can be authorised to adopt is an implementing act.[49] Implementing acts are distinct from delegated acts. They can be used to adopt measures of general application and individual measures.[50] Moreover, implementing acts have a particular purpose.[51] They are concerned with the uniform implementation of European acts and will need to be adopted when it is necessary to ensure 'uniform conditions for implementing legally binding Union acts'.[52] Before the Commission can exercise its powers pursuant to Article 291, a regulation will need to be adopted by the Council and the EP in order to define an overarching framework governing the exercise of implementing powers.[53] Once adopted, this regulation will succeed the current Comitology Decision.[54] As in the case of the Comitology Decision, the regulation will specify the decision-making procedures that have to be followed and require Member State officials to be involved in the decision-making procedures.

Delegated and implementing acts and the role of the EP The choice between delegated and implementing acts is not politically benign, especially for the EP. From the EP's point of view, the new provisions on delegated acts, as opposed to implementing acts, achieved a satisfactory result by equating its powers to those of the Council. Having said that, the proposed practical implementation of these provisions, especially the Commission's intention to involve national experts, did not go unnoticed with the EP.[55] Recall that committees made up of national officials have traditionally given Member States a good deal of influence over the adoption of comitology measures. In response to the Commission's Lisbon declaration that it would continue consulting national officials in the financial services field,[56] the EP was quick to point out that the new arrangements

[49] TFEU Art 291.

[50] 'Commission Communication on Article 290' 4.

[51] See also *ibid.*, 3. [52] TFEU Art 291(2). [53] TFEU Art 291(3).

[54] See European Commission, 'Proposal for a regulation of the European Parliament and of the Council laying down the rules and general principles concerning mechanisms for control by Member States of the Commission's exercise of implementing powers' (COM(2010) 83 final, 9 March 2010).

[55] European Parliament, 'Report on the power of legislative delegation' (A7–0110/2010, 29 March 2010) 12.

[56] 'Declaration 39 on Article 290'.

could not prejudice the Parliament's existing rights, in particular its rights regarding early communication of documents or information.[57] The Commission, on the other hand, was keen to avoid a repetition of the 'sunset clause' practice, stressing that although the legislature must pursuant to Article 290(1) TFEU decide on the duration of a delegation, this provision should not be interpreted as endorsing 'sunset clauses'.[58] But the EP, in its resolution on legislative delegation, did not rule it out.[59] For the time being, the legislature seems to be content with a 'watered-down' version of the sunset clause. As seen earlier, the PD, as amended, includes a clause that allows the delegation of powers to be automatically extended at the end of a cut-off period of four years.

As far as the TFEU's provisions on implementing acts are concerned, the EP's powers as co-legislator were also constitutionally endorsed by the TFEU which states that an overarching regulation will need to be adopted by the Council and the EP under the ordinary legislative procedure in order to establish the necessary control mechanisms.[60] But because of the nature of implementing acts, the TFEU does not make the exercise of implementing powers subject to a right for the EP (or, for that matter, the Council) to revoke the delegation of implementing powers. Nor does it make the adoption of implementing measures subject to a legislative veto. Member State interests are to some degree safeguarded because the regulation, which will define the decision-making procedures that the Commission will need to respect when exercising its powers, will specify arrangements for Member States to oversee the Commission's use of implementing powers.[61] National officials will, therefore, continue being closely involved in the implementation process. But the EP will not be put on an equal footing with Member States. To be fair, the fact that the right to oversee the Commission is reserved to Member States is not an attempt to deny the Parliament its place, but a necessary and logical consequence of the distribution of competences between the EU and Member States. The implementation of European acts is, in general, a matter for Member States rather than European institutions.[62] The Parliament's powers

[57] European Parliament resolution of 5 May 2010 on the power of legislative delegation (P7_TA(2010)0127), para G ('EP Resolution on delegation').

[58] 'Commission Communication on Article 290' 5.

[59] 'EP Resolution on delegation' para 8.

[60] TFEU Art 291(3). [61] *Ibid.*

[62] See TFEU Art 291(1) and TEU Art 4(3) second sub-para. Under Art 291(2), the Council can also in certain cases be entrusted with implementing powers.

cannot, therefore, be equal to those of the Member States. For delegated acts, the matter is different given that a delegated act amends a legislative act, even though only non-essential elements.[63] The role of the EP as co-legislator, must therefore be protected. Because the Parliament has a lesser say over the adoption of implementing measures, it can safely be assumed that, whenever possible, the EP, as an institution and co-legislator, will prefer vesting delegated powers in the Commission.

III Collective securities actors

By all accounts, it is Level 3 of the Lamfalussy process which has become the centre of attention in the post-FSAP period and in the wake of the financial crisis.[64] As initially conceived by the Lamfalussy committee, Level 3 was meant to be a pole for cooperation between national securities authorities and thus a crucial part of Lamfalussy's strategy to ensure that EU regulatory output was properly implemented and applied by competent authorities.[65] At the heart of this network of competent authorities – the 'node of the network',[66] if you will – was CESR. CESR started operating on 7 June 2001. It ceased operating when it was replaced by a new, more powerful supervisory authority, i.e. ESMA, on 1 January 2011. While CESR no longer exists, its experience as a collective securities actor, has nevertheless something to teach us. Indeed, one of the core messages of this section and later chapters is that ESMA is not fundamentally different from CESR. Understanding CESR's experience is, therefore, valuable for appreciating the challenges that ESMA will face. I begin by examining CESR (A), after which I will turn to ESMA (B).

[63] See also Piris, *The Lisbon Treaty* 103.

[64] Level 3 has commanded much interest among legal scholars, but also among scholars of European governance. See, for example, C. de Visscher, O. Maiscocq and F. Varone, 'The Lamfalussy reform in the EU securities markets: fiduciary relationships, policy effectiveness and balance of power' (2008) 28 *Journal of Public Policy* 19; D. Coen and M. Thatcher 'Network governance and multi-level delegation: European networks of regulatory agencies' (2008) 28 *Journal of Public Policy* 49; M. Thatcher and D. Coen, 'Reshaping European regulatory space: an evolutionary analysis' (2008) 31 *West European Politics* 806.

[65] The network is also anchored in various directives which impose specific legal obligations to cooperate on competent authorities.

[66] I borrow the expression from G. Majone, 'The credibility crisis of Community Regulation' (2000) 38 *Journal of Common Market Studies* 273, 295 (using it in the context of European agencies and transnational regulatory networks).

A CESR

I start by examining CESR's nature and organisation (1), and then turn to the problems that CESR has faced (2).

1 The nature and organisation of CESR

In a sense, CESR was a peculiar actor. Although a crucial part of the Lamfalussy process, it was not a body with legal personality under EU law, but instead a non-profit association under French law.[67] What is more, it was a collective actor.[68] Scharpf defines a collective actor as an actor that does not decide independently over the preferences that will shape its activities, but instead depends on the preferences of its members.[69] In the case of CESR, these members were national financial markets authorities or 'competent authorities' in EU jargon.

CESR's internal organisation was also fairly simple. CESR was a small committee. Its members were not permanently based in Paris and there is a question mark about the frequency of their interactions. CESR had no strong executive, but only a small secretariat headed by a secretary general. It was chaired by a member of CESR. It had a number of permanent employees, but it also had to rely on the staff of its members. Moreover, CESR decided, at least initially, not to recruit from outside its member organisations, 'in order to preserve the spirit of the network'.[70] Arguably, this environment did not offer much incentive for common organisational values or a common culture to develop between these competent authorities.[71] In short, CESR was, in a sense, a type of 'club', but one to which entry was restricted, exit not foreseen and, in any event, highly

[67] See Annex B of the Decision No 716/2009/EC of the European Parliament and of the Council of 16 September 2009 establishing a Community programme to support specific activities in the field of financial services, financial reporting and auditing [2009] OJ L 253/8.

[68] I borrow the concept of collective actors from Scharpf, *Games Real Actors Play* 54–6. I have described CESR as a collective actor elsewhere. See P. Schammo, 'Comments on abuse of rights' in R. de la Feria and S. Vogenauer (eds.), *Prohibition of Abuse of Law – A New General Principle of EU Law* (Hart Publishing, Oxford, 2011).

[69] Scharpf, *Games Real Actors Play* 54–5.

[70] CESR, 'Interim report on the activities of the Committee of European Securities Regulators to the European Commission […]' (CESR/03-147b, July 2003) 2. To be fair, CESR's limited budget meant, in any event, that it had limited resources for recruitment purposes.

[71] CESR's efforts were, arguably, one-dimensional, in that it sought to build a common culture in a functional way, by mainly promoting common training or staff exchange programmes or joint inspections between authorities.

problematic given the requirements of the Lamfalussy process and various obligations of cooperation between competent authorities under EU legislation.

As far as CESR's approach to its work at Level 3 was concerned, it seemed to prefer a 'pragmatic' or 'practical' approach.[72] On the whole, this appears to have been successful. But while supposed to deal with technical issues at Level 3, it would be mistaken to think that these technical issues could not have important wider implications, such as for the overall attractiveness or competitiveness of national markets. There are ready examples in later chapters.[73] Indeed, in practice, it is apparent that CESR often filled in for the Court of Justice and *de facto* provided interpretations of EU legislation. A case in point are CESR's 'questions and answers' on the PD that were often nothing short of interpretations of the PD.[74] To be sure, CESR's quasi-interpretations were not legally binding. But they nevertheless benefited from CESR's authority and, therefore, from the authority of its members.

2 Problems with CESR

Before examining problems with CESR in more detail, it is fair to begin with a qualification. As with most things, it is important to keep a sense of perspective when examining CESR's record. The fact is that its establishment was a significant improvement on the pre-Lamfalussy situation. What is more, given the benefits of supervision at the grass-roots level and the fact that in Europe national markets have different orientations, there is a good case to be made in favour of decentralised supervision and enforcement through competent authorities. But nevertheless, Level 3 suffered from a number of weaknesses. In this part, I will focus especially on two problems with CESR.[75] The first concerns the fact that CESR had no legally binding powers. The second has to do with the behaviour of its members.[76]

[72] Interviews 25-EUR and 33-EUR (see Chapter 10 for details on the interview methodology); cf., L. Quaglia, 'Financial sector committee governance in the European Union' (2008) 30 *Journal of European Integration* 563, 573 (referring to the style of decision-making of Level 3 committees as 'evidence based').

[73] See e.g., CESR's work on employee share schemes or retail cascades in Chapters 3 and 4.

[74] e.g., CESR, 'Frequently asked questions regarding prospectuses: common positions agreed by CESR members' (CESR/10-830, July 2010) (hereinafter, 'CESR Q&A July 10').

[75] On issues of transparency and accountability, see Moloney, *EC Securities Regulation* 1135–8.

[76] Note that in the wake of the financial crisis, the role of Level 3 committees was questioned more vigorously. I will return to this later. See section III, B.1, below.

a The absence of legally binding powers When political leaders endorsed the Lamfalussy process in 2001, it was on the understanding that the Lamfalussy approach would respect the balance of powers between institutions.[77] At the moment of CESR's institutional creation, this brought important limits to bear on its formal remit and powers.[78] Level 3 was meant to become a subordinate level of competence. CESR was expected to play 'an important role in the transposition process' by promoting cooperation, perform peer reviews and encourage best practice.[79] But, crucially, CESR's decisions and measures were not legally binding; they had no legal authority. Instead, competent authorities and market actors were expected to respect CESR's measures and decisions because of CESR's intrinsic authority, arising from its membership and from its place within the Lamfalussy process.

One implication of the fact that political leaders were not prepared to grant CESR legal powers, was that the establishment of CESR never truly challenged the EU's institutional balance of powers *as a constitutional principle upheld by the Court of Justice* (as opposed to a political concept used as a means to justify what EU actors consider to be a politically acceptable delegation of powers). Admittedly, attempts were made to strengthen CESR in the years that followed its institutional creation. In the wake of an intensifying banking crisis, the Commission launched a consultation, largely under the theme of the need to align the decisions establishing the three Level 3 committees.[80] These actions ultimately culminated in a rewrite of the Commission Decision establishing CESR.[81] For the first time, the role of CESR at Level 3 was written into the body of the legally binding text of a Commission decision. CESR was given new powers (e.g., mediation). Moreover, the Commission decision also addressed the way in which CESR decided on common action or common measures. The fact that CESR made decisions by way of consensus – that is unanimity

77 European Council, 'Presidency Conclusions' (Stockholm, 23 and 24 March 2001) Annex I, www.consilium.europa.eu/ueDocs/cms_Data/docs/pressData/en/ec/00100-r1.%20ann-r1.en1.html.

78 See also Coen's and Thatcher's analysis in 'Network governance and multi-level delegation'.

79 European Council, 'Presidency Conclusions' (Stockholm, 23 and 24 March 2001) Annex I.

80 European Commission, 'Public consultation paper on amendments to Commission Decisions establishing CESR, CEBS & CEIOPS' (23 May 2008), http://ec.europa.eu/internal_market/finances/docs/committees/consultation_en.pdf.

81 Commission Decision of 23 January 2009 establishing the Committee of European Securities Regulators (2009/77/EC) [2009] L25/18.

'minus one or two'[82] – had, for some time, been seen as an obstacle to Level 3 decision-making. To remedy the threat of deadlocks or decisions at the lowest common denominator, the Commission Decision provided for decisions to be adopted by qualified majority. To be more specific, as a matter of principle, CESR was permitted to continue operating by way of consensus,[83] but the Commission Decision made it plain that CESR members should vote by qualified majority if no consensus could be found.[84] The decision-making arrangements remained, however, peculiar, for the simple reason that the Commission Decision did not vest legally binding powers in CESR. Any decision, taken by consensus or not, could not, at any rate, bind CESR members. To somewhat lessen incentives for members to simply disregard (non-binding) recommendations, standards and so on, the Commission Decision stated that a member should explain its reasons if it decided not to comply with a CESR measure.[85] This provision was as much a recognition of the limits of CESR's authority, as an attempt to deal with its consequences.

b Adverse behaviour My second point about problems with CESR is in many ways more complex to assess. As noted, CESR was a collective actor.[86] It had no independent, overriding choice over its preferences.[87] Instead, it depended on the preferences of its members. These members were national securities actors which had long operated independently at national level. They had, and continue to have, separate organisational objectives or mandates which define their *raison d'être* and, as it were, are the prism through which they interpret a complex world.[88] What is more, while meant to act in the public interest, competent authorities also have distinct self-interest which can be understood in terms of their 'organizational survival, autonomy, and growth'.[89] Hence, because CESR was a collective actor whose members depended for their survival and growth on a national context and on national actors (national Parliaments or

[82] CESR, 'A proposed evolution of EU securities supervision beyond 2007' (CESR/07-783, November 2007) 4 ('CESR 2007 Report').

[83] Commission Decision of 23 January 2009 establishing the Committee of European Securities Regulators, Art 14.

[84] *Ibid.* [85] *Ibid.*

[86] I borrowed the concept of a collective actor from Scharpf, *Games Real Actors Play*.

[87] See text to nn. 68 and 69.

[88] A similar point is made in relation to the SEC in E. Tafara and R. Peterson, 'A blueprint for cross-border access to US investors: a new international framework' (2007) 48 *Harvard International Law Journal* 31, 42.

[89] Scharpf, *Games Real Actors Play* 64 (reference omitted).

governments) to which they were accountable, CESR was not unambiguously driven by an overriding collective or European interest.[90]

To be sure, if the preferences of its members were aligned, CESR could be expected to be at its best, sourcing effectively expertise from its members. On the other hand, on institutionally significant questions which risked conflicting with the separate interests of its members, the matter was arguably different. Thus, because CESR was a collective actor, CESR could be expected to ultimately safeguard, for better or worse, the interests of its members.[91] The most obvious example is the fact that CESR did not support its own transformation into a fully fledged European securities authority which would have threatened the autonomy of national authorities.[92] Likewise, it did not support a wholesale transfer of day-to-day supervision away from national authorities,[93] which would also have led to a significant erosion of the competences of its members. On the other hand, CESR had long called for its members to be given equivalent powers at national level,[94] which, assumedly, is best understood as a call for national authorities with weaker powers to be given greater powers.

On other issues, however, it seems more difficult to make sense of CESR positions. For example, its members have supported centralising

[90] Or in the more plainspoken words of E. Wymeersch, CESR's former chairman: '... national supervisors pursue national interests and will be held accountable to their national authorities (governments, parliaments) if they divergence [sic] from that objective'. See E. Wymeersch, 'Presentation at the International Conference of the "Giordano Dell'Amore"' (S&C 2010–01, January 2010) 2 www.law.ugent.be/fli/wps/pdf/S&C2010–01.pdf.

[91] Cf., Quaglia, 'Financial sector committee governance in the European Union' 574 (noting that 'on issues that directly affect the tasks and powers of the supervisory authorities, the members of the committees might be inclined to defend their (bureaucratic) preferences').

[92] 'CESR 2007 Report' 6 (noting that '... CESR is not advocating for the creation of an EU single regulator embedded in the Treaty').

[93] See the testimony of E. Wymeersch (former chairman of CESR) in front of the House of Lords, European Union Committee (HL European Union Committee, 'The future of EU financial regulation and supervision – vol II: Evidence' (14th Report of Session 2008–09), www.publications.parliament.uk/pa/ld200809/ldselect/ldeucom/106/106ii.pdf, noting at 146 '[o]ne thing that is clear to me at least in the securities field is that at CESR, there is no ambition to engage in do day-to-day supervision except perhaps for credit rating agencies, but that is very specific' ('House of Lords Report – Evidence')).

[94] CESR, 'Preliminary progress report – which supervisory tools for the EU securities markets? An analytical paper by CESR' (CESR/04-333f, October 2004) 21 (hereinafter, the 'Himalaya Report'); 'CESR 2007 Report' (CESR/07-783) 3. See also CESR's contribution to the discussions on the *de Larosière* report (CESR/08-289b), published in '3L3 Joint Contribution to the European Commission's consultation on the improvement of supervision for the financial services sector' (CESR/09-356, April 2009) 12 (hereinafter, 'CESR's *de Larosière* contribution').

regulatory decision-making (as opposed to supervision).[95] This seems, ostensibly, to contradict my earlier observation. But not necessarily so, given that, when CESR came of age, most regulatory decision-making in the securities field was, at any rate, made at EU level. Finally, on other matters, CESR's position on how Level 3 should develop appears simply to be evidence of differences in the integrationist preferences of its members.[96] For example, its members had different preferences on the *de Larosière* proposal to transform the three Level 3 committees into new supervisory authorities.[97] Neither did they unanimously support the idea of Level 3 measures being given binding authority.[98] Likewise, they were divided on the merit of home country control.[99] Moreover, at least some CESR members seem to have had reservations about entrusting the supervision of credit agencies to a new EU securities authority.[100]

These points are well worth highlighting, for CESR's *raison d'être* was precisely to find *common* ways. Indeed, given that CESR was made up of a group of experienced professionals, mainly dealing with technical matters, one should expect CESR to be the place where good arguments and ideas can gain currency. Majone has long argued that regulatory networks have intrinsic qualities which help to alleviate conflicts and ensure that national regulators cooperate sincerely with each other. He has highlighted the fact that network members are professionals who are likely to be concerned about maintaining their reputation vis-à-vis their peers within the network.[101] For him, 'the function of a network is not only to permit an efficient division of labour and exchange of information, but

95 'CESR's *de Larosière* contribution' 13 ('[m]embers are in favour of centralised rule-making and decentralised supervision').

96 See also 'CESR 2007 Report' 6.

97 'CESR's *de Larosière* contribution' 12 (noting that '*most of them* support the transformation of the committees into new independent EU authorities' (emphasis added)).

98 'CESR 2007 Report' 7 (noting that '[i]n the view of *some* members an additional step would be confer to some of CESR's Level 3 measures a binding nature' (emphasis added)); 'CESR's *de Larosière* contribution' 13 (noting that '[*s*]*ome* members are of the view that L1 rules should be more general/principles-based granting to the new Authorities the competence to issue binding rules' (emphasis added)).

99 'CESR's *de Larosière* contribution' 12 ('[*s*]*ome* members are of the view that the home country control system should be revisited' (emphasis added)).

100 *Ibid.*, 13 ('[m]ost members are of the view that credit rating agencies should be supervised by a central authority').

101 Majone, 'The credibility crisis of Community regulation', 298; G. Majone *Dilemmas of European integration* (Oxford University Press, 2009) 101; G. Majone 'The new European agencies: regulation by information' (1997) 4 *Journal of European Public Policy* 262; G. Majone, 'The future of regulation in Europe' in G. Majone, (ed.), *Regulating Europe* (Routledge, London, 1996) 265, 273. Drawing on Majone, see also B. Eberlein and

also to facilitate the development of behavioural standards and working practices that create shared expectations and enhance the effectiveness of the social mechanisms of reputational enforcement'.[102] Majone might be right on the whole, but in specific instances, such as CESR, one should caution against drawing deterministic conclusions on the basis of a general argument about regulatory networks. As Quaglia notes, Lamfalussy committees (meaning both Level 2 and Level 3 committees) are 'neither "epistemic communities" of experts … nor simply "intergovernmental" forums for political negotiations'.[103] She notes further that while expertise and arguments have good currency within CESR most of the time, the decision-making dynamics can nevertheless vary depending on the issue at stake and, especially, depending on how politically salient an issue is perceived to be.[104] What is more, ultimately, the behaviour of CESR members must be examined empirically[105] and here the evidence is somewhat mixed. In my field of interest, it is possible to identify two types of behaviour that testify to CESR's limits. I will refer to them as 'no action' and 'defection'. I will return to this behaviour in later chapters where I will provide other examples (e.g., with respect to mediation or equivalence-based regulation).

No action 'No action' describes situations where CESR members failed to agree a shared course of action or simply agreed to disagree when dealing with a given problem-situation. I will slightly stretch the meaning of 'no action' by also including examples where CESR members failed to agree common positions when, for instance, commenting on proposed EU actions at Level 3. Absent a positive obligation to disclose 'no action' cases, reporting on such behaviour is bound to be difficult. What is more, the reasons for a lack of action are difficult to interpret *ex post*. But it is not impossible. CESR may voluntarily decide to disclose the reasons for a lack of action or state that it was unable to reach agreement among its members. An example is CESR's comment paper on the Commission's pre-consultation on amending the PD.[106] CESR did not provide views on

A. Newman, 'Escaping the international governance dilemma? Incorporated transgovernmental networks in the European Union' (2008) 21 *Governance* 25, 36.

102 Majone, 'The credibility crisis' 298.

103 Quaglia, 'Financial sector committee governance in the European Union' 575.

104 *Ibid.* 105 In this sense, *ibid.*

106 European Commission, 'Background Document – Review of Directive 2003/71/EC […]' (undated), http://ec.europa.eu/internal_market/consultations/docs/2009/prospectus/background_en.pdf (hereinafter 'Commission Background Document').

most of the questions raised by the Commission because, it noted, it had decided to 'restrict itself only to those issues where CESR members are in common agreement'.[107] In particular, it did not provide views on the question of the EUR 1,000 threshold found in Article 2(1)(m)(ii) of the directive which contributes to determining whether issuers benefit from a choice of competent authority. The question is of direct interest to CESR's members as it affects the distribution of competences between them.[108] CESR also failed to provide answers on other sensitive issues such as, for example, on the harmonisation of civil liability or the definition of a public offer. These issues too have proven controversial in the past among Member States for reasons which have to do with different integrationist preferences or differing approaches to investor protection. CESR has also disclosed the fact that its members have in the past disagreed on basic interpretations of the PD, for example in the context of CESR's 'questions and answers' which are intended 'to provide market participants with responses (…) to "everyday" questions'.[109] Admittedly, there seem to have been few disagreements and they were resolved in subsequent Q&A updates. But there are other examples. CESR's comments on the *de Larosière* report, to which I referred already earlier, testify to a similar type of behaviour.[110] The *de Larosière* report made recommendations on how financial supervision should evolve in the wake of the financial crisis. While CESR underlined that there was 'a broad consensus of CESR members on several issues of the Report',[111] it is also apparent that CESR was unable to agree a common position on many issues.[112] As mentioned earlier, there are a few other examples of 'no action' behaviour. Mediation comes to my mind. But I will examine the matter only in Chapter 6 when turning to enforcement.

Defection Defection, the second type of behaviour worth mentioning, refers to situations where CESR members simply failed to act at national level on previously agreed courses of action; for example, when ignoring agreed Level 3 recommendations or standards. In Chapter 6, the implementation, or better, non-implementation of CESR's Standard No. 1 and Standard No. 2 on financial information will provide tangible evidence

[107] CESR, 'CESR's comments on the European Commission's background and consultation document on the review of Directive 2003/71/EC' (CESR/09-240, March 2009) 1.

[108] See, for details, Chapters 3, section IV, and 10.

[109] CESR, 'Frequently asked questions regarding prospectuses' (CESR/06-296d, July 2006). See the positions on questions 1, 2, 3 and 14.

[110] 'CESR's *de Larosière* contribution'.

[111] *Ibid.*, 12. [112] See above for details.

of this type of behaviour.[113] Suffice it to say here that competent authorities have taken a somewhat cavalier approach in applying the standards. There is also evidence to suggest that CESR members, on occasions, simply failed to observe the provisions of the PD. Market actors have commented on various practices at national level which are suspect, if not plainly out of line with the provisions of the PD.[114] Whatever the accuracy of these views, the practice of ignoring agreed, albeit non-binding, Level 3 standards is hard to dispute. CESR itself reported on this behaviour.[115]

B ESMA

Notwithstanding the limitations of CESR, it is fair to say that CESR has made a lasting contribution to improving regulation and supervision in the securities sector. But on 1 January 2011, ESMA succeeded CESR. It marked a new stage on the evolutionary road towards greater centralisation and consolidation of competence. ESMA is a more complex organisation than CESR. It has greater competence and powers. That said, ESMA is not fundamentally different from CESR. Like CESR, ESMA is a collective securities actor. Moreover, ESMA needs to find its place between existing institutions and actors and respect the institutional balance of powers. In this subsection, I will examine the implications of these facts. I begin with the *de Larosière* recommendations (1), after which I will turn to the constitutional limits of a delegation of powers (2). Once these points have been discussed, I will examine ESMA's nature and organisation (3) and finally, its tasks (4).

[113] CESR, 'Standard No. 1 on financial information – enforcement of standards on financial information in Europe' (CESR/03-073, March 2003); CESR, 'Standard No. 2 on financial information – coordination of enforcement activities' (CESR/03-317c, April 2004).

[114] See CESR, 'CESR's report on the supervisory functioning of the Prospectus Directive and Regulation' (CESR/07-225, June 2007) (hereinafter 'CESR's Report on the PD'); ESME, 'Report on Directive 2003/71/EC of the European Parliament and of the Council on the prospectus to be published when securities are offered to the public or admitted to trading' (Brussels, September 2007) 5–6 (hereinafter 'ESME Report'). See also more generally, E. Wymeersch, 'Preparing for the Future' (CESR/09-203, Speech, 23 February 2009) 1–2 ('… market participants regularly draw attention to the fact that they are confronted with many local differences … and that even harmonised rules are interpreted differently and sometimes – what is even worse – that some national regulators do not seem to care much about the European harmonisation, and apply their own views without further ado').

[115] See Chapter 6, section IV, A.2, for details.

1 Beginnings: the *de Larosière* proposals

Until the financial crisis began to hit real economies in 2008, reforms dealing with financial markets oversight had followed an evolutionary path.[116] But as the crisis unfolded, the functioning of Level 3 started increasingly being questioned. EU institutional arrangements, among which was also the Level 3 Lamfalussy network architecture, were viewed as having failed to perform adequately and, therefore, in need of review. The setting-up of the *de Larosière* group was a sign of this change of heart.[117] The group published its report in February 2009. Like Lamfalussy, *de Larosière* proposed changes to the institutional framework. But while the Lamfalussy Committee was instructed to ignore prudential supervision,[118] the financial crisis had brought prudential supervision into sharp focus, making it a core issue for *de Larosière* and its group of experts. The *de Larosière* group identified eight issues as having had detrimental effects on supervision: an absence of macro-prudential supervision; an absence of means to alert policy actors to macro-prudential risks; supervisory malfunctions at national level; inadequate mechanisms for challenging the measures of national authorities having cross-border implications; insufficient cooperation and frankness between national authorities; national authorities with inadequate powers; insufficient resources for Level 3 committees; and finally insufficient legal powers for them to take common decisions.[119] As far as the supervisory architecture is concerned,[120] *de Larosière* responded by making proposals that had two main points of focus. It proposed addressing macro-prudential supervision by establishing a European Systemic Risk Council which was subsequently renamed 'European Systemic Risk Board' ('ESRB'). Meanwhile, a second set of proposals was aimed at micro-supervision and at transforming the Level 3 committees, i.e., CESR, CEBS and CEIOPS,[121] into new European

[116] European Commission, 'Mandate for the high-level expert group on financial supervision in the EU' annexed to the Report of the high-level group on financial supervision in the EU (Brussels, 25 February 2009) 69, http://ec.europa.eu/internal_market/finances/docs/de_larosiere_report_en.pdf (noting that '[s]upervisory reform has so far relied on an evolutionary approach' (hereinafter, the '*de Larosière* Report')).

[117] '*de Larosière* Report'.

[118] 'Committee of Wise Men's terms of reference given by the European Union's economic and finance ministers on 17 July 2000' annexed to the 'Lamfalussy Report' 99.

[119] '*de Larosière* Report' 39–42.

[120] The *de Larosière* group not only dealt with institutional reforms, but also made proposals concerning substantive reforms and external (international) action.

[121] CEBS stands for Committee of European Banking Supervisors; CEIOPS stands for Committee of European Insurance and Occupational Pensions Supervisors.

Supervisory Authorities ('ESAs'). By doing so, the *de Larosière* report did not reject the network approach. Indeed, it endorsed it, but referred to it as 'European System of Financial Supervision' ('ESFS'),[122] with the three new ESAs as the nodes of the ESFS.

Political leaders endorsed the *de Larosière* conclusions on the ESFS.[123] Ecofin resolved that CESR should be transformed into and renamed the European Securities and Markets Authority ('ESMA').[124] It would work alongside the new European Banking Authority and the European Insurance and Occupational Pensions Authority that would take the place of CEBS and CEIOPS, respectively.[125] The Commission came forward with a formal package of proposals in September 2009 which was formally adopted in 2010 at first reading. Given the subject matter of this chapter, I will skip over the rules governing the new ESRB and focus instead on ESMA, CESR's successor.

2 Establishing ESMA: constitutional limits

The institutional balance of powers as a constitutional principle governing the delegation of powers As noted in the previous subsection, when political leaders endorsed the Lamfalussy process in 2001, it was on the understanding that it would respect the balance of powers between institutions.[126] CESR was, as a result, left without binding powers. As the financial crisis worsened, however, proposals to give greater powers to new supervisory authorities gained momentum and greater acceptance among political leaders, so much so that by 2010, the main constraint on the delegation of powers to ESMA was no longer an overwhelming political opposition to granting ESMA binding powers – in other words, the need to respect the balance of powers between institutions as a political expression of will – but, increasingly, the need to respect the balance of powers as a constitutional principle upheld by the Court of Justice. The

[122] '*de Larosière* Report' 47.

[123] Council of the European Union (Ecofin), 'Council conclusions on strengthening EU financial supervision' (Luxembourg, 9 June 2009), para. 7, www.consilium.europa.eu/uedocs/cms_Data/docs/pressdata/en/ecofin/108389.pdf; European Council, 'Presidency Conclusions – 18/19 June 2009' (ref. 11225/2/09 REV2), para. 20, http://register.consilium.europa.eu/pdf/en/09/st11/st11225-re02.en09.pdf.

[124] Ecofin, 'Council conclusions on strengthening EU financial supervision', para. 8.

[125] *Ibid.*

[126] The fact that the balance of powers has an important political dimension (besides its legal dimension), has also been highlighted elsewhere. See P. Craig, *EU Administrative Law* (Oxford University Press, 2006) 274.

whys and wherefores of the Court's case law need to be explained in more detail.

The constitutional limits on the delegation of powers: the Court's case law Save for the odd reference to subsidiarity and proportionality, the *de Larosière* group sidestepped constitutional issues. It concluded that new supervisory authorities with binding powers were needed, but it came to this conclusion without considering the Court's case law on the delegation of powers to outside bodies.[127] For many decades, the Court's decisions have shaped the law on the issue.[128] In *Meroni*, the Court made it plain that in order to uphold the balance of powers between institutions, any delegation of powers had to be non-discretionary. Thus, a delegation of powers could not involve a 'discretionary power, implying a wide margin of discretion'.[129] Any delegation of this nature would be tantamount to handing over responsibility to a delegatee and admit that the latter could substitute its own choices to those of the delegator.[130] The principle of the balance of powers would be rendered meaningless.[131] Consequently, a delegation could only involve 'clearly defined executive powers', as the exercise of such powers could be subject to review according to 'objective criteria determined by the delegating authority'.[132] What is more, the

[127] See on the issue of delegation, S. Griller and A. Orator, 'Everything under control? The "way forward" for European agencies in the footsteps of the Meroni doctrine' (2010) 35 *European Law Review* 3; K. Lenaerts, 'Regulating the regulatory process: "delegation of powers" in the European Community' (1993) 18 *European Law Review* 23.

[128] Interestingly, the question of the proper legal basis for establishing ESMA (as opposed to the question of the constitutional limits to the powers which can be delegated) proved to be less problematic because of the Court's case law. See the Court's decision on the establishment of the European Network and Information Security Agency (ENISA) (Case C-217/04 *United Kingdom v European Parliament and Council* [2006] ECR I-03771). In ENISA, the Court confirmed that Art 95 EC could be used for establishing a European agency (or 'Community body') that participates in the implementation of the harmonisation process, if certain conditions were met. The Court reached its conclusion despite some solid counter-arguments and the recommendations of AG Kokott who, given the tasks of ENISA, concluded that ENISA's planed activities were not sufficient to conclude that the setting up of the agency was justified under Art 95 (see Opinion of AG Kokott in C-217/04, *United Kingdom v European Parliament and Council*, paras 28ff).

[129] Case 9/56 *Meroni v High Authority* [1958] ECR 133, 152. Specifically, what the Court had in mind were powers which could, depending on their use, make it possible to execute policy.

[130] *Ibid.*

[131] *Ibid.*, 152 ('[t]o delegate a discretionary power, by entrusting it to bodies other than those which the Treaty has established to effect and supervise the exercise of such power each within the limits of its own authority, would render that guarantee [i.e., the balance of powers] ineffective').

[132] *Ibid.*

delegating institution could not, in any event, delegate powers which were different from its own powers derived from the Treaty.[133] The Court returned to the limits of a delegation of powers in later cases. One of these cases is *Romano*, in which it held, although without mentioning *Meroni*, that it was not permissible to delegate powers which allowed a body to adopt acts 'having the force of law' ('*revêtant un caractère normatif*').[134] For the Court, the body in question – the Administrative Commission of the European Communities on Social Security for Migrant Workers – could, therefore, not make decisions that required national authorities to observe specific methods or certain interpretations when applying Community legislation.[135]

Romano was an important case, but *Meroni* was a seminal one. Its premise is simple and compelling; its practical implications are severe. It established an absolute boundary: discretionary powers cannot be delegated to outside bodies.[136] Absent treaty amendment, the boundary could not be crossed. Although the implications of the decision are increasingly impractical, the Court's reasoning is convincing from a constitutional point of view. Moreover, it can easily be applied across EU policy fields. Thus, *Meroni* sets a significant boundary on what is a permissible delegation of powers in the securities markets fields. More specifically, compliance with *Meroni* presupposes that one answers two questions in the affirmative: first, has the delegator delegated powers that are within the scope of its own powers; second, is the delegation properly structured in order to ensure that the powers are not discretionary?

To answer the first question, one would need to have regard to the Treaties, as the ultimate source of EU law. In *Meroni*, the Court concluded that because the delegated powers were more extensive than those that belonged to the delegating authority, the delegation was not permissible.[137]

[133] *Ibid*., 150. See also Case C-301/02 P *Carmine Salvatore Tralli v European Central Bank* [2005] ECR I-4071, para. 43.

[134] Case 98/80 *Romano v Institut national d'assurance maladie-invalidité* [1981] ECR 1241, para. 20; Case C-102/91 *Knoch v Bundesanstalt für Arbeit* [1992] ECR I-04341, para. 52; Case 21/87 *Borowitz v Bundesversicherungsanstalt für Angestellte* [1988] ECR 3715, para. 19.

[135] Case 98/80 *Romano*, para. 20. See also Case C-102/91 *Knoch*, para. 52.

[136] Note that the Commission has spelled out its understanding of the limits to a delegation of powers to regulatory agencies in its White Paper on European Governance. See European Commission, 'European governance – a White Paper' (COM(2001) 428 final, 25 July 2001) 24.

[137] Case 9/56 *Meroni v High Authority* 150.

This reasoning should apply *a fortiori* in a situation where a delegating authority attempted to delegate powers that are of an altogether different nature to its own powers. It is relevant to note in this context that each of the EU's institutions must act within the limits of the powers that it is entrusted with by the Treaties.[138] This principle echoes the principle of conferral in Article 5(2) of the TEU according to which the EU can only act within the scope of the powers which are vested in it by the Treaties.[139] Competences not vested with the EU belong to the Member States.[140] If an institution does not act within the limits of the Treaties, the delegation would necessarily be unlawful, as it would infringe the Treaties.

Assuming that we overcome this first obstacle, there is still a second issue to address: does the delegation involve discretionary powers? It is worth pausing a moment and considering in more detail the dimensions of the problem. *Meroni* and its ban on a delegation of discretionary powers affect two types of measures, i.e., legislative measures (i.e., measures of general application) and individual decisions, whether they are addressed to market actors or competent authorities.[141] As far as the delegation of legislative powers to an EU agency is concerned, *Meroni* stands firm against such a delegation. The exercise of legislative powers involves a wide margin of discretion. Policy judgments and legislative choices are intrinsically linked. Besides, *Romano* ruled this type of delegation explicitly out. As far as the delegation of individual decision-making powers is concerned, the matter is arguably more complex. On the one hand, a number of agencies have already been vested with *binding* powers to take individual decisions, i.e., powers to take individual measures binding on third parties.[142] Among those more powerful authorities is, for example, the European Aviation Safety Agency.[143] On the other hand, there is no reason to think that the exercise of such decision-making powers, as opposed to the exercise of legislative power, is, by its nature, incompatible with the exercise of discretion and policy calculations involving competing considerations, public values or interests. In coming to a decision, the delegatee might, for instance, have to balance different and, indeed, possibly conflicting considerations. The implication is that even though it might be

[138] TEU Art 13(2). [139] TEU Art 5(2). [140] *Ibid.*

[141] On the distinction between legislative and individual measures, see Case C-345/00 P *Fédération nationale d'agriculture biologique des régions de France* [2001] ECR I-3811, para. 45.

[142] European Commission, 'Communication from the Commission – the operating framework for the European regulatory agencies' (COM(2002) 718 final, 11 December 2002) 4 (hereinafter, 'Commission Communication on European Regulatory Agencies').

[143] *Ibid.*

possible to vest agencies with individual decision-making powers, it will be necessary to significantly pre-structure the delegation in order to ensure that the delegation does not involve 'a wide margin of discretion' allowing, for example, policy considerations to be taken into account. It will presuppose that the tasks which are delegated are clearly defined. In particular, it will require clearly defined 'objective criteria' on the basis of which an agency will be able to make a decision.[144] Indeed, for the delegation to be '*Meroni* compliant', the delegatee should be able, when exercising its delegated decision-making power, to come to a decision *in an almost mechanical way*, on the basis of the criteria or requirements determined by the delegator. If an agency were, for instance, delegated a power to approve or license a product (assuming that such a delegation would be considered permissible under the first test, discussed above), but would in the course of its decision-making process be required to balance or reconcile competing policy considerations or interests (instead of, say, simply 'ticking boxes' to come to a decision), the delegation would fall foul of the *Meroni* principles. The delegatee would no longer exercise strict executive powers, but make decisions that imply a wide margin of discretion. On the other hand, the exercise of executive powers might very well involve a degree of *technical* discretion when examining, for instance, whether a product satisfies (or not) specified regulatory requirements.[145] This does not seem to contradict the *Meroni* principles. In *Meroni*, the situation was different because the agencies had a real power of appreciation over the principles that guided their decisions. This delegation was not permissible. Indeed, this was so notwithstanding the fact that the delegator had the power to replace the delegatee's decisions with its own. Since the delegator was, in fact, unable to question the information provided by the delegatee, the delegator's power was not sufficient, in the opinion of the Court, to call into question its conclusions.[146]

[144] In the case of *Meroni*, such objective criteria lacked. It meant that the assessment to be carried out by the delegatee was not akin to 'mere accountancy procedures', but implied a wide margin of discretion. See Case 9/56 *Meroni v High Authority* 153.

[145] See e.g., in this context, European Commission, Proposal for a regulation of the European Parliament and of the Council on establishing common rules in the field of civil aviation and creating a European Aviation Safety Agency (COM(2000) 595 final, 27 September 2000) 5.

[146] Case 9/56 *Meroni v High Authority* 154. Note that the Court also referred to two earlier instances where the delegator had adopted a decision on its own in lieu of the delegatees. The Court did not agree that this was relevant evidence of an effective exercise of decision-making powers by the delegating authority because the delegator had not, in any event, exercised its power in order to prevent discretionary behaviour.

Although the Court found in *Meroni* that the delegator's right to refuse approval was inadequate, it does, arguably, not automatically follow that a power of approval, which the delegator reserves to himself, will necessarily serve no purpose. In other words, if a delegator retains a real power of approval, which makes the delegation effectively non-discretionary, the delegation should arguably pass the *Meroni* test. But based on *Meroni*, this power must be real. It is plain that mere 'rubberstamping' by the delegator would not be sufficient. The delegator must have a real power of decision. He must form his own views on the matters at issue.[147]

Incidentally, assuming again that the delegation would pass the first test discussed above, there is no reason to believe that the second test would not apply with equal force to the delegation of enforcement powers. Enforcement can be a policy instrument, just as much as legislation. Thus, if an agency had, for example, a discretionary say in determining a financial sanction (e.g., the amount of a fine), the delegation would not seem to be '*Meroni* compliant', given that the exercise by a regulatory agency of such a discretionary power could make policy choices possible. The regulation establishing the European Aviation Safety Agency (EASA) includes, for instance, a provision on fines.[148] But it is apparent that the EASA does not have the power to impose fines. Instead, it must ask the Commission to impose the fines or periodic penalty payments.[149] The latter's decision is discretionary.[150]

This ends my analysis of the Court's case law on the delegation of powers to EU agencies. It is apparent that *Meroni* and the need to respect the institutional balance of powers set a number of constraints on the nature and scope of the powers that can be delegated to ESMA. The next paragraphs will examine the nature, organisation and the powers of ESMA. As far as powers are concerned, I will mainly introduce them, but I will

[147] For an example of a case where the Court of First Instance seemed content to accept that the Commission had retained sufficient powers over the decision of an outside body, see Joined cases T-369/94 and T-85/95 *DIR International Film and others* [1998] ECR II-357, paras 52–3; on appeal, Case C-164/98 P *DIR International Film and others* [2000] ECR I-447, para. 6. Note, however, that the issue was not primarily about whether the delegation was '*Meroni* compliant' or not, but whether the decision in question could be ascribed to the Commission in order to bring an action against the latter in front of the Court of Justice.

[148] Regulation (EC) 216/2008 of the European Parliament and of the Council of 20 February 2008 on common rules in the field of civil aviation and establishing a European Aviation Safety Agency (…) [2008] OJ L79/1, as amended.

[149] Regulation (EC) 216/2008 Art 25(1).

[150] *Ibid.* (Art 25(1) reads: '… the Commission may', as opposed to the Commission shall).

return to them in later chapters, especially in Chapter 6 where I will also return to *Meroni* and its implications for the delegation of powers to ESMA.

3 The nature and organisation of ESMA

In comparison to CESR, ESMA is, as an organisation, a good deal more sophisticated. To begin with, ESMA has legal personality under European law.[151] It is an EU body,[152] although not a Union institution such as, for example, the European Central Bank. ESMA is part of a Commission web of European agencies and, more importantly, it is part of the ESFS whose main purpose is to ensure a proper implementation of EU rules in the financial sector.[153]

Decision-making is mainly in the hands of a Board of Supervisors,[154] which takes decisions by simple or qualified majority, depending on the measures to be adopted.[155] It is composed of the heads of competent authorities (i.e., the relevant national *public* authorities which have competence to supervise market actors[156] at Member State level) who are vote holders, but also of a number of persons representing mostly other bodies and institutions who have no voting rights (i.e., the Commission, the ESRB, EBA and EIOPA).[157] ESMA's Chairperson is also a part of this second group.[158] The latter is elected to his or her full-time position for five years.[159] S/he represents ESMA.[160] Moreover, s/he prepares the board's work and presides over its meetings,[161] without having the right to vote.[162]

Besides its Board of Supervisors, ESMA has a Management Board that is made up of ESMA's Chairperson who chairs the board's meetings,[163] and six members chosen 'by and from the voting members of the Board of Supervisors' for two and a half years.[164] The Management Board takes its

[151] Regulation (EU) No 1095/2010 of the European Parliament and of the Council of 24 November 2010 establishing a European Supervisory Authority (European Securities and Markets Authority), amending Decision No 716/2009/EC and repealing Commission Decision 2009/77/EC [2010] OJ L331/84, Art 5(1) (hereinafter, 'ESMAReg').

[152] *Ibid.* [153] Art 2(1). [154] Rec (52).

[155] Art 44(1). Simple majority voting is based on the principle of 'one member; one vote'. The rules defining a qualified majority are those of the Treaties.

[156] Note that the regulation refers to market actors as either a 'financial market participant' or a 'key financial market participant'. Both are defined terms (Art 4(1) and (2)). For convenience purposes, I will continue referring to market actors, hereinafter.

[157] Art 40(1). [158] *Ibid.*

[159] Art 48(3). His mandate can be renewed once (*ibid.*).

[160] Arts 5(3) and 48(1).

[161] Art 48(1). [162] Art 40(1)(a). [163] Art 48(1).

[164] Art 45(1). The mandates of the six elected members can be renewed once (*ibid.*).

decisions on the basis of a majority of the members that are present.[165] The Commission and ESMA's Executive Director can also attend the meetings of the board, but they have no voting rights, except that the Commission can vote on budgetary matters.[166] The role of the Management Board is to make sure that ESMA fulfils its mission and its tasks.[167] It is empowered to propose ESMA's annual and multi-annual work programmes to the Board of Supervisors.[168] It also has budgetary powers[169] and certain decision-making powers for staff matters and over the arrangements governing access to ESMA documents.[170] It has the power to propose ESMA's annual report to the Board of Supervisors for approval.[171] Finally, it is empowered to appoint a number of persons to the Board of Appeal which has competence to review ESMA's measures.[172] It can also remove them, as a disciplinary sanction, after consulting the Board of Supervisors.[173]

The day-to-day management of ESMA rests, meanwhile, with its Executive Director, a 'full-time independent professional' elected for five years by the Board of Supervisors.[174] S/he is in charge of implementing ESMA's budget, but also its work programme (guided by the Board of Supervisors and under the supervision of the Management Board).[175] S/he manages the functioning of the Authority by, for example, adopting the necessary internal measures.[176] Besides these execution tasks, the Executive Director prepares the work of the Management Board, contributes to budgetary matters by preparing an initial draft budget, prepares ESMA's work programmes and draws up a draft report which the Management Board uses as a basis for proposing ESMA's annual report to the Board of Supervisors.[177] The Executive Director can also attend the meetings of the Board of Supervisors and the Management Board, but without being able to vote on any matters.[178]

The ESMA Regulation also makes provision for the establishment of a Joint Committee of European Supervisory Authorities which is supposed

[165] Art 45(2). [166] *Ibid.* [167] Art 47(1).
[168] Art 47(2). [169] Art 47(3). [170] Art 47(4) and (5).
[171] Art 47(6). The proposed annual report must be based on a draft report prepared by ESMA's Executive Director.
[172] Art 47(8). It must first consult the Board of Supervisors (Art 58(3)).
[173] Art 47(8). It presupposes 'serious misconduct' by the Board of Appeal member (Art 58(5)).
[174] Art 51(1), (2) and (3); Art 53(1). Its mandate can be renewed once (Art 51(3)).
[175] Arts 53(2) and (6).
[176] Art 53(3). The Executive Director has also certain powers over staff matters (Art 58(8)).
[177] Art 53(1), (4), (5), (6) and (7). [178] Arts 40(6) and 45(2).

to become a place for cooperation and for ensuring cross-sector consistency among ESAs.[179] Another institutional innovation is the establishment of a Board of Appeal which is set up as a 'joint body' among the three ESAs.[180] The establishment of an appeal's board is a response to the fact that the ESAs decisions will have greater authority than the former Level 3 measures. The procedure allows a person (or a competent authority) to appeal a decision taken by ESMA when exercising its powers to deal with EU law breaches, emergency actions or the settlement of disputes between competent authorities under the provisions of its founding regulation, or when ESMA adopts any other decision in accordance with its Framing Acts,[181] provided that the appeal is made by the addressee of the decision.[182] In addition, the procedure is also available to a person who is not the addressee when this person is directly and individually affected by ESMA's decision.[183] Of course, the establishment of the Board of Appeal does not prejudice the TFEU's provisions governing direct actions in front of the Court of Justice which has competence to deal with the decisions of the Board of Appeal or ESMA.[184]

Hence, ESMA's internal structure testifies to the fact that it is a far more developed organisation than CESR ever was. ESMA will also benefit from greater financial and human resources to carry out its tasks. But despite changes to the internal structure, the fact is that in terms of its nature, ESMA is not fundamentally different from CESR. Like CESR, it is a collective securities actor. National securities authorities, acting as ESMA members, share among them most of the decision-making power. To deal with potentially adverse behaviour, the ESMA Regulation includes a number of arrangements and safeguards. The regulation attempts, first of all, to ensure that European actors have some grip on the operation of ESMA. Thus the regulation makes it plain that ESMA is accountable to European actors, i.e., the Council and the European Parliament.[185] What is more, the EP has an important say on the choice of ESMA's chairman. It is empowered to veto his designation.[186] In addition, the chairman can only be removed from his position by the EP (on the basis of a decision of the Board of Supervisors).[187] The EP also has a crucial say on the choice of Executive Director, as the Board of Supervisors can only appoint the

[179] Art 54(1) and (2). It also plays a dispute resolution role under Art 54(4) (see section III, B.4).

[180] Art 58(1).

[181] For the meaning of Framing Acts, see section III, B.4, below.

[182] Art 60(1). [183] *Ibid.* [184] Art 61. [185] Art 3.

[186] Art 48(2). [187] Art 48(5).

director 'after confirmation by the European Parliament'.[188] Finally, both the Council and the EP are entitled to hear ESMA's Chairperson.[189]

As far as decision-making is concerned, the regulation also introduces a series of noteworthy principles and provisions. The regulation explicitly states that ESMA's Chairperson and the heads of national securities authorities in the Board of Supervisors must act 'independently and objectively' in the European interest when fulfilling their tasks under the regulation.[190] Note that there is a corresponding obligation for Member States, European actors and other public/private bodies to abstain from attempting to influence members of the Board of Supervisors.[191] The fact that the Board of Supervisors will generally vote by simple majority should *a priori* expedite decision-making. Admittedly, however, in some specified cases, other arrangements can apply.[192] For instance, ESMA votes by qualified majority when it decides on draft technical standards, guidelines and recommendations;[193] when it votes on budgetary matters under Chapter VI of the regulation;[194] or in the particular case where ESMA has taken a decision to temporarily ban or limit certain market activities and a Member State has asked it to rethink its decision.[195]

These arrangements, especially the voting requirements, make real progress towards ensuring effective decision-making. The fact that ESMA can be held responsible for its inactions in front of the Court of Justice when it is legally obliged to act, is also worth mentioning.[196] The 'think European' rule is, meanwhile, interesting. In theory, it has significant implications for the accountability structure of national authorities. ESMA's members will be required by law to 'think European' when fulfilling their duties in ESMA. But they continue to be separately accountable for their common actions at Member State level where national interests dominate. The main benefit for competent authorities of the 'think European' rule is that it provides them with a justification to defend their actions in front of national actors. Whether the rule will, in practice, have a noticeable

[188] Art 51(2). [189] Art 50.

[190] Art 42. Nor can they solicit or take instructions from EU actors, Member States or public/private bodies. See also Arts 1(5) and 46 in relation to ESMA (as a whole) and the Management Board; Arts 49 and 52 on the independence of the Chairperson and the Executive Director.

[191] Art 42. Similar obligations are found in Art 46 (with respect to the Management Board), Art 49 (Chairperson) and Art 52 (Executive Director).

[192] See Art 44(1) for details.

[193] Art 44(1) referring to Arts 10–16.

[194] Art 44(1). [195] Art 44(1) and Art 9(5). [196] Art 61(3).

effect on attitudes of competent authorities is uncertain. In any event, an obligation to 'think European', does not and should not prevent disagreements about what actually is in the best interest of the EU.

As a more general comment, it is apparent that ESMA's founding regulation makes a certain assumption about the future behaviour and interaction of competent authorities in ESMA: competent authorities must be ready to confront and challenge each other. This arguably presupposes a certain shift in attitudes. Recall that CESR's members tended, as a matter of principle, to vote by consensus.[197] ESMA's members, on the other hand, must be prepared to make effective use of the new voting arrangements instead of spending, in practice, unreasonable amounts of time and effort on reaching consensus between them in the shadow of a vote. Other arrangements too presuppose that competent authorities are willing to challenge and stand up to each other – think, for instance, of dispute settlement. Indeed, ESMA is expected to stand its ground even against political leaders; for instance, in the context of a crisis situation or when ESMA considers it necessary to ban or limit financial activities for a certain period of time.

4 Tasks and functions

Introduction I examine ESMA's tasks and functions next. When exercising its tasks, ESMA must act in accordance with the powers that were conferred upon it by its founding act. In addition, it must act within the scope of various legislative acts and subordinate measures in the field in which it operates, and any further binding EU acts that vest powers in ESMA.[198] In order to ease the presentation, I will refer to all of these acts hereinafter as 'Framing Acts'. Note that in areas of activities of market actors, ESMA can also take action with respect to issues that are not 'directly covered' by the Framing Acts, as long as its actions ensure that the Framing Acts are effectively and consistently applied.[199] Clearing and settlement or matters pertaining to derivatives and take-over bids are expressly mentioned as fields where ESMA can take 'appropriate action'.[200]

[197] See section III, A.1, above. [198] Art 1(2).

[199] Art 1(3). The regulation mentions fields such as 'corporate governance, auditing and financial reporting' as also being included (*ibid.*)

[200] *Ibid.*

Level- and circuit-switchers In order to ensure that ESMA can act effectively within its scope of activities and that the institutional balance of powers (or the distribution of competence) is not undermined, ESMA's founding regulation enacts a number of 'level-switcher' and 'circuit-switcher' rules. To explain the meaning of level- and circuit-switchers, I begin by describing a simple model in which decision-making is made at two levels. At a first level, decisions are made by EU institutions, i.e., the Commission, the Council or the European Parliament. At a second level, decision-making is in the hands of supervisors, i.e., ESMA or competent authorities acting individually. Each of these levels includes a number of circuits. In other words, a level is made of circuits; decisions made by actors operating at the same level (e.g., at the supervisory level) can be made by using different circuits. A circuit represents a specific configuration of actors making decisions. For instance, at the supervisory level, decisions can be made by competent authorities acting individually in their respective Member States, or by ESMA. In the latter case, competent authorities act collectively. Likewise, at the first level, decisions can be made in different institutional configurations (e.g., the Commission acting alone, the Council acting alone, institutions acting together, and so on).

Switching levels means switching between the first and second level of decision-making; switching circuits means switching between circuits at a given level. It is worth noting that the difference between levels does not correspond to the difference between the EU level and the Member State level. This difference is irrelevant in the present context. Instead what matters is the nature of the actor that takes the decision: EU actors (in the sense of Union institutions) or supervisory actors. The criterion for distinguishing between circuits is the specific configuration of actors at a given level.

The concept of level-switching and circuit-switching is useful for at least two reasons. First, it is at the heart of ESMA's founding regulation; second, circuit-switcher and level-switcher rules are among the main innovations of the ESFS. Specifically, level-switching and circuit-switching is the EU legislature's solution to the conundrum of creating a more powerful collective securities authority whilst making the delegation of powers to ESMA politically and constitutionally acceptable. The purpose of circuit-switching is to deal with weaknesses at the supervisory level. It is a response to the failings of the previous Level 3 committee structure and is supposed to ensure that ESMA has the means to take action if competent authorities fail to act. The purpose of level-switching is mostly to safeguard the EU's institutional balance of power (as a constitutional principle or as a political concept expressing what EU institutions consider to be an acceptable delegation), or simply to safeguard the interests of Member States. It is important to appreciate that the purpose of level-switching can as much have a constitutional as a political reason. Indeed, some level-switching rules have a lesser bearing on the question of *Meroni* compliance,[201] and were rather added in order to make the founding texts of the ESAs acceptable among Member States.[202] With this in mind, I turn to ESMA's main tasks.

A single rulebook – regulatory technical standards One of the major innovations of the ESMA Regulation is that it empowers ESMA to play a significant role in fashioning a single European rulebook. ESMA can develop 'draft regulatory technical standards'. It presupposes that the Council and the Parliament authorise the Commission to adopt regulatory technical standards by way of delegated acts.[203] The aim is to 'ensure consistent harmonisation' in areas identified in the Framing Acts.[204]

The regulation seeks to ensure that the adoption of such technical standards is compliant with the principles in *Meroni* or, for that matter, *Romano* through, at least, two means. First, the regulation states explicitly that the standards cannot involve 'strategic decisions or policy choices'.[205] Moreover, their content must be structured by the acts from which they derive.[206] There is a second safeguard in the form of a level-switcher rule: the Commission must endorse ESMA's draft standards;[207] ESMA has no power to adopt rules of general application. This power is vested with the Commission which exercises it by using its powers to adopt delegated acts.

When considering whether to endorse ESMA's draft standards, the Commission has a number of options: it can endorse them in full or in part; it can amend them; or it can reject them.[208] In order to strike a proper balance between the competence of ESMA, which is in its field after all

[201] *A priori*, there are other means that are supposed to ensure '*Meroni* compliance'; for instance, the provisions on appeals (ESMAReg Art 60). The fact that the Treaty of Lisbon made changes to the Treaty rules governing direct actions in front of the Court of Justice, by providing that third parties can, in certain circumstances, question the legality of decisions of agencies is also worth mentioning (TFEU Art 263).

[202] See the discussion on the safeguard clauses, below.

[203] ESMAReg Art 10(1). Note that the Framing Acts in question must be legislative acts.

[204] *Ibid.* [205] *Ibid.* [206] *Ibid.*

[207] *Ibid.* [208] *Ibid.*

the repository of expertise, and the prerogatives of the Commission, the regulation adds a number of requirements. If the Commission is not willing to endorse a proposed standard or if it intends only to endorse it in part or after amendment, the Commission must justify its decision.[209] ESMA has, meanwhile, the right to resubmit a draft standard in amended form, taking the Commission's proposed amendments as a basis.[210] But the Commission has to make the final decision on the draft standard. Moreover, if ESMA fails to produce an amended draft standard or produces one that is not amended in a manner which is 'consistent' with the Commission's amendments, the latter can adopt a standard with those amendments that it considers pertinent or turn down the draft standard.[211] The only requirement is that any changes to ESMA's draft standards are preceded by 'prior coordination' with ESMA.[212]

The Commission has other prerogatives. It can, for instance, extend the time limit within which ESMA is expected to produce a standard, if the latter plainly fails to submit a draft standard during the time period that was defined by the EU legislature.[213] But the Commission's right to press ahead in this case without ESMA's contribution is curtailed by the fact that the Commission can only adopt a technical standard without ESMA's participation, if ESMA fails to produce the draft standard within the extended time period.[214] What is more, before adopting its own technical standard, the Commission must submit it to ESMA.[215] The latter is entitled to propose amendments.[216] But even so, the Commission is not bound by ESMA's amendments.[217] The only requirement is that changes to any draft standards produced by ESMA are preceded by 'prior coordination' with ESMA.[218]

Given that the standards are adopted as delegated acts, the Council and the EP also have certain powers. Each has the power to revoke the delegation.[219] The delegation is limited to four years, but is extended automatically, except where the Council or Parliament decides to revoke it.[220] Each institution is entitled to be kept informed and be forwarded or notified

[209] *Ibid*. See also Art 14(1).
[210] ESMA will submit them in the form of a formal opinion (Art 10(1)).
[211] *Ibid*.
[212] *Ibid*. The requirement is satisfied if the Commission acts in accordance with Art 10(1).
[213] Art 10(2). [214] Art 10(3).
[215] It must also forward it to the EP and the Council (Art 10(3)).
[216] *Ibid*. [217] *Ibid*.
[218] *Ibid*. The requirement is satisfied if the Commission acts in accordance with Art 10(1).
[219] Art 12. [220] Art 11.

of the necessary documents.[221] They can hear ESMA's chairman and the relevant Commissioner in cases where the Commission intends to amend or to turn down ESMA's draft standards.[222] Finally, each institution has a right to veto an adopted technical standard.[223]

It is apparent that these provisions, especially the level-switcher rule, seek to strike a balance between ensuring that ESMA can put its expertise to good use and that the delegation of powers does not fall foul of the Court's case law. Whilst the regulation puts in place checks and balances, it leaves the Commission a true power of appreciation. To be sure, the recitals of the regulation adopt a somewhat more cautious tone with respect to the power of the Commission to depart from ESMA's draft standards. They stress that the Commission should only exceptionally and in limited cases amend the standards.[224] Moreover, they record the Commission's intention to rely, as a matter of principle, on ESMA to develop standards.[225] It is obvious that the Commission should rely on ESMA's work. Politically, the Commission would find itself in an uncomfortable position if it were to plainly, or consistently, ignore ESMA's advice. Indeed, entrusting ESMA with work on technical standards would otherwise serve little purpose. The legislature might just as well use the ordinary route by entrusting the Commission with the power to adopt 'ordinary' delegated acts at Level 2. But because of *Meroni* the legislature was, arguably, right not to write strict restrictions on the exercise of the Commission's powers into the legally binding text of the regulation.

Implementing technical standards Technical standards can also be adopted as implementing acts.[226] Although delegated and implementing acts have different Treaty bases and are subject to different Treaty requirements, the procedures for endorsing implementing technical standards and regulatory technical standards are alike under the ESMA Regulation. The procedure for adopting implementing technical standards is, therefore, also based on the same level-switcher rule. But there are a few differences and I will highlight the two main ones. First, the regulation insists on the content of implementing technical standards. They are supposed to specify the 'conditions of application' of ESMA's Framing Acts.[227] Second, the Council and the Parliament are not given any powers to revoke the delegation of powers or veto an adopted standard. Nor is the delegation

[221] Arts 10(1), 10(3) and 11(2) and 14(1).
[222] Art 14(2). [223] Art 13(1). [224] Rec (23).
[225] Rec (24). [226] Art 15. [227] Art 15(1).

limited in time. The reason for these differences is mainly based on the legal difference between delegated and implementing acts. Recall that in the case of implementing acts, control over the Commission's powers is supposed to be exercised by Member States.[228]

Proper application of European rules and supervisory practices ESMA is expected to play a crucial role in fostering a 'common, uniform and consistent application of Union law' and in developing 'consistent, efficient and effective supervisory practices'.[229] For these purposes, ESMA can develop guidelines and recommendations for competent authorities and market actors.[230] These measures are not binding. But their addressees are expected to 'make every effort to comply' with them.[231] Besides, the regulation puts in place arrangements intended to make it more difficult for addressees to simply ignore them. First, competent authorities must disclose, within two months of the release of ESMA's guidelines/recommendations, whether they comply or, at least, expect to comply, with the relevant measure.[232] This requirement creates a positive obligation for competent authorities; keeping silent is not good enough. They must explain their reasons if they fail to comply or do not expect to comply.[233] ESMA is required to 'name and shame' such competent authorities by making a publication to this effect.[234] Moreover, it is expected to name competent authorities, which fail to comply, in its annual report and to take some responsibility for their behaviour by explaining how it expects to deal with such behaviour in the future.[235] Note that market actors can also be asked to disclose whether they comply with the relevant measures.[236]

Remedying breaches of EU law ESMA will play a role in policing the application of its Framing Acts and its regulatory and implementing technical standards.[237] More specifically, if a competent authority fails to apply ESMA's Framing Acts or its technical standards, or applies them in a manner which seems to breach EU law, especially because it is failing to ensure that a market actor complies with its legal requirements, ESMA can investigate the matter and, if necessary, issue a recommendation to the competent authority stating which actions the latter should take in

[228] See section II, B, above.
[229] Art 16(1). [230] Art 16. [231] Art 16(3).
[232] *Ibid.* [233] *Ibid.* [234] *Ibid.*
[235] Art 16(4). [236] Art 16(3). [237] Art 17.

order to redress the situation.[238] The competent authority is obliged to let ESMA know how it will remedy the situation.[239]

The difficulty with ESMA taking more forceful action against a competent authority is that ESMA is not the guardian of the Treaties, or for that matter, EU law. Thus, in order to ensure that the balance of powers is respected, the regulation includes another level-switcher rule: if the competent authority does not redress the situation, the regulation makes provision for the Commission to take matters into its own hands by issuing a formal opinion requiring the contravening authority to take the necessary steps to comply with the relevant EU law provisions.[240]

Once the Commission has taken action, ESMA is not, by the same token, relieved from its duties. In order to ensure maximum compliance, the regulation enacts a circuit-switcher rule. If the competent authority fails to comply within the time period set by the Commission, ESMA can effectively replace the contravening competent authority and address an individual decision to a market actor who, given the ongoing failings of the competent authority, does not comply with relevant EU law provisions.[241] The conditions that must be met before ESMA can take action appear fairly strict.[242] First, it must be necessary to 'remedy in a timely manner [the] non-compliance' in order to 'maintain or restore neutral conditions of competition in the market or ensure the orderly functioning and integrity of the financial system'.[243] What is more, ESMA can only take action if the relevant requirements found in its Framing Acts are directly applicable to the market actor(s).[244] Thus, ESMA can exercise its powers only with respect to rules found in a regulation, as opposed to a directive which requires implementation in national law.[245] Recall also in this context that the Treaty reserves, as a general rule, the implementation of EU law to Member States.[246] ESMA's discretion will be further curtailed by the fact that the decision that it addresses to a market actor must conform to the Commission's formal opinion.[247] Once the individual decision is adopted by ESMA, it will 'prevail' over any earlier decision taken by the competent authorities.[248] The latter will be bound to comply with it (or, for that matter, the Commission's opinion).[249] Note that ESMA

[238] Art 17(1), (2) and (3). [239] Art 17(3).

[240] Art 17(4). [241] Art 17(6).

[242] Rec (29) also underlines the exceptional nature of this power by stating that it should only be used 'as a last resort', in the case of 'persistent inaction by the competent authority'.

[243] Art 17(6). [244] *Ibid.*

[245] The term 'directly applicable' can be ambiguous. See Rec (29) for clarification.

[246] TFEU Art 291(1).

[247] Art 17(6). [248] Art 17(7). [249] *Ibid.*

is also expected to identify any contravening competent authority/market actor in its annual report.[250]

Promoting a common supervisory culture and consistency in the work of authorities To promote, *inter alia*, a shared supervisory culture and consistency in the supervisory practices between competent authorities, the regulation lists a number of minimum tasks that ESMA is expected to carry out. Specifically, it can address opinions to competent authorities; work on an effective exchange of information; help define supervisory standards; assess the application of technical standards, guidelines and recommendations and suggest amendments where necessary; develop common training programmes; and promote staff exchanges and secondments.[251] In order to promote shared supervisory arrangements, the regulation also provides that ESMA should develop 'new practical instruments and convergence tools'.[252]

Conciliation and dispute settlement powers Conciliation and dispute settlement is another noteworthy innovation. Admittedly mediation was already part of CESR's toolkit, but under the ESMA Regulation the matter is taken to an altogether new level. ESMA's founding text sets out a multi-stage procedure which ties (non-binding) conciliation and binding dispute settlement together.[253] ESMA can exercise its powers in relation to disagreements between competent authorities in the same sector;[254] or, as part of the joint committee, in relation to disputes across sectors;[255] or in relation to disagreements between competent authorities in colleges.[256]

Under the regulation, ESMA first plays the role of a mediator in order to attempt to 'assist the authorities in reaching an agreement'.[257] Specifically, ESMA can take action if there is a disagreement between competent authorities from different Member States on the 'procedure or content of an action or inaction' in the cases specified in ESMA's Framing Acts.[258] It presupposes that ESMA is being asked to intervene by a competent authority that is concerned by the disagreement.[259] There is, however, a second scenario under the regulation where there is no need for ESMA

[250] Art 17(8). [251] Art 29(1). [252] Art 29(2).
[253] Art 19. [254] *Ibid.*
[255] Art 20. See also Art 56 in this context.
[256] Art 21(4). [257] Art 19(1).
[258] *Ibid.* Given the internal market legal basis on which the regulation is based, the procedure is obviously meant to deal with disagreement in a cross-border context only (see Rec (32)).
[259] Art 19(1).

to be asked to intervene. If provided for in the legislation which is part of ESMA's Framing Acts and where the existence of a disagreement can be established on the basis of 'objective criteria', ESMA can intervene in the disagreement 'on its own initiative'.[260] The reference to 'objective criteria' was probably inspired by the Court's reasoning in *Meroni*. Its aim is to constrain ESMA's discretion in the case where it has the power to intervene on its own initiative. There will be more to say about this in Chapter 6. For now it suffices to note that if competent authorities fail to resolve their dispute with the help of ESMA, the matter is supposed to be resolved by switching circuits. In other words, ESMA can take matters into its own hands by, first of all, adopting a legally binding decision requesting the competent authorities to take action or abstain from action in order to resolve the matter and, by the same token, comply with EU law.[261] What is more, if a competent authority does not comply with ESMA's decision and, as a result, a market actor fails to comply with obligations that are directly applicable to it pursuant to ESMA's Framing Acts, ESMA can address an individual decision to the market actor requesting it to comply with EU law by either taking an action or ending a practice, as the case may be.[262] ESMA's decision with respect to the market actor will prevail over any earlier decision of the competent authorities.[263] Any action by the latter must henceforth comply with ESMA's decisions.[264]

Entrusting ESMA with the power to resolve disagreements by taking a binding decision against a competent authority, especially in colleges, proved to be a contentious proposal during the negotiations. For some Member States, it was a step too far. They saw it as affecting their 'fiscal responsibilities'.[265] The argument was well chosen in the wake of the banking crisis when questions about who should bear the cost of a failing cross-border financial institution loomed large. To find a solution agreeable to all Member States, the legislature added a safeguard clause. Under this clause, ESMA must first of all, as a preventive measure, ensure that it does not impinge 'in any way' on the fiscal responsibilities of Member States.[266] Where a Member State is, nonetheless, of the opinion that its fiscal responsibilities are affected and that, therefore, its competent authority will not comply with ESMA's decision, the regulation provides that the Member State should inform ESMA and the Commission of this fact and state its reasons.[267] This notification

260 *Ibid.* 261 Art 19(3). 262 Art 19(4).
263 Art 19(5). 264 *Ibid.*
265 European Council, 'Presidency Conclusions – 18/19 June 2009', para. 20.
266 Art 38(1). 267 Art 38(2).

will suspend ESMA's decision and oblige the latter to reassess its decision.[268] Where ESMA decides to maintain its decision, the ESMA Regulation builds into the safeguard clause a level-switcher rule. The matter is brought in front of the Council,[269] which decides by a majority of the votes that are cast whether to maintain ESMA's decision.[270] The Council will thus settle the matter.

The meaning of 'fiscal responsibility' was not defined in the regulation, but the regulation nevertheless states that Member States, which seek to oppose ESMA's decision, must state their reasons for believing that their fiscal responsibilities are affected.[271] If ESMA decides not to withdraw its decision, there is a corresponding obligation for ESMA to state why it thinks otherwise.[272] There is another provision that arguably helps to specify the concept of fiscal responsibility. The regulation stresses that the safeguard clause should not be abused, especially by challenging a decision which has no 'significant or material fiscal impact'.[273] In other words, if the decision has a *de minimis* impact on the fiscal responsibility of a Member State, the safeguard clause cannot be used. Indeed, using it for this purpose would be unlawful and 'incompatible with the internal market'.[274] The result is that although ESMA is under an obligation not to affect 'in any way' the fiscal responsibility of Member States, Member States can only switch levels in order to challenge ESMA's assessment and decision if there is more than a *de minimis* impact.

Emergency situations One important lesson from the financial crisis was that a proper mechanism was needed for dealing with crisis situations. ESMA's founding text includes such a provision. The level of detail and the twists in the agreed text suggest, however, that the provision was not easily agreed. The regulation provides for ESMA to play a role in facilitating and coordinating the actions of competent authorities where adverse events risk seriously endangering the proper functioning and integrity of markets, or the stability of the EU financial system.[275] But the crux of the new arrangements concerns ESMA's power to take individual decisions. First, ESMA is empowered to address individual decisions to competent authorities.[276] The aim is to ensure that, exceptionally, when coordinated action is required in order to deal with events that could pose a serious

268 *Ibid.* 269 *Ibid.*

270 *Ibid.* ESMA's decision will be terminated if the Council does not decide to maintain it.

271 *Ibid.* 272 *Ibid.* 273 Art 38(5). 274 *Ibid.*

275 Art 18(1). 276 Art 18(3).

danger to the proper functioning or integrity of markets or the stability of the EU financial system, ESMA can request competent authorities to take action to address such events and, thereby, make sure that market actors/competent authorities meet their legislative obligations in the Framing Acts.[277]

Second, where a competent authority ignores ESMA's decision, ESMA is empowered to address an individual decision to a market actor. This second rule is a circuit-switcher rule: ESMA can, effectively, take decisions in place of the contravening authority. Its decision will prevail over any earlier decision of the competent authorities.[278] The aim is to ensure that, where legislative requirements found in ESMA's Framing Acts or requirements found in its technical standards are directly applicable to a market actor, ESMA can instruct a market actor to take an action or end a practice in order to comply with its legal requirements.[279]

ESMA's powers are significant, but their exercise is, nevertheless, subject to various conditions and safeguards, including two level-switcher rules. The first level-switcher rule applies with respect to the power to determine the existence of an emergency situation, which is a prerequisite for ESMA to be able to exercise its powers. In its proposal on establishing ESMA, the Commission had suggested that it should be the institution to decide on this matter. Member States were not impressed. As adopted, the power is mainly in the hands of the Council. The Commission, the ESRB or ESMA must request the Council to take such a decision.[280] But it is the Council who has the power to declare an emergency situation[281] and to terminate its decision.[282] Note that until it comes to the latter conclusion, the Council must re-examine regularly (at a minimum, each month) its decision.[283] If it fails to renew the decision 'at the end of a one-month period', the decision will automatically come to an end.[284]

The power to address a decision to a market actor is subject to additional conditions. As mentioned, it presupposes that a competent authority does not abide by a decision taken by ESMA. It also presupposes that the competent authority has failed to apply any of the legislative acts that are part of ESMA's Framing Acts (or any of the technical standards made under the authority of such acts), or applies them in a manner which seems to be a 'manifest breach' of the acts.[285] Moreover, addressing this

[277] *Ibid.* [278] Art 18(5). [279] Art 18(4). [280] Art 18(2).

[281] *Ibid.* In taking its decision, the Council is only required to consult the Commission, the ESRB and, if necessary, the ESAs.

[282] *Ibid.* [283] *Ibid.* [284] *Ibid.* [285] Art 18(4).

state of affairs must be considered urgent for re-establishing the proper functioning and integrity of the markets or the stability of the EU financial system.[286]

If these conditions were not stringent enough, the ESMA Regulation enacts a second level-switcher rule; a safeguard clause similar to the one which I examined above in relation to dispute settlement. It allows a Member State to call upon the Council to reconsider a decision taken by ESMA against a competent authority, on the grounds that the decision affects its fiscal responsibility.[287] The Council will decide by a simple majority whether to end ESMA's decision.[288] While awaiting the decision of the Council, ESMA's decision will be suspended.[289] If at the outcome of the vote, the Council decides not to end ESMA's decision, the Member State in question can call upon the Council a second time to re-assess its case.[290] The Council will have to vote again and decide whether or not to confirm its earlier decision. Note that the use of this level-switcher (safeguard) rule is subject to the same no-abuse clause as is the safeguard clause that applies for decisions taken by ESMA in the context of the settlement of disagreements between competent authorities.[291]

Consumer protection and policing financial activities The role that ESMA plays with respect to consumer protection and the monitoring and policing of financial activities, can also be seen as a legislative response to the financial crisis.[292] ESMA has soft-law powers in order to ensure that the financial markets for consumer products and services are, in essence, consumer friendly.[293] ESMA is, for example, expected to play a role in coordinating and evaluating initiatives aimed at educating investors.[294] It is also supposed to keep an eye on financial activities and where necessary send out warnings if it believes that such activities might pose a risk to its objectives.[295] But one power, in particular, stands out. ESMA is empowered to ban, or restrict, for a limited time market activities that risk affecting the proper functioning and integrity of markets or the stability of the EU financial system.[296] Admittedly, the regulation seeks to somewhat structure the delegation of powers, presumably in order to ensure '*Meroni* compliance'. It makes plain that ESMA can only take such

[286] *Ibid.* [287] Art 38(3). [288] *Ibid.*

[289] *Ibid.* The suspensive effect will end if the Council cannot agree to revoke ESMA's decision

[290] Art 38(4). [291] Art 38(5). [292] Art 9. [293] Art 9(1).

[294] Art 9(1)(b). [295] Art 9(2) and (3). [296] Art 9(5).

measures if ESMA's Framing Acts provide for this and the conditions specified in these acts are met, or if such an action is necessary in order to deal with an emergency situation.[297] In the latter case the regulation's requirements on emergency situations are applicable, including the conditions that apply thereunder. ESMA must also regularly (at a minimum every three months) reassess its decision. If not reaffirmed after three months, the decision ends automatically.[298] On the other hand, there is no level-switcher rule.[299] A Member State can ask ESMA to reconsider the ban or restriction, but ESMA is not required to overturn its decision as a result.[300] It remains to be seen how these provisions will be put into practice and how, precisely, ESMA's Framing Acts will structure this type of delegation in order to ensure that the delegation complies with the constitutional principles discussed earlier.

Day-to-day supervision The exercise of day-to-day supervision represents in many ways the boundary between the competences of national authorities and the new ESAs. Day-to-day supervision continues being organised around the home country model, although colleges play an important role for supervising cross-border financial firms. *De Larosière*, recommended that for certain institutions which have an EU wide impact, the ESAs should be entrusted with licensing and direct oversight powers.[301] The proposals proved controversial in the run-up to the Commission's formal proposals on the ESFS and the ESRB. But in June 2009, the European Council agreed that the ESAs should be given oversight powers over credit rating agencies, provided that decisions taken by the ESAs did not encroach on the fiscal responsibility of Member States.[302] In a concession to the UK government, the Council conclusions did not, however, refer to post-trading facilities as a type of institution that should be subject to direct ESA supervision.[303] The question of ESMA's powers over credit rating agencies, which will be specified in separate legislation, continued to prove controversial during the negotiations of ESMA's founding text in 2010, but EU institutions finally

[297] *Ibid.* [298] *Ibid.*

[299] A market actor might, however, be able to rely on the provisions governing appeals. See Arts 60 and 61.

[300] Art 9(5). [301] '*de Larosière* Report' 53.

[302] European Council, 'Presidency Conclusions – 18/19 June 2009', para. 20.

[303] EurActiv 'EU leaders back financial supervision overhaul' (19 June 2009), www.euractiv.com/en/financial-services/eu-leaders-back-financial-supervision-overhaul/article-183341 (noting that the concession concerned 'clearing houses for derivatives').

agreed that ESMA would have supervisory competence for credit rating agencies. Note that the Commission stated in a declaration that, in the future, the ESAs might be given supervisory competence in other fields (e.g., for certain market infrastructure).[304]

Additional tasks: peer reviews, tasks with respect to colleges, etc. ESMA has various other important tasks which cannot be examined exhaustively within the scope of this chapter. For instance, like its predecessor, ESMA carries out peer reviews which may materialise in recommendations or guidelines.[305] They may also inform its work on technical standards.[306] ESMA carries out various tasks with respect to colleges.[307] I have already mentioned its dispute settlement role. *Inter alia*, it is also expected to participate in improving the operation of colleges and to promote a coherent application of EU rules among colleges.[308] ESMA's founding text also includes important new provisions on delegation. Thus, competent authorities can, in certain cases, delegate powers to ESMA or indeed to other competent authorities.[309] ESMA is meant to encourage and make it easier for competent authorities to delegate powers between them.[310] ESMA also carries out various tasks in an effort to address and deal with the consequences of systemic risk.[311] It has a general coordinating function to play among competent authorities, especially when there is a risk to the proper functioning and integrity of the markets or the stability of the EU financial system.[312] Moreover, it has an important role to play in watching, evaluating and reporting on market developments, including on micro-prudential trends and on the existence of risks and weaknesses in its field.[313] In this context, it is also expected to work together with the ESRB, on launching and coordinating evaluations of how resilient market actors are to adverse events.[314] It can address opinions to EU actors on any matter that is within its competence.[315] Last but not least, it has a role to play in the external field. It can establish contacts with third-country or international actors and conclude external administrative arrangements.[316] Moreover, it is also

304 Commission Statement annexed to 'Position of the European Parliament adopted at first reading on 22 September 2010 with a view to the adoption of Regulation (EU) No .../2010 of the European Parliament and of the Council establishing a European *Supervisory* Authority *(European Securities and Markets Authority)*' (P7_TC1-COD(2009)0144).

305 Art 30(1) and (3). 306 Art 30(3). 307 Art 21.

308 Art 21(1). 309 Art 28(1). 310 Art 28(2).

311 Art 22. 312 Art 31. 313 Art 32.

314 Art 32(2). 315 Art 34(1). 316 Art 33(1).

expected to participate in drawing up equivalence decisions regarding third-country supervisory regimes.[317]

IV National securities authorities

So far, this chapter has focused on the role of EU actors and collective actors in the securities field. Before concluding, this section turns briefly to actors at national level, i.e., competent authorities. Often known by their acronyms – the BaFIN (the German *Bundesanstalt für Finanzdienstleistungsaufsicht*), the Consob (the Italian *Commissione Nazionale per le Società e la Borsa*), the AFM (the Dutch *Autoriteit Financiële Markten*), and so on – they are the main actors involved in supervising market actors on a day-to-day basis and play a crucial role in enforcing EU securities laws. Within the scope of their competences, they have general rule-making powers, individual decision-making powers, and a toolkit of investigatory and enforcement powers. They were established by national law which determines their *raison d'être*, defines their scope of competences and the means for carrying out their tasks.

The fact that supervision and enforcement rests largely with national authorities is characteristic of the way in which the EU operates. On the one hand, it means that competent authorities are embedded closely in the markets that they regulate and supervise. Over the years, they have developed different sets and levels of skills, depending on the way in which national securities markets have developed. The establishment of CESR and ESMA allowed pooling this expertise together. On the other hand, however, competent authorities in Europe have had, at least in the past, a fairly different appreciation of their role. As a result, authorities have liked to do things differently.[318] One of the challenges for ESMA is to find common ways among these authorities.

To be sure, the reason why competent authorities might like to do things differently can have multiple causes. There are interest-based considerations at play here, not least because there has traditionally been a level of competition between financial market places in Europe. But other factors also matter; for instance, values, norms, beliefs or even identities and culture, which are often defined loosely in the political science literature as different types of 'ideas', as opposed to interests.[319] These 'ideas' can have

[317] Art 33(2).

[318] Cf., CESR, 'Himalaya Report' 12.

[319] On the role of ideas, see, e.g., J. Campbell, *Institutional Change and Globalization* (Princeton University Press, Princeton, 2004). See also Chapter 9.

a noteworthy impact on how authorities define their role. Granted, differences in role disposition (or 'role orientation'[320]) are generally differences in emphasis. All authorities, for example, have concerns about (retail) investor protection. But in Europe, they have nevertheless tended to have different views about the relative emphasis that should be placed on this goal. For example, when judged by its objectives and second-order principles of good regulation, the FSA, when acting as the UK Listing Authority (UKLA),[321] emerges as quite a different organisation than, say, the French AMF. The UKLA must, for example, have regard to (second-order) principles, such as 'the international character of capital markets' and the 'desirability of maintaining the competitive position of the United Kingdom'.[322] The FSA has separate objectives and principles of good regulation, but the latter are similar to those of the UKLA.[323] On the other hand, the AMF's statutory objectives focus, in essence, on ensuring investor protection and preserving market integrity.[324] Note that the AMF's institutional mandate has a long history. For the most part, it was that of the Cob, the French stock exchange commission (*Commission des opérations de bourse*),[325] one of the authorities that the AMF replaced in 2003. As an organisation, the Cob was known for a more 'administrative',[326] never mind, 'bureaucratic'[327] decision-making style.

Based on this account of objectives and statutory principles, the AMF and the FSA/UKLA appear, at a root level, to be different types of

320 I borrow the term from Scharpf, *Games Real Actors Play* 64.

321 The UKLA agrees general and specific objectives with the UK Treasury. Until the change of government in the UK, these objectives were available on the Treasury's webpage. They are archived at http://webarchive.nationalarchives.gov.uk/+/www.hm-treasury.gov.uk/fin_list.htm. For a more detailed analysis, see P. Schammo, *The Prospectus Directive – New Perspectives on Issuer's Choice and Regulatory Competition* (D. Phil. dissertation, unpublished, Oxford University, 2006) 186–95.

322 FSMA s 73(1).

323 FSMA s 2(3).

324 C. monét. fin. Art L. 621-1. states that the AMF 'deals with protection of the savings invested in financial instruments and all other investments which give rise to public offerings, the information provided to investors, and the proper functioning of the financial instruments markets. It lends its support to the regulation of those markets at a European and an international level'.

325 See H. de Vauplane, 'L'Autorité des marchés financiers' in H. de Vauplane and J-J. Daigre (eds.), *La Loi sur la Sécurité Financière* (Revue Banque édition, Paris, 2004) 15, 20.

326 *Ibid.*, 19.

327 P-H. Conac, 'La fusion de la Cob et du CMF' in H. de Vauplane and J.-J. Daigre (eds.), *Droit Bancaire et Financier – Mélanges AEDBF-France III* (Revue Banque Editeur, 2002, Paris) 59, 67.

organisations with different overall orientations. As mentioned earlier, it is ESMA's task to develop common ways among such authorities. In this endeavour, it might be helped by the fact that changes in role orientations can, *prima facie*, take place. But as shown in the case of the FSA, the main influences on the way in which competent authorities define and develop their role, whether interest- or idea-based, appear so far at least, to have had a national origin, as opposed to an EU origin. I will return to the point in Chapter 6. Suffice it to say that since the collapse of Northern Rock and Lehman Brothers and the high profile Turner review,[328] the FSA has been subject to intense public criticism in the UK. It conceded that it had failed to be 'tough enough'[329] and felt it necessary to re-evaluate its role as the UK financial markets authority. For the FSA, this change was the result of a change in expectations of the public.[330]

But it is also apparent that in the case of the FSA the change was one of truly revolutionary magnitude. It was exceptional and its likelihood is probably best seen as such. Indeed, if changes of this magnitude were a common occurrence, role orientations would arguably be of no particular significance for explaining the behaviour of competent authorities. ESMA would have no cause for concern, as it would have no difficulties in reconciling differences in the way in which competent authorities define their role.[331] Moreover, the recent events that have affected the FSA, although exceptional, also drive the point home that national actors (i.e., the national Parliament and governments) decide the fate of competent authorities. Notwithstanding the will of the FSA to change, the new UK coalition government, which came to power in 2010, intends to break up the FSA and replace it with new authorities.

There is a final point to address. Given the changes that the FSA has gone through, is it still proper to talk of the AMF and the FSA as organisations with different overall orientations? The question is well worth asking because the AMF, although concerned about retail investor protection, is not the mirror image of the Cob.[332] The AMF is nowadays signalling

[328] FSA, 'The Turner review – a regulatory response to the global banking crisis' (March 2009), www.fsa.gov.uk/pubs/other/turner_review.pdf.

[329] H. Sants in front of the Treasury Committee of the House of Commons stating that 'I readily agree with you that historically the FSA was not tough enough'. See House of Commons, 'Banking Crisis – Volume I' (Treasury Committee, 1 April 2009) 294, www.publications.parliament.uk/pa/cm200809/cmselect/cmtreasy/144/144i.pdf.

[330] FSA, 'A regulatory response to the global banking crisis' (DP09/2, March 2009) 186.

[331] Of course, interest-based factors might still matter and complicate agreement between ESMA members.

[332] The fact that, unlike the Cob, a majority of the members of the AMF's *collège*, its general decision-making body, must be chosen because of their professional expertise and that,

openly the need to integrate the competitiveness of the Paris market within its overall strategy defined by its mission statement.[333] Hence, by signalling its intention to be more sensitive to competitiveness concerns, the AMF's discourse seems nowadays to be informed by considerations that are similar to those which have informed the FSA/UKLA. But an instinctive thought is that differences are likely to persist between the general orientations of the UK authority and the French authority. Their incentive makeup is simply different because UK markets are mostly wholesale markets. What is more – arguably – the two authorities do not, necessarily, see competition in the same light. In Chapter 4, we will see how the AMF's concern with competitiveness has persuaded it to fashion reforms which were designed for Euronext Paris. This approach, which focuses on improving the conditions for French market champions, seems consistent with Mark Thatcher's findings on how French policy-makers focus on promoting 'French international champions'.[334] Moreover, this is, for Thatcher, fairly different from the UK, where policy-makers focus instead on creating international competitive markets.[335] Indeed, this general concern for competition is also evident in the case of the UKLA or, for that matter, the FSA.[336]

ESMA will need to steer a course through the maze of considerations and factors that motivate competent authorities. It might just be that focusing on technical issues will insulate ESMA members from other questions. If not, ESMA will ultimately have to find ways of reconciling separate national interests for the benefit of a common overarching EU interest.

V Conclusion: evolutionary or revolutionary change?

This chapter discussed the institutional framework governing the regulation of securities markets and introduced the different actors participating in the creation, application and enforcement of EU prospectus

as a result, market professionals are given a say in the AMF's decisions has been much discussed in the literature. See, e.g., Conac, 'La fusion de la Cob et du CMF' 68–70. For details on the composition of the *collège*, see T. Bonneau and F. Drummond, *Droit des marchés financiers* (Economica, Paris, 2010) 350–52.

333 See e.g., AMF, 'Meilleure Régulation: un premier bilan et programme de travail 2008–2009' (25 avril 2008) 2–3, www.amf-france.org/documents/general/8288_1.pdf.

334 M. Thatcher, 'Regulatory agencies, the state and markets: a Franco-British comparison' (2007) 14 *Journal of European Public Policy* 1028, 1043.

335 *Ibid.*

336 FSMA ss 2(3)(f) and (g); 73(1)(e) and (f).

law. It is apparent that the institutional framework governing securities markets has developed significantly over the years. But how, by way of conclusion, should one characterise these changes?[337] Grundfest, for example, describes the development of US securities regulation as consistent with a pattern of 'sudden evolutionary spurt between relatively tranquil periods of common law interpretation'.[338] This is consistent with the logic of punctuated equilibria,[339] which if transferred into an institutional context, links patterns of prolonged institutional stability with patterns of swift but dramatic change.[340] But in a European context, this description has little fit. Throughout the chapter, I have alluded to the evolutionary nature of change.[341] It is now possible to be more specific, beginning with the changes that Lamfalussy introduced.[342] While the adoption of the Lamfalussy process was a significant development, it did not fundamentally call into question an existing model where regulatory competences are being increasingly centralised at EU level, but the implementation, day-to-day application and enforcement of these rules were more or less left to Member States and their national authorities. At Level 1, the Lamfalussy report did not fundamentally call into question co-decision. It criticised it for being too cumbersome, but unable to replace it, sought to address its problems by relying on comitology decision-making, a well-established practice in many sectors of activities. The establishment of CESR and Level 3 were admittedly innovations, but here too, the Lamfalussy committee sought to build on existing solutions, i.e.,

[337] See also Moloney's analysis on the evolution of EC securities regulation in Moloney, *EC Securities Regulation*.

[338] J. Grundfest, 'Punctuated equilibria in the evolution of United States securities regulation' (2002) 8 *Stanford Journal of Law, Business & Finance* 1, 1.

[339] The concept stems from evolutionary biology. See S. Gould, *The Structure of Evolutionary Theory* (Harvard University Press, Harvard, 2002); N. Eldredge and S. Gould, 'Punctuated equilibria: an alternative to phyletic gradualism' in T. Schopf (ed.) *Models in Paleobiology* (Freeman, Cooper & Co., San Francisco 1972) 82–115.

[340] See P. Genschel, 'The dynamics of inertia: institutional persistence and change in telecommunications and health care' (1997) *Governance* 43, 45; J. Campbell, *Institutional change and globalization* 5; M. Howlett and B. Cashore, 'The dependent variable problem in the study of policy change: understanding policy change as a methodological problem' (2009) 11 *Journal of Comparative Policy Analysis* 33, 34. See also S. Krasner, 'Approaches to the State: alternative conceptions and historical dynamics' (1984) 16 *Comparative Politics* 223, 240–44.

[341] The evolutionary pattern in the securities sector is now well documented. In the governance literature, see M. Thatcher and D. Coen, 'Reshaping European regulatory space: an evolutionary analysis' (2008) 31 *West European Politics* 806. See also NewGov, 'European Regulatory Networks' (Final Report Ref 06/D07, August 2008), www.eu-newgov.org.

[342] See also Thatcher and Coen, 'Reshaping European regulatory space'.

FESCO (the Federation of European Securities Commissions) in particular, which already brought together financial markets authorities.[343] CESR was given few real powers. At Level 3, its power was meant to be the power of argument and persuasion. At Level 4, the Lamfalussy process did not innovate, but merely re-emphasised the role of the Commission. Hence, the Lamfalussy Committee's *tour de force* was to build upon an existing *acquis* in order to design an inclusive approach to securities regulation. As Coen and Thatcher have noted, the changes in the securities field were consistent with an evolutionary or incremental logic of change.[344] In other words, '[c]hange is evolutionary in the sense that today's institutional arrangements differ from but still closely resemble yesterday's because they have inherited many of the predecessors' characteristics' (references omitted).[345]

In trying to explain this pattern of change, one is inevitably drawn to the preferences of existing actors,[346] but also the Treaties' rules and the Court's case law which set limits on the menu of choices that policy actors can envisage pursuing – think of *Meroni* in this context. But what is striking is the pace with which actors were willing to consider changes; indeed so much so that one can, arguably, speak of a form of incremental activism at EU level.[347]

To be sure, the financial crisis has, as an exogenous factor, provided a fresh impetus for reforms. But these reforms do not testify to a revolutionary change in institutional terms. Instead, they represent the next step on a continuum towards greater centralisation and consolidation of decision-making authority within the EU's constitutional framework. *De Larosière* built upon existing institutional solutions, especially the Lamfalussy Level 3 arrangements and the network architecture. The Commission's proposals, which built on the *de Larosière* recommendations, did not create a fundamental rupture with the past either. As established, ESMA is not a single European securities authority. Member State authorities are still the main decision-makers within ESMA. The home-country control

343 'Lamfalussy Report', 31.

344 Thatcher and Coen, 'Reshaping European regulatory space'.

345 Campbell, *Institutional change and globalization* 33.

346 See also Thatcher and Coen, 'Reshaping European regulatory space' 829 (noting that '[o]nce in place, a regulatory organisation limits radical changes and provides incentives to build on existing institutions').

347 Incrementalism is a long-established concept in the political science literature. See the original work by C. Lindblom, 'The science of 'muddling through' (1959) 19 *Public Administration* 79, C. Lindblom, 'Still muddling, not yet through' (1979) 39 *Public Administration Review* 517.

model has not been abandoned either. Colleges, another noteworthy feature of the EU's strategy, were already being used before the financial crisis. Where *de Larosière* innovated such as in the case of the ESRB, actors decided against vesting real powers and legal personality in the new body. Of course, even if the financial crisis did not usher in a paradigmatic sea change, this does not imply that the proposals are not significant. On the contrary, in comparison to CESR, ESMA has significantly enhanced powers over its members and over market actors, although these powers are to some extent reined in by level-switcher rules. But in any event, giving ESMA legal powers, without abandoning the network approach, is precisely what one would expect the next step to be on an evolutionary path towards a continuously progressing consolidation of powers at EU level.

PART II

Prospectus disclosure regulation

2

Introduction

Part I discussed the institutional framework governing European securities regulation and identified the main actors that are involved in prospectus disclosure regulation and enforcement. Part II deals with EU prospectus disclosure regulation and the regulatory strategies that it implements. This introductory chapter discusses the main issues that disclosure regulation has raised for the literature and defines the perspective that I will adopt in the coming chapters.

Prospectus disclosure regulation is about information disclosure; it is about mandating issuers to disclose information when they seek to have securities admitted to trading on a regulated market or raise capital with the public. Mandatory information obligations are so familiar in every day life that the question of whether disclosure should be mandated when a firm seeks to raise capital strikes one as somewhat odd. Yet, historically, the question has been much debated, especially in the USA. Mandatory disclosure was first questioned and criticised during the 1960s and 1970s by authors such as Stigler or Benston.[1] For Benston, for example, the Securities Exchange Act of 1934 had no meaningful positive impact and, therefore, seemingly no *raison d'être*.[2] In the 1980s, the discussion moved forward as influential law and economics scholars adopted a less sanguine view, but still had reservations.[3] At the end of the 1990s, the debate on mandatory disclosure spilled over and gained new momentum as proponents and opponents of regulatory competition sought to make their case in favour of or against issuer choice in the field of securities

[1] E.g., G. Stigler, 'Public regulation of the securities markets' (1964) 37 *Journal of Business* 117; G. Benston, 'The value of the SEC's accounting disclosure requirements' (1969) 44 *Accounting Review* 515; G. Benston, 'Required disclosure and the stock market: an evaluation of the Securities Exchange Act of 1934' (1973) 63 *American Economic Review* 132.

[2] Benston, 'Required disclosure and the stock market' 153.

[3] See J. Coffee, 'Market failure and the economic case for a mandatory disclosure system' (1984) 70 *Virginia Law Review* 717; F. Easterbrook and D. Fischel, 'Mandatory disclosure and the protection of investors' (1984) 70 *Virginia Law Review* 669.

regulation.[4] A number of arguments emerged from these debates and discussions. For law and economics scholarship, mandatory disclosure was necessary to deal with third-party externalities.[5] It was beneficial because it contributed to information standardisation.[6] It also improved corporate governance by prescribing the disclosure of information items which (say) managers would otherwise be reluctant to disclose to shareholders (e.g., because such disclosure may shed a negative light on their performance and, therefore, potentially have a negative impact on their remuneration or employment prospect).[7] Mandatory disclosure has also been described as a 'bonding device' – i.e., a means for issuers to show their commitment to high standards of disclosure[8] – or as a 'cost reduction strategy',[9] which allows research analysts to mitigate their research costs and reduces prodigal research duplication by competing firms in search of trading profits.[10] But while endorsing mandatory disclosure, it is fair to say that the overall mood of this scholarship was one of confidence in the functioning of securities markets and one of restraint when advocating regulatory intervention. The bedrock of the law and economics/finance debate has been the efficient market hypothesis (EMH) which states that securities prices will reflect, without bias,[11] all available information.[12]

[4] E.g. R. Romano, 'Empowering investors: a market approach to securities regulation' (1998) 107 *Yale Law Journal* 2359; M. Fox, 'Retaining mandatory securities disclosure: why issuer choice is not investor empowerment' (1999) 85 *Virginia Law Review* 1335; M. Fox, 'The issuer choice debate' (2001) 2 *Theoretical Inquiries in Law* 563.

[5] Easterbrook and Fischel, 'Mandatory disclosure and the protection of investors' 685 and 697. The argument has also been discussed at length in the regulatory competition literature, see e.g., Fox 'The issuer choice debate'.

[6] G. Hertig, R. Kraakman and E. Rock, 'Issuers and investor protection' in R. Kraakman, P. Davies, H. Hansmann, G. Hertig, K. Hopt, H. Kanda and E. Rock (eds.), *The Anatomy of Corporate Law – A Comparative and Functional Approach* (Oxford University Press, 2004) 193, 205–6.

[7] Hertig *et al.*, 'Issuers and investor protection', 204; P. Mahoney, 'Mandatory disclosure as a solution to agency problems' (1995) 62 *University of Chicago Law Review* 1047.

[8] J. Coffee, 'The future as history: the prospects for global convergence in corporate governance and its implications' (1999) 93 *Northwestern University Law Review* 641. See also E. Rock, 'Securities regulation as lobster trap: a credible commitment theory of mandatory disclosure' (2002) 23 *Cardozo Law Review* 675.

[9] Coffee, 'Market failure and the economic case for a mandatory disclosure system' 722. See also Z. Goshen and G. Parchomovsky, 'The essential role of securities regulation' (2006) 55 *Duke Law Journal* 711, 738.

[10] Coffee, 'Market failure and the economic case for a mandatory disclosure system' 728 and 733.

[11] M. Fox, 'Required disclosure and corporate governance' (1999) 62 *Law and Contemporary Problems* 113, 115.

[12] See E. Fama, 'Efficient capital markets: a review of theory and empirical work' (1970) 25 *Journal of Finance* 383. The actual means that allow information to be absorbed into the

The EMH not only provided a positive underpinning, but also contributed to rebutting the claim that mandatory disclosure was necessary in order to improve investor protection.[13] Instead of protecting investors, disclosure was seen as a means for improving the accuracy of security prices.[14]

This scholarship offered much valuable insight on disclosure and its purpose. But its underpinnings, especially the EMH and the conventional neoclassical paradigm, were soon put to the test by the behavioural economics and finance literature.[15] The behavioural literature questioned some of the standard assumptions of the conventional economic paradigm, especially the premise that individuals are rational actors. For behavioural economists, given the findings on the intricacies of human judgment in cognitive psychology,[16] the rational economic actor was hardly made in the likeness of an actual human actor whose judgment

pricing were famously identified by R. Gilson and R. Kraakman, 'The mechanisms of market efficiency' (1984) 70 *Virginia Law Review* 549. The authors revisited their claims in R. Gilson and R. Kraakman, 'The mechanisms of market efficiency twenty years later: the hindsight bias' (2003) 28 *Journal of Corporation Law* 715.

[13] Law and economics scholars have argued that ordinary investors are protected by the trading activities of informed professional investors. See Easterbrook and Fischel, 'Mandatory disclosure and the protection of investors' 694. Of course, the argument presupposes that markets are deep and vibrant (see Hertig *et al.* 'Issuers and investor protection' 206). See also M. Fox, 'The securities globalization disclosure debate' (2000) 78 *Washington University Law Quarterly* 567, 573 (rebutting the investor protection argument); M. Fox, 'Civil liability and mandatory disclosure' (2009) 109 *Columbia Law Review* 237, 252.

[14] E.g., Fox, 'Retaining mandatory securities disclosure: why issuer choice is not investor empowerment' 1369–70 ('[m]ore information ... will increase the expected accuracy of the price, i.e., the likelihood that the price will be relatively close, one way or the other, to the share's actual value' (reference omitted)); M. Kahan, 'Securities laws and the social costs of "inaccurate" stock prices' (1992) 41 *Duke Law Journal* 977, 985.

[15] In the behavioural finance literature, see the early contributions of W. De Bondt and R. Thaler, 'Does the stock market overreact?' (1984) 40 *Journal of Finance* 793; W. De Bondt and R. Thaler 'Do security analysts overreact?' (1990) 80 *American Economic Review* 52. In the law and economics literature, see C. Sunstein, 'Behavioral law and economics: a progress report' (1999) 1 *American Law and Economics Review* 115; C. Jolls, C. Sunstein and R. Thaler, 'A behavioral approach to law and economics' (1998) 50 *Stanford Law Review* 1471.

[16] See e.g., D. Kahneman and A. Tversky 'Judgment under uncertainty: heuristics and biases' (1974) 185 *Science* 1124; D. Kahneman and A. Tversky, 'Prospect theory: an analysis of decision under risk' (1979) 47 *Econometrica* 263; T. Gilovich, D. Griffin and D. Kahneman (eds.), *Heuristics and Biases – The Psychology of Intuitive Judgment* (Cambridge University Press, 2002). See also the earlier work on bounded rationality by H. Simon, 'A behavioral model of rational choice' (1955) 69 *Quarterly Journal of Economics* 99.

under conditions of uncertainty was clouded by cognitive biases.[17] As far as the EMH is concerned, the literature took exception with the rationality assumption that underpinned the EMH, but also with the faith that the EMH put into arbitrage by sophisticated investors as a mechanism to correct the impact which trading by irrational investors might have on securities prices.[18] For the law and economics literature interested in disclosure, behavioural economics/finance also provided new insights.[19] Prentice, for example, argued that the insights gained from the behavioural literature supported arguments in favour of a mandatory, as opposed to a voluntary, disclosure system.[20]

The final major episode of the scholarly debate on disclosure was the 2008 economic crisis and the housing bubble that preceded it. For many, it struck another serious blow to the conventional economic paradigm and the faith in the functioning of markets. It led authors writing in various traditions to re-evaluate conventional economic wisdom.[21] For influential authors such as Posner, the financial crisis had shown that both the EMH and the rationality assumptions were based on, as he put it, 'a

[17] In their earlier work, Kahneman and Tversky identified the importance of heuristic principles as a way to deal with complex problems under conditions of uncertainty and identified a number of cognitive biases that were related to the use of these heuristics. They showed that the outcome could be serious and systematic mistakes. See Kahneman and Tversky, 'Judgment under uncertainty' 1124.

[18] For details, see A. Shleifer, *Inefficient Markets – An Introduction to Behavioral Finance* (Oxford University Press, 2000) 10–16.

[19] E.g., R. Prentice, 'Whither securities regulation? Some behavioral observations regarding proposals for its future' (2002) 51 *Duke Law Journal* 1397. See also S. Bainbridge, 'Mandatory disclosure: a behavioral analysis' (2000) 68 *University of Cincinnati Law Review* 1023; D. Langevoort, 'Taming the animal spirits of the stock markets: a behavioral approach to securities regulation' (2002) 97 *Northwestern University Law Review* 135; S. Choi and A. Pritchard, 'Behavioral economics and the SEC' (2003) 56 *Stanford Law Review* 1. Finally, see the work of Sunstein and Thaler who built on behavioural economics in order argue in favour of a new form of paternalism which they coined 'libertarian paternalism' – a form of gentle, 'nonintrusive' form of paternalism which 'steer[s] people's choices in directions that will improve the choosers' own welfare'. See C. Sunstein and R. Thaler, 'Libertarian paternalism is not an oxymoron' (2003) 70 *University of Chicago Law Review* 1159, 1162; R. Thaler and C. Sunstein, *Nudge – Improving Decisions about Health, Wealth and Happiness* (Penguin Books, London, 2009).

[20] Prentice, 'Whither securities regulation?' 1511.

[21] Among prominent converts is R. Posner, 'Reply to comments' (2010) 6 *Journal of Institutional Economics* 139, 139–40. See also A. Greenspan, 'Testimony of Dr. Alan Greenspan' (U.S. House of Representatives, Committee on Oversight and Government Reform, 23 October 2008), http://oversight.house.gov/images/stories/documents/20081023100438.pdf, noting in a much-quoted statement that 'those of us who have looked to the self-interest of lending institutions to protect shareholder's equity (myself especially) are in a state of shocked disbelief'.

dangerously exaggerated belief in the ability of investors and consumers to acquire and process necessary information'.[22] Likewise, for the literature interested in behavioural approaches a full picture of the origins of the crisis not only included telltale signs of bounded rationality affecting the capacity of market actors to appreciate complex products, but also herding, overconfidence in the operation of the markets or loss aversion following the first signs of distress of banks.[23] The question of the merit of mandatory disclosure was also raised again; not, as at the beginning of the story on mandatory disclosure, because it was considered unnecessary in a world in which markets could be trusted, but because it was seen as an insufficient regulatory strategy in a world of imperfect markets.[24]

Yet, despite widespread recognition of the flaws of the conventional economic paradigm, behavioural scholarship has not been powerful enough to oust for good an established paradigm. Indeed, for those that are in the business of making predictions, the usefulness of behavioural economics remains limited.[25] Calls have been made for a unifying theory, with authors noting that otherwise behavioural economics is no more than 'a collection of interesting insights'.[26]

The reality of EU disclosure regulation – problematic It might well be that disclosure regulation needs to be fundamentally rethought following the financial crisis. But from the present perspective, the EU disclosure paradigm is given and, in any event, the nature of the European policy-making

[22] Posner, 'Reply to comments' 140.

[23] See (in the behavioural law and economics literature), E. Avgouleas, 'The global financial crisis and the disclosure paradigm in European financial regulation: the case for reform' (2009) 6 *European Company and Financial Law Review* 440; E. Avgouleas, 'The global financial crisis, behavioural finance and financial regulation: in search of a new orthodoxy' (2009) 9 *Journal of Corporate Law Studies* 23.

[24] See in the behavioural law and economics literature, e.g., Avgouleas, 'The global financial crisis and the disclosure paradigm in European financial regulation'. On the merit of disclosure in the subprime mortgage market, S. Schwarcz, 'Disclosure's failure in the subprime mortgage crisis' (2008) 3 *Utah Law Review* 1109. See also O. Bar-Gill, 'The law, economics and psychology of subprime mortgage contracts' (2009) 94 *Cornell Law Review* 1073.

[25] But see Sunstein, 'Behavioral law and economics: a progress report' 149 who takes a less sanguine view.

[26] S. Levitt and J. List, 'Homo economicus evolves' (2008) 319 *Science* 909, 910 ('researchers should integrate the existing behavioral models and empirical results into a unified theory rather than a collection of interesting insights'). See also D. Fudenberg, 'Advancing beyond advances in behavioral economics' (2006) 44 *Journal of Economic Literature* 694, 697 (noting that '[t]here are too many behavioral theories, most of which have too few applications').

process makes a simple transmission of normative ideas into policy reality difficult.[27] Instead of questioning the merit of mandatory disclosure which, as an endeavour, has little to offer from my perspective, I will, in the next chapters, set out on a different track and focus on the shape of the disclosure regime and the institutional choices that underpin it. In other words, my primary interest is the reality of disclosure regulation in the EU and the question of who – the EU or Member States – does what under which constraints and conditions. Specifically, I will suggest that prospectus disclosure regulation in the EU uses a mixture of regulatory techniques, including (maximum) harmonisation but also equivalence-based regulation.[28] I approach my tasks in the next chapters with two lessons from the financial crisis in mind. They concern the need to ensure transparency and to find ways for dealing with disclosure complexity for investors. Chapter 3, the largest chapter of the book, begins by examining prospectus disclosure harmonisation. Chapter 4 deals with equivalence-based regulation.

[27] What is more, it is apparent that in the real world the level and quantity of disclosure is increasingly being driven by efforts of issuers and market actors to protect themselves *ex ante* against any potential liability claims that might arise *ex post*.

[28] Of course, both strategies are based on harmonisation instruments, but the point is that these instruments enact different strategies for regulating issuers or market actors. Under the first model, issuers have to comply with uniform requirements and standards that apply in each Member State. Under the second model, third-country issuers can rely on different requirements and standards which are foreign to the EU, but which are deemed to be equivalent to the uniform standards applying in the EU.

3

(Maximum) harmonisation

I Introduction

Among the FSAP directives in the financial markets field, it is perhaps the Prospectus Directive ('PD') that is most often associated with the concept of maximum harmonisation, the most ambitious form of harmonisation.[1] Paradoxically, however, the directive does not explicitly pin down the basis of the maximum harmonisation regime. It is more readily apparent in the PD's implementing legislation, the Level 2 Prospectus Regulation ('PR')[2] that requires a person, who wishes to make a public offer or seek admission to trading on a regulated market, to comply with specific and detailed disclosure requirements.[3] These disclosure requirements – or information items – form the core of a first prospectus disclosure model, a maximum harmonisation model, which is meant to ensure a level playing field and ultimately contribute to the EU's integrationist ambitions. The EU, as opposed to the Member States acting individually, emerges as the main actor, or the main force, shaping this disclosure model. The purpose of this chapter is to examine the harmonised content of this regime (or model) and the various obligations that relate to it.[4] In the maze of rules and requirements, it identifies three core obligations on which the regime is built: (i) the obligation to draw up a prospectus in accordance with the rules of the PD and PR, (ii) the obligation to seek approval of the

[1] Directive 2003/71/EC [2003] OJ L345/64.

[2] Commission Regulation (EC) No 809/2004 [2004] OJ L149/1.

[3] Generally, the directive differentiates between three categories of persons: an issuer, an offeror and a person requesting admission to trading. An issuer is defined as a 'legal entity which issues or proposes to issue securities' (PD Art 2(1)(h)). An offeror is 'a legal entity or individual which offers securities to the public' (Art 2(1)(i)). The meaning of a person requesting admission to trading is not defined, but the term seems fairly self-explanatory. For convenience purposes, I will mainly use the term issuer hereinafter.

[4] Earlier contributions include: Moloney, *EC Securities Regulation*; D. Van Gerven (ed.), *Prospectus for the Public Offering of Securities in Europe – Vol. I* (Cambridge University Press, 2008); E. Ferran, *Building an EU Securities Markets* (Cambridge University Press, 2004).

prospectus with the competent authorities of the issuer's home Member State, and (iii) the obligation to publish the prospectus and comply with the PD's and PR's rules and principles governing advertisement. In return, the directive has a mutual recognition system to offer – the single passport for prospectuses – that was designed to succeed where previous directives had failed, by making cross-border capital raising a reality.

Another way to look at this chapter is as a foundational chapter on prospectus regulation from which later chapters will 'branch off' in order to explore more specific aspects; for example, equivalence-based regulation or enforcement. Section II begins by examining constitutional questions and the broader choices underpinning the PD. The sections that follow examine the main obligations of the directive. Thus, section III focuses on the obligation to prepare a prospectus. Section IV discusses the obligation to seek approval of a prospectus with the issuer's home Member State. Section V focuses on the obligation to publish the prospectus and comply with the rules and principles governing advertising. Section VI finally turns to the single passport for prospectuses, the *pièce de résistance* of the directive. Section VII concludes by examining whether the changes, which the PD introduced, were evolutionary or rather more revolutionary.

II Harmonisation and prospectus disclosure

I begin this chapter with a few observations about the EU legislature's competence to legislate in the field of prospectus regulation. The EU legislature has no unbounded competence to legislate.[5] It is subject to the principle of conferral under Article 5(2) of the Treaty on European Union ('TEU') which provides that the EU can only act within the scope of the powers which it was vested with under the Treaties. The legislature must also respect the principles of subsidiarity (in areas of shared competence, such as the internal market)[6] and proportionality under Article 5(3) and (4) of the TEU. But within these formal constitutional limits that structure its actions and helped by the integrationist case law of the Court of Justice, the legislature has enjoyed a good deal of discretion when taking action and, as long as the EU's integrationist objectives in the internal market field were met, when determining the substance of a common

[5] See generally on the constitutional principles governing EU competence following the entry into force of the Lisbon Treaty, S. Weatherill, *Cases and Materials on EU Law* (Oxford University Press, 2010); Piris, *The Lisbon Treaty*.

[6] TFEU Art 4(2)(a).

harmonised regulatory regime. Among the Court's case law, the much-cited *Tobacco Advertising* case, in which the ECJ sanctioned the legislature for having failed to comply with the principle of attributed competence, continues being the odd exception.[7] Moreover, the Court has not shown an avid interest in enforcing forcefully the principles of subsidiarity[8] or proportionality either.[9] As far as the PD is concerned, this relative constitutional freedom meant that the directive was able to translate three broad sets of choices into regulatory policy.

Maximum harmonisation and home country competence The PD is based on the twin principles of maximum harmonisation and home country competence.[10] 'Maximum harmonisation' means that the PD generally seeks to regulate the prospectus disclosure field exhaustively. Maximum harmonisation promises a simple solution to defining the division of powers between the Union and Member States in the prospectus disclosure field: once the EU occupies the regulatory space exhaustively, Member States are pre-empted from departing from the common rules. Admittedly, the text of the directive offers few clues about the legislature's overall choice in favour of maximum harmonisation.[11] There is no

[7] Case C-376/98 *Germany v European Parliament and Council* [2000] ECR I-8419. Subsequent cases where the Court did not sanction the legislature for failure to comply with the principle of Art 5(1) EC are, among others, Case C-491/01 *The Queen v Secretary of State for Health, ex parte British American Tobacco (Investments) Ltd and Imperial Tobacco Ltd* [2002] ECR I-11453; Case C-210/03 *Swedish Match AB and Swedish Match UK Ltd v Secretary of State for Health* [2004] ECR I-11893; Joined Cases C-154/04 and C-155/04 *The Queen, on the application of Alliance for Natural Health and Others v Secretary of State for Health and National Assembly for Wales* [2005] ECR I-6451. For a critical assessment of the Court's case law, see D. Wyatt, 'Community competence to regulate the internal market' in M. Dougan and S. Currie (eds.), *50 Years of the European Treaties: Looking Back and Thinking Forward* (Hart Publishing, Oxford, 2009).

[8] E.g., G. Bermann, 'Proportionality and subsidiarity' in C. Barnard and J. Scott (eds.), *The Law of the Single Market – Unpacking the Premises* (Hart Publishing, Oxford, 2002) 75, 85–6; G. Howells and S. Weatherill, *Consumer Protection Law* (Ashgate, Hants, 2005) 133.

[9] The Court has preferred not to get involved in areas which require the legislature to make 'political, economic and social choices' and which involve 'complex assessments'. See Case C-491/01 *The Queen v Secretary of State for Health*, para. 123.

[10] Home country competence also applies to enforcement. See Chapter 6, section III, A, for details.

[11] In the literature, authors have had conflicting views on whether the PD is a maximum harmonisation directive. See e.g., M. Tison, 'Financial market integration in the post FSAP era – In search of overall conceptual consistency in the regulatory framework' in G. Ferrarini and E. Wymeersch (eds.), *Investor Protection in Europe – Corporate Law Making, the MiFID and Beyond* (Oxford University Press, 2006) 443; Moloney, *EC*

reference to maximum harmonisation in the directive.[12] Indeed, the directive includes various provisions which make exception to maximum harmonisation. In the absence of any explicit reference to maximum harmonisation, the question of whether the directive achieves complete harmonisation is, therefore, one of interpretation and the answer must, according to the Court, be ultimately deduced from the directive's 'wording, purpose and structure'.[13] What is more, when carrying out this assessment, it matters for the Court whether a directive explicitly authorises Member States to adopt measures on top of the EU common requirements.[14] The Court has previously pointed to the absence of such a provision as one of the reasons why a directive did not achieve complete harmonisation.[15] Thus, absent such a provision, it is reasonable to assume that the Court is more likely to find that a directive regulates a given field exhaustively. The point is relevant for our purposes because, unlike other directives such as, for example, the Consolidated Admissions and Reporting Directive ('CARD') which the PD partially replaced, or the Transparency Directive ('TD'),[16] the PD does not give Member States broad or general powers to adopt requirements on top of those of the directive. To be sure, the directive includes derogations and exceptions, and at times leaves matters to be decided by national law.[17] But this fact is not necessarily such as to undermine the maximum harmonisation nature of a directive, as long as the matters which are subject to national law or which allow for derogations are carefully circumscribed.[18] Moreover, the

Securities Regulation 114. CESR has concluded that the PD is a maximum harmonisation directive. See 'CESR's Report on the PD' 5.

12 Note that as far as the disclosure items of the Level 2 PR are concerned, the PR, however, makes it plain that they are meant to be maximum harmonisation items. For details, see section III, B.1, below.

13 Case C-154/00 *Commission v Hellenic Republic* [2002] ECR I-03879, para. 12. See also Case C-402/03 *Skov and Bilka* [2006] ECR I-199, para. 22; Case C-52/00 *Commission v France* [2002] ECR I-3827, para. 16; Case C-183/00 *Sánchez v Medicina Asturiana SA* [2002] ECR I-3901, para. 25.

14 Case C-154/00 Commission v Hellenic Republic, para. 14.

15 *Ibid.*

16 Directive 2001/34/EC [2001] OJ L184/1, Art 8; Directive 2004/109/EC [2004] OJ L390/38, Art 3(1).

17 E.g., Arts 6(2) and 21(3).

18 The Court has confirmed that a directive can regulate a field exhaustively while providing for exceptions or leaving a specific matter to be governed by national law. See Case C-154/00 *Commission v Hellenic Republic*, para. 15. According to the Court, that was so because the derogations were confined to 'matters exhaustively specified', were 'narrowly defined' and subject to possible future harmonisation. See *ibid.*, para. 16. To be sure, where securities are admitted to trading on a regulated market, Rec (15) allows

fact that the directive makes it plain that its purpose is to 'harmonise' prospectus requirements, as opposed to, say, merely coordinate national requirements is, arguably, also evidence of its maximum harmonisation nature.[19]

The adoption of the home country principle complemented the choice in favour of maximum harmonisation. The PD thus locates regulatory and enforcement competence overwhelmingly with the so-called home Member State of an issuer.[20] As a principle governing the distribution of competences between Member States, the home country principle is meant to prevent a multiplication of regulatory or enforcement efforts among Member States. It therefore also fits well with the Treaties' integrationist objectives and, not surprisingly, has been widely used in internal market law,[21] despite the fact that the Treaties do not explicitly make provision for home country control.[22]

It is apparent that like maximum harmonisation, the home country principle is of great consequence for the division of competences in the EU. By locating competence with the home Member State, it promises a simple solution to the *horizontal* division of competence between Member States. Commonly, however, the home country principle is not an absolute principle in the internal market field. Some matters are typically left to host Member States to decide – as an example, think of MiFID which entrusts some matters to host Member States (e.g., conduct of business rules in relation to branches[23]), even though it is based on the home country principle.[24] In the case of the PD, the home country principle is not

Member States, competent authorities or exchanges to define in a rulebook 'other particular requirements'. But, in my view, the recital only clarifies that, as long as a particular matter is outside the scope of the directive (e.g., corporate governance requirements), Member States are free to adopt unilateral measures, provided that such measures do not interfere with the matters that are dealt with in the directive.

19 PD Art 1(1).

20 For details, see section IV, below.

21 For a more detailed assessment, see S. Weatherill, 'Pre-emption, harmonisation and the distribution of competence to regulate the internal market' in C. Barnard and J. Scott (eds.), *The Law of the Single European Market — Unpacking the Premises* (Hart Publishing, Oxford, 2002) 41.

22 See e.g., Case C-233/94 *Germany v Parliament and Council* [1997] ECR I-2405, para. 64 (noting, in relation to home country supervision, that it 'is not a principle laid down by the [EC] Treaty').

23 MiFID Art 32(7).

24 For details, see Moloney's analysis of MiFID in Moloney, *EC Securities Regulation*.

absolute either.[25] Some matters are governed by ordinary territorial rules of jurisdiction, even though this is not necessarily apparent on the face of the directive. The relevant provisions will be discussed in the coming chapters.[26] Suffice it to note for now that, as long as the legislature does not undermine the legitimate expectations of interested parties, it benefits from a good degree of discretion when defining the rules governing the distribution of competence between home and host Member States.[27]

A 'product-driven' directive The PD is a 'product-driven' directive.[28] In other words, the type of product (equity securities, non-equity securities, etc.) contributes importantly to determining the disclosure requirements of the prospectus.[29] Given the subject matter of the directive – securities disclosure – this was in many ways a self-evident choice. Nonetheless, the point is worth noting because it differentiates the PD from other directives such as, for example, MiFID, which is more service oriented.[30]

Market access for issuers and investor protection Facilitating market access for issuers and ensuring investor protection is the final set of choices which the PD seeks to translate into regulatory output.[31] The Commission's proposal for a directive on prospectuses was partly prompted by a general feeling that the earlier Listing Particulars Directive ('LPD') and Public Offers Directive ('POD') had failed to stimulate cross-border capital raising and that a new mutual recognition system was required for cross-border capital raising to become a reality.[32] At the same time, the proposal was presented as an instrument of investor protection, especially retail investor protection.[33] The latter concern is not only reflected in the formal

[25] Admittedly, in practice, the importance of home state competence is somewhat reduced for regulatory matters, at least for those which are governed by the Level 2 PR. This is because the PR is a regulation and hence directly applicable in Member States. Moreover, unlike the PD, the Level 2 PR is more outspoken on maximum harmonisation.

[26] See Chapter 6, section III, A.

[27] C-233/94 *Germany v Parliament and Council*, para. 64.

[28] ESME, 'Differences between the definitions of "qualified investor" in the Prospectus Directive and "professional client" and "eligible counterparty" in MiFID – is alignment needed?' (November 2008) 10, http://ec.europa.eu/internal_market/securities/docs/esme/report-qualified-investor_en.pdf (hereinafter, 'ESME Differences Report').

[29] See the annexes to the Level 2 PR.

[30] 'ESME Differences Report' 10.

[31] This set of concerns dominated discussions well before Rec (10), which sets out the formal aims of the directive (i.e., investor protection and market efficiency), was added.

[32] See also PD Rec (1). Note that the LPD was integrated into CARD.

[33] See also Moloney, *EC Securities Regulation* 117.

objectives of the directive,[34] but also in the substantive requirements of the PD and the Level 2 PR.[35]

Retail investor protection, as a choice of policy discourse, also emerged forcefully during the negotiations of the directive. It resonated well with Member States whose domestic markets were mainly frequented by retail investors and whose competent authorities saw themselves as (retail) investor champions. It had comparatively less resonance with Member States whose markets were dominated by professional investors and/or which viewed conduct of business rules, instead of prospectus disclosure, as a better means to protect retail investors. Many of the PD's provisions can be seen as reflecting the outcome of a certain contest between these different concerns and preferences. The fact that this outcome was not always satisfactory is reflected in some ungainly compromises – I think, for example, of the provisions which define the 'home Member State' of an issuer of non-equity securities and especially the EUR 1,000 threshold which determines whether an issuer of non-equity securities can benefit from a choice of competent authority.[36] In 2009, the Commission proposed to deal with some of these compromises when putting forward its proposal to amend the PD.[37] Interestingly, the Commission's proposal also reflected a certain change in discourse. Thus, the recitals of the 2010 Prospectus Amending Directive ('PAD') place greater emphasis on reducing 'administrative burdens' for companies.[38] But concerns over investor protection were clearly not absent during the negotiations in 2009 and 2010.[39] In fact, as finally adopted, the PAD raises various threshold amounts, seemingly in order to protect retail investors (e.g., the thresholds which determine whether a person is obliged to prepare a prospectus).[40] Moreover, the PAD did not remove the EUR 1,000 threshold mentioned above, notwithstanding the Commission's proposal to remove it.

[34] Rec (10) and (16).

[35] See, for example, the provisions governing the prospectus summary, the language provisions applying to summaries or the high threshold amount for non-equity securities whose purpose is to draw a line between the ordinary disclosure regime and the one aimed at wholesale investors.

[36] PD Art 2(1)(m)(ii).

[37] European Commission, 'Proposal for a Directive of the European Parliament and of the Council amending Directives 2003/71/EC on the prospectus' (COM(2009) 491 final, 23 September 2009).

[38] Directive (EU) 2010/73 [2010] OJ L327/1, Rec (1), (2), (3) and (4).

[39] See e.g., PAD Rec (9).

[40] PD Art 3(2)(b), (c) and (d).

Choice of legal bases The choices discussed above were translated into regulatory policy on the basis of Article 44 EC which is one of the provisions found in the chapter on the right of establishment of the (former) EC Treaty and which provides for the adoption of directives '[i]n order to attain freedom of establishment' for companies. As a 'product-driven' directive which seeks to improve investor protection and investor confidence,[41] it was also adopted on the basis of the general harmonisation provision of Article 95 EC which provides for the adoption of measures having 'as their object the establishment and functioning of the internal market'. The PAD, meanwhile, was adopted on the basis of Articles 50 and 114 of the Treaty on the Functioning of the European Union ('TFEU'), which replaced Articles 44 and 95 of the EC Treaty following the entry into force of the Lisbon Treaty.

Hence, the PD is an internal market measure whose market integration objectives are evidenced by, *inter alia*, Recital (4) which states that the directive is 'an instrument essential to the achievement of the internal market' and seeks to make it easier for issuers to have 'the widest possible access to investment capital on a Community-wide basis'.[42] Substantively, it pursues its market integration objectives by providing for a single passport for prospectuses[43] and by providing for a greater level of standardisation of prospectus regulation, in accordance with Article 1(1) which states that the purpose of the PD is to 'harmonise requirements for the drawing up, approval and distribution of the prospectus'.[44] These objectives do not raise particular objections. There are ready arguments for greater standardisation and increased uniformity in the disclosure field. Requiring issuers to comply with diverging sets of prospectus requirements can be a cost factor for them and, as such, an obstacle to raising capital which in turn might affect their ability to develop activities abroad.[45] Furthermore, the benefits of greater standardisation extend to investors too, for disclosure standardisation promises to improve transparency, as well as make it easier for investors to compare disclosure.[46] In theory, harmonisation

[41] E.g., Recs (10), (16), (18) or (21).

[42] The PD also pursues two more specific goals which are to ensure market efficiency and investor protection (Rec (10)).

[43] PD Arts 17 and 18.

[44] PD Art 1(1).

[45] See also Rec (35) which highlights prospectus language requirements at Member State level as 'discourag[ing] cross-border offers or multiple trading' or Rec (30) which identifies differences at the level of prospectus approval as hampering cross-border activities.

[46] This reasoning also underpins the adoption of Regulation (EC) No 1606/2002 of the European Parliament and of the Council of 19 July 2002 on the application of

of prospectus disclosure should, therefore, not only benefit issuers seeking access to capital abroad, but also make investors more willing to look beyond national boundaries when searching for investment opportunities.[47] To be sure, the link between objectives such as improving investor protection or investor confidence and the ultimate constitutional goal of market building can sometimes seem tenuous. Moloney has been critical of this relationship for the reason that it is built on assumptions rather than empirical evidence.[48] But the Court of Justice is likely to be content with assumptions. In *Dionik*, in which the Court was asked to examine certain provisions of CARD,[49] the Court did not take issue with the investor protection/confidence objectives of CARD, although admittedly, it did not elaborate on the point.[50]

III Obligation to draw up a prospectus

So far, I have discussed constitutional questions and examined the broad policy choices which the PD translated into a common harmonised regime. The remainder of this chapter will deal with the substance of this regime. As mentioned in the introductory section, it is built on three core obligations: the obligation to draw up a prospectus; the obligation to seek approval of the prospectus with the issuer's home Member State; and

international accounting standards [2002] OJ L243/1 ('IAS Regulation'). See IAS Regulation, Art 1.

[47] Cf., IAS Regulation, Art 1. See also European Central Bank, 'Opinion of the European Central Bank of 16 November 2001 at the request of the Council of the European Union on a proposal for a Directive of the European Parliament and of the Council on the prospectus to be published when securities are offered to the public or admitted to trading (COM(2001) 280 final)' [2001] OJ C344/4, para. 5 (noting that '[t]he introduction of harmonised and enhanced disclosure standards in line with international standards for public offer of securities and admission to trading is likely to increase investor confidence, in particular as regards investing on an EU-wide basis'). For a critical view of the investor confidence argument, see Moloney, *EC Securities Regulation* 98–101.

[48] Moloney, *EC Securities Regulation* 98 (speaking of the 'notoriously nebulous objective of investor confidence, which permeates the EC regime due to the assumed, but not evidenced, synergy between investor confidence and market interpenetration').

[49] CARD is another disclosure directive whose provisions have now, by and large, been replaced.

[50] Case C-430/05 *Dionik and others* [2007] ECR I-05835, para. 44 (stating that 'it is clear from recitals (5), (11) and (31) in the preamble to Directive 2001/34 that the purpose of that directive is, *inter alia*, to ensure adequate information of investors in the field of transferable securities in order to improve investor protection, to increase investors' confidence in securities markets and thus to ensure that those markets function correctly').

finally, the obligation to file and publish the prospectus, and comply with the PD's and PR's rules governing advertising. This section discusses the first of these obligations. If securities are to be admitted to trading on a regulated market or are offered to the public in a Member State, the PD makes provision for a prospectus to be prepared in accordance with its provisions and its implementation legislation. The obligation to prepare a prospectus raises five questions which will be examined in separate subsections. I will first deal with the question of the scope of the directive (A). Next, the PD's requirements regarding the content of the prospectus, its format and its period of validity will be examined (B). The requirements dealing with incorporation by reference are discussed in a third subsection (C). The question of whether information can be omitted from the prospectus will be addressed in a fourth subsection (D). Prospectus language requirements will be examined in a final subsection (E).

A Scope and exceptions

1 Scope

Admission of securities to trading on a regulated market and public offers The material scope of the directive is, first and foremost, defined by two core concepts: (i) an admission of securities to trading on a regulated market and (ii) an offer to the public.[51] In defining the scope of the PD along these lines, the PD sought to consolidate and upgrade the disclosure requirements of two separate directives, the POD and LPD, which governed the drawing-up of public offer prospectuses and listing particulars, respectively. Note that the PD sees an admission to trading on a regulated market and a public offer as separate concepts. An admission to trading on a regulated market can, for example, take place independently of a public offer. Each concept is worth examining separately.

Admission to trading on a regulated market As mentioned, the directive states that a prospectus must be prepared when securities are to be admitted to trading on a regulated market.[52] The term 'admission to trading of securities' does not have a special or specified meaning in EU law. But a 'regulated market' is an EU law concept. MiFID defines a regulated market in a somewhat convoluted fashion as a

> multilateral system operated and/or managed by a market operator, which brings together or facilitates the bringing together of multiple third-party

[51] Art 1(1). [52] *Ibid.*

> buying and selling interests in financial instruments – in the system and in accordance with its non-discretionary rules – in a way that results in a contract, in respect of the financial instruments admitted to trading under its rules and/or systems, and which is authorised and functions regularly and in accordance with the provisions of [MiFID].[53]

In short, regulated markets are generally Europe's flagship markets. They are those that are exposed to the full might of EU securities regulation. They include markets such as, for example, Euronext Paris, the *Frankfurter Wertpapierbörse* (regulated market), the London Stock Exchange (regulated market), derivative markets such as the *marché des options négociables de Paris* (MONEP), or the London International Financial Futures and Options Exchange (LIFFE).

Whilst an 'admission to trading' has no specified meaning in EU law, it is an essential concept in EU securities law. Under the PD, it replaced an earlier concept, the concept of an 'admission to official listing', which was found in the LPD (and continues to survive in CARD). While this conceptual change was intended to improve the scope of harmonisation, the switchover represented a noticeable change for some markets which had hitherto benefited from more flexible regulatory requirements under national law. Also, in an effort to stay outside the scope of the PD and other FSAP directives, exchanges throughout the EU began, following the adoption of the PD, to set up so-called exchange-regulated markets which are not regulated markets under EU law. One of the more prominent exchange-regulated markets is the Alternative Investment Market (AIM), a market of the London Stock Exchange for smaller companies. Initially launched in 1995, it converted into an exchange-regulated market in October 2004. Exchange-regulated markets have become a permanent fixture of the regulatory landscape. Other markets, which followed suit, are, for instance, the Euro MTF of the Luxembourg Stock Exchange (July 2005) or NYSE Alternext of NYSE Euronext (May 2005).

Public offer The second concept, which contributes to defining the scope of application of the directive, is the concept of an offer to the public.[54] The POD, which governed disclosure requirements for public offer prospectuses before the PD, had failed to define the meaning of a public offer.[55]

[53] MiFID Art 4(1)(14). [54] Art 2(1)(d).

[55] European Commission, 'Proposal for a Directive of the European Parliament and of the Council on the prospectus to be published when securities are offered to the public or admitted to trading' (COM (2001) 280 final, 30 May 2001) 7 (hereinafter, 'Initial Commission Proposal').

Member States were, consequently, left with the task of defining the concept unilaterally. It soon became apparent that they adopted fairly different approaches. One and the same operation could be treated differently depending on the Member State; for example, as a private placement in one Member State and a public offer in another Member State.[56] In order to solve this conundrum, the PD laid down a common definition. Article 2(1)(d) defines an offer of securities to the public as:

> a communication to persons in any form and by any means, presenting sufficient information on the terms of the offer and the securities to be offered, so as to enable an investor to decide to purchase or subscribe to these securities.[57]

Under the definition the support or medium used to communicate an offer does not matter. What matters is that the communication presents 'sufficient information on the terms of the offer and the securities to be offered' and that it 'enable[s] an investor to decide to purchase or subscribe to these securities'. The definition remains intentionally wide.[58] Accordingly, it did not fully level the playing field between Member States.[59] It is worth examining the constituent elements of a public offer in more detail.

Public offer – 'sufficient information on the terms of the offer and the securities to be offered' Save for stating in broad terms that a communication, in the sense of Article 2(1)(d), must include information regarding the terms of the offer and the securities being offered, the directive does not specify what is deemed to be 'sufficient information'.[60] The Commission has taken a pragmatic view on the matter and suggested that Member States have some leeway to determine the meaning

[56] See also Rec (5).

[57] In order to make sure that the public offer requirements cannot be ignored outright by financial intermediaries claiming that they merely seek to place securities with, say, a selected number of their existing clients, the directive stresses that the definition also applies when securities are placed with investors through financial intermediaries (see Art 2(1)(d)).

[58] European Commission, '3rd informal meeting on prospectus transposition' (summary record, 26 January 2005) 3, http://ec.europa.eu/internal_market/securities/docs/prospectus/summary-note-050126_en.pdf (hereinafter, '3rd Transposition Meeting').

[59] In some Member States, for example, a public offer must be a contractual offer under national law. Other Member States do not consider this to be a requirement. See 'Commission Background Document' 14.

[60] Note that according to the Court, 'the meaning and scope of terms for which Community law provides no definition must be determined by considering the general context in which they are used and their usual meaning in everyday language'. See Case C-164/98 *DIR International Film Srl and others* [2000] ECR I-00447, para. 26.

of sufficient information.[61] It is apparent that Member States have, in practice, made use of this relative freedom. The UK, for example, anxious that the display of information on trading screens could potentially be treated as a communication in the sense of Article 2(1)(d),[62] has made sure that a communication, which is made in connection with trading on, *inter alia*, a regulated market or a multilateral trading facility, can be excluded from the scope of a public offer.[63] The Commission has subsequently taken a similar view on screen trading and noted that the display of limited information on trading screens would generally not constitute a communication in the sense of the directive.[64]

Public offer – 'enable an investor to decide to purchase or subscribe to these securities' For a communication to be treated as a public offer, it must convey sufficient information so as to make it possible for an investor to make a decision about whether or not to buy or subscribe to securities. Thus, what precisely is deemed to be 'sufficient information' and, hence, what type of communication qualifies as a public offer must ultimately be assessed from the perspective of an investor. The definition is thus in a sense 'outcome based'. Instead of insisting on the nature of the communication (i.e., is the communication contractual?), the definition insists on the outcome that the communication is expected to produce (i.e., does it enable a person to make an investment decision?). In practice, it will often be a matter for competent authorities to decide, on a case-by-case basis and having regard to the specific elements of each case, which information enables investors to make investment decisions. If information is too general in nature and plainly not meant to allow investors to decide on whether or not to buy securities, the communication should not be treated as a public offer.[65] The Commission has also inferred that a person must have some choice about whether to accept (or refuse to accept) an

[61] '3rd Transposition Meeting' 3.

[62] HM Treasury, 'UK implementation of the Prospectus Directive 2003/71/EC – a consultation document' (HM Treasury, October 2004) 22, http://webarchive.nationalarchives.gov.uk/+/www.hm-treasury.gov.uk/d/DFE27339-BCDC-D4B3-16FD311B308ABF54.pdf (hereinafter, 'HM Treasury Consultation Document').

[63] FSMA, s 102B(5).

[64] 'Commission Background Document' 15 (fn 28).

[65] D. Van Gerven, 'General provisions of Community law relating to the prospectus to be published when securities are offered to the public or admitted to trading' in D. Van Gerven (ed.), *Prospectus for the Public Offering of Securities in Europe – Vol. I* (Cambridge University Press, 2008) 3, 17.

offer.[66] If securities are being allocated without a person making a decision (think of the case of free shares), there can be no public offer in the sense of the directive.[67]

Transferable securities The scope of the PD is further defined by the concept of 'securities'. The directive defines securities as 'transferable securities'.[68] The definition of transferable securities was initially found in the Investment Services Directive ('ISD').[69] MiFID replaced the ISD and now defines transferable securities as 'classes of securities which are negotiable on the capital market, with the exception of instruments of payment'.[70] Note that the PD adds that money market instruments are excluded from the definition of securities under the directive, if they have a maturity of less than twelve months.[71] But the directive also states explicitly that Member States may apply national law to such instruments.[72] This means presumably that Member States may include money market instruments within the scope of the national legislation implementing the PD.[73] Otherwise the explicit reference to national law would have little purpose, as it is plain that national law will continue applying for instruments that are outside the scope of the directive.

In practice, it may happen that the transferability of securities is restricted by agreement. This raises the question of whether such securities are still transferable securities within the meaning of the directive. Recall that the main feature of transferable securities under MiFID is that they are, as a class, negotiable on capital markets.[74] CESR has taken the view that where the transferability is limited by contractual agreement (e.g., selling restrictions which are applicable in a Member State), this is generally not so as to change the status of the securities for the purposes of the application of the directive.[75] Nonetheless, if the restrictions are too extensive, the securities may indeed no longer be treated as transferable securities for the purposes of the PD.[76] When exactly this

[66] 'CESR Q&A July 10' Question 6.

[67] *Ibid.* [68] Art 2(1)(a).

[69] Council Directive 93/22/EEC of 10 May 1993 on investment services in the securities field [1993] OJ L141/27 (repealed).

[70] MiFID Art 4(1)(18). [71] Art 2(1)(a). [72] *Ibid.*

[73] In this sense, Van Gerven, 'General provisions of Community law relating to the prospectus to be published' 12.

[74] European Commission, 'Your questions on MiFID' cited in 'CESR Q&A July 10', Question 67.

[75] 'CESR Q&A July 10', Question 67. [76] *Ibid.*

is the case, is left to competent authorities to decide on a case-by-case basis.[77]

Equity and non-equity securities The PD further subdivides securities into equity and non-equity securities. The adoption of this distinction represented both a change in language and substance from previous directives. The meaning of equity securities is broader than the meaning of shares and includes 'shares and other transferable securities equivalent to shares in companies', but also any other form of transferable securities 'giving the right to acquire any of the aforementioned securities as a consequence of their being converted or the rights conferred by them being exercised, provided that securities of the latter type are issued by the issuer of the underlying shares or by an entity belonging to the group of the said issuer'.[78] 'Non-equity securities' are defined by reference to equity securities, as securities which are not caught under the definition of equity securities.[79]

The definitions must accommodate a multitude of instruments, including derivative and hybrid instruments (e.g., covered warrants, options, convertible or exchangeable securities).[80] Convertible bonds, for instance, are debt securities which, upon conversion, are exchanged for equity of the issuer, its parent company or a subsidiary of the issuer.[81] Convertibles have been popular in the international debt market. Their key features are adjustable. The conversion itself may be at the option of the investor or the issuer. In the case of mandatory convertibles, conversion takes place mandatorily.[82] Depending on characteristics such as call protection, the price of conversion or the maturity date, convertibles are either more equity-like or debt-like products.[83]

Under the PD, convertible securities are treated as equity or non-equity securities depending on whether they allow their holder to gain access to the capital of the issuer (or an entity which is part of the issuer's group) or of a third-party company. In other words, what matters is

[77] *Ibid.* [78] Art 2(1)(b). [79] Art 2(1)(c).

[80] As far as derivative securities are concerned, ESME noted the absence of a clear definition. See ESME Report 12.

[81] P. Wood, *Law and Practice of International Finance* (Sweet & Maxwell, London, 2008) 173.

[82] M. Ammann and R. Seiz, 'Pricing and hedging mandatory convertible bonds' (2006) 13 *Journal of Derivatives* 30–46, 30.

[83] F. Bancel and U. Mittoo, 'Why do European firms issue convertible debt' (2004) 10 *European Financial Management* 339, 357. See also C. Lewis, R. Rogalski and J. Seward,

the identity of the entity that issues the underlying shares. Convertible bonds are equity securities under the directive if the underlying shares are issued by the issuer of the convertible or an entity which is part of the issuer's group.[84] Characteristics such as those mentioned above (e.g., the conversion price or maturity) are not relevant. Likewise, it is irrelevant whether the decision to convert is entirely in the hands of the investor.[85] Admittedly, Recital (12) creates confusion. It provides *in fine* that securities, which are convertible 'at the option of the investor', are deemed to be non-equity securities. It thus implies that *all* convertible securities are non-equity securities, as long as the conversion can be triggered by the investor. Recital (12) was added as a concession to the UK delegation during the negotiations of the directive.[86] It is unfortunate that the recital survived the recent revisions of the directive, but, at any rate, recitals are not legally binding and cannot make exception to the application of a provision of an EU directive.[87] They can be useful for interpretative purposes, but in the present case, interpreting the definition of equity securities in the light of Recital (12) would unnecessarily strain the (legally binding) text of the directive. To be sure, CESR attempted to reconcile Recital (12) with the text of the PD by suggesting that the recital was meant to refer to securities which are convertible into shares of another issuer, that is an issuer other than the issuer of the convertible securities or one that is part of the issuer's group.[88] The type of convertible securities to which CESR referred is also known as an exchangeable, but, in practice, the terminological distinction between convertibles and exchangeables is not always made.[89] Recital (12) certainly does not use this term. In any event, under the directive, exchangeables are, by default, deemed to be non-equity securities. Moreover, even if one follows CESR's reasoning, it is apparent that the recital continues to create confusion because it is plainly irrelevant under the text of the directive whether the decision to convert is in the hands of the investor or not.

'Understanding the design of convertible debt' (1998) 11 *Journal of Applied Corporate Finance* 45.

[84] Art 2(1)(b).

[85] 'CESR Q&A July 10', Question 28.

[86] See Chapter 10, section IV, B.

[87] E.g., Case C-162/97 *Criminal proceedings against Gunnar Nilsson* [1998] ECR I-07477, para. 54.

[88] 'CESR Q&A July 10', Question 28.

[89] E.g., Clifford Chance, 'The Prospectus Directive and its likely impact – Part 3: convertible bonds and exchangeable bonds' (Newsletter February 2004, on file) 1 (noting that

EUR 100,000 wholesale regime for non-equity securities The classification of securities into equity or non-equity securities is important because of the different disclosure requirements that apply to these different types of securities, but also because issuers of non-equity securities, which have a denomination per unit that is at least equal to EUR 1,000, benefit from a (limited) choice of competent authority.[90] Moreover, the directive establishes a separate, lighter, regime for non-equity securities which are to be admitted to trading on a regulated market and which have a denomination per unit that is at least equal to EUR 100,000 (the 'prospectus wholesale regime'). The prospectus wholesale regime relaxes certain requirements of the directive. Issuers are only required to provide a prospectus summary as a matter of exception.[91] Prospectus translation requirements are also relaxed and separate disclosure requirements are applicable.[92]

The existence of separate arrangements for non-equity securities of a certain denomination testifies to the importance of the international debt market in Europe and the legislature's attempts, admittedly after much negotiation and discussions, not to excessively disturb existing practices on this market. But the adoption of the prospectus wholesale regime for non-equity securities also testifies to the fact that the PD sought to level the playing field beyond the boundaries set by previous directives. Indeed, before the PD was adopted, Member States with a stake in the Eurobond or international debt market (e.g., the UK or Luxembourg) took advantage of the fact that the LPD, and subsequently CARD, allowed Member States to provide for lighter disclosure requirements for debt securities which, while admitted to official listing, were 'because of their nature', almost all '... bought and traded in by a limited number of investors who are particularly knowledgeable in investment matters'.[93] The PD replaced this provision when it introduced a new prospectus wholesale regime. This latter regime is a lighter, but – crucially – a harmonised regime that sets sharper limits on the discretion of Member States.

The PD's rules governing the prospectus wholesale regime no longer require investors to be especially 'knowledgeable'. The threshold amount

'[c]onvertible bonds and exchangeable bonds are often talked about in the same breath and market participants often use the same terms to mean both types of bonds').

[90] For details, see section IV, below.

[91] Art 5(2) last sub-para. For details, see section III, B.2.b below. Note that according to CESR, the PD does not prevent issuers from preparing a summary if they wish so, as long as the requirements of the PD and PR with respect to summaries are met. See 'CESR Q&A July 10', Question 41.

[92] PD Arts 19(4) and 7(2)(b).

[93] LPD Art 10, CARD Art 27 (repealed).

effectively replaced this requirement. The underlining rationale appears to be that a high threshold allows fencing off the regime from retail investors.[94] When adopted in 2003, this threshold was fixed at EUR 50,000. But during the revisions of the directive in 2010, it was raised to EUR 100,000.[95] Interestingly, a EUR 100,000 threshold had originally been rejected when the text of the directive was negotiated in 2002 and 2003. But as evidence emerged in 2010 that retail investors were, in fact, making investments in excess of EUR 50,000 in a single transaction, the mood changed.[96] Policy actors agreed that the EUR 50,000 threshold was no longer likely to fulfil its purpose.

2 Exceptions

So far, we have studied the scope of the directive and various definitions and concepts which contribute to defining it. The rules that make exception to the application of the directive are examined next. Article 1(2) is the relevant provision. Securities which fall under one of the exceptions in Article 1(2) are simply outside the scope of the directive. As a result, Member States are free to decide how to treat them under national law, provided, of course, that the securities are not caught under any other EU law provision.[97]

There may be cases, however, where a person might wish to take advantage of the provisions of the PD, especially its passport system. To deal with such cases, the directive also includes certain 'opt-in' arrangements.[98] By opting in, all of the directive's provisions will become applicable,[99] including the provisions governing disclosure, approval and the publication of a prospectus. In examining which securities are outside the scope of the directive and when a person can 'opt-in', it is helpful to differentiate between three types of exceptions.

Exceptions that were included in order to deal with special legal arrangements in Member States Some exceptions were added to the directive in order to deal with certain legal arrangements that exist only in some

[94] European Commission, 'Amended proposal for a Directive of the European Parliament and of the Council on the prospectus to be published when securities are offered to the public or admitted to trading and amending Directive 2001/34/EC' (COM(2002) 460 final, 9 August 2002) 4 (hereinafter, 'Commission Amended Proposal').

[95] See PD Arts 7(2)(b) and 19(4), as amended.

[96] PAD Rec (9). [97] See '3rd Transposition Meeting' 5.

[98] Art 1(3). [99] '3rd Transposition Meeting' 2.

Member States and that, because of their particular nature, were seen as justifying an exception to the application of the directive. Article 1(2)(g), for example, was included in order to deal with situations, such as in Finland, where the right to occupy an apartment or property is connected to ownership of a share in a housing association.[100] These (non-fungible) shares of capital are outside the scope of the directive. Article 1(2)(i) was included in order to make sure that the PD would not apply to a traditional form of Swedish mortgage bonds, known as 'bostadsobligationer'.[101] They are excluded if certain conditions are met and unless a person chooses to opt into the PD's provisions.[102] Finally, Article 1(2)(c) was included in order to deal with cases in which central banks take the form of shareholding companies in Member States.[103] Shares in the capital of central banks are, therefore, not caught under the directive's provisions.[104]

Exceptions that were included because of the nature of the issuer or guarantor Some securities were excluded from the scope of the PD on account of the nature of the issuer or guarantor. Thus, non-equity securities issued by Member States or their regional/local authorities,[105] EU central banks, or public international institutions (provided that, at least, one Member State is a member of the institution in question) are excluded.[106] Non-equity securities issued by the ECB are also excluded from the scope of the directive.[107] Likewise, are excluded securities that are 'unconditionally and irrevocably guaranteed' by a Member State or one of its regional/local authorities.[108] For all of these exceptions, an opt-in remains, however, possible.[109]

Securities issued by associations or non-profit bodies which a Member State has duly recognised are also excluded when the securities are issued with a view to contributing to realising their organisational (non-profit) goals.[110] Units issued by a collective investment undertaking that is not of the closed-end type[111] are also outside the scope of the directive. Likewise

[100] Common Position (EC) No 25/2003 [2003] OJ C 125E/21, 48.
[101] *Ibid.* [102] Art 1(3).
[103] Common Position (EC) No 25/2003 [2003] OJ C 125E/21, 48.
[104] Art 1(2)(c).
[105] But securities that are issued by third countries or their regional/local authorities are not excluded (PR Rec (20)).
[106] PD Art 1(2)(b). [107] *Ibid.* [108] Art 1(2)(d).
[109] Art 1(3). [110] Art 1(2)(e).
[111] Art 1(2)(a). A definition of this type of undertaking is found in Art 2(1)(o).

are non-equity securities that are issued by credit institutions 'in a continuous or repeated manner' as long as the securities which are issued meet a number of conditions.[112]

Exceptions that were included because of the size of the offer The final class of exceptions deals with securities that are outside of the scope of the directive because of the amount of the consideration of an offer. Deemed small, the treatment of these offers is left to Member States to decide;[113] that is, unless a person chooses to 'opt-in'.[114]

The first 'small offer' exception is found in Article 1(2)(j). It applies to non-equity securities issued by credit institutions 'in a continuous or repeated manner' for which the total consideration amounts to less than EUR 75,000,000.[115] The amount was raised from EUR 50,000,000 to EUR 75,000,000 when the PD was amended in 2010. The amended text now also clarifies that this figure must be calculated on an EU-wide basis.[116] As previously, it must be calculated over a time span of twelve months.[117] In addition, the securities that are issued must meet certain conditions. They must not be subordinated.[118] Nor must they be convertible or exchangeable.[119] And finally, they must not grant rights of subscription or acquisition to other types of securities, and be connected to derivatives.[120]

The second exception is found in Article 1(2)(h) of the directive and concerns securities for which the total consideration amounts to less than EUR 5,000,000.[121] Like the previous exception, the provision was amended in 2010 by raising the maximum amount, which amounted initially to EUR 2,500,000, and by specifying that the total consideration should be calculated for the whole of the EU.[122] As previously, the amount must be

[112] According to Art 1(2)(f), the securities are excluded as long as they '(i) are not subordinated, convertible or exchangeable; (ii) do not give a right to subscribe to or acquire other types of securities and that they are not linked to a derivative instrument; (iii) materialise reception of repayable deposits; (iv) are covered by a deposit guarantee scheme under Directive 94/19/EC of the European Parliament and of the Council on deposit-guarantee schemes'.

[113] See also Common Position (EC) No 25/2003 [2003] OJ C 125E/21, 48 and 49.

[114] Art 1(3). [115] Art 1(2)(j), as amended.

[116] See also PAD Rec (6). The amendment was prompted by the fact that before the adoption of the PAD, there was some uncertainty about whether the amount should be calculated per Member State or on an EU wide basis. See European Commission, 'Proposal for a Directive of the European Parliament and of the Council amending Directives 2003/71/EC on the prospectus ...' (COM(2009) 491 final, 23 September 2009), 5.

[117] Art 1(2)(j). [118] Art 1(2)(j)(i). [119] *Ibid.*

[120] Art 1(2)(j)(ii). [121] Art 1(2)(h), as amended.

[122] *Ibid.* See also PAD Rec (6).

calculated over a time span of twelve months,[123] separately for different sorts of securities (e.g., shares or debt securities).[124] For the avoidance of doubt, offers of free shares (offers of 'zero consideration') can also benefit from this exception.[125]

The interplay between Article 1(2)(h) and other provisions of the directive, especially the 'EUR 100,000 exemption' of Article 3(2)(e) which is examined below,[126] has given rise to some questions. The 'EUR 100,000 exemption' exempts offers with a total consideration that amounts to less than EUR 100,000 from the obligation to prepare a prospectus.[127] Article 1(2)(h), on the other hand, not merely exempts issuers from publishing a prospectus; it is an exception to the application of the directive. The interplay between these two provisions can lead to odd results. Recall that Member States are free to specify unilaterally the treatment to be given to securities which fall under Article 1(2)(h). Because the securities are outside the scope of the directive, the PD does not express any preference for the treatment to be given to such securities and whether (or not) they ought to be subject to a lighter regime. Member States are, consequently, also free to make offers of such securities subject to the prior publication of a prospectus *under national law*. From an EU law perspective, this is entirely unobjectionable, as long as EU primary law is respected. But for exempt offers of less than EUR 100,000, Member States cannot require publication of a prospectus because the directive expressly prohibits it.[128] Hence, Member States can only require, as a matter of national law, publication of a prospectus for offers with a total consideration between EUR 100,000 and EUR 5,000,000.[129] In the case of a free offer (an 'offer for zero consideration'), for example, which is caught under Article 1(2)(h) and

123 Art 1(2)(h). According to the Commission, the period should, generally, begin running when the offer is opened. For offering programmes, the period runs from the start of the programme until it ends. See European Commission, '4th informal meeting on prospectus transposition' (summary record, 8 March 2005) 1, http://ec.europa.eu/internal_market/securities/docs/prospectus/summary-note-050308_en.pdf (hereinafter, '4th Transposition Meeting').

124 *Ibid.*, 1.

125 'CESR Q&A July 10', Question 6. Note that Art 3(2)(e) would also be applicable. On the interplay between Art 1(2)(h) and Art 3(2)(e), see below. Moreover, as noted earlier in relation to public offers, there is no public offer in the sense of the directive, if securities are being allocated without a person having to make a decision about whether to accept the offer. If so, the PD would also not be applicable (*ibid.*).

126 See Section V, A.3.a, below.

127 Art 3(2)(e).

128 Art 3(2).

129 In this sense, '3rd Transposition Meeting' 5 (note that the reference to EUR 2,500,000 was the figure in Art 1(2)(h) before that it was amended in 2010).

Article 3(2)(e), a Member State would not be able to ask for a prospectus to be published under national law.[130]

B Content, format and validity of the prospectus

1 Content

I will begin by examining the factors affecting the disclosure content of a prospectus, after which I will step back and take some time to examine ways to help investors make more sense of increasingly complex and technical disclosure in the future.

a Factors affecting the disclosure content of a prospectus The information content of a prospectus is affected by three broad factors: (i) the disclosure requirements of the Level 2 PR; (ii) the general disclosure principle of Article 5(1); and (iii) liability risk.

Level 2 information items The main instrument determining the disclosure content of a prospectus is the Level 2 PR. It lays down detailed disclosure requirements. As a Lamfalussy measure, the PD only defined broad disclosure principles.[131] These principles were implemented by the European Commission when adopting the Level 2 PR.[132] The disclosure requirements take the form of specific information items, set out in various schedules, which require an issuer to disclose information on various items such as, for example, risk factors, property and equipment, research activities, trend information, and so on. The Level 2 items are based on the requirements of an earlier directive (CARD), but also on international standards which have been set by the International Organization of Securities Commissions ('IOSCO').[133] Moreover, following the adoption of IFRS – the International Financial Reporting Standards – as the common EU financial reporting standards, the PR now also makes provision

130 See 'CESR Q&A July 10', Question 6.

131 PD Art 7.

132 Note that ESMA is now also empowered to prepare draft implementing technical standards 'in order to ensure uniform conditions of application of the delegated acts adopted by the Commission'. See PD Art 7(4), as amended by Directive (EU) 2010/78 of the European Parliament and of the Council of 24 November 2010 amending Directives ... 2003/71/EC ... in respect of the powers of [ESMA] [2010] OJ L331/120 (the 'Omnibus Directive').

133 PR Rec (2).

for historical financial information to be prepared in accordance with IFRS.[134]

The PR and the directive refer to these information items as *minimum* information requirements.[135] That is not meant to be a reference to the level of harmonisation (e.g., minimum harmonisation). In fact, as far as the disclosure requirements are concerned, the maximum harmonisation nature of the PD is, for once, very obvious. This is because the PR states that the home state authority cannot, generally, ask for information items, which are not found in the regulation, to be added to a prospectus.[136] Admittedly, this rule is subject to a number of adjustments and derogations. Competent authorities may thus ask for 'adapted information' for certain types of issuers – i.e., property, mineral and investment companies, as well as scientific research companies, start-ups and shipping firms[137] – which because of the nature of their activities, benefit from an exceptional treatment. For wholly new kinds of securities products for which the PR does not lay down appropriate disclosure requirements, competent authorities are also given discretion.[138] Meanwhile, for securities which, albeit not identical, are similar to several types of securities, the PR allows adjustments to be made.[139] An information item may also, occasionally, be omitted where such an item (or any equivalent information) is deemed not to be 'pertinent'.[140] Finally, following an amendment in 2007,[141] a new exception was added to the PR in order to deal with issuers having a complex financial history or having made a financial commitment that is deemed to be significant.[142] In relation to these issuers, a competent authority is empowered to ask for items of financial information, which relate to another company that would not otherwise be disclosed by the issuer, to be added to the issuer's registration document.[143] The PR states that these items will 'be deemed to relate to the issuer'.[144]

[134] Certain third country issuers can benefit from special arrangements. For details, see Chapter 4, section III.

[135] PD Art 7 (heading), PR Rec (2) and Arts 1(2), 2(1), 3, 22 and 23.

[136] Arts 3 (second para) and 22(1) (second sub-para).

[137] PR Art 23(1), Rec (22) and Annex XIX.

[138] Art 23(3), Rec (23). [139] Art 23(2). [140] PR Art 23(4), Rec (24).

[141] Commission Regulation (EC) No 211/2007 of 27 February 2007 amending Regulation (EC) No 809/2004 implementing Directive 2003/71/EC of the European Parliament and of the Council as regards financial information in prospectuses where the issuer has a complex financial history or has made a significant financial commitment [2007] OJ L 61/24.

[142] Art 4a(1). [143] *Ibid.* [144] *Ibid.*

These adjustments and derogations to the prospectus disclosure requirements of the PR do not, however, undermine the general principle of maximum harmonisation. They are not open-ended, and substantive or procedural requirements are attached to their use. Information items can, for example, be omitted only if the item or any equivalent information is deemed not to be 'pertinent to the issuer, to the offer or to the securities'.[145] For new types of securities, authorities benefit from discretion only to the extent that the type in question has characteristics that are wholly different from those for which the PR makes provision and only if a combination of existing items would not provide an appropriate solution.[146] Moreover, competent authorities are required to inform the Commission if they choose to exercise their discretion and depart from the PR's schedules.[147] Likewise, the Commission must be informed if a competent authority asks for adapted information in relation to issuers which benefit from a special treatment because of the nature of their activities (e.g., property companies, start-ups, etc.).[148] And finally, the derogations for issuers with a complex financial history or a significant financial commitment are carefully circumscribed by the PR too; for instance, by defining the meaning of 'complex financial history' or 'significant financial commitment',[149] or by setting certain base requirements on the disclosure that competent authorities can require.[150]

Disclosure principle of Article 5(1) PD The second factor which affects the information content of the prospectus is the disclosure obligation of Article 5(1) of the PD. Article 5(1) states, in broad and general terms, that the prospectus must include all information which, given the specific nature of the issuer and the securities that are issued, is necessary for investors to make 'an informed assessment' of the financial credentials of the issuer, the guarantor (if any) and the securities' rights. It also provides that the information should be presented in a manner which is 'easily analysable and comprehensible'. The open-ended language of Article 5(1) might appear, at first, to somewhat contradict the PR which does not allow competent authorities to ask for information items to be added to a prospectus if these items are not found in the PR. But there is no contradiction. Article 5(1) essentially plays a threefold role. First, it is useful for interpreting the provisions of the Level 2 regulation, or for that matter,

[145] Art 23(4). [146] Art 23(3). [147] *Ibid.*
[148] Art 23(1). [149] See Art 4a(4) and (5). [150] Art 4a(2).

the directive.[151] Second, Article 5(1) is supposed to guide issuers and their advisers when making decisions about the information that should be disclosed under each disclosure item. Note that issuers are not prevented from adding information 'going beyond the information items', as long as such additional disclosure is deemed to be appropriate.[152] Finally, Article 5(1) also informs investor expectations about the level and extent of the disclosure.

Liability risk Liability risk is the final factor worth highlighting. It contributes importantly to determining the extent and amount of disclosure that issuers are prepared to provide. Indeed, liability risk is generally seen as the crucial factor for issuers and their advisers. The flipside, however, is that liability risk may lead to excessive levels of disclosure which are potentially at the expense of the clarity of the prospectus. Admittedly, there is a certain onus on competent authorities to ensure that the disclosure is comprehensible when they vet prospectuses.[153] Given that excessive levels of disclosure can have a detrimental effect on the comprehensibility of the prospectus, competent authorities might be able to address this problem. However, they might be reluctant to do so,[154] if they themselves are concerned about their own liability risk.

b How to deal with increasingly complex disclosure It is common to observe that disclosure regulation in the securities field is a somewhat ineffective means to protect retail investors. Investors, who have no specialised knowledge, face obvious limitations when trying to make sense of technical and complex disclosure language. What is more, the length of a prospectus, which typically has many hundreds of pages, is likely to deter them from trying to read it in the first place. These problems have been widely acknowledged. ESME, for instance, noted in its report on the PD that: 'many investors have difficulties in understanding the technical language and the complex structure of information as well as analyzing the importance of various types of information'.[155] Likewise, CESR reported

[151] It also informed the drafting of the PR's disclosure requirements at Level 2. See e.g., Rec (3) of Commission Regulation (EC) No 211/2007 which amended the PR. Note that the legal basis for adopting implementing legislation is found elsewhere (e.g., PD Art 5(5) and 7(3)).

[152] PR Rec (5). [153] PD Art 2(1)(q).

[154] Cf., 'ESME Report' 10 (noting that '... there is some evidence that issuers have decided to provide (and competent authorities have decided to impose) more disclosure to minimize legal risk and potential court action').

[155] 'ESME Report' 10.

on the comments of market actors who highlighted problems associated with reading detailed and lengthy prospectus disclosure.[156] Outside the EU, IOSCO has stressed that many investors face difficulties in assimilating printed information.[157]

For the European Commission, the prospectus summary has been part of the solution for dealing with this type of problem. The recent revisions of the directive have sought to improve the rules governing summaries.[158] But summaries are, by definition, incomplete. Also, instead of seeking to summarise complex and technical information, the future of dealing with the type of challenges that disclosure raises might lie elsewhere. In the age of the Internet and ever more powerful computers, the answer to information overload and complexity might eventually be the more effective use of software and web-based services. The use of applications such as text mining and, especially, sentiment analysis offers a first glimpse into the possibilities that software-based solutions might eventually be able to offer. Text mining allows identifying information, information patterns and correlations in vast piles of documents and thereby offers a way to deal with problems such as information overload.[159] Sentiment analysis is related to the field of text mining.[160] It has been described as 'a type of subjectivity analysis … that focuses on identifying positive and negative opinions, emotions, and evaluations expressed in natural language'.[161] Specifically, it allows identifying and highlighting the polarity of documents or specific phrases.[162] Thus, sentiment analysis can be used to pinpoint statements, in vast amounts of textual information which express, for instance, a

[156] 'CESR's Report on the PD' 16.

[157] IOSCO, 'Principles on point of sale disclosure' (Consultation Report, November 2009) 13–4, www.iosco.org/library/pubdocs/pdf/IOSCOPD310.pdf.

[158] See section III, B.2.b, below.

[159] See on text mining, M. Hearst, 'Untangling text data mining' in *Proceedings of the 37th Annual Meeting of the Association for Computational Linguistics* (Maryland, US, June 1999) 3; R. Feldman and J. Sanger, *The Text Mining Handbook – Advanced Approaches in Analyzing Unstructured Data* (Cambridge University Press, 2006); S. Ananiadou and J. McNaught (eds.), *Text Mining for Biology and Biomedicine* (Artech House, Boston MA, 2006).

[160] See generally, B. Pang and L. Lee, 'Opinion mining and sentiment analysis' (2008) 2 *Foundations and Trends in Information Retrieval* 1; S. Piao, Y. Tsuruoka and S. Ananiadou, 'Sentiment analysis with knowledge resource and NLP Tools' (2009) 4 *International Journal of Interdisciplinary Social Sciences* 17.

[161] T. Wilson, J. Wiebe and P. Hoffmann, 'Recognizing contextual polarity: an exploration of features for phrase-level sentiment analysis' (2009) 35 *Computational Linguistics* 399, 399 (reference omitted).

[162] T. Wilson, J. Wiebe, and P. Hoffmann, 'Recognizing contextual polarity in phrase-level sentiment analysis' in *Proceedings of the Conference on Human Language Technology*

positive, neutral or negative message. For prospectuses, sentiment analysis could potentially be useful. One could imagine the use of an application whose purpose is to draw investors' attention to statements that have a particular polarity and that may, consequently, be of varying interest to them. Possibly one could, in the future, also think of combining sentiment analysis with other tools such as, for example, educational tools for investors. Attempts to apply sentiment analysis to securities prospectuses do not appear to have been made so far.[163] Developing a sufficiently ripe application will presuppose that the technology develops further. Sentiment analysis requires, *inter alia*, the polarity of language to be accurately identified and appreciated in its context.[164] Besides, it would seem to require significant pre-processing of disclosure. Other features of prospectus disclosure might however, in fact, be helpful. Prospectuses are highly formatted documents and their content is harmonised to a good extent. Moreover, whilst the language used in prospectuses is technical and specialised, it is also relatively homogeneous. To be sure, sentiment analysis can only be a first step on the road towards a more IT-driven way of dealing with prospectus disclosure. Ultimately, the answer to the problems that were described above is likely to require a combination of different strategies, including conduct-of-business rules as a means to ensure that investors get effective advice on their investment decisions,[165] and prospectus summaries. As far as sentiment analysis is concerned, much work still needs to be done in this field. But given the limitations of the current solutions and the nature of the problem, it arguably offers a promising starting point for exploring what information technology has to offer.

2 Formats

The PD introduced new rules governing the format of a prospectus. It also added rules on prospectus summaries and on a common format for correcting and updating a prospectus.

and Empirical Methods in Natural Language Processing (Vancouver, Canada, October 2005) 347.

[163] Sentiment analysis has been used in relation to legal blogs. See J. Conrad, J. Leidner, F. Schilder and R. Kondadadi, 'Query-based opinion summarization for legal blog entries' in *Proceedings of the 12th International Conference on Artificial Intelligence and Law* (ACM Press, New York, 2009) 167; J. Conrad and F. Schilder, 'Opinion mining in legal blogs' in *Proceedings of the 11th International Conference on Artificial Intelligence and Law* (ACM Press, New York, 2007) 231.

[164] See on this, Wilson *et al.*, 'Recognizing contextual polarity: an exploration of features for phrase-level sentiment analysis'.

[165] See also PD Rec (18) which refers to the importance of conduct-of-business rules.

a Prospectus formats *Common format* The directive provides for a prospectus to be prepared as a single or as a tripartite document.[166] If a prospectus is drawn up as a tripartite document, it will take the form of a registration document which will include information about the issuer, a securities note which incorporates information about the securities, and a summary note.[167] The tripartite prospectus creates a shelf-registration system in EU law whose purpose is to offer issuers a more efficient way to raise capital.[168] The benefit of shelf-registration is that the registration document may be filed with competent authorities independently of any issue of securities. If authorities have already approved the registration document, a person will only be required to seek approval of the securities and summary notes when they decide to raise capital.[169]

In some Member States, shelf-registration was an established practice well before the PD was adopted. Indeed, in some Member States, companies simply filed their annual report as a registration document. Neither the PD, nor the PR makes provision for this, but as long as the annual report complies with the relevant disclosure requirements, including the requirements regarding the presentation of the information,[170] this practice does arguably not raise objections.

Special formats In order to accommodate certain market practices, the PD also laid down rules on a third, special, prospectus format, known as a base

[166] Art 5(3). Note that the PR lays down a number of requirements regarding the presentation of the information in a prospectus. In the case of a single prospectus it, *inter alia*, requires the prospectus layout to follow the following order: a table of contents which must be followed by a summary, the risk factor section and, finally, all other information items which are found in the schedules/building-blocks. Likewise, in the case of a tripartite document, the securities note and the registration document must follow a prescribed layout which is as follows: a table of contents, which, as the case may be, is followed by a risk factor section, and all other information items in the schedules. This order of presentation is mandatory, but the order of the information items in the schedules/building-blocks may be altered. If so, a competent authority may, however, ask for a cross-reference list to be provided. See PR Art 25(1), (2) and (3). For the base prospectus layout, see (n. 171) below. Note that CESR has taken the view that, whilst one cannot make exception to the order in which the table of contents, the summary and risk factor section is presented, issuers are not prevented, if they wish, to first include a 'brief cover note' giving general information on the issuer and the securities issue. See 'CESR Q&A July 10', Question 9.

[167] Art 5(3). [168] See Moloney, *EC Securities Regulation* 146.

[169] PD Art 12. If the registration document was filed but was not approved by the competent authority, the registration document will need to be approved together with the securities and summary notes (Art 12(3)).

[170] See (n. 166), above.

prospectus.[171] Base prospectuses are commonly used in the context of offering programmes in the international debt market. Under a programme, an issuer will be able to make several issues of debt securities (for example, medium term notes) over a period of time. Programmes provide issuers with flexibility. They allow them to tap markets quickly because most of the disclosure will be set out in the base prospectus and, consequently, the documentation burden for each issue under the programme will be reduced.[172] Under the PD, a base prospectus can be used in relation to programmes of non-equity securities (including all forms of warrants),[173] and, if certain conditions are met, for non-equity securities issued by credit institutions 'in a continuous or repeated manner'.[174] Note that the PD does not make the use of a base prospectus mandatory. It is an optional arrangement.[175]

The fact that the PD creates different types of prospectus formats raises the question of whether these separate formats can be mixed or combined. As initially adopted, the directive did, for instance, not make it possible to use shelf-registration for a base prospectus.[176] But during the 2010 amendments of the directive, the legislature made a subtle change to the wording of Article 5(3) which, as finally adopted, no longer prevents issuers from using shelf-registration for base prospectuses. The PD's rules on incorporation by reference[177] can also be used in relation to base prospectuses. Thus, it is possible to use these rules in order to incorporate by reference information included in an approved and filed registration document, into a base prospectus.[178] It is also possible to put different base prospectuses together in order to create a single document.[179]

[171] Art 5(4). Note that the layout requirements which are applicable to prospectuses are also applicable to base prospectuses (PR Art 26(1), (2) and (3)). See also (n. 166) above.

[172] Clifford Chance, 'The Prospectus Directive and its likely impact – Part 2: MTN programmes' (Newsletter, January 2004, on file) 1.

[173] PD Art 5(4)(a).

[174] PD Art 5(4)(b). Two conditions must be met: '(i) … the sums deriving from the issue of the said securities, under national legislation, are placed in assets which provide sufficient coverage for the liability deriving from securities until their maturity date; (ii) … in the event of the insolvency of the related credit institution, the said sums are intended, as a priority, to repay the capital and interest falling due, without prejudice to the provisions of Directive 2001/24/EC of the European Parliament and of the Council of 4 April 2001 on the reorganisation and winding up of credit institutions' (*ibid.*). The meaning of 'securities issued in a continuous or repeated manner' is defined in Art 2(1)(l) as 'issues on tap or at least two separate issues of securities of a similar type and/or class over a period of 12 months'.

[175] PD Rec (23), Art 5(4).

[176] See also CESR, 'CESR's advice on level 2 implementing measures for the Prospectus Directive' (CESR/03-300, September 2003) 11.

[177] Art 11. [178] See for details, PR Art 26(4). [179] PR Art 26(8).

A distinctive feature of base prospectuses is that the final terms of an offer of securities, which might not be known at the time of the drafting of the base prospectus, do not need to be included in the base prospectus.[180] They may be included in a supplement.[181] They can also be filed separately.[182] If the final terms are not included in a base prospectus or in a supplement, the directive only provides that they should be made available to investors, filed with the home competent authority and communicated by the issuer to host competent authorities,[183] 'when each public offer is made as soon as practicable and, if possible, in advance of the beginning of the public offer or admission to trading'.[184] What is more, if the final terms are provided separately, they do not need to be approved by the competent authority.[185]

In practice, the directive's provisions on the final terms have given rise to some uncertainty. The PD states that if the final terms are provided separately, the base prospectus will need to include 'the criteria, and/or the conditions in accordance with which the [final offer price and amount of securities] will be determined or, in the case of price, the maximum price'.[186] But there were question marks over what exactly could be included in the final terms. Competent authorities appeared to adopt different practices.[187] The point was clarified when the PD was amended in 2010. As amended, the directive states that only information which concerns the securities note can be included in the final terms.[188] In addition, it says explicitly that the final terms cannot be used in order to supplement a base prospectus.[189] A recital puts some flesh on these requirements by adding that the final terms might, for example, include information on the issue price, the maturity or exercise date, and the international securities identification number.[190] Any new information, which could have an impact on the evaluation of the issuer or the securities, should generally be disclosed in a prospectus supplement.[191]

180 PD Arts 2(1)(r) and 5(4) final sub-para.
181 Art 5(4) final sub-para. 182 *Ibid.*
183 Although the directive does not say it explicitly, the latter requirement is presumably meant to address the case where an issuer seeks to use the directive's passport system.
184 PD Art 5(4) last sub-para, as amended.
185 PR Rec (21). While the final terms do not need to be formally approved, the Commission has taken the view that this does not mean that they should not be checked by the competent authority. See '4th Transposition Meeting' 4.
186 PD Art 5(4) last sub-para, cross-referring to Art 8(1)(a)).
187 'CESR Q&A July 10', Question 57.
188 PD Art 5(4) final sub-para, as amended.
189 Art 5(4) final sub-para, as amended.
190 PAD Rec (17). 191 *Ibid.*

Hence, it would not be appropriate to include in the final terms information which concerns, for instance, risk factors.

Prior to the adoption of the PAD, the PR already provided some guidance on the content of the final terms in order to ensure that the greater freedom which a base prospectus offers to issuers is not at the expense of access to information for investors.[192] Thus, Article 22(2) of the PR sets out a broad rule-based principle which states that information items may be omitted from the base prospectus provided that the relevant items 'are not known when the base prospectus is approved' and can only be ascertained 'at the time of the individual issue'. Besides, the base prospectus will need to identify the type of information that will be added to the final terms (e.g., by listing in the base prospectus the information that is missing, or by leaving blanks that allow identifying the type of information that will be added).[193] The publication method of the final terms, or at least an indication of the manner in which investors will be informed about the publication method, will need to be disclosed as well.[194] Moreover, a statement must be added to the final terms which stresses that both the base prospectus and the final terms are needed for investors to be fully informed.[195] It must also state where the base prospectus is available.[196] Where the final terms reproduce information which is found in the base prospectus, it must be ensured that the final terms can be easily differentiated from the reproduced base prospectus information.[197]

b Summaries The prospectus summary is meant to provide investors with an overview of essential information. It is an integral part of a prospectus (i.e., a single or tripartite prospectus) or a base prospectus.[198] It is mainly intended for retail investors.[199] As such, there is no need to prepare a summary under the EUR 100,000 (wholesale) regime for non-equity securities, unless an issuer wishes to do so[200] or a Member State provides by law for a summary to be translated into the state's official language in accordance with the language requirements of the directive.[201] The rules

[192] PR Rec (25). [193] PR Rec (26), Art 22(5)(1).
[194] Art 22(5)(2). [195] Art 26(5) last sub-para.
[196] *Ibid.* [197] Art 26(5) second sub-para.
[198] For base prospectuses, PR Art 26(6) states that only a single summary needs be prepared, even if the base prospectus concerns different types of securities. But the summary will need to clearly differentiate between the information which relates to the different securities.
[199] PAD Rec (15). [200] 'CESR Q&A July 10', Question 41.
[201] Art 5(2) last sub-para.

governing summaries have recently been revised, after much debate and discussions. Although the changes are intended to make summaries more useful for retail investors, the rules themselves are now more complex than before. The directive sets out the first set of rules. Further measures will have to be adopted at Level 2.[202] In addition, ESMA is also expected to prepare draft implementing technical standards.[203]

As amended, the new arrangements governing summaries build on the concept of 'key information'. The directive states that the summary should provide 'in a concise manner and in non-technical language … key information in the language in which the prospectus was originally drawn up'.[204] It adds that the 'format and content of the summary … shall provide, in conjunction with the prospectus, appropriate information about essentials elements of the securities concerned in order to aid investors when considering whether to invest in such securities'.[205] 'Key information' is a defined concept under the directive. The latter defines it as information which is 'essential and appropriately structured' and which is intended to enable investors to appreciate the nature and risks associated with the issuer (and guarantor) as well as the securities and to choose which offers to give further consideration.[206] A list of more detailed requirements specifies the concept further. Thus, key information must include (i) a brief description of the essential characteristics of the issuer (and any guarantor), the risks associated with the issuer/guarantor as well as their financial credentials; (ii) the essential characteristics and risks involved in the investment, including the securities' rights; (iii) the terms of the offer which also includes an estimate of the costs that an investor might be asked to bear; (iv) details regarding the admission to trading; and (v) the motives for the offer as well as the use of the proceeds. Given the wording of the relevant article, the list is non-exhaustive. Finally, in order to make it easier for investors to compare summaries, the directive now also insists on greater standardisation. It thus states that summaries should be prepared in a 'common format'.[207]

202 PD Art 5(5), as amended. See also PAD Rec (27) which clarifies that these measures should be aligned with future measures adopted in the context of the Commission's initiative on packaged retail investment products.

203 PD Art 5(2), as amended by the Omnibus Directive.

204 Art 5(2), as amended. 205 *Ibid.* 206 Art 2(1)(s).

207 Art 5(2), as amended. A recital clarifies that the format of a summary should make it possible to compare summaries by making sure that 'equivalent information always appears in the same position in the summary' (see PAD Rec (15)).

It is important to stress that the aim of the summary is not to allow investors to make a decision on whether to invest or not. Under the directive, this decision must be made in light of the full prospectus.[208] The directive, as amended, reiterates these basic principles when stating that the summary is meant to 'aid investors when considering whether to invest'.[209] Likewise, when defining the meaning of key information, the directive stresses that key information is merely intended to enable investors to 'decide which offers of securities to consider further'.[210] Whether these precisions have any legal teeth is doubtful, but they are likely to satisfy market actors concerned about the scope of their obligations under the new rules governing summaries.

Whilst the changes regarding summaries are significant, a number of the directive's original provisions on summaries survived the overhaul. A recital continues stating that the summary should generally not include more than 2,500 words,[211] despite calls from market actors to remove the recital. The directive also continues to forbid a person to incorporate information by reference into summaries.[212] The rules governing summary language requirements have also survived.[213] The provisions governing the translation of summaries, in cases where capital is raised abroad, remain in place too.[214] Moreover, the directive continues making provision for the summary to include a number of warnings. To address the risk that investors might exclusively focus on the summary and stop short of reading the full prospectus, the summary must state that it is meant to be read as if it were an 'introduction to the prospectus'[215] and that investment decisions should be made on the basis of the prospectus 'as a whole'.[216] It must also state that if investors need to bring an action before a court in connection with prospectus disclosure, prospectus translation costs might be at their expense.[217] The summary must make the limits of liability for information disclosed in the summary plain.[218] Finally, the PD's annexes also remain substantially the same as far as summaries are concerned.[219] But note that they are not meant to be binding and are non-exhaustive.[220]

208 E.g., Art 5(2)(b). 209 Art 5(2), as amended. 210 Art 2(1)(s).
211 Rec (21). 212 PD Art 11(1).
213 The rule is that the language of the summary is that of the prospectus (Art 5(2)).
214 Art 19. For details on language requirements, see section III, D, below.
215 Art 5(2)(a). 216 Art 5(2)(b). 217 Art 5(2)(c).
218 Art 5(2)(d). See Chapter 6, section V, for details on prospectus liability.
219 PAD Art 1(22). 220 '4th Transposition Meeting' 6.

c Formats for correcting or updating prospectus disclosure *Purpose of prospectus supplements.* The common method for updating or correcting prospectus disclosure is to publish a prospectus supplement. Like prospectuses, prospectus supplements are subject to approval by the relevant competent authority.[221] Moreover, they must be published and can be 'passported' into host Member States.[222] While the basic principles regarding approval and publication are thus the same, a prospectus supplement is not an alternative to a prospectus. It fulfils a specific function. It is a means to communicate new or corrective information to an investor after a prospectus has been published, but before an offer closes or trading begins.[223] The supplement thus concerns an ongoing operation. It is supposed to convey information which is relevant for assessing the securities. It cannot be used for communicating information on an entirely new offer.[224]

More specifically, two factors, i.e., the type of information and the moment when it becomes apparent, will determine whether a prospectus supplement is required. A prospectus supplement is only required where a 'significant new factor, material mistake or inaccuracy' which concerns the information content of the prospectus 'is capable of affecting the assessment of the securities'.[225] Consequently, no supplement is required if, for instance, a mistake is not material or a new factor is not significant. The onus will be on issuers to decide when a supplement must be produced.[226] In case of doubt, issuers are well advised to produce a supplement.[227]

[221] PD Art 16(1).

[222] Arts 16(1) and 17(1). The directive states that the supplement must be published 'in accordance with at least the same arrangements as were applied when the original prospectus was published' (Art 16(1)).

[223] PD Rec (34), Art 16(1).

[224] 'CESR Q&A July 10', Question 34.

[225] PD Art 16(1).

[226] CESR has provided some guidance. With respect to interim financial statements, CESR has responded to the question of whether the publication of such statements is a significant new factor by noting that the matter had to be decided on a case-by-case basis ('CESR Q&A July 10', Question 19). For profit forecasts made prior to the final closing of an offer, CESR, meanwhile, noted that there was a presumption, especially in the case of share issues, that such information was material and hence that a supplement was required ('CESR Q&A July 10', Question 20).

[227] Note that ESMA is empowered to prepare draft regulatory technical standards in order to identify cases where a supplement is needed (PD Art 16(3), as amended by the Omnibus Directive).

The second factor concerns the moment when a new (significant) factor, material mistake or inaccuracy becomes apparent. A prospectus supplement is only required if a new factor, material mistake or inaccuracy 'arises or is noted between the time when the prospectus is approved and the final closing of the offer to the public or, as the case may be, the time when trading on a regulated market begins, *whichever occurs later*' (emphasis added).[228] The fact that the directive identifies the relevant event, which forecloses the possibility to produce a supplement, as the later event, is meant to resolve problems of legal certainty.[229] Indeed, by adding the phrase 'whichever occurs later', the legislature ensures that a person can no longer find himself in a situation where he is being prevented from preparing a prospectus supplement in, say, the period after the securities were admitted to trading, but before the offer is finally closed (because the admission to trading is considered to be the relevant event). Under the amended directive, only the later event (in our case, the final closing of the offer) will foreclose the possibility to prepare a supplement.

Use of supplements for prospectuses, registration documents and base prospectuses Prospectus supplements can be used in order to update or correct prospectuses and, if necessary, prospectus summaries (and any translation of the summary).[230] But there have, in the past, been complications for registration documents. A registration document can be supplemented by a securities note if a 'material change' or 'recent development' has occurred that is relevant to investors.[231] But opinions have differed on whether a prospectus supplement could also be used, separately, for updating or correcting a registration document.[232] The legislature addressed these uncertainties when revising the directive in 2010. As amended, the directive allows prospectus supplements to be used in relation to registration documents.[233]

Base prospectuses can be supplemented too. The PR, which has yet to be brought into line with the directive's amended provisions, states that a

228 Art 16(1), as amended. Note that, according to CESR, issuers should prepare and file the supplement 'as soon as practicable' after the new factor, mistake or inaccuracy which requires disclosure is noticed. See 'CESR Q&A July 10', Question 22.

229 PAD Rec (23).

230 PD Art 16(1). The directive states that a summary can be supplemented 'if necessary to take into account the new information included in the supplement'.

231 PD Art 12(2).

232 'CESR's Report on the PD' 25.

233 PD Art 12(2), as amended. See also Art 9(4), as amended, which cross-refers to Art 16.

supplement must be prepared and published where a significant new factor, material mistake or inaccuracy, which has the potential of affecting the assessment of the securities, has occurred in the timeframe between the approval of the base prospectus and 'the final closing of the offer of each issue of securities under the base prospectus or, as the case may be, the time that trading on a regulated market of those securities begins'.[234] A prospectus supplement may also be required for the summary of a base prospectus.[235] Indeed, there may be cases where the final terms may need correcting or updating. Recall that the final terms may not necessarily be included in the base prospectus. They may be included in a supplement, but they may also be filed separately. CESR suggested that to correct final terms or update them with necessary information, issuers should prepare a supplement to the base prospectus which should make reference to the amended final terms.[236] Strictly speaking, the supplement thus supplements the base prospectus rather than the final terms. Note, however, that CESR also suggested that, in order to avoid any ambiguity, a new set of final terms should also be prepared and filed with the relevant competent authority.[237]

Prospectus supplements: right of withdrawal for investors While a supplement is useful for correcting or updating information, it may not be sufficient to redress the consequences of faulty disclosure. Investors should also therefore be able to reconsider and indeed retract in certain circumstances, a previous acceptance of an offer. Yet having said this, not all information that is supplemented is necessarily bad news that affects an investment negatively.[238] Nor is the supplemented information necessarily unknown to investors prior to being supplemented. Indeed, in practice, supplements appear to have been prepared even in the absence of any significant new factor, material mistake or inaccuracy for the mere sake of consistency.[239] A right of withdrawal may, hence, not always be justified or desirable. The PD enacts a right of withdrawal for investors.[240] The text

[234] PR Art 22(7). The PR adds that, in this case, the supplement must be published 'prior to the final closing of the offer or the admission of those securities to trading' (PR Art 22(7)).

[235] PR Art 25(5). [236] 'CESR Q&A July 10', Question 64.

[237] *Ibid.* [238] See also 'ESME Report' 21.

[239] ICMA, 'Consultation on the review of the Prospectus Directive' (letter to the European Commission, 10 March 2008) 5, www.icmagroup.org/ICMAGroup/files/54/54d09f97–1137–402b-8cc4-c554e6229908.pdf (hereinafter, 'ICMA Comment Letter').

[240] Note that besides the right of withdrawal of Art 16(2), there is another right of withdrawal under Art 8(1), where the final offer price and amount of securities offered to the public are not stated in the prospectus. See for details section III, C.2.a, below.

of the relevant provision, Article 16(2), was recently amended. Although the amendments are important, it is apparent that the legislature did not wish to dilute the withdrawal right by introducing additional distinctions regarding the type and nature of the information that prompts a person to publish a supplement and subsequently triggers the right for a person to withdraw his acceptance. As amended, the right of withdrawal is only applicable where a prospectus is prepared for a public offer of securities. Hence, if an offer is caught under Article 3(2), which exempts persons from publishing a prospectus (e.g., for an offer to qualified investors) and a prospectus is prepared merely for the purposes of having securities admitted to trading, Article 16(2) will not be available.[241] The amendments also concern the time periods within which the withdrawal right can be exercised. In the past, Member States adopted different practices. To improve consistency, the PD now states that investors can withdraw their acceptances 'within two working days' following the publication of the supplement, as opposed to a minimum of two working days, as it was previously the case.[242] This time period can be extended, but only by the issuer or the offeror.[243] The date by which the right of withdrawal ends, must be mentioned in the supplement.[244] Finally, the directive now explicitly ties the right of withdrawal to the events that trigger the publication of a supplement and canvasses more clearly the period within which this event must occur. Thus, the right of withdrawal is only available if a new factor, mistake or inaccuracy, which is such as to trigger the requirement to prepare a supplement, arises 'before the final closing of the offer to the public and the delivery of the securities'.[245]

3 Validity of the prospectus

The PD sets time limits to the validity of a prospectus, registration document and base prospectus.[246] Provided that the prospectus is updated when necessary by a prospectus supplement, the period of validity of a prospectus is twelve months.[247] This period starts running from the date of the prospectus approval (rather than the date of the publication of the prospectus, as it was previously the case).[248] A registration document,

[241] In this sense, see also Linklaters 'Amendments to Prospectus Directive published' (10 July 2010), www.linklaters.com/pdfs/publications/PDReview_ClientNote.pdf.
[242] Art 16(2), as amended. [243] Art 16(2), as amended. [244] *Ibid.* See also PAD Rec (24).
[245] Art 16(2). See also 'CESR Q&A July 10', Question 21 (stating that '[w]ithdrawal is no more possible when the securities have been issued and delivered/allotted to investors').
[246] Art 9. [247] Art 9(1). [248] Art 9(1), as amended.

which has been filed and approved by the home state competent authority, will also be valid for a (maximum) period of twelve months.[249] For offering programmes, the period of validity of a base prospectus is also a maximum of twelve months, save for base prospectuses which concern 'Article 5(4)(b)' securities, i.e., non-equity securities which are issued by credit institutions in a 'continuous or repeated manner'.[250] For such securities, the base prospectus will remain valid until there are no securities left to be issued in a 'continuous or repeated manner'.[251]

C *Incorporation by reference*

Incorporation by reference is allowed under Article 11 of the directive. Before the PD was adopted, incorporating information in a prospectus by simply making a reference to a document containing the relevant information was possible in some Member States. Luxembourg even allowed incorporating future documents by way of a reference. The advantage of incorporation by reference is that it makes it cheaper for issuers to prepare a prospectus or, for that matter, a base prospectus.[252] As elsewhere, the PD's rules on incorporation by reference attempted to balance the interests of issuers and investors.[253] In its amended form, the directive states that published documents, which have been approved or filed with the home state competent authority pursuant to the PD or the TD, can be incorporated by reference.[254] In addition, the PR, which implements the directive's provisions, includes an open-ended list of documents whose content can be fully or partially incorporated by reference.[255] Among the information that can be incorporated by reference is information included in financial statements, articles of associations or audit reports.[256] Information contained in a prospectus or base prospectus,

[249] Art 9(4), as amended. [250] Art 9(3).

[251] *Ibid.* CESR has pointed out that the same rule applies where a prospectus, as opposed to a base prospectus, is used to issue securities in a continuous or repeated manner. Thus, the prospectus will be valid until 'no more of the securities concerned are issued in a continuous or repeated manner' (Art 9(3)), regardless of the twelve-month period of validity which applies to prospectuses under Art 9(1). See 'CESR Q&A July 10', Question 37.

[252] PR Rec (30); PD Rec (29). [253] *Ibid.* [254] Art 11(1), as amended.

[255] PR Art 28(1). If the information content of the document is incorporated only in part, the prospectus/base prospectus must state that the information which is not incorporated by reference is either irrelevant or dealt with somewhere else in the prospectus (PR Art 28(4)).

[256] PR Art 28(1).

which has been approved and published previously, can also be incorporated by reference into a new prospectus/base prospectus.[257] It is also possible to incorporate information found in a registration document by reference into a base prospectus.[258]

Incorporation by reference is subject to a number of conditions and restrictions. As already noted, information, which is to be incorporated by reference, must be included in a published document that has either been approved or filed with the home competent authority pursuant to the PD or the TD.[259] The information must be the most recent available.[260] Moreover, the directive does not allow future documents such as, for example, forthcoming financial statements, to be incorporated by reference.[261] This practice, which was common in some Member States, is thus no longer permissible under the terms of the directive.

To ensure that incorporation by reference does not prejudice the quality and clarity of the disclosure, the PR also lays down a guiding principle according to which issuers should make every effort to ensure that incorporation by reference is not at the expense of investor protection.[262] The PD and PR also seek to promote disclosure clarity by other means and measures, for example by mandating that a list of cross-references be provided in order to make it easier for investors to identify particular information items,[263] or by ruling out the possibility to incorporate information by reference in summaries.[264] Moreover, incorporation by reference does not make exception to the rules governing the language of the prospectus.[265] The documents incorporated by reference must therefore also comply

[257] *Ibid.* According to CESR, it is also possible to incorporate by reference information included in a base prospectus whose period of validity has come to an end, into a new base prospectus (see 'CESR Q&A July 10', Question 8).

[258] PR Art 26(4). [259] PD Art 11(1).

[260] *Ibid.* If material changes have affected the information which is included in the document that is incorporated by reference, the prospectus/base prospectus must disclose this fact and provide updated information (PR Art 28(3)).

[261] The PD only allows information to be incorporated by reference if the information has been published 'previously or simultaneously' (PD Art 11).

[262] Art 28(5). Compliance with this principle is meant to be ensured by the home state authority. See 'CESR's Report on the PD' 30.

[263] PD Art 11(2). According to the Commission, the list aims at 'inform[ing] an investor, in a clear and easily accessible manner, whether the prospectus is complete in itself, or whether he will need access to other documents to complete the prospectus'. See '3rd Transposition Meeting' 9.

[264] PD Art 11(1).

[265] PR Art 28(2). That is, however, not to say that information which is incorporated by reference may necessarily have to be drawn up in the same language as the prospectus.

with the latter rules.[266] Finally, it should be recalled that incorporation by reference of information does not make exception to the overriding disclosure principle of the directive which requires, among other things, information to be laid out in the prospectus in a form which is both easy to analyse and comprehensible.[267]

D Omission of information

1 Main issues

For a piece of legislation which sought to level the playing field and whose aim was, *inter alia*, to contribute to protecting investors and promoting investor confidence through disclosure,[268] allowing issuers to omit information from the prospectus was bound to be a sensitive matter. On the one hand, broad and unconditional provisions allowing issuers (and competent authorities) to exclude information items would not have squared with the PD's and PR's objectives and principles. On the other hand, however, full disclosure may not always be possible or, indeed, desirable. There are good reasons for allowing, at times, issuers to omit information. The PD and PR seek to balance these different concerns and interests. The outcome of this balancing act is that information can only be omitted as a matter of exception. However, it is also apparent that the rules governing omissions often use undefined concepts or terms (for instance, is the disclosure 'seriously detrimental' or not 'pertinent'?). These terms raise questions of interpretation and questions of fact. But because the rules governing omissions make exceptions to two overriding principles of the directive, full disclosure and maximum harmonisation, these terms or concepts must ultimately be interpreted strictly.

2 Grounds for omitting information

a Omission of information under the PD *Unavailable information* There may be occasions where certain information items – the final offer price and the amount of securities to be offered to the public – are unavailable at the time when the prospectus is prepared. The PD allows

What matters is that the PD's language requirements are complied with. Thus, a translated document can also be incorporated by reference provided that the language rules of the directive are still satisfied (see 'CESR Q&A July 10', Question 7).

[266] See section III, D below. [267] PD Art 5(1). See also PR Rec (30).

[268] PD Rec (18).

these items to be omitted from the prospectus.[269] But requirements and conditions apply. Once the information on the offer price and amount of securities becomes available, the missing information will need to be filed with the home state authority and be published.[270] According to CESR, it should also be given to host state authorities.[271] To be sure, the requirement to communicate this information to host state authorities is not a legally mandated requirement under the directive. Nevertheless, host state authorities are pursuant to the rules governing the passport system entitled to a copy of the prospectus[272] and that being so, they should also be entitled to any information that is missing from the prospectus.[273] During the recent revisions of the directive, the legislature clarified in relation to base prospectuses that, as far as the final terms of an offer are concerned, host state authorities should be communicated the missing terms once they become available.[274] But unfortunately, the legislature missed the opportunity to make a similar adjustment to the provisions governing the omission of information.

Moreover, the prospectus will also need to meet certain additional requirements prior to the information being available. Thus, it will need to specify criteria or conditions according to which the final offer price and the amount of securities will be determined,[275] or, if the offer price is omitted, state a maximum price.[276] Alternatively, investors must be offered a right to withdraw their acceptances to purchase or subscribe to the securities. The directive states that the period during which investors can exercise this right cannot be shorter than two working days.[277] The period starts running from the time that the missing information is filed with the home competent authority.[278] For the avoidance of doubt, the PD does not express a preference for either of these arrangements. They are alternatives.

Disclosure which is not in the public interest, or is seriously detrimental to the issuer, or is unimportant Information may also be omitted from the prospectus if the disclosure would not be in the public interest.[279] There is no definition of public interest under the PD, but pursuant to the directive,

[269] Art 8(1). For the avoidance of doubt, Art 8(1) also applies where only one of these items is omitted. See '4th Transposition Meeting' 4.

[270] Art 8(1), final sub-para. [271] 'CESR Q&A July 10', Question 1.

[272] Art 18(1).

[273] Such information does not need, however, to be officially filed with host state authorities.

[274] Art 5(4), final sub-para, as amended. [275] Art 8(1)(a).

[276] *Ibid.* [277] Art 8(1)(b). [278] *Ibid.* [279] Art 8(2)(a).

it is the home state authority which has the say on whether the omission of information is a matter of public interest.[280] Likewise, if the disclosure would be 'seriously detrimental to the issuer', a home state authority is entitled to authorise a person to omit the information in question as long as it is satisfied that the omission would not be such as to mislead the public.[281] Finally, a home state authority is entitled to authorise the omission of unimportant information – that is, information of 'minor importance' in the language of the PD – but only for a specific offer or admission to trading.[282] Moreover, the home state authority must be satisfied that the information in question does not matter for assessing the financial position and the future of the issuer (or offeror, or any guarantor).[283]

Inappropriate disclosure If exceptionally, information is deemed to be inappropriate 'to the issuer's sphere of activity or to the legal form of the issuer or to the securities to which the prospectus relates', it can be omitted from the prospectus,[284] provided a set of conditions and requirements are met. The omission of information must not undermine the proper information of investors.[285] Moreover, omitted information must, where possible, be replaced by equivalent information.[286] The directive does not state explicitly who is meant to decide on equivalence. The issuer appears to be entitled to decide in the first place on the matter.[287] But given that the prospectus will need to be vetted,[288] the home competent authority will have the final say on the matter.

b Omission of information under the PR While the bulk of the PR is about defining detailed disclosure items, the PR also includes certain rules which allow information items to be omitted from a prospectus.

Information items which are not pertinent An information item (or information deemed to be equivalent) may exceptionally be omitted from a prospectus on the grounds that it is not 'pertinent' to the issuer, the offer or the securities that are being issued.[289] When exactly information is not deemed to be pertinent is an open question. CESR gave little guidance on

[280] Arts 8(2) and 8(2)(a). In the future, the concept of public interest might conceivably be specified by way of delegated acts. See Art 8(4), as amended.

[281] Art 8(2)(b). [282] Art 8(2)(c). [283] *Ibid.*

[284] Art 8(3). [285] *Ibid.* [286] *Ibid.*

[287] Van Gerven, 'General provisions of Community law relating to the prospectus to be published when securities are offered to the public or admitted to trading' 41.

[288] Art 13(1). [289] PR Art 23(4).

the matter, save for stating that the 'risk factor' item of a prospectus could never be omitted.[290] But, in any event, there are safeguards, given that the prospectus will require vetting by the home state authority and that, accordingly, the application of the provision will not go unchecked.

Unknown information items for base prospectuses Given that it is not uncommon for base prospectuses to omit information, special rules on the omission of information are applicable to them. The relevant provisions were examined earlier when discussing prospectus formats.[291] Recall that Article 22(2) of the PR states that information items may be omitted from the base prospectus where they are unknown at the time of the approval of the base prospectus and are only available when each issue is made. Recall also that the legislature has sought to clarify the rules on the final terms of an offer when amending the directive in 2010.[292]

c The use of the rules governing disclosure omissions as a 'short-term fix' The rules governing disclosure omissions have at times been used rather creatively as a quick fix in order to attend to unforeseen problems caused by the application of the directive. Article 23(4) of the PR, which allows information that is not deemed to be pertinent to be omitted, has, for instance, been used in order to address unexpected problems with retail cascades and employee share schemes.[293] The rules on omissions have also been used in the wake of the banking crisis. CESR suggested that competent authorities should rely on Article 23(4) of the PR or Article 8 of the PD (which also deals with information omissions) in order to facilitate securities issues guaranteed by Member States.[294] This type of operation is generally outside the scope of the directive,[295] but, as mentioned earlier, the directive allows a person to opt into the provisions of the directive if he wishes to do so.[296] In this case, the PD's provisions become applicable, including the disclosure requirements of the directive. Given that credit institutions, which turned to Member States for help in the wake of the banking crisis, often wished to continue benefiting from the passport system, CESR recommended that, in order to ease the ensuing disclosure obligations for credit institutions, competent authorities should rely on the rules on disclosure omissions and decide on a case-by-case

[290] 'CESR Q&A July 10', Question 11. [291] See section III B.2, above.
[292] See *ibid.* [293] For retail cascades, see section V, A.3.a, below.
[294] 'CESR Q&A July 10', Question 70.
[295] PD Art 1(2)(d). [296] Art 1(3).

basis whether certain information could be omitted from the prospectus if a Member State unconditionally and irrevocably guaranteed the securities.[297] As in the case of employee share schemes and retail cascades, the solution provided a short-term fix to an unexpected problem. The legislature duly examined the issue when reviewing the functioning of the directive in 2010. It added a new article which states that an issuer should not be required to provide information in the prospectus about an EU Member State which acts as a guarantor of an offer of securities.[298]

E Language requirements

The PD's rules governing language requirements determine both the language and translation requirements governing prospectuses. Their purpose is mainly to facilitate cross-border operations.[299] Translation requirements can be an important cost factor and have, in the past, led issuers to reconsider their listing decisions. The most evocative illustration of this fact goes back to a decision of the French *Conseil d'Etat*, the highest administrative court in France. The details of the case do not need to concern us. Suffice it to say that in December 2000, it partially annulled the provisions of a ministerial order that officially sanctioned a decision by the *Commission des opérations de bourse* (Cob) to ease translation requirements in France for certain issuers.[300] The Court's ruling led to a staggering drop in the number of admissions of non-equity securities on the Paris market (see Table 1). Between January and April 2000 and January and April 2001, the total amount of bond issues fell from EUR 33 billion to EUR 11 billion, with many large foreign, but also French issuers turning their back on the Paris market in favour of other financial centres such as Luxembourg (see Table 2).[301] Just a year after the decision of the

[297] 'CESR Q&A July 10', Question 70.

[298] PD Art 8(3a). The legislature had in mind a specific scenario, i.e., of an issuer that relies on the 'opt-in' mechanism of PD Art 1(3).

[299] PD Rec (35). They appear to have had a positive impact on the cost burden of preparing a prospectus. See CSES (Centre for Strategy & Evaluation Services), 'Study on the impact of the prospectus regime on EU financial markets' (Final Report, July 2008) 53, http://ec.europa.eu/internal_market/securities/docs/prospectus/cses_report_en.pdf (hereinafter, 'CSES Report').

[300] Décision du Conseil d'Etat n°213415 (20 December 2000), www.conseil-etat.fr; COB, 'Bulletin mensuel d'information de la Commission des opérations de bourse' (no. 352, December 2000) 43, www.amf-france.org/affiche.asp?id=5726.

[301] See P. Marini, 'Rapport fait au nom de la commission des finances, du contrôle budgétaire et des comptes économiques de la Nation (1) sur le projet de loi, adopté part l'Assemblée

Table 1 *Admission to listing of so-called 'international' bonds*[302] *(limited to qualified investors)*

	1998	1999	2000	2001
January	14	7	7	5
February	36	13	22	6
March	21	17	18	4
April	22	18	13	14
Total for four months	93	45	60	29
Total over the year	235	192	186	Ns

Original Source (and copyright holder): Euronext

French *Conseil d'Etat*, the French legislature responded to the outflow of issuers by adopting the *loi MURCEF* on urgent reform measures of economic or financial nature, which gave the Cob the necessary legislative support for enacting more flexible language requirements.[303]

The ruling of the *Conseil d'Etat* and its impact on capital-raising activities in France is a telling example of regulatory arbitrage. Following the entry into force of the PD, the rules governing the translation of prospectuses are now determined exhaustively by the directive. The directive seeks, *inter alia*, to ease translation requirements by allowing issuers, in cross-border situations, to draw up a prospectus in a 'language customary in the sphere of international finance' such as, for example, English.[304] More specifically, the rules are based on three basic distinctions. The first distinction relates to the respective competence of home and host competent authorities. The essential thrust is to limit the competence of host competent authorities to insist on a translation of a prospectus in the official language of the host state when issuers seek to raise capital – by making a public offer or seeking admission to trading on a regulated market – in the

nationale, après déclaration d'urgence, portant mesures urgentes de réformes à caractère économique et financier' (Rapport n°336, Session Ordinaire de 2000–2001) 102, www.senat.fr/rap/l00–336/l00–3361.pdf (hereinafter, 'Senate Report').

302 Translated from 'Senate Report' 102.

303 COB, 'Bulletin mensuel d'information de la Commission des opérations de bourse' (no. 367, April 2002) 5, www.amf-france.org/affiche.asp?id=5709.

304 The decision to recognise a language as being customary in international finance belongs to competent authorities. There is nothing to prevent languages other than English from being recognised as such. See '3rd Transposition Meeting' 10.

Table 2 *Amount of bond issues (comparison January–April 2000 and January–April 2001)*[305]

	2000			2001			
Numbers at the end of	Numbers	Amounts B euros	Total	Numbers	Amounts B euros	Total	**Variation**
— January	15	4,714	4,714	9	675	675	**-86%**
— February	25	7,867	12,581	15	6,000*	6,675	**-15%**
— March	22	7,875	20,456	7	1,626	8,301	**-59%**
—April	21	12,671	33,127	11	2,525**	10,826	**-67%**
Total for the four months	83	33,127		42	10,826	—	

* of which 2.7 billion euros for exchangeable FT on Orange of 12/02/01
** issuers: CADES, RFF, SAGESS, Dexia, SG
No foreign issuer in 2001
Original Source : COB

host Member State(s). Thus, the directive states that a prospectus will need to be produced either in a language accepted by the host state authority or in a language customary in international finance.[306] The issuer (offeror or person asking for admission) will be free to choose between these alternatives. The host state authority will only be able to insist that a summary be translated into the host state's official language or languages.[307] The second distinction concerns home Member States. To make sense of the distinction, it must be borne in mind that under the home country control principle, the home competent authority is entrusted with prior approval of prospectuses, regardless of whether a public offer or admission to trading takes place at 'home'. The directive therefore differentiates between two situations. Where capital is raised at home, the home Member State is given full discretion to set language requirements,[308] whether or not an issuer seeks also to raise capital in host Member States. However, where no capital raising activities take place at home, the discretion of the home state authority is limited and it will need to accept a prospectus prepared in a language customary in international finance.[309] Finally,

305 Translated from 'Senate Report' 102.
306 PD Art 19(2), 19(3). 307 *Ibid.*
308 Art 19(1), 19(3).
309 PD Art 19(2), sub-para 2. The home competent authority can also ask for a prospectus to be prepared in another language, but in any event, the issuer is free to choose a language of international finance.

the PD introduces separate rules governing the EUR 100,000 (wholesale) regime. Thus, for non-equity securities with a denomination (per unit) of at least EUR 100,000, both home and host state authorities are required to accept a prospectus drawn up either in a language that they accept or that is customary in international finance.[310] The issuer (offeror or person asking for admission) is free to choose between these alternatives, but home and host competent authorities can ask for a prospectus summary to be prepared in their official language(s), provided that this requirement is enacted in national law.[311]

As far as the *quality* of the translation is concerned, the person responsible for making sure that the translation of a prospectus is satisfactory is the person who is responsible for the prospectus.[312] CESR recommended that any translation should mention this fact.[313] It also stressed that it was not for the host state authority to assess the quality of a translation. The latter cannot interfere with the passport system.[314] The directive's passport allows a person to rely on an approved prospectus for capital raising purposes in host Member States. If a host state authority finds inaccuracies in a translated text, it will have to rely in the first place on the home state authority for taking action under the precautionary measures principle.[315] Note that CESR provided few clues about the appropriate action to be taken in cases where a translation of a prospectus was found to be faulty. It only suggested that the home and host competent authority should find a solution together with the issuer.[316]

IV Obligation to seek prior approval with the competent authority of the home Member State

Once the prospectus has been drawn up, the competent authority of the issuer's home Member State must approve it before it can be published.[317] The obligation to seek prior approval is hence the second core obligation under the directive. The nature and content of prior approval will be examined in Chapter 6 when turning to means of enforcement. This

[310] PD Art 19(4), as amended. [311] *Ibid.*

[312] 'CESR Q&A July 10', Question 33.

[313] *Ibid.* [314] *Ibid.*

[315] PD Art 23. A host state authority's actions are restricted under this principle. Art 23 only allows it to take action after having informed the home state authority and ESMA and only if the actions of the home state authority have proven to be insufficient or inadequate.

[316] 'CESR Q&A July 10', Question 33.

[317] PD Art 13.

section will accordingly be fairly short. It suffices to focus here on the rules governing the determination of the home Member State. The directive identifies the home Member State of an issuer as 'the one best placed to regulate the issuer'.[318] Because of the importance of the home country principle under the directive, the rules allocating competence between Member States are crucial. As finally adopted, the rules reflect a hard-fought compromise.[319] Before examining the relevant rules, it is helpful to briefly look at the principles which underpinned the distribution of competence under the LPD (as consolidated into CARD) and the POD which were both replaced by the PD.[320]

Determination of competence under the LPD and POD Unlike the PD, the LPD was not based on the home state principle. Instead, competence was settled according to territorial jurisdiction: issuers submitted their listing particulars to the competent authority of the Member State where the stock exchange, on which they intended to list, was situated or was operating. But if an issuer sought to make use of the LPD's mutual recognition system,[321] the mutual recognition provisions of the directive affected the distribution of competence.[322] Thus, if an admission to official listing was sought on stock exchanges in at least two Member States *including the Member State where the issuer had its registered office*, the LPD settled the distribution of competence in favour of the latter Member State.[323] Where an issuer used mutual recognition in order to raise capital in Member States other than the Member State where it had its registered office, it could choose among these Member States, the one which would have rule-making and enforcement competence.[324] Hence, under these rules, the LPD settled the distribution of competence in a manner which gave priority to the Member State in which the issuer's registered office was situated (hereinafter, the 'registered-office-primacy rule'), unless, of course, the Member State of the place of the issuer's registered office was not affected by the capital raising activities. The POD included a similar

[318] Rec (14).

[319] Chapter 10 examines the point in more detail.

[320] Council Directive 80/390/EEC [1980] OJ L100/1, as consolidated in Directive 2001/34/EC [2001] OJ L184/1; Council Directive 89/298/EEC [1989] OJ L124/8 (repealed).

[321] CARD Arts 38 and 39 (LPD Arts 24 (a) and (b)).

[322] For a more comprehensive review of the different mutual recognition scenarios and the historical background of these rules, see Moloney, *EC Securities Regulation*.

[323] CARD Art 37 (LPD Art 24, after amendment).

[324] *Ibid.*

provision, but the rules were slightly more complicated. Essentially, however, Article 20(1) of the POD, which envisaged the case of a person seeking to make a public offer in at least two Member States, applied the registered-office-primacy rule. Article 20(2) dealt with situations in which the registered-office-primacy rule did not apply – for example, because the Member State of the place of the issuer's registered office did not vet public offer prospectuses. For these cases, a person could choose a competent authority among the Member States on whose territory the public offer was made and which vetted public offer prospectuses.[325]

Hence, whilst the registered-office-primacy rule was not an absolute rule, it is nevertheless fair to say that, if a person sought to make use of mutual recognition, the registered-office-primacy rule was the crux of the distribution of competence under the LPD and POD. This is because it was the Member State of the place of the issuer's registered office which was seen as having the most legitimate jurisdictional claim over an issuer. One crucial consequence of the registered-office-primacy rule was that issuers were effectively prevented from circumventing the competent authorities of the Member State in which their registered office was located by seeking approval of their prospectus/listing particulars abroad and subsequently using mutual recognition to raise capital in the Member State of the place of their registered office.

Determination of home state competence under the PD Unlike the LPD and POD, the PD no longer includes *separate* provisions governing jurisdictional competence in case where the passport system (i.e., mutual recognition) is being used. There is only one set of rules, Article 2(1)(m) and (n), which determines the home Member State of an issuer as well as the host Member States. By defining the home Member State, these rules also determine the issuer's home state competent authority. To determine competence, the rules differentiate between the type of securities which are being offered to the public or admitted to trading on a regulated market, and their denomination.[326] Thus, for non-equity securities which have a denomination per unit of at least EUR 1,000, including certain types of hybrid or derivative securities which are treated as non-equity

[325] POD Art 20(2).

[326] Issuers incorporated in third countries that wish to raise capital in the EU are partially subject to separate rules under Art 2(1)(m)(iii). See Chapter 4, section V.

securities,[327] the PD allows a person to choose a home Member State, and therefore a home state authority, among the following Member States:

(i) the Member State where the issuer's registered office is located;
(ii) the Member State where the regulated market, on which the securities are to be admitted to trading, is located; or
(iii) the Member State on whose territory the securities are offered to the public.[328]

For equity securities and any other type of securities that are not caught under the above provision, a person is denied a choice of home Member State and as a result subject, for matters governed by the home state principle, to the sole competence of the Member State in which the issuer's registered office is located, regardless of where the securities are offered or admitted to trading.[329] The same rules governing competence apply to base prospectuses.[330] Thus, if non-equity securities with a denomination of at least EUR 1,000 are expected to be issued under a programme, a person benefits from a choice of competent authority for the approval of the base prospectus.[331] If, on the other hand, non-equity securities with a denomination of less than EUR 1,000 are expected to be issued under the programme, a person will need to seek approval of the base prospectus with the competent authority of the Member State in which the issuer's registered office is located.[332]

If one compares the PD's rules governing the horizontal allocation of competence with those of the LPD or POD, one is struck by the difference in approach. *De jure*, the PD's rules are not consistent with those of the LPD or POD. But nor are they, for that matter, consistent with the conventional rules governing home country control which, for legal persons,

[327] More specifically, Art 2(1)(m)(ii) also applies to 'any issues of non-equity securities giving the right to acquire any transferable securities or to receive a cash amount, as a consequence of their being converted or the rights conferred by them being exercised, provided that the issuer of the non-equity securities is not the issuer of the underlying securities or an entity belonging to the group of the latter issuer'.

[328] Art 2(1)(m)(ii). If non-equity securities are issued in another currency, a person benefits of the same choice as long as 'the value of such minimum denomination is nearly equivalent to EUR 1 000' (*ibid.*). This assessment is, according to CESR, to be made when the draft prospectus is being submitted. See 'CESR Q&A July 10', Question 13.

[329] Art 2(1)(m)(i).

[330] 'CESR Q&A July 10', Question 46.

[331] According to CESR, a person must at least have a 'reasonable expectation' that securities will be issued with a view to their admission to trading on a regulated market, or a public offer, in the chosen home Member States (*ibid.*).

[332] *Ibid.*

are typically based on the registered office criterion. Importantly, the registered-office-primacy rule is no longer fully respected under the PD. Indeed, Article 2(1)(m)(ii), which offers issuers a choice of home Member State and hence a choice of competent authority, no longer settles the distribution of competences in a manner which prevents an issuer – say, a French issuer – from seeking approval with, say, the UK FSA when applying for admission to trading of non-equity securities on a UK regulated market and subsequently to 'passport' its FSA-vetted prospectus back to France in order to make a public offer to French retail investors, without having to seek approval with the French securities markets authority.[333]

V Obligation to publish a prospectus and comply with the PD's provisions relating to advertisement

Once the prospectus has been approved, it must be filed with the home state authority and be published according to the rules of the PD.[334] Any advertising material must also comply with the principles set out in the directive and the Level 2 PR. The requirement to publish the prospectus and comply with the relevant rules governing advertisement is the third core obligation of the directive. This section examines the relevant provisions. It begins with the PD's and PR's rules on the publication of prospectuses (A), after which it examines the rules on advertisement (B).

A Obligation to publish a prospectus

The PD sets out detailed rules regarding the publication of prospectuses. The publication is a crucial requirement under the directive. It is a condition for making a public offer or having securities admitted to trading on a regulated market.[335] The publication follows the approval of the prospectus and must take place 'as soon as practicable', but in any event 'at a reasonable time in advance of, and at the latest at the beginning of, the offer to the public or the admission to trading of the securities'.[336] Note

[333] There is empirical evidence that the passport system has been used to this effect. See CRA International 'Evaluation of the economic impacts of the Financial Services Action Plan' (Report commissioned by the European Commission, March 2009) 170, http://ec.europa.eu/internal_market/finances/docs/actionplan/index/090707_economic_impact_en.pdf (hereinafter, the 'CRA Report').

[334] PD Art 14(1). The prospectus must also be made available to ESMA by the competent authority (*ibid.*, as amended).

[335] PD Art 3(1) and (3).

[336] Art 14(1).

that special requirements apply for IPOs that concern a class of shares not yet admitted to trading on a regulated market and which is to be admitted for the first time.[337] In such a case, the prospectus must be made available a minimum of six working days before the offer ends,[338] even where an offer is, in fact, open for less than six working days.[339]

The directive and the regulation define publication arrangements (1), but also seek to facilitate access to the published prospectus and to make sure that the integrity of the published information cannot be compromised (2). In certain circumstances, issuers can also benefit from an exemption to publish a prospectus (3).

1 Publication arrangements

The directive sets out a number of alternative means for publishing a prospectus or a base prospectus.[340] A prospectus can, first, be published through a printed medium, i.e., in one or several newspapers which are circulated or broadly distributed in the Member State(s) in which the public offer is made or the admission to trading is taking place.[341] The newspaper(s) in question can be either of a general nature or specialise in financial matters, as long as they have 'national or supra-regional scope'.[342] Second, the obligation to publish a prospectus will also be satisfied if printed copies of the prospectus are made available, at no charge, at the issuer's registered office and at the offices of financial intermediaries and paying agents, or at the offices of the regulated market on which admission is sought.[343] Third, the directive allows prospectuses to be published electronically on the issuer's web page or, where applicable, on the web pages of financial intermediaries and paying agents who are involved in the operation, or on the web page of the relevant regulated market in

337 *Ibid.* 338 *Ibid.*

339 '3rd Transposition Meeting' 10.

340 The rules governing the publication of a prospectus under PD Art 14 also apply to base prospectuses. See 'CESR's advice on Level 2 implementing measures for the Prospectus Directive' 13.

341 PD Art 14(2)(a). Note that PR Rec (32) adds that the newspaper should have both a 'wide area of distribution' and a 'high circulation'.

342 PR Art 30(1). The home state authority is entitled to question the choice of a newspaper, if it considers that it does not meet the requirements of Art 30(1) (see Art 30(2); 'CESR Q&A July 10', Question 3). According to the PR, it may choose itself a newspaper which has an appropriate circulation 'taking into account, in particular, the geographic area, number of inhabitants and reading habits in each Member State' (Art 30(2)).

343 PD Art 14(2)(b).

the case of an admission of securities to trading, or finally, on the home state authority's web page if this service is made available by the latter.[344]

Admittedly, these different methods of publication are not perfect alternatives. Issuers using a printed medium for the publication of their prospectus (i.e., a newspaper publication or printed copies) must also make their prospectus available electronically on the issuer's web page or on the web pages of any financial intermediaries and paying agents.[345] On the other hand, if the prospectus is published electronically, investors are entitled to ask for a printed copy of the prospectus at no charge.[346]

Although the above rules apply generally to all prospectus formats including supplements,[347] there are a few additional rules for tripartite prospectuses, base prospectuses and for prospectuses which incorporate information by reference. If, for instance, a prospectus is made up of several documents or incorporates information by reference, the PD allows for the separate publication and circulation of the documents and information forming the prospectus, as long as the documents are made available at no cost to the public and in a manner which complies with the PD's publication arrangements.[348] Additional rules also apply for base prospectuses or, more precisely, for the final terms of an offer. Recall that the final terms may not be included in the base prospectus and may need, therefore, to be published separately. If so, the publication method for the final terms can be different from the method used for the base prospectus, provided that the final terms are published in accordance with the PD's arrangements governing the publication of a prospectus.[349]

[344] Art 14(2)(c) (as amended), (d) and (e). Note that the home state authority is authorised to delegate the web page publication of prospectuses to other bodies (e.g., stock exchanges) (Art 21(2)).

[345] Art 14(2) final sub-para., as amended. For the avoidance of doubt, there is no obligation to inform host competent authorities of the manner in which the prospectus is published. See 'CESR Q&A July 10', Question 1.

[346] Art 14(7). According to the Commission, the prospectus will need to be 'sent free of charge' to investors in order for this requirement to be satisfied. See '3rd Transposition Meeting' 10.

[347] Supplements must be published 'with at least the same arrangements as were applied when the original prospectus was published' (Art 16(1)).

[348] Art 14(5). The different documents that form the prospectus will need to mention where each part is available (*ibid.*).

[349] PR Art 33. The base prospectus will need to disclose the publication method of the final terms or, at least, mention how investors will be informed about the publishing method (PR Art 22(5)(2)).

2 Ensuring access to the prospectus and the integrity of the information.

Both the directive and the Level 2 PR include rules that seek to ensure easy access to, and an effective distribution of, a published prospectus or a base prospectus.[350] To make sure that investors are aware of the manner in which a prospectus has been published and where they can get it, home Member States are entitled to ask for a notice to be published for this purpose.[351] If a home state authority decides to exercise this power, the notice must be published in a newspaper that has national or supra-regional coverage and be published at the latest the (working) day which follows the date of publication of the prospectus.[352]

In the same spirit of making prospectuses accessible, the directive also provides for the home state authority to publish on its Internet site all those prospectuses that it has approved or, at least, publish a list of them (together with a hyperlink to the prospectus on the issuer's web page or the web page of the regulated market).[353] ESMA too must publish electronically a list of approved prospectuses and, if possible, hyperlink users to the Internet pages of the home competent authority, the issuer or the regulated market where such prospectuses are accessible.[354] What is more, the directive requires ESMA and host competent authorities to maintain a list of certificates of approval which they have been notified of by the home authority, on their Internet sites and hyperlink users to the prospectuses and prospectus supplements that are published on the Internet sites of the home state authority, the issuer or the regulated market.[355] Finally, in an effort to protect the integrity of the disclosure, the directive prescribes that any published prospectus and prospectus supplement

[350] For convenience purposes, I will refer, hereinafter, mainly to prospectuses, instead of base prospectuses.

[351] PD Art 14(3). Details on the content of the notice are found in PR Art 31(3). According to PR Rec (33), where a base prospectus is used, the home Member State should also be entitled to ask for a notice to be published in relation to the final terms. Note that host Member States cannot ask for a notice to be published. See 'CESR Q&A July 10', Question 2.

[352] PR Art 31(1) and (2). Special arrangements apply where the notice concerns prospectuses (or base prospectuses) which are published 'for the only purpose of admission of securities to trading on a regulated market where securities of the same class are already admitted'. PR Art 31(1), sub-para. 2 states that in this case, the notice can also be published in the regulated market's gazette.

[353] PD Art 14(4). Note that the publication requirements expire after a year.

[354] Art 14(4a).

[355] Art 18(3). The list must be kept up-to-date and the reference to each certificate must be maintained for a minimum of twelve months (*ibid.*).

must be strictly identical to the documents that were originally approved by the home state authority.[356]

Admittedly, the publication of prospectuses on the Internet is, in itself, an effective means to ensure access to information. But the wealth of material, which can be made available electronically, also creates problems. The PR seeks to address these issues by a few practical measures. It provides, *inter alia*, for prospectuses to be 'easily accessible' on entry to the web page, to be downloadable and fit for printing.[357] Moreover, in order to guarantee the integrity of the disclosure, a prospectus is supposed to be in a format which does not allow for modifications to its file.[358] Finally, the PR also deals with the flipside of greater access to prospectuses via the worldwide web. Whilst the Internet is an invaluable information resource, its global reach is posing new challenges to regulators wary of making sure that investors are not targeted by offers that do not comply with domestic regulatory requirements. Article 29(2) of the PR must be seen in this light. It states that:

> [i]f a prospectus or base prospectus for offer of securities to the public is made available on the web sites of issuers and financial intermediaries or of regulated markets, these shall take measures, to avoid targeting residents in Members States or third countries where the offer of securities to the public does not take place.

In order to prevent targeting investors outside the Member State where the offer takes place, Article 29(2) suggests that a disclaimer be displayed which identifies those to which the offer is addressed. But Article 29(2) does not specify exhaustively the type of measures that may be taken. Note that the provision only requires issuers, financial intermediaries or regulated markets to take such measures. Competent authorities, which may also decide to publish approved prospectuses on their web pages, are not required to take measures in accordance with Article 29(2). For CESR, treating competent authorities differently was legitimate, given that they are not participating in a public offer.[359] But, arguably, this reasoning is

[356] Art 14(6).

[357] PR Art 29(1)(1) and (4). Moreover, Art 29(1)(3) adds that the prospectus should not include hyperlinks save for links that give access to web pages where information, which was incorporated by reference, is found. Material, which is incorporated by reference, must then be accessible with 'easy and immediate technical arrangements' (Art 29(1) last sub-para).

[358] PR Art 29(1)(2). See also PR Rec (31).

[359] See also 'CESR Q&A July 10', Question 4.

somewhat formalistic. At any rate, the requirements of Article 29(2) do not extend to competent authorities.

The fact that Article 29(2) seeks to prevent investors in Member States or third country jurisdictions from being targeted by an offer which takes place elsewhere, does not mean that these investors are prohibited from acquiring or subscribing to the securities. An investor may, for example, become aware of a public offer, which takes place in another Member State, following his or her own investigations. If so, s/he is free to purchase or subscribe to the securities. Moreover, the fact that this investor might wish to buy the securities will not trigger an obligation to publish a prospectus in the Member State in which s/he resides,[360] if this decision was not preceded by a communication in the latter state which qualifies as a public offer.[361] Recall that under the definition of a public offer, the decision to buy securities viewed in isolation (i.e., absent a communication of sufficient information) is not sufficient to draw conclusions on the existence of a public offer.[362]

3 Exemptions from the obligation to publish a prospectus

a Private placements Article 3(2) of the PD – as recently amended – exempts from the requirement to publish a prospectus (i) an offer which is limited to qualified investors,[363] (ii) an offer to less than 150 persons in each Member State who are not treated as qualified investors,[364] (iii) an offer to investors if they buy securities for a total consideration of a minimum of EUR 100,000, calculated for each investor and for each separate offer,[365] (iv) an offer of securities where the denomination per unit is at least EUR 100,000,[366] and finally (v) an offer of securities where the total consideration in the EU does not amount to EUR 100,000.[367]

Nature and scope of the exemptions For the avoidance of doubt, the exemptions of Article 3(2) apply for offers which would otherwise be treated as public offers. They are exemptions to Article 3(1) which requires

360 'CESR Q&A July 10', Question 43.

361 Admittedly, even if there was a public offer in the Member State of residence of the investor, the PD's requirements regarding the publication of a prospectus are fairly flexible and allow a person to publish a prospectus electronically.

362 See for details section III, A.1, above.

363 Art 3(2)(a). 364 Art 3(2)(b), as amended.

365 Art 3(2)(c), as amended. 366 Art 3(2)(d), as amended.

367 Art 3(2)(e), as amended. The threshold must be calculated 'over a period of 12 months'.

a prospectus to be published when securities are offered to the public. They do not exempt issues of securities which are meant to be admitted to trading on a regulated market. As a consequence, a prospectus will need to be drawn up, published and approved if the securities are also admitted to trading on a regulated market.[368]

Article 3(2) was intended to make a break with the past. Under the POD and LPD, loosely worded exemptions and definitions contributed to creating a patchy regulatory framework which affected the functioning of mutual recognition.[369] Under the PD, exemptions were fleshed out[370] and important terms (e.g., the meaning of qualified investor) defined. The adoption of Article 3(2) thus represented a step forward in terms of levelling the playing field. But as a new, untested, provision, it has inevitably also raised fresh issues. Questions have, for instance, been asked about whether the exemptions could be combined.[371] Moreover, the scope of Article 3(2) has also been a source of debate. Exempt offers are not altogether outside the scope of the directive.[372] Article 3(2) merely states that the requirement to 'publish a prospectus' does not apply to exempt offers. But are exempt offers, thereby, also exempted from other requirements such as the obligation to prepare and file a prospectus or the obligation to seek prior approval? Although the term 'publish' is not a defined term under the directive, it is generally understood as meaning that a prospectus must be 'made available to the public' in accordance with the rules governing the publication of a prospectus.[373] In the context of Article 3(2), such a reading appears, however, excessively literal and restrictive. The reason for Article 3(2) is that for certain types of offers, full prospectus disclosure and the ensuing expenditure of preparing a prospectus is more difficult to justify; either because of the type of investor who is likely to acquire securities or

368 In this sense, see '3rd Transposition Meeting' 5.

369 See also K. Hopt and H-C. Voigt, 'Grundsatz- und Reformprobleme der Prospekt- und Kapitalmarktsinformationshaftung' in K. Hopt and H-C. Voigt (eds.), *Prospekt- und Kapitalmarktinformationshaftung – Recht und Reform in der Europäischen Union, der Schweiz und den USA* (Mohr Siebeck, Tübingen, 2005) 9, 16; Moloney, *EC Securities Regulation* 139.

370 E.g., Art 3(2)(b), as amended, which limits an offer to 'fewer than 150 natural or legal persons'. The POD simply excluded offers of securities which were made to 'a restricted circle of persons' (POD Art 2(1)(b)).

371 ESME, 'Report on Directive 2003/71/EC … – Annex to the Report' (Brussels, 5 September 2007) 11, http://ec.europa.eu/internal_market/securities/docs/esme/05092007_annex_en.pdf (hereinafter, 'ESME Report Annex').

372 See Common Position (EC) No 25/2003 [2003] OJ C125E/21, 50 (confirming that the EU legislature did not intend to exclude these offers from the scope of the Directive).

373 Art 14(1) and (2).

because of the size of the offer. Disclosure should be tailored to the needs of investors, a point which the directive takes to its logical conclusion when stating that prospectus disclosure is simply not necessary for certain types of investors, such as qualified investors.[374] If offers were under Article 3(2) merely exempted from the requirement to make a prospectus available to the public, but would otherwise continue being subject to, say, the obligation to draw up and file a prospectus, the objectives pursued by Article 3(2) would be frustrated and its application rendered nugatory. The exemption from the obligation to 'publish a prospectus' should, therefore, be interpreted in a broader sense, i.e., as exempting issuers from preparing a prospectus. Investors will, consequently, not only be exempted from the obligation to draw up a prospectus, but also from the requirement to seek prior approval with the competent authority.[375]

Qualified investors As part of the effort to avoid gaps in the public offer regime, the PD harmonised the definition of 'qualified investor'.[376] As a reminder, offers addressed to qualified investors can benefit from an exemption to publish a prospectus under Article 3(2). The rules defining the meaning of qualified investor were substantially reworked during the initial negotiations of the directive and, in 2010, extensively revamped, in order to bring them into line with the requirements of MiFID.[377] The status of a qualified investor is reserved to seasoned investors whose level of expertise, experience and knowledge is such that they do not require the same level of protection as ordinary investors. Initially, the PD set out its own criteria for identifying seasoned investors. It effectively established a two-tier regime. Under this two-tier system, certain types of investors were automatically given qualified investor status because of the nature of their activities or their status. Others were not, as a general matter, given qualified investor status, but could 'opt-in' under certain conditions. The new rules introduced in 2010 are based on a similar distinction, but simply cross-refer to the rules which are found in MiFID.[378] The directive

[374] PD Rec (16).

[375] See also in this sense, Van Gerven, 'General provisions of Community law relating to the prospectus to be published when securities are offered to the public or admitted to trading' 18. See also European Commission 'Call for evidence regarding private placement regimes in the EU' (Brussels, April 2007) 9–10, http://ec.europa.eu/internal_market/investment/docs/consultations/private_placement_en.pdf (hereinafter, 'Call for Evidence Regarding Private Placements').

[376] PD Art 2(1)(e), as amended.

[377] *Ibid.* [378] *Ibid.*

mainly draws on the classification of professional clients in Annex II of MiFID.[379] MiFID differentiates between categories of persons who are treated either, by default, as professionals, but who can expressly ask not to be treated as such; and persons who may ask to be treated as professionals but who are, by default, not treated as such. Included within the first category are, *inter alia*, firms that must be 'authorised or regulated to operate in the financial markets' (e.g., credit institutions, investment banks, collective investment schemes, pension funds, etc.); and firms of a substantial size which satisfy two of the following criteria: their balance sheet totals EUR 20,000,000; they have a net turnover of EUR 40,000,000; their own funds amount to EUR 2,000,000. Governmental actors, public bodies which deal with public debt, central banks and various international and supra-national actors are also given 'professional client' status. Finally, other institutional investors that mainly invest in financial instruments are also treated as professional clients.

Persons – natural or legal – that fall in the second category can only be treated as professionals if they ask to be treated as such and provided that they are considered, after evaluation, to be capable of making their own decisions to invest which also means that they are capable of appreciating the risks that are involved. It also pre-supposes that they meet at least two out of the three following criteria: (i) they must have performed transactions 'in significant size' on markets 'at an average frequency of 10 [transactions] per quarter over the previous four quarters'[380], (ii) their portfolio of financial instruments must amount to more than EUR 500,000 and (iii) they must have at least one year of work experience in the financial sector in a professional occupation that demands knowledge of transactions or services.

Besides drawing on MiFID's categories of professional clients, the PD also accords qualified investor status to persons treated as 'eligible counterparties' pursuant to MiFID's rules,[381] provided, however, that they have not asked to be treated as non-professionals.[382] Finally, the PD also takes account of MiFID's transitional arrangements[383] and, therefore, allows investment firms to continue, for the purposes of the PD's qualified investor regime to treat as qualified investors, persons recognised as having 'professional client' status before the entry into force of MiFID.

379 Directive 2004/39/EC [2004] OJ L145/1.
380 MiFID Annex II. 381 MiFID Art 24. 382 PD Art 2(1)(e).
383 MiFID Art 71(6).

The 2010 amendments of the PD also removed the requirement to establish a separate qualified investor register. Under the previous rules, each competent authority was required to set up such a register and enter natural persons or SMEs that were treated as qualified investors into the register.[384] Under the new regime, issuers are expected to take advantage of the lists of professional clients and eligible counterparties prepared by investment firms and credit institutions. Upon request, these actors are expected to communicate the relevant information to issuers.[385]

Retail cascade The use of exemptions for offers that involve retail investors has long been a sensitive issue between Member States. Only recently, various thresholds were raised,[386] seemingly in an effort to better fence off offers that are, effectively, intended for professional investors, from the common regime applying to retail investors.[387] But retail investors have also long participated in the Eurobond or international debt market. Before the PD was adopted, it was not uncommon for offers to be made to retail investors outside a public offer framework. In Member States such as Luxembourg, for example, credit institutions were, under certain conditions, able to offer securities to retail customers without such offers being treated as a public offer.[388] Deeming such practices undesirable, the PD set out to deal with them by introducing for the first time a legally binding and harmonised definition of a public offer[389] and by addressing directly the case of a resale of securities to investors which follows an exempt offer (i.e., an offer benefiting from one of the exemptions found in Article 3(2)). Article 3(2) thus provides that if, following an exempt offer, securities are resold, a resale will be treated as a discrete offer and may, therefore, be caught under the definition of public offer. If so, the directive's requirements regarding public offers will also become applicable. Moreover, the directive states that where securities are placed through financial intermediaries, a prospectus must also be published if the final placement of the securities does not qualify as an exempt offer under Article 3(2). The provision was meant to be an '"anti-avoidance"

384 Art 2(3) (deleted). 385 Art 2(1)(e); PAD Rec (7).

386 See Art 3(2)(b) (raising the threshold from 100 to 150 persons); Art 3(2)(c) and (d) (raising the thresholds from EUR 50,000 to 100,000).

387 PAD Rec (9) (in relation to the former EUR 50,000 threshold).

388 E.g., H. Wagner and M. Limpach, 'Debt restructurings in connection with Luxembourg listed securities' (2003) 18 *Journal of International Banking Law and Regulation* 453, 456. Investors were, nevertheless, not altogether unprotected, given that conduct-of-business rules continued applying (*ibid.*).

389 See section III, A.1, above.

provision'.[390] It was intended to make sure that public offer requirements could no longer be circumvented by making an exempt offer, say, to qualified investors, who would subsequently resell the securities to retail investors outside the public offer framework.

Together with the definition of a public offer and the stricter conditions applying to private placement exemptions, Article 3(2) introduced major changes. But the changes somewhat overshot the mark in terms of protecting retail investors and created unexpected new problems for resales of debt securities to retail investors.[391] The practice of reselling securities to retail investors is generally known as a retail cascade. A retail cascade usually involves an underwriter selling securities to financial intermediaries which then resell them to retail customers.[392] Resales are treated as a public offer and the offer will be subject to the publication of a prospectus, notwithstanding the fact that the offer, which preceded the resale to retail investors, was an exempt offer.

Although the directive's aim of ensuring that public offer requirements cannot be circumvented was laudable, the PD did not satisfactorily address several key questions and problems. More specifically, the questions concerned the precise moment when a prospectus would have to be produced and at what level of the retail cascade (e.g., at the level of the offer to retail investors or at the level of the distribution to financial intermediaries or even when the securities were initially sold by the issuer?).[393] Additional problems concerned the precise information content of the prospectus,[394] given that certain information about the various suboffers made under the retail cascade were not necessarily available at the outset.

CESR attempted first to find a solution to these questions and problems at Level 3. It suggested that one should effectively differentiate between cases where financial intermediaries were acting 'in association' with an issuer and where they were not.[395] CESR recommended that, in the former case, intermediaries should be allowed to rely on the issuer's prospectus and not be asked to prepare a separate prospectus.[396] Any prospectus supplements would need to be prepared by the issuer, as long as

[390] 'Commission Background Document' 6.

[391] *Ibid.*, 6–7; 'ESME Report' 13–5; 'CESR's Report on the PD' 20–1; 'CSES Report' 62–4. In the literature, see also L. Burn and B. Wells, 'The pan-European retail market – are we there yet?' (2007) 2 *Capital Markets Law Journal* 263; H. Schneider and H. Haag, 'Retail cascading in Germany – a model for a revision of the PD' (2007) 2 *Capital Markets Law Journal* 370.

[392] 'ICMA Comment Letter' 3.

[393] E.g., 'CESR's Report on the PD' 20.

[394] *Ibid.*, 21.

[395] 'CESR Q&A July 10', Question 56.

[396] *Ibid.*

any offers made by intermediaries under the cascade subsisted.[397] On the other hand, if an intermediary acted on its own, rather than in association with an issuer, CESR recommended that a prospectus, including any prospectus supplements, would need to be prepared by the offeror.[398] In order to address problems caused by an initial lack of information on suboffers, CESR suggested relying on Article 23(4) of the PR.[399] Recall that it allows information to be omitted which is not deemed to be 'pertinent'. But CESR added that the missing information would, nevertheless, need to be produced subsequently (i.e., when the suboffers were made).[400]

CESR's distinction between financial intermediaries who act in association with issuers and those that do not do so, was meant to provide a workable solution and a quick fix to an unforeseen problem. But with no legal grounding, it was a temporary solution awaiting legislative action. Article 3(2) was duly amended in 2010. A new sub-paragraph was added to Article 3(2) which now states that no other prospectus is required for a 'resale of securities or final placement of securities through financial intermediaries', provided that there is a valid prospectus and that the issuer or the person who was responsible for preparing it, agrees 'by means of a written agreement' to the prospectus being used. Given that the preparation of prospectus supplements is a condition to the validity of a prospectus, supplements will also need, if necessary, to be filed and published.[401] In the absence of an agreement, the financial intermediaries involved in the retail cascade will have to publish a new prospectus.[402]

b Article 4 Additional exemptions from the obligation to publish a prospectus are provided for under Article 4 of the directive. Article 4 mostly covers very specific operations such as, for example, securities that are offered at the occasion of a merger or takeover, or which are offered to employees by their employer, or free of charge to current shareholders.[403] Like offers which benefit from an Article 3(2) exemption, offers under Article 4 are not altogether outside the scope of the directive. They are exempted from the obligation to publish (that is, to prepare) a prospectus.[404] But unlike Article 3(2), Article 4 not only applies to transactions that would otherwise have to comply with the PD's requirements regarding public offers; it also covers operations in which securities are to be

[397] *Ibid.* [398] *Ibid.* [399] *Ibid.*
[400] *Ibid.* [401] See also PAD Rec (10). [402] See *ibid.*
[403] Note that ESMA is empowered to prepare draft technical standards with respect to the exemptions of Art 4 (see Art 4(3), as amended).
[404] '4th Transposition Meeting' 3.

admitted to trading on a regulated market. Another distinctive feature of Article 4 is that many of its exemptions are available only under the proviso that in place of the prospectus, an alternative information document is made available. This information document will not be subject to the PD's disclosure requirements[405] or, for that matter, its rules governing the approval, filing and publication of a prospectus. But, given that it is not a prospectus, it will not be able to benefit from the single passport either.

Article 4(1). Article 4(1) covers five different types of operations:

- offers of shares which are issued 'in substitution for shares of the same class already issued' without an ensuing increase in the issued capital;[406]
- securities of all kinds[407] offered at the occasion of a takeover if those securities are offered by way of an exchange offer;[408]
- securities that are offered or allocated at the occasion of a merger or a division;[409]
- dividends which are paid out to present shareholders as shares, if these shares are of the same class as the ones for which the dividends are paid;[410]
- securities which are offered or allocated to present or previous directors or employees by their employer (or an affiliated undertaking), if the company has its head office or its registered office in the EU.[411]

Save for the first exemption (i.e., offers of securities which are issued in substitution for shares of the same class), Article 4(1) requires an information document to be prepared in replacement of the prospectus.[412] But, as noted, the EU legislature stopped short of demanding that this document be published in accordance with the PD's requirements.[413] Moreover, the legislature did not specify the information content of this alternative document. For securities offered in the context of a takeover, merger or

[405] See also 'Call for Evidence Regarding Private Placements' 10 (noting that the document will be a lighter version of a prospectus).

[406] Art 4(1)(a).

[407] In this sense, '3rd Transposition Meeting' 6.

[408] Art 4(1)(b). [409] Art 4(1)(c), as amended.

[410] Art 4(1)(d), as amended.

[411] Art 4(1)(e), as amended. Note that Art 4(1)(e) also applies with respect to firms that are established outside the EU. The relevant rules are, however, more complex. They will be discussed in detail in Chapter 4, section IV, B. The term 'affiliated undertaking' should be given a wide meaning according to the Commission (see '3rd Transposition Meeting' 6).

[412] Art 4(1)(b), (c), (d) and (e).

[413] See also Common Position (EC) No 25/2003 [2003] OJ C125E/21, 51.

division, the PD merely states that the competent authority will have to satisfy itself that the information content of the document is equivalent to that of a prospectus.[414] For securities that are offered to employees or directors by a company having its head office or registered office in the EU, as well as for payments of dividends in the form of shares, the PD adopts a 'very "light touch"'[415] approach and only requires information to be provided with respect to the number and nature of the securities to be offered, including details on the offer and the reasons for making it.[416] To be sure, for offers of securities to directors or employees, the directive's rules governing exemptions have grown more complicated since they have been amended in 2010; but only as far as third-country firms are concerned. As amended, the directive thus sets out separate arrangements for third-country companies that wish to offer securities to employees or directors in the EU and that, for this purpose, seek to rely on Article 4. The relevant rules will be discussed in Chapter 4. Suffice it to note that in relation to third-country firms, the rules, as amended, enact an equivalence clause whose purpose is ultimately to make it possible for such firms to offer employee share schemes in Europe under better conditions than was previously the case. For EU companies, the EU legislature also sought to facilitate employee share schemes. It did so by no longer requiring employers to already have securities admitted to trading on a regulated market. While this requirement was originally meant to ensure transparency (an admission to trading ensures that issuers are subject to ongoing disclosure requirements), the EU legislature ultimately considered it to be too restrictive.[417] However, the legislature also added, albeit only in a non-binding recital, that EU firms taking advantage of the revised arrangements of Article 4(1)(e) should update the alternative information document in a way that ensures that the securities can be properly evaluated.[418] But given that the legislature did not make provision for it in the legally binding text of the directive, it is somewhat uncertain whether this requirement will have any teeth.

414 Art 4(1)(b) and (c). The Commission has the power to adopt Level 2 measures in order to specify the meaning of 'equivalence'. But it has not taken action so far. It has only made the fairly obvious point that the information content of this alternative document does not need to be identical to that of a prospectus. See '3rd Transposition Meeting' 5.

415 '3rd Transposition Meeting' 6.

416 Art 4(1)(d) and (e).

417 See also PAD Rec (14). See also Chapter 4, section IV, for further details.

418 PAD Rec (14).

Article 4(2) While Article 4(1) deals with offers that, absent an exemption, are caught under the directive's rules governing pubic offers, Article 4(2) deals with securities that are meant to be admitted to trading on a regulated market. Like Article 4(1), it exempts certain securities operations from the requirement to publish a prospectus. Indeed, many of the operations that are exempted under Article 4(2) correspond to the ones found in Article 4(1). More precisely, Article 4(2) applies to:

- securities which are offered at the occasion of a takeover if those securities are offered by way of an exchange offer;[419]
- securities that are offered or allocated at the occasion of a merger or division;[420]
- shares that are issued in substitution for shares of the same class and which have already been admitted to trading on the same regulated market, without there being an ensuing increase in issued capital;[421]
- shares that are offered or allocated at no charge to present shareholders, including dividends paid out as shares which are of the same class as the ones for which dividends are paid;[422]
- securities which are offered or allocated to present or previous directors or employees by their employer or by an affiliated undertaking, if the securities in question are of the same class as those that have already been admitted to trading on the same regulated market.[423]

In addition to the above exemptions, Article 4(2) also exempts the following operations from the obligation to publish a prospectus:

- shares that over a time period of twelve months, do not amount to 10 per cent of the number of shares of the same class which have already been admitted to trading on the same regulated market;[424]
- shares which are the consequence of other securities being converted or exchanged, or which result from the rights granted by other securities being exercised, as long as the shares in question are of the same class as the shares that have already been admitted to trading on the same regulated market;[425] and
- securities which have already been admitted to trading on a different regulated market,[426] subject to various conditions intended to ensure that investors benefit from a sufficient level of information.[427]

[419] Art 4(2)(c). [420] Art 4(2)(d), as amended.
[421] Art 4(2)(b). [422] Art 4(2)(e). [423] Art 4(2)(f).
[424] Art 4(2)(a). [425] Art 4(2)(g). [426] Art 4(2)(h).
[427] Common Position (EC) No 25/2003 [2003] OJ C125E/21, 51. Pursuant to Art 4(2)(h) the conditions are that '(i) that these securities, or securities of the same class, have been

Some of the exemptions under paragraph (2) require an information document to be made available in lieu of the prospectus. This is, for instance, the case for securities issued at the occasion of a takeover, a merger or a division. The directive provides no detail on the information content of this document. Article 4(2) only requires that competent authorities deem the information to be equivalent.[428] For shares offered free of charge to shareholders, or securities offered to employees or directors, the disclosure document will need to provide information on the number and nature of the shares or securities.[429] Details on the offer will need to be provided and the reasons for making the offer will need to be explained.[430]

B Advertisement

1 Basic provisions

Non-exhaustive principles and requirements Besides the rules governing publication arrangements, the PD also laid down rules governing advertisements made in connection with a public offer or an admission to trading on a regulated market. Before the directive was adopted, Member States approached advertising in significantly different ways.[431] Differences concerned, for example, the type of communications that was

admitted to trading on that other regulated market for more than 18 months; (ii) that, for securities first admitted to trading on a regulated market after the date of entry into force of this Directive, the admission to trading on that other regulated market was associated with an approved prospectus made available to the public in conformity with Article 14; (iii) that, except where (ii) applies, for securities first admitted to listing after 30 June 1983, listing particulars were approved in accordance with the requirements of Directive 80/390/EEC or Directive 2001/34/EC; (iv) that the ongoing obligations for trading on that other regulated market have been fulfilled; (v) that the person seeking the admission of a security to trading on a regulated market under this exemption makes a summary document available to the public in a language accepted by the competent authority of the Member State of the regulated market where admission is sought; (vi) that the summary document referred to in (v) is made available to the public in the Member State of the regulated market where admission to trading is sought in the manner set out in Article 14(2); and (vii) that the contents of the summary document shall comply with Article 5(2). Furthermore the document shall state where the most recent prospectus can be obtained and where the financial information published by the issuer pursuant to his ongoing disclosure obligations is available'.

[428] Art 4(2)(c) and (d), as amended.

[429] Art 4(2)(e) and (f). [430] *Ibid.*

[431] See generally CESR, 'Summary of the answers to the questionnaire on factual information regarding advertisement practices and relevant legislation in the Member States' (CESR/03-494, December 2003).

treated as a form of advertising or the tasks which authorities were supposed to perform with respect to advertising.[432] The PD sought to address advertising in an effort to deal with legislative loopholes.[433] But, paradoxically, it did not do so exhaustively.[434] Rather the directive, together with the PR, set broad principles and basic rules which are intended to establish minimum guarantees with respect to advertising activities.

The directive does not define the meaning of advertising, but a definition of 'advertisement' is found in the Level 2 PR.[435] The definition is helpful in that it narrows down the type of communications that competent authorities will treat as a form of advertising. It defines advertisement, by reference to the material scope of the directive, as an 'announcement' that relates to a 'specific offer to the public of securities or to an admission to trading on a regulated market'.[436] This announcement must, in addition, have a specific purpose in the sense that it must be intended to 'specifically promote the potential subscription or acquisition of securities'.[437] A communication of a general nature, which is made outside the context of a public offer or an admission to trading, should therefore not be treated as a form of advertising.[438] The type of medium that is used for communicating advertising messages or for circulating advertising material matters little. The PR envisages the distribution of advertisements by various means, including by way of radio or television announcements, electronic mail, telephone, posters, in printed form, and so on.[439] The list is non-exhaustive.

The PD's contribution to regulating advertising is limited to a number of broad and basic principles, mainly included for the sake of investor protection. Advertisements must disclose that a prospectus has been published and where it is available.[440] Advertising material must be identifiable as such.[441] Information that is included in advertisements must not be wrong or misleading.[442] Nor must it be inconsistent with prospectus disclosure.[443] Indeed, the directive insists especially on consistent

[432] *Ibid.*; CESR, 'CESR's advice on Level 2 implementing measures for the Prospectus Directive' (CESR/03-399, December 2003) 15–6.

[433] Rec (33).

[434] Other directives, such as MiFID, are, however, also relevant to consider in this context. See Moloney, *EC Securities Regulation* 163.

[435] PR Art 2(9). [436] Art 2(9)(a). [437] Art 2(9)(b).

[438] CESR explicitly excluded this type of communication from its Level 2 advice. See, 'CESR's advice on Level 2 implementing measures for the Prospectus Directive' 16.

[439] Art 34.

[440] PD Art 15(2). If the prospectus has not yet been published, the directive must state where the prospectus will be published and where it will be available.

[441] Art 15(3). [442] *Ibid.* [443] *Ibid.*

information. Consistency must be ensured even if information, which concerns a public offer or an admission to trading, was not disclosed with the intention to advertise.[444] Finally, the directive also seeks to ensure equal treatment among investors. Any material information that is disclosed selectively among only a part of the investor population must be communicated to all other investors as well.[445] In order to ensure that this obligation is met, the directive requires the information to be disclosed either in the prospectus or in a supplement to the prospectus.[446]

2 Exempt offers: selective disclosure

While most of the rules that have to do with advertising concern issues of securities for which a prospectus must be prepared, advertising of exempt offers – that is, offers which are exempted from the requirement to publish a prospectus – are not ignored altogether. The main concern with respect to these offers is to make sure that material information is not distributed selectively among the persons to whom such an offer is addressed. The requirement to ensure equal treatment among investors, which was discussed above in relation to offers that are subject to an obligation to publish a prospectus, is therefore also applicable to exempt offers. Specifically, when an exempt offer is made to qualified investors or to other particular categories of investors, issuers or offerors who have disclosed material information selectively among a part of this population of investors – say, during a road show – must ensure that the same information will be disclosed to all of them.[447] For the avoidance of doubt, the type of exempt offers that this provision targets are those that are found in Articles 3(2) and 4(1).[448] As a reminder, these offers are exempted from the obligation to prepare a prospectus, but are not excluded from the scope of the directive. Note that the PD does not prescribe the means through which material information must be communicated to the whole population of investors.

While supposed to ensure equality among investors, the rules do not go as far as requiring material information, which was disclosed selectively at the occasion of an exempt offer, to be released to the public at large. Such a requirement was initially included in the Commission proposal, but was later abandoned on the grounds that it would create an undesirable burden for issuers or offerors.[449] Of course, however, if a prospectus

[444] Art 15(4). [445] Art 15(5). [446] *Ibid.*

[447] Art 15(5). [448] In this sense, '3rd Transposition Meeting' 10.

[449] Common position (EC) No 25/2003 [2003] C125E/21, 54.

needs to be published (because an offer is not exempted), material information will need to be communicated to the public, either in the prospectus or in a prospectus supplement.[450]

VI The passport system

Sections III, IV and V discussed the core obligations of the PD and PR. As a reminder, they are (i) to prepare a prospectus according to the rules of the PD and PR; (ii) to submit the prospectus for approval to the home state authority of an issuer; and (iii) to publish (and file) the prospectus and comply with the PD's and PR's rules governing advertising. The prize, if you will, for all these efforts is the single passport for prospectuses. The passport was intended to be the *pièce de résistance* of the PD. It replaced the POD's and LPD's earlier mutual recognition arrangements which were said to have failed cross-border capital raising activities. The basis of the passport system is a single provision, Article 17 of the directive, which provides that a prospectus and any supplements that have been approved by the home state authority, are valid in any Member State in the context of a public offer or an admission to trading on a regulated market, as long as ESMA and the host state authority have been notified of the use of the passport.[451]

The passport system is based on the home state principle. In other words, it is the home state authority which must deliver the certificate of approval, which is necessary for a prospectus to be successfully 'passported' to host Member States,[452] regardless of whether an offer to the public is made, or an admission to trading is sought, at home. The certificate will state that the prospectus complies with the requirements of the directive.[453] The procedure for notifying a host state authority is meant to be simple, swift and uncomplicated. The certificate will be notified by the home state authority within three working days following a request made by the issuer or the persons in charge of preparing the prospectus.[454] The host state authority is also entitled to a copy of the prospectus and, where applicable, a translation of the prospectus summary.[455] If the passport request was put to the home state authority at the time when the draft prospectus was submitted for approval, the home state authority is

450 Art 15(5). 451 PD Art 17(1), as amended.

452 Art 18(1). 453 *Ibid.* 454 *Ibid.*

455 *Ibid.* If information was omitted from the prospectus under Art 8(2) and (3), this fact must be disclosed and justified in the certificate (see Art 18(2)).

required to notify the certificate of approval (together with a copy of the prospectus and any translation of the summary) within one working day following the approval of the prospectus.[456] ESMA must be notified too.[457] Once notified the prospectus will be valid for any public offer or admission to trading of securities on a regulated market in the host Member State(s).[458] The passport will materialise in an administrative decision by the relevant competent authority which will create individual rights for the applicant, i.e., the right to passport the prospectus.

Whilst a competent authority would be in breach of its obligations if it failed to meet the time delays mentioned above, the directive does not grant issuers any automatic right to use their passport abroad at the end of the time period. In order to avoid exposing issuers, unaware of the absence of a decision, to unnecessary risk, the notification procedure was recently amended. The home state authority must now inform the issuer, or the person in charge of preparing the prospectus, about the approval certificate 'at the same time as the competent authority of the host Member State'.[459] CESR too has, in the past, sought to improve the notification procedure by developing a standardised certificate of approval.[460] It also put in place a procedure for the notification of certificates under which the notification and the subsequent receipt confirmation were made in electronic form according to a standardised email format.[461] ESMA is likely to continue working on improving this procedure. It has the power to prepare draft implementing standards in order to develop 'standard forms, templates and procedures' which apply to the notification of certificates, but also prospectuses, supplements and the translation of summaries.[462]

In practice, the passport system seems to have worked fairly well,[463] mainly in the debt markets.[464] It has not worked perfectly. CESR used to monitor the functioning of the passport. It produced at different intervals statistics on the use of the passport[465] and surveyed both competent

[456] Art 18(1). [457] Art 18(3).

[458] Note that the directive requires ESMA and host competent authorities to maintain a list of certificates of approval on their Internet sites. If possible, they must hyperlink users to the prospectuses and prospectus supplements that are published on the Internet sites of the home state authority, the issuer or the regulated market (*ibid.*).

[459] Art 18(1), as amended. [460] 'CESR's Report on the PD' 41.

[461] *Ibid.* [462] Art 18(4).

[463] E.g., 'ESME Report' 4 noting that 'unlike the previous "mutual recognition system", the new passporting mechanism has delivered a real benefit to issuers'; 'CRA Report' 16.

[464] 'CSES Report' 17.

[465] CESR, 'CESR data on prospectuses approved and passported – July 2009 to December 2009' (CESR/10-282, March 2010).

authorities and market actors on the working of the directive, including the passport system. Thus, market actors have commented on various obstacles which have affected them.[466] Whilst some of the reported obstacles simply breached the directive, some limitations were, admittedly, caused by the terms of the directive.[467] Nevertheless, notwithstanding any remaining obstacles, the bottom line – and my final observation – is that the passport system has contributed to making cross-border capital raising more accessible to issuers. It was without doubt a significant improvement on the POD's and LPD's mutual recognition arrangements.

VII Conclusion: evolutionary or revolutionary change?

The purpose of this chapter was to examine and discuss the harmonised obligations and requirements of the PD and PR. It focused on three core obligations of the disclosure regime: (i) the obligation to prepare a prospectus, (ii) the obligation to seek approval with the competent authority of the issuer's home Member State,[468] and (iii) the obligation to publish the prospectus and ensure that advertisement complies with the provisions of the regime. In return, the PD offers issuers a means to access EU markets more easily by using, for the purposes of their capital raising activities, a prospectus approved by their home competent authority in any number of host Member States, without having to make alterations to the content of the prospectus. The PR's information requirements, i.e., the Level 2 disclosure items, are at the heart of this regime. They apply, by default, to securities transactions that come within the scope of the directive and, together, form the basis of the first of two prospectus disclosure models in EU law. They also epitomise, in the most apparent and forceful manner, the maximum harmonisation approach for which the PD has become known.

466 'CESR's Report on the PD' 39–40.

467 For example, market participants have pointed out that registration documents cannot be 'passported' into host Member States. But for CESR, there was no scope under the directive to extend the passport to a registration document (*ibid.*, 25), notwithstanding the fact that the registration document, *together* with the securities note and summary note, form a valid prospectus (PD Art 9(4)).

468 I mainly focused on the rules governing the determination of the home Member State. The rules governing prior approval will be examined in Chapter 6 when discussing enforcement of prospectus disclosure.

Before drawing this chapter to a close, a few final words are warranted on the broader direction of the changes and reforms that have taken place in the prospectus disclosure field. Despite the fact that the directive gave birth to a new regime which, in terms of its sophistication and comprehensiveness, was unprecedented, it is apparent that by introducing maximum harmonisation or, for that matter, a single passport for prospectuses, the PD did not result in any revolutionary re-orientation of the existing disclosure regime. Whilst the EU legislature has been the main force shaping the requirements and obligations of this disclosure model, its choices represented, in many respects, the natural and logical continuation of the EU's ambitions in the securities field. The PD thus built on the legacies of the LPD (as integrated into CARD) and POD whose minimum harmonisation and mutual recognition arrangements had, in a sense, prepared the ground for a more exhaustive disclosure regime and a more aggressive single passport system. Where earlier directives had failed – think, for example, of the absence of a definition of a public offer in the POD – the PD made first progress. Where inroads in national law had already been made – think of the common disclosure requirements found in CARD – the directive set out to close gaps and level the playing field comprehensively and exhaustively. To be sure, when first proposed, the Commission proposal included one jurisdictional rule, the home state principle which, if adopted *as initially presented by the European Commission*, would have led to a revolutionary change by concentrating jurisdictional competence in the hands of the Member State of the place of the issuer's registered office, instead of the Member State of the place where a public offer was made or where the stock exchange, on which admission to listing was being sought, was situated.[469] As finally agreed, however, the Commission's original rules governing the determination of the home Member State are significantly changed, so much so that it would be mistaken to characterise them as revolutionary, as opposed to evolutionary. In fact, the rules follow closely the *de facto* distribution of competence between Member States: first, by concentrating competence with respect to issues of equity securities in the hands of the Member State in which a company is most likely to raise capital when issuing shares (i.e., the Member State in which a company's registered office is situated); second, by allowing competence for issues of non-equity securities to be shared. These rules allowed the jurisdictional competence of Member States, which are active in the

[469] See section IV, above. See also Chapter 10 for further details.

international debt market, to be safeguarded. There will be more to say about these rules and Chapter 10 will, in due course, return to the reasons underpinning the distribution of competence between Member States when turning to the negotiations of the directive. For now, however, it is time to close the chapter and to turn to the second disclosure model under the directive which is based on equivalence provisions. This is the subject matter of Chapter 6.

4

Equivalence-based regulation

I Introduction

One of the distinctive features of the Prospectus Directive ('PD') is that its provisions apply to companies incorporated in a Member State ('EU issuers')[1] *and* outside the EU ('third country issuers') that wish to raise capital in the EU by making a public offer or seeking admission of securities to trading on a regulated market in a Member State.[2] Where applicable, the PD provides for a prospectus to be prepared, approved and published according to its provisions and its implementing legislation (the 'Prospectus Regulation' or 'PR').[3] Recall that the latter lays down the 'maximum harmonisation' disclosure requirements that apply to EU issuers and, generally, third country issuers. But there is a special set of arrangements for third country issuers. First, when preparing financial information, third country issuers may be able to rely on third country accounting standards that are deemed to be equivalent to the relevant European standards. In other cases, they may not have to comply with the common EU disclosure items at all. They may instead be allowed to rely on third country prospectus documentation for a public offer or an admission to trading on a regulated market in the EU (a 'third country prospectus' as opposed to an 'EU prospectus' when prepared in accordance with EU disclosure standards), provided that the third country requirements are, *inter alia*, considered to be equivalent to European requirements. Finally, for particular types of operations, commonly known as employee share

[1] For the sake of accuracy, note that the PD's provisions are also applicable in EEA states. For convenience purposes, I will continue referring to the EU, rather than the EEA, hereinafter.

[2] Note that the PD is a 'product driven' Directive (see 'ESME Differences Report' 10). Rec (36) PD states *in fine* that '[i]n order to ensure that the purposes of this Directive will be fully achieved, it is also necessary to include within its scope securities issued by issuers governed by the laws of third countries'.

[3] Commission Regulation (EC) No 809/2004 [2004] OJ L149/3.

schemes, third country issuers may be exempted altogether from having to produce a fully-fledged prospectus upon a finding of equivalence, as long as they prepare a simple information document.[4] For lack of better words, I will refer, hereinafter, to these different types of arrangements as 'equivalence-based regulation' and talk where relevant of 'equivalence provisions'.[5]

Equivalence-based regulation is thus the second regulatory arrangement (or model) in the EU prospectus disclosure field. Equivalence provisions are increasingly common in EU law. Their emergence reflects a growing awareness among policy makers that financial markets no longer operate in isolation. There is a need to deal with the regulatory implications of this fact, especially as the EU's legislative ambitions continue to grow, and equivalence-based regulation provides a way forward.[6] But this type of regulation is also special for another reason. It can have a noteworthy 'external' dimension. It is, indeed, not uncommon for equivalence decisions to be preceded by negotiations with third countries. When approaching equivalence-based regulation, it is therefore important to bear in mind that it not only promises to facilitate access to EU markets by reducing overregulation and lowering the cost of access for third country actors, but that it is potentially also an effective tool for the EU to negotiate, in return for recognising third country rules or standards, better access terms to third country markets. As one author puts it, '[e]quivalence assessments are not a unilateral process, they are a negotiation exercise'.[7]

[4] For the sake of accuracy, note that EU issuers can also be exempted from having to produce a prospectus in the case of employee share schemes (see PD Art 4(1)(e)). In this case, however, the equivalence clause does not apply. For details, see Chapter 3, section V, A.3.b.

[5] On equivalence-based regulation, see also T-b. Wei, 'The equivalence approach to securities regulation' (2007) *Northwestern Journal of International Law & Business* 255. In the EU context, see O. Girard, 'Les méthodes de suppression des frontières au plan mondial dans le domaine bancaire et financier' (2007–2008) 3 *Revue Européenne de droit bancaire & financier* 349.

[6] In EU law, equivalence provisions have taken many different forms. Girard identifies three types of 'equivalence clauses' which he coins "'national' equivalence clauses", "'decentralised' equivalence clauses" and "'centralised' equivalence clauses". Each type has different consequences for the allocation of competence between the EU and Member States. For the first type, national competence dominates. For the third type, EU competence dominates. The second type takes an intermediary position. See Girard, 'Les méthodes de suppression des frontières au plan mondial dans le domaine bancaire et financier' 361–364.

[7] *Ibid.*, 363.

The aim of this chapter is to examine equivalence-based regulation in the prospectus field.[8] The main arrangements that will be discussed have already been mentioned. The first concerns financial reporting. In this field, EU requirements are based on international standards, the so-called International Accounting Standards ('IAS') or International Financial Reporting Standards ('IFRS'),[9] which become applicable within the European regulatory space following their endorsement at EU level ('EU IFRS'). The PD and its implementing legislation testify to these developments. Historical financial information must now be prepared in compliance with EU IFRS. But in an effort to limit the impact on third country issuers of the adoption of IFRS as the EU's common standards, Article 35(5) and (5a) of the Prospectus Regulation provides that third country issuers may continue drawing up historical financial information in accordance with accounting standards of certain selected third countries ('third country GAAP') on a temporary or indeed permanent basis.[10] The second arrangement concerns employee share schemes. Article 4(1)(e) of the PD allows a third country issuer whose securities are not admitted to trading on an EU regulated market, but on a third country market, to be exempted from producing a prospectus if the third country market benefits from a finding of equivalence. The provision was added during the recent revisions of the PD and is meant to resolve the problems that third country issuers have faced when attempting to offer employee share schemes in the EU. Finally, the third provision concerns Article 20 of the PD. Following a finding of equivalence under Article 20, a third country issuer may be allowed to use a third country prospectus when seeking to raise capital in the EU. It is this latter provision that will mostly interest us, for it is the legal basis of a shadow prospectus disclosure regime; in other words, a regime that exists in the shadow of the PD's 'maximum harmonisation' disclosure regime whose kernel is the PR. It enacts a complex interplay of competence between Member States and the EU, and, by the same

[8] The PD also uses the term 'equivalent' in different other contexts which are not examined hereinafter. See, for example, Art 2(1)(b), Art 4(1)(b) and (c), Art 4(2)(c) and (d), and Art 8(3). But in these cases, equivalence is more a term than a concept whose purpose is to deal with third country issuers.

[9] The standards were initially coined IAS, but are now known as IFRS. See Rec (7) of Regulation (EC) No 1606/2002 of the European Parliament and of the Council of 19 July 2002 on the application of international accounting standards [2002] OJ L243/1 ('IAS Regulation'). I will refer only to 'IFRS' or 'EU IFRS', hereinafter.

[10] Third country issuers can also prepare historical financial information according to IFRS, as opposed to EU IFRS, if they satisfy the requirements of Art 35(5)(b) of the PR.

token, preserves decision-making powers for Member State authorities. The means that allows safeguarding Member State competence is the prospectus approval system. The nature of the PD's approval system has a number of implications for the exercise by home competent authorities of their decision-making powers. This chapter will seek to elucidate these implications. Already worth noting is that prior approval does not contribute to improving transparency. I will consider three possible solutions to improving the operation of Article 20: (i) improving transparency through simple procedural means, (ii) achieving process uniformity and (iii) achieving substantive uniformity. I reject the two latter for the time being, but advocate greater transparency as a minimum requirement.

The chapter proceeds as follows. Section II clarifies constitutional questions first. The fact that the PD, as an internal market measure, applies to third country issuers is not insignificant from a constitutional point of view. Moreover, the addition of equivalence provisions, such as Article 20, also requires one to re-assess the distribution of decision-making competence between the EU and Member States under the directive. The sections that follow examine the different equivalence arrangements. Section III discusses equivalence-based regulation in relation to third country GAAP. Section IV deals with the new equivalence clause under Article 4(1)(e) of the PD which is supposed to facilitate employee share schemes. Section V examines Article 20.[11] Section VI concludes with some final thoughts on equivalence-based regulation and Article 20, in particular.

II Equivalence-based regulation and prospectus disclosure

Two questions precede the enquiry into the PD's provisions. The first regards the competence of the EU to adopt measures that concern third country actors in internal market legislation. The second question concerns the precise division of competence between the EU and Member States for matters concerning third country issuers.

Attributed competence (the principle of conferral) The PD is among a subset of secondary legislative measures which were adopted as internal

[11] A version of this section was published as P. Schammo, 'Equivalence-based regulation and EU prospectus law – the shadow regime' in D. Prentice and A. Reisberg (eds.), *Corporate Finance Law in the UK and the EU* (Oxford University Press, 2011).

market acts, but include measures that concern third country actors.[12] The content of these measures can vary. They may seek to regulate cooperation with third country authorities, or entrust the Commission, in the field covered by internal legislation, with powers to negotiate better market access terms to third countries.[13] But they may also simply extend the scope of harmonisation to third country actors that wish to exercise activities within the internal market. This is the case of the PD. It not only defines the regulatory position of EU issuers, but also the position of third country issuers if they wish to raise capital in the EU.

One would be forgiven for thinking that extending the scope of the PD to third country issuers is constitutionally insignificant. The EU's actions need to be based on an adequate legal basis or face the prospect of being struck down by the European Court for failure to comply with the principle of conferral under Article 5(2) TEU. Given that the PD was adopted as an internal market measure on the basis of Articles 44 and 95 EC (now Articles 50 and 114 TFEU), the principle of conferral raises for our purposes the question of whether the European legislature could validly extend the PD's scope to securities issued by third country issuers. Questions over the adequacy of internal market bases for adopting measures which concern third country actors have been considered by the European Court at various times. The latter has, at least until the entry into force of the Lisbon Treaty, been the main actor in developing the EU's external competence through incremental steps.[14] This approach has resulted in a noticeably convoluted series of decisions, but which have mostly been enabling for the EU. Indeed, it is fair to say that, all in all, the European Court has been generous with the legislature. In *Opinion 1/94*,[15] it noted that whilst primary freedoms such as the right of establishment

[12] See generally on external relations (prior to the Treaty of Lisbon), P. Eeckhout, *External Relations of the European Union – Legal and Constitutional Foundations* (Oxford University Press, 2005); P. Koutrakos, *EU International Relations Law* (Hart Publishing, Oxford, 2006). Following the entry into force of the Lisbon Treaty, see J. Wouters, D. Coppens and B. De Meester 'The European Union's external relations after the Lisbon Treaty' in S. Griller and J. Ziller (eds.), *The Lisbon Treaty – EU Constitutionalism without a Constitutional Treaty?* (Springer, Vienna, 2008) 143.

[13] E.g., MiFID Arts 63 and 15.

[14] P. Koutrakos, 'Primary law and policy in EU external relations: moving away from the big picture' (2008) 33 *European Law Review* 666, 683. EU primary law now effectively codifies some of the Court's case law in the external relations field. See, e.g., TFEU Arts 3(2) and 216(1). For a first appraisal of the issues and questions that these provisions raise, see (*ibid.*, 683–5). See also Wouters *et al.*, 'The European Union's external relations after the Lisbon Treaty'.

[15] *Opinion 1/94* [1994] ECR I-5267, paras 90–94.

or the free movement of services had a single objective which is to ensure the free movement for Member State nationals,[16] the legislature was not therefore prevented from using harmonisation powers found in the treaty chapters on the right of establishment and free movement of services in order to determine the regulatory treatment of third country nationals.[17] Indeed, in *Tobacco Labelling*, the ECJ found in relation to Article 95 EC, that it was lawful for an internal market act to include a provision on exports to third countries which was not 'aimed directly at improving the conditions for the functioning of the internal market'.[18]

There is clearly a certain spillover logic at work in the Court's case law when it accepts that internal market legislation can include provisions with external orientations. But the Court's approach is not fully open-ended either. Thus, the legislature has not the green light to add external measures whose purpose is wholly detached from, or which bear no relation to, the objectives pursued by the legal basis on which the internal market act is based. Referring to *Opinion 1/94*, Dashwood, for example, argues in relation to the Treaty titles on the right of establishment and freedom to provide services, that the European legislature can claim competence as long as the relevant 'external provisions' are 'an accessory and integral element of measures which, considered as a whole, are very firmly targeted on internal market objectives'.[19] Meanwhile, in *Tobacco Labelling*, the Court made it clear that an internal market act adopted on the basis of Article 95 EC could only include a measure not aimed directly at ameliorating the operation of the internal market if it was possible to show that the purpose of the provision in question was 'to ensure that certain prohibitions concerning the internal market and imposed in pursuit of that object are not circumvented'.[20]

[16] *Ibid.*, para. 81. See also Case C-492/04 *Lasertec v Finanzamt Emmendingen* [2007] ECR I-3775, para. 27 (in relation to the right of establishment); Case C-452/04 *Fidium Finanz AG v Bundesanstalt für Finanzdienstleistungsaufsicht* [2006] ECR I-9521, para. 25 (in relation to the free movement of services).

[17] *Opinion 1/94*, para. 90.

[18] Case C-491/01 *The Queen v Secretary of State for Health, ex parte British American Tobacco (Investments) Ltd and Imperial Tobacco Ltd* [2002] ECR I-11453, paras 82 and 91.

[19] A. Dashwood, 'The attribution of external relations competence' in A. Dashwood and C. Hillion (eds.), *The General Law of E.C. External Relations* (Sweet & Maxwell, London, 2000) 115, 130. Eeckhout concurs by underlining that internal legislation based on the chapters on the right of establishment and free movement of services can include measures which concern third country actors 'in so far as this is connected with internal market harmonization'. See Eeckhout, *External Relations* 80.

[20] *Tobacco Labelling*, para. 82. On the ECJ's reasoning, see also paras 83–91.

We have yet to explain and justify the extension of the PD's scope to securities issued by third country issuers. The point is that capital markets are largely interconnected. Securities issued by third country issuers and EU issuers trade alongside regulated markets within the EU. Hence, if standardisation of disclosure has positive effects on the functioning of the internal market – think, for example, of the benefits of increased transparency and comparability for investors – then securities issued by third country issuers, which trade on European markets, should indeed be included within the scope of the directive. But one can also think of other reasons for extending the PD's scope. Excluding third-country securities and leaving it to Member States to define unilaterally their treatment could, for example, lead to distortions of competition between regulated markets located in different Member States. The point is not negligible because the cost of complying with prospectus regulation is a factor – albeit a factor among others – which issuers are likely to consider when deciding on which market to seek admission to trading. Moreover, it is important not to lose sight of the broader aims pursued by way of market integration. Capital markets which attract a wide range of issuers from Europe and beyond are a key ingredient to a striving financial industry which contributes both to economic growth and employment. Improving access to EU markets for third-country issuers therefore also contributes to the Union's broader objectives.[21]

Relational competence The PD's provisions on third-country issuers not only raise special considerations from a competence conferral point of view, but also require us to revisit the question of the distribution of powers between the EU and Member States in the prospectus disclosure field. Recall that in an area of shared competence such as the internal market,[22] the question of whether competence rests with the EU or Member States will necessarily be affected by the precise arrangements (maximum harmonisation, minimum harmonisation, etc.) which the European legislature decides to lay down.[23] If a directive or a regulation is found to be

[21] Unfortunately, the PD itself is rather brief with respect to the reasons for extending its scope. Rec (36) merely states *in fine* that it is necessary for 'ensur[ing] that the purposes of [the PD] will be fully achieved'.

[22] TFEU Art 4(2)(a).

[23] See generally on the subject, S. Weatherill, 'Beyond preemption? Shared competence and constitutional change in the European Community' in D. O'Keeffe and P. Twomey (eds.), *Legal Issues of the Maastricht Treaty* (Chancery Law Publishing, London, 1994) 13; Weatherill, 'Pre-emption, harmonisation and the distribution of competence to regulate the internal market' 41.

of a maximum harmonisation nature, the EU will occupy the regulatory space exhaustively and Member States will be pre-empted – the Court prefers the term 'precluded' – from departing unilaterally from the common course of action.[24] Moreover, this type of internal market harmonisation also impacts on the distribution of competence between the EU and Member States in *external matters*, that is in the dealings of Member States and the EU with third countries. In external matters, preemption is generally discussed in the language of 'exclusivity'[25] and questions about the exclusive competence of the EU typically arise in relation to the conclusion of international agreements. The point about international agreements is relevant because, as I mentioned in the introductory section, it is not uncommon for equivalence-based regulation to have an external dimension in the sense that Member States or the EU may wish to enter into negotiations with third countries prior to deciding on equivalence. Among the Court's rulings on exclusivity, which are, since the entry into force of the Lisbon Treaty, reflected (for better or worse) in the Treaties,[26] are also a number of decisions in which the Court established that exclusive external competence could also follow from internal market harmonisation which covers the same area.[27] Thus, the Court has, *inter alia*, held that if the European legislature has achieved full harmonisation internally or has specified the treatment to be given to third-country actors in internal legislation, the Community would benefit from exclusive external competence.[28]

Given that the PD is generally thought to be a maximum harmonisation directive, the position with respect to relational competence appears to be quite clear: competence rests with the Union; Member States are precluded from taking unilateral action concerning matters which fall

[24] In seeking to establish whether harmonisation is complete or whether Member States retain discretion, the Court will generally examine the 'wording, purpose and structure' of the measure. For examples, see Case C-154/00 *Commission v Hellenic Republic* [2002] ECR I-03879, para. 12; Case C-402/03 *Skov and Bilka* [2006] ECR I-199, para. 22; Case C-52/00 *Commission v France* [2002] ECR I-3827, para. 16; Case C-183/00 *Sánchez v Medicina Asturiana SA* [2002] ECR I-3901, para. 25.

[25] The latter concept has been profoundly shaped by the European Court's case law. See D. O'Keeffe, 'Exclusive, concurrent and shared competence' in Dashwood and Hillion, *The General Law of E.C. External Relations* (Sweet & Maxwell, London, 2000) 79. See also generally Koutrakos, *EU International Relations Law*; Eeckhout, *External Relations*.

[26] TFEU Art 3(2).

[27] E.g., *Opinion 1/94* [1994] ECR I-05267, paras 95–96; Case C-476/98 *Commission v Germany* [2002] ECR I-9855, paras 109–110; *Opinion 1/03* [2006] ECR I-1145, para. 122.

[28] *Ibid.*

within the scope of the directive. Yet, upon reflection, the matter is a bit more complicated. This is mainly because of Article 20 of the PD and the equivalence arrangements that it lays down for third-country issuers. The detail of Article 20 and its implications for the distribution of competence will require more careful examination. But already worth noting is that because of Article 20, the directive effectively makes provision for two prospectus disclosure models: (i) an ordinary regime that applies with respect to securities issued by EU issuers and, generally, third-country issuers and whose kernel is the Level 2 PR; and (ii) an equivalence-based prospectus disclosure regime for certain third-country issuers. As far as the former is concerned, Articles 3 (second paragraph) and 22(1) (second sub-paragraph) of the PR prevent, as a matter of principle, competent authorities from departing from the common disclosure items set out in the PR and, thereby, give the ordinary disclosure regime its maximum harmonisation character.[29] The second disclosure regime, based on Article 20, allows competent authorities to recognise third-country prospectuses by exercising their power to approve a prospectus. Thereby, Article 20 effectively preserves Member State competence to decide unilaterally on equivalence, albeit under a set of conditions and in the shadow of the exercise by the Commission of delegated and implementing powers, but which powers the Commission has not yet used. The implication is that Member State authorities are currently benefiting from a greater degree of freedom to make unilateral decisions over third country disclosure requirements (within the scope of their powers under Article 20(1)) than over EU disclosure requirements where the Level 2 PR prevents, as a matter of principle, competent authorities from exercising discretion.

III Third country GAAP

I now turn to an examination of equivalence-based regulation in relation to third country GAAP. In recent years, the regulation of financial reporting has become one of the main fields of application of equivalence provisions.[30] In the EU context, its rise must be seen in the light of the adoption of IFRS as the new common EU standards,[31] a process which was initiated

[29] The PR makes some adjustments and exceptions to the maximum harmonisation principle. See PR Arts 4a and 23.

[30] See also Moloney, *EC Securities Regulation* 223–8; Ferran, *Building an EU Securities Market* 160–4.

[31] See generally Moloney, *EC Securities Regulation* 212–23.

by the adoption of Regulation No 1606/2002 on the application of international accounting standards ('IAS Regulation').[32] The IFRS are made by the International Accounting Standards Board.[33] They become applicable within the EU regulatory space only following their endorsement by the European Commission.[34] The adoption of IFRS heralded a new time for issuers seeking to make a public offer or intending to apply for an admission of securities to trading on a regulated market. Following the end of a transitional period, historical financial information provided in prospectuses has to be prepared in accordance with EU IFRS.[35] For third country issuers, however, the PR makes separate arrangements.[36] Initially, it put in place two types of transitional arrangements. First, the PR allowed, for a limited period of time, third country issuers to continue relying on standards other than EU IFRS.[37] Second, it provided that equivalence arrangements should be adopted in order to make it possible for third country issuers to continue relying on third country GAAP if the latter were judged equivalent to EU IFRS.[38] The adoption of these arrangements proved lengthier than expected. In December 2008, however, the Commission adopted its first decisions regarding the recognition of equivalence of third country GAAP.[39] These decisions brought a purely transitional regime to its end and resulted in the PR being amended by the insertion of a new Article 35(5) and (5a).[40] While these provisions no longer make any reference to the recognition of equivalence, their content reflects the Commission measures of December 2008. As we will see later, some transitional arrangements remain nevertheless in place.

The EU's approach to equivalence-based regulation, which has emerged from this process, takes the form of a two-stage process. The first part consists in assessing whether third country GAAP is equivalent to EU IFRS (A). The second part consists in the recognition of

32 [2002] OJ L243/1. 33 IAS Regulation, Rec (7). 34 IAS Regulation, Art 3.

35 The requirement is laid down in various information items found in the Annexes to the Level 2 PR.

36 See also PR Rec (28). 37 PR Art 35(3) and (4).

38 PR Art 35(5), before amendment.

39 Commission Decision of 12 December 2008 on the use by third countries' issuers of securities of certain third country's national accounting standards and International Financial Reporting Standards to prepare their consolidated financial statements [2008] OJ L340/112. See also, Commission Regulation (EC) No 1289/2008 of 12 December 2008 amending Commission Regulation (EC) No 809/2004 implementing Directive 2003/71/EC of the European Parliament and of the Council as regards elements related to prospectuses and advertisements [2008] OJ L340/17 ('Regulation No 1289/2008'), Art 1.

40 Following amendment by Regulation No 1289/2008.

equivalence *sensu stricto* (B). Each part of the process is worth investigating further.

A Assessment of equivalence

In order to allow an assessment of equivalence to be carried out, the Commission adopted Regulation No 1569/2007 which defines the meaning of equivalence and lays down certain procedural requirements.[41]

Meaning of equivalence Like maximum harmonisation, the concept of equivalence is not a terribly precise concept.[42] The term 'equivalent' can be used in ordinary language as a synonym for similar, comparable or identical. It can be defined in the abstract, but also by reference to a benchmark such as, for example, decisions of investors who may or may not be proficient in IFRS. These and other questions informed the enquiry of CESR, which was entrusted by the Commission with the preparatory work on equivalence, into how to approach and assess equivalence. Some of the questions were resolved by simply defining the meaning of equivalence. Thus, CESR adopted the view that third country GAAP should be considered equivalent:

> when financial statements prepared under such third country GAAP enable investors to take similar decision [sic] in terms of whether to invest or divest, as if they were provided with financial statements prepared on the basis of IAS/IFRS.[43]

The definition does not draw a distinction between professional and retail investors. Nor does it specify any level of investor proficiency with

[41] Commission Regulation (EC) No 1569/2007 of 21 December 2007 establishing a mechanism for the determination of equivalence of accounting standards applied by third country issuers of securities pursuant to Directives 2003/71/EC and 2004/109/EC of the European Parliament and of the Council [2007] L340/66 ('Regulation No 1569/2007').

[42] See Wei, 'The equivalence approach to securities regulation' 257–63 (examining the various meanings of equivalence).

[43] CESR, 'Concept paper on equivalence of certain third country GAAP and on description of certain third countries mechanisms of enforcement of financial information' (CESR/04-509C, February 2005) 8. See also CESR, 'CESR's technical advice on a mechanism for determining the equivalence of the generally accepted accounting principles of third countries' (CESR/07-289, May 2007) 8 'investors should be able to make a similar decision irrespective of whether they are provided with financial statements based on IFRS or on third country GAAP'; CESR, 'CESR's advice to the European Commission on the work programmes of the Canadian, Japanese and US standard setters, the definition of equivalence and the list of third country GAAPs currently used on the EU capital markets' (CESR/07-138, March 2007) 18.

regard to IFRS. CESR, however, made clear that it would not differentiate between types of investors when assessing equivalence and that it would assume that investors are reasonably knowledgeable about IAS/IFRS.[44] The Commission subsequently adopted its own, binding, definition of 'equivalence' in Regulation No 1569/2007. According to Article 2, third country GAAP should be deemed to be equivalent to EU IFRS if:

> ... the financial statements drawn up in accordance with Generally Accepted Accounting Principles of the third country concerned enable investors to make a similar assessment of the assets and liabilities, financial position, profit and losses and prospects of the issuer as financial statements drawn up in accordance with IFRS, with the result that investors are likely to make the same decisions about the acquisition, retention or disposal of securities of an issuer.

In comparison with CESR's definition, the language chosen by the Commission is, arguably, unnecessarily complicated. CESR's definition was plainly 'outcome-based'.[45] What mattered for CESR was that financial information drawn up in accordance with third country GAAP enabled investors to 'take similar decision[s]' about whether to invest or not. Moreover, CESR's definition focused on the enabling capacity of financial information. That is to say, for CESR, financial statements drawn up with third country GAAP should 'enable' – i.e., make it possible for – investors to make similar decisions. For the Commission, on the other hand, financial statements drawn up with third country GAAP should 'enable investors to make a similar assessment' of the financial credentials of the issuer, but in addition, investors should as a consequence 'be likely to make the same decisions' about whether to invest. The reference to 'investors' instead of 'an investor' in the Commission definition is a bit unfortunate because it gives the impression that a finding of equivalence is premised on the idea that different investors should be likely to make, at the outcome of the assessment process, the same decisions. This, of course, is erroneous given that different investors make decisions according to different investment calculations and, therefore, may not even be likely to make the same decisions if all had a perfectly identical appreciation of the financial position of an issuer.[46] CESR's definition does not raise the

[44] CESR, 'Concept paper' (CESR/04-509c) 9.

[45] CESR, 'Technical advice on equivalence of certain third country GAAP and on description of certain third countries mechanisms of enforcement of financial information' (CESR/05-230b, June 2005) 4.

[46] Cf., CESR, 'Concept paper' 8 noting that '[e]ven when provided with exactly the same information, different investors might still take completely different decisions'.

same issue because it focuses on the enabling capacity of financial information. Whether investors are actually likely to make the same decisions is entirely irrelevant under its definition.

The adoption of Article 2 also raised some alarm bells with market actors who expressed concerns over the language used by the Commission. Among other comments, it was the use of the word 'same' in the Commission definition which was a source of anxiety.[47] The combination of the word 'same' with the word 'likely' somewhat alleviates these concerns. At any rate, although the choice of definitional language is not entirely satisfactory, the definition has not, in practice, become an obstacle to the recognition of equivalence.

Assessing equivalence Commission Regulation No 1569/2007 not only laid down a definition of equivalence, but also established a so-called 'equivalence mechanism'. The equivalence mechanism is, in essence, the procedure which needs to be followed in order to make a decision on equivalence.[48] The Commission Regulation itself is remarkably brief on the form and content of this mechanism. It includes a single article, entitled 'equivalence mechanism', that identifies the actors that can launch the assessment process. Article 3 provides for a 'decision on the determination of the equivalence' of third country GAAP to be taken by the Commission on its own initiative, or following an application by a Member State authority or a third country authority. Once initiated, CESR, which was consulted in an advisory capacity in accordance with the Lamfalussy arrangements for Level 2 decision-making, assessed equivalence first.[49] Admittedly, ESMA has now succeeded CESR. But ESMA will need to address issues similar to those that affected CESR. CESR's work on equivalence remains therefore relevant. One of the issues which ESMA might, in the future, have to address is how precisely equivalence should be assessed. There are various ways and methods for doing this. They include a straight comparison of different rules or standards, or a more 'holistic' approach in lieu of a detailed assessment. The assessment scope can also give rise to questions. Should an assessment of equivalence, for

[47] ICMA and SIFMA, Letter to the Commission, dated 21 August 2007, www.icmagroup.org/ICMAGroup/files/97/97ece018-e5b9–4c45-acdc-b4cba102bd07.pdf.

[48] European Commission, 'Request for advice on equivalence under the Transparency Directive and Prospectus Regulation' (letter to CESR, undated), annexed to CESR, 'CESR's technical advice' (CESR/07-289) 14, 17.

[49] Commission Regulation No 1569/2007, Rec (3). CESR provided the Commission with (non-binding) advice on US, Japanese, Chinese, Canadian, South Korean and Indian GAAP.

instance, include an evaluation of the manner in which third country GAAP is being implemented and applied? There is the question of reciprocity. Should a finding of equivalence be premised on the idea that third countries offer similar advantages to EU actors? In examining these questions, CESR's methodology reveals a number of constants. First of all, CESR provided technical advice. The question of reciprocity was outside its remit and a matter for the Commission to consider.[50] Moreover, CESR took the view that a 'pre-requisite' for recognising equivalence was the existence of so-called 'filters' at the level of the third country and 'audit assurance and enforcement at the entity level' which were adequate for investors to place reliance on.[51] Filters were meant to address potential defects at the level of the implementation, application or enforcement of third country GAAP. While stressing the importance for such filters to be in place, CESR generally worked on the basis of assumptions. Thus, it repeatedly stated that:

> [f]or the purposes of establishing equivalence, CESR assumes that third country GAAPs are properly applied including the provision of any rectifying disclosures necessary. CESR further assumes that the necessary filters for ensuring market confidence are in place for third country issuers using or participating in the EU capital markets.[52]

[50] CESR, 'Concept paper on equivalence of certain third country GAAP and on description of certain third countries mechanisms of enforcement of financial information – Feedback statement' (CESR/05-001, January 2005) 5.

[51] CESR, 'CESR's technical advice' (CESR/07-289) 9. Note that CESR described audits as '[o]ne of the key filters' (*ibid.*, 10). In this context, it also drew attention to the adoption of the 8th Directive (2006/43/EC [2006] OJ L 157/87) noting that the 'assessment of the audit filter … is dealt with exclusively through the assessment of compliance with the 8th Directive' (*ibid.*). In its subsequent advice on third country GAAP, CESR pointed to the fact that the Commission was in the process of assessing the status of third country auditors under the 8th Directive and noted that it had 'not attempted to perform its own assessment of such matters'. See CESR, 'CESR's advice on the equivalence of Chinese, Japanese and US GAAPs' (CESR/08-179, March 2008) 15; CESR, 'CESR's advice on Canadian and South Korean GAAPs' (CESR/08-293, May 2008) 14; CESR, 'CESR's technical advice to the European Commission on Indian GAAP' (CESR/08-859, November 2008) 11.

[52] CESR, 'CESR's technical advice' (CESR/07-289) 9. See also CESR, 'CESR's advice' (CESR/08-179) 15; CESR, 'CESR's advice' (CESR/08-293) 14; 'CESR's technical advice' (CESR/08-859) 11. But note that in relation to Chinese GAAP, CESR recommended that a decision on equivalence should be deferred on the grounds that there was yet insufficient evidence on how Chinese GAAP was being implemented. See CESR, 'CESR's advice' (CESR/08-179) 14. The Commission concurred. See Commission Regulation 1289/2008, Rec (10).

Despite these common factors, it is apparent that the manner in which CESR carried out its assessments developed significantly over time. In tracing this change or development, three moments are worth highlighting. The first moment was the adoption by CESR of its concept paper on equivalence which was followed by its first technical advice on the equivalence of US, Canadian and Japanese GAAP in June 2005.[53] The manner in which CESR sought to measure equivalence was based on a 'direct comparison of standards'.[54] As a result, CESR set out on a detailed and work intensive examination of US, Canadian and Japanese GAAP. It revisited its approach when requested by the Commission to advise on an equivalence mechanism.[55] In its advice, CESR suggested that in the context of an application for recognition of equivalence, the assessment of equivalence should in the first place be made by the relevant authorities of the third country.[56] According to CESR, the third country authority should provide an 'honest assessment of whether the disclosures, measurement and recognition principles, and financial statement presentation required by the third country GAAP concerned are materially the same as IFRS and where they are not an assessment of the differences'.[57] In case of 'significant differences' between third country GAAP and IFRS, CESR suggested that third country issuers should nevertheless be allowed to rely on their local GAAP, provided that differences could be remedied by way of additional disclosures.[58] It proposed that it, CESR, should be entrusted with the task of making sure that the disclosures were adequate and non-complex.[59] Finally, CESR advised the Commission that the latter should conduct an '"overall" assessment of equivalence' as a final step of the procedure.[60] But CESR also suggested that the Commission extend transitional arrangements for a number of third countries, which were in the process of adapting local GAAP to IFRS, until 2012.[61] The publication of CESR's advice led to the third and final moment worth highlighting: the adoption by the Commission of Regulation No 1569/2007. Besides defining the meaning of equivalence and laying down certain procedural rules, the Commission Regulation followed CESR's advice on transitional arrangements and put a new transitional regime in place for third countries which are in the process of moving towards IFRS. Under the Commission Regulation,

[53] CESR, 'Concept paper' (CESR/04-509C); CESR, 'Technical advice' (CESR/05-230b).
[54] CESR, 'Technical advice' (CESR/05-230b) 4.
[55] CESR, 'CESR's technical advice' (CESR/07-289).
[56] *Ibid.*, 6. [57] *Ibid.*
[58] *Ibid.*, 7. Disclosures would only be accepted if audited (*ibid.* 3).
[59] *Ibid.*, 8. [60] *Ibid.* [61] *Ibid.*, 9.

third country issuers are allowed to continue using for a finite period – that is, until the 31st December 2011 – third country GAAP in order to prepare historical financial information.[62] But the Regulation provides that third country standards will be accepted only if the relevant third country authority has publicly committed itself to *converge* local GAAP with IFRS by the end of 2011,[63] or has committed itself to *adopt* IFRS by the end of 2011,[64] or finally if the third country authority and the EU have agreed a mutual recognition arrangement.[65] The public commitments to converge with, or adopt, IFRS had to be made by the end of June 2008.[66] The mutual recognition arrangements, meanwhile, were supposed to be agreed by the end of 2008.[67] The transitional regime is therefore, in fact, no longer available for new candidate states.

The adoption of Commission Regulation No 1569/2007 is also a crucial moment for the reason that it led CESR to revisit its methodology. In its advice to the Commission, CESR cast doubts on the appropriateness of comparing standards individually and went on to express a preference for a 'more *holistic* outcome-based approach to third country GAAP equivalence'[68] (emphasis added). For CESR, this approach was in line with the Commission's understanding of equivalence in Regulation No 1569/2007.[69] Crucially, this holistic methodology is firmly tied to the efforts of third countries to converge with, or adopt, IFRS. Thus, CESR summarised its position by noting that it:

> now believes that it is best to base a decision on equivalence on an holistic assessment of the ability of investors to make similar decisions on investments irrespective of the existence of potential lingering differences in presentation and measurement, as long as such differences are taken into account in a sensible long-term work programme between the standard setters concerned and the IASB and there is evidence of such programmes being active [sic] pursued.[70]

In short, in assessing third country GAAP, CESR decided that it was best to rely on the efforts of third countries to bring their domestic GAAP in line with IFRS.[71] In trying to make sense of this methodological

[62] Commission Regulation 1569/2007, Art 4(1). Note that the transitional arrangements of Art 4 also apply in relation to the TD.

[63] Art 4(1)(1). [64] Art 4(1)(2). [65] *Ibid.*

[66] Art 4(1)(1) and (2). [67] Art 4(1)(2).

[68] CESR, 'CESR's advice' (CESR/08-179) 9.

[69] *Ibid.* [70] *Ibid.*

[71] See also Girard, 'Les méthodes de suppression des frontières au plan mondial dans le domaine bancaire et financier' 367 (noting that 'for CESR … the degree of convergence

evolution, CESR highlighted a number of different factors, including the text of the Commission's definition of equivalence which post-dated CESR's first efforts to assess third country GAAP.[72] But it is also fair to say that by relying on a more holistic approach and a third country's efforts to bring national GAAP in line with IFRS, CESR was able to considerably reduce its workload. Recall, in this context, that CESR had limited resources and had to rely on the expertise of its members. But whilst beneficial in terms of managing its workload, CESR's approach also raised a few questions about the purpose and future of equivalence-based regulation. The adoption of a convergence programme or a commitment to adopt IFRS is not, as such, a condition for the recognition of equivalence under Commission Regulation No 1569/2007. It is only a condition to benefit from transitional arrangements under Article 4. Yet, obviously the adoption of a convergence programme will be an effective means for a third country to make sure that its domestic GAAP satisfies the test of equivalence of Article 2. But if a third country is, as a result, prompted to abandon local GAAP in favour of IFRS, equivalence-based regulation is also arguably quite a redundant concept. Indeed, considering the growing prominence of IFRS and given that third country issuers are under Commission Regulation No 1289/2008 allowed to rely on IFRS when preparing financial disclosure,[73] there may very well be no need for equivalence assessments to be performed in the future. Having said this, this is less a criticism than an observation. In the field of accounting standards, the case for greater standardisation is arguably especially strong.[74]

B *Recognition of equivalence*

While CESR advised on the recognition of equivalence, it is the Commission that has the legal power to decide whether third country GAAP is equivalent to European standards. It adopted the first

between IFRS and the accounting standard under review should be a key element in any equivalence assessment').

[72] For CESR, the approach adopted at EU level 'potentially require[d] a more holistic outcome-based approach to third country GAAP equivalence'. See CESR, 'CESR's advice' (CESR/08-179) 9. CESR's reasoning is detailed in paras. 25–42.

[73] See also PR Art 35(5)(b).

[74] I do not attempt to assess whether IFRS is superior to a given third country GAAP. On differences between IFRS and US GAAP, see W. Bratton and L. Cunningham, 'Treatment differences and political realities in the GAAP-IFRS debate' (2009) 95 *Virginia Law Review* 989. See also J. Cox, 'Coping in a global marketplace: survival strategies for a 75-year-old SEC' (2009) *Virginia Law Review* 941.

equivalence decisions in December 2008.[75] Article 35 of the Level 2 PR was subsequently amended and, as a result, provides that third country issuers are allowed to rely on EU IFRS, IFRS, US or Japanese GAAP in order to prepare historical financial information. Moreover, under the regulation, Chinese, Canadian, South Korean and Indian GAAP continue benefiting from transitional arrangements.[76]

With respect to the issue of reciprocity, recall that CESR did not consider it when examining third country GAAP (even though it encouraged convergence with IFRS). As far as the Commission is concerned, Commission Regulation No 1569/2007, as finally adopted, does not include a legally binding obligation for the Commission to make recognition of third country GAAP subject to reciprocity. But there are a number of statements and provisions which are worth mentioning. Among them is first and foremost, Recital (3) which provides *in fine* that the Commission's decision on equivalence 'will have to be such that Community issuers are permitted to use IFRS adopted pursuant to [the IAS Regulation] in the third country concerned'.[77] In a similar spirit, Recital (3) also states that the Commission 'will actively monitor ongoing progress ... to eliminate any requirement for Community issuers accessing the financial markets of a third country to reconcile financial statements'. Meanwhile, Article 2 of Commission Regulation No 1289/2008 requires the Commission to alert the Council and the European Parliament if EU issuers are made subject to reconciliation requirements in one of the third countries concerned. Last but not least, following lengthy discussions in the European Securities Committee, the Commission adopted a declaration which testifies to the broader issues which equivalence-based regulation raises for Member States and to the rationale for insisting on reciprocity. It is worth setting out the declaration in full:

> *In its deliberations on the determination of equivalence of accounting standards applied by third country issuers of securities pursuant to [Commission Regulation No 1569/2007], the Commission will base its decision on technical criteria and take into account the importance of avoiding competitive disadvantages for European companies operating*

[75] Commission Decision of 12 December 2008 on the use by third countries' issuers of securities of certain third country's national accounting standards and International Financial Reporting Standards to prepare their consolidated financial statements [2008] OJ L340/112.

[76] PR Art 35(5a).

[77] See also Commission Regulation 1289/2008, Rec (3).

in the global marketplace and the need to maintain the attractiveness of European capital markets.[78]

The European Securities Committee issued a positive opinion on draft Commission Regulation 1289/2008 in November 2008 which amended Art 35 of the PR. France decided to abstain from the vote.[79]

IV Employee share schemes

In section III, we saw how equivalence-based regulation was used as a means to avoid overregulation and reconciliation of accounting standards in the wake of the decision to adopt IFRS as the common financial reporting language of the EU. But financial reporting is, by no means, the sole field where the EU legislature has used equivalence provisions as a means to mitigate the impact of its legislative ambitions. It only recently added a new equivalence clause to the PD in relation to employee share schemes. I begin by examining the problems which preceded the adoption of this new arrangement for third country companies, after which I will examine the equivalence provision in more detail.

A Article 4(1)(e) and employee share schemes

Problems with employee share schemes Employee share schemes, i.e., offers of securities by an employer (or an affiliated company) to employees, have long benefited from special arrangements at EU level. Before the PD was adopted, the Public Offers Directive ('POD'), which the PD eventually replaced, excluded from its scope securities offered by employers to their employees.[80] The PD no longer excludes offers to employees from its scope. But it attempts, nonetheless, to facilitate such offers by exempting employers from the obligation to publish a prospectus. Specifically, Article 4(1)(e) allows employers, or an affiliated company, to offer securities to present or previous directors/employees without such an offer triggering an obligation to publish a prospectus. The directive adds certain conditions. In particular, it obliges the offeror to prepare a lighter

[78] ESC, 'Draft summary record of the 57th meeting of the European Securities Committee (members)' (3 December 2007) 4, http://ec.europa.eu/internal_market/securities/esc/index_en.htm.

[79] ESC, 'Summary record of the 62nd meeting of the European Securities Committee (members)' (14 November 2008) 2, http://ec.europa.eu/internal_market/securities/esc/index_en.htm.

[80] POD Art 2(2)(h).

information document in place of a prospectus.[81] Moreover, before the PD was amended in 2010, employers could only benefit from Article 4(1)(e), if they already had securities admitted to trading on a regulated market, i.e., an (EU) market in the sense of Article 4(1)(14) of MiFID. If that was not the case and an employer was unable to take advantage of another exemption,[82] the offer was a public offer in the sense of the directive and, accordingly, subject to all the requirements applying to public offers.

The requirement to have securities admitted to trading on a regulated market was intended to ensure transparency. Given that companies, whose securities have been admitted to trading on a regulated market, are subject to ongoing disclosure obligations, it was thought that such a requirement would ultimately benefit employees.[83] Whatever the merit of this argument, Article 4(1)(e) caused, in practice, unforeseen problems for companies which were not listed on a regulated market or listed on an exchange-regulated market. In particular, Article 4(1)(e) became an issue for companies incorporated in third countries that wished to offer securities to staff in Europe. The reason why third country companies, in particular, felt that the requirements of Article 4(1)(e) were onerous was plainly obvious. They were generally less likely to be trading their securities on a regulated market in Europe.[84]

To be sure, some employee share schemes were altogether outside the scope of the directive.[85] But many schemes were caught and, if a company did not have securities admitted to trading on a regulated market, it was faced with the choice of bearing the cost of preparing a prospectus or simply abandoning the scheme altogether.

Solutions to employee share schemes Fearing that employers would, as a result, abandon employee share schemes, the European Commission instructed CESR to find a solution.[86] CESR members responded by

[81] Art 4(1)(e). [82] E.g., PD Arts 3(2)(b) or 1(2)(h).

[83] Common Position (EC) No 25/2003 [2003] OJ C125E/21, 51.

[84] 'European Commission, 'Background Document – Review of Directive 2003/71/EC' (undated) 7.

[85] For example, offers of non-transferable options are outside the scope of the directive. See European Commission, 'Request for assistance on employee share schemes' (letter to CESR) attached to CESR, 'CESR starts work on employee share scheme prospectuses' (CESR/07-825, December 2007) 2. Non-transferable options are outside the scope of the directive because the PD only covers transferable securities (Art 2(1)(a)). Note that the actual exercise of the (non-transferable) option will not trigger public offer requirements either. This is because it does not constitute an offer in the sense of the directive. See 'CESR Q&A July 10', Question 5.

[86] CESR, 'CESR starts work on employee share scheme prospectuses'.

agreeing to allow issuers, which are admitted to a market, but which is not a regulated market in the sense of MiFID, to draw up a prospectus under a 'short-form disclosure regime'.[87] Under this regime, issuers were allowed to omit various information items on the basis of Article 23(4) of the PR which permits information to be omitted, if it is not deemed to be pertinent.[88] This solution allowed containing the problem, but it was also plainly in contradiction with the premise of Article 4(1)(e), which was that a full prospectus was necessary to ensure transparency in the absence of an admission to a regulated market. The conundrum was finally resolved by the legislature in 2010.[89] For EU companies, the legislature decided to simply remove the obligation to have securities admitted to trading on a regulated market. As a result, EU companies – i.e., a company having its head office or registered office in the EU – will only be obliged to prepare an alternative information document.[90] The concern about transparency, which originally prompted the legislature to oblige employers to have securities admitted to trading on a regulated market, did not, however, vanish completely. A recital to the directive amending the PD ('PAD') notes that the alternative information document should, if necessary, be updated in order to ensure that the securities can be properly evaluated.[91] Of course, the recital does not create legally binding obligations. But this might be just as well. A legally binding obligation to update the information document if the securities are not admitted to trading on a regulated market, might have opened the door to new requirements being added through the 'back door', so to speak. At any rate, competent authorities will, in all probability, have a say on the matter, especially as Article 4(1)(e) is fairly vague on the content of the alternative information document.

Most of the amended text of Article 4(1)(e) does not deal, however, with EU employers, but with third country companies – i.e., companies established outside the EU regulatory space. It is perhaps somewhat paradoxical that the legislature's efforts to make the prospectus exemption of Article 4(1)(e) more accessible to third country issuers has made it considerably more complex. Under the amended provision, separate arrangements now apply to third country companies that wish to offer

[87] 'CESR Q&A July 10', Question 71.

[88] *Ibid.* [89] PD Art 4(1)(e), as amended.

[90] This information document must include details on the number and nature of the securities, as well as on the offer and the reasons for making it.

[91] Directive (EU) 2010/73 [2010] OJ L327/1, Rec (14).

employee share schemes in the EU. Like EU companies, a third country company will be obliged to prepare a lighter information document. But the obligation to have securities admitted to trading has not been removed for third country companies. Instead, the requirement has been weakened. Thus, a third country company will only benefit from Article 4(1)(e) if it has securities admitted to trading on a regulated market or – crucially – on a third country market. In the latter case, two additional conditions must be met. First, adequate information must be available in, at least, a language which is customary in international financial circles. The PD does not specify the meaning of 'adequate information'. But given the wording of Article 4(1)(e), it is apparent that the obligation to provide an alternative information document will not, in itself, be sufficient to satisfy this requirement. The second condition that needs to be satisfied is that the third country market benefits from a decision on equivalence. Thus, in short, the *quid pro quo* for widening the conditions of Article 4(1)(e) was the adoption of a new equivalence provision. In the remaining part of this section, I will examine this provision and, by the same token, return to questions that have been raised earlier when examining third country GAAP, i.e., how is equivalence assessed and which actor has competence to decide on equivalence?

B The equivalence condition of Article 4(1)(e)

We have seen so far that after the PD was amended in 2010, a third country company can benefit from Article 4(1)(e) even if it has no securities admitted to trading on an EU regulatory market. More specifically, a third country company wishing to offer share schemes to its staff (i.e., former/previous employees or directors) in the EU can benefit from a derogation to publish a prospectus, if it prepares an alternative information document and if it has securities admitted to trading on a regulated market *or* a third country market. Third country markets are not, by definition, regulated markets in the sense of MiFID. They are, therefore, not subject to the same legal and supervisory requirements. To ensure adequate levels of regulation, supervision and enforcement, the EU legislature added an equivalence condition. As amended, Article 4(1)(e) thus states that a third country company, wishing to take advantage of an employee share scheme exemption, can only benefit from the fact that it has securities admitted to trading on a third country market if the third country market benefits from an equivalence decision. The new equivalence provision requires closer examination.

Assessment of equivalence. Like other equivalence clauses, the crucial issue, which will ultimately determine how useful and effective equivalence-based regulation is going to be, concerns the manner in which equivalence is assessed. We have as yet no experience with this assessment process. Although the European Commission is empowered to lay down measures by way of delegated acts in order to put flesh on the requirements of the directive,[92] the equivalence process is, for the time being, only loosely structured by a set of principles and requirements found in Article 4(1)(e). The directive, first of all, specifies the subject matter of the assessment. Under investigation are the regulatory requirements, including the supervisory and enforcement arrangements, that are applicable in a third country and which constitute the framework in which the foreign market operates. Specifically, the regulatory requirements must be deemed to be equivalent to the requirements of the TD, the MAD and MiFID's provisions on regulated markets.[93] This analysis is tied to an assessment of enforcement and supervisory arrangements in the third country. A finding of equivalence will, in other words, presuppose that the relevant third country regulatory requirements are also subject to proper enforcement and supervision. But these enforcement and supervisory arrangements are not subject to a separate equivalence condition. They must merely be considered 'effective'.[94]

The scope of this equivalence assessment is obviously especially broad. The directive gives a few further clues about the requirements that the third country market must meet in order to benefit from a decision on equivalence. First, it must be established that the third country market is subject to authorisation requirements and to 'effective' ongoing supervision and enforcement arrangements. Second, 'clear and transparent' provisions governing the admission of securities to trading must be in place in order to ensure that securities can be traded 'in a fair, orderly and efficient manner, and are freely negotiable'. Third, issuers on the third country market must be subject to periodic and ongoing disclosure obligations that ensure a 'high level of investor protection'. Finally, the legal and supervisory framework of the third country must ensure market transparency and market integrity by addressing market abuse (i.e., insider dealing and market manipulation). These four requirements go some way towards

92 PD Art 4(1)(e), final sub-para., as amended.

93 Directive 2004/109/EC [2004] OJ L390/38; Directive 2003/6/EC [2003] OJ L96/16; Directive 2004/39/EC [2004] OJ L145/1.

94 To borrow the terminology that CESR used in relation to third country GAAP, enforcement and supervision act as a type of 'filter'.

specifying the content of the assessment exercise. Admittedly, *prima facie*, they appear to diminish the meaning of equivalence. This is because none of the four requirements necessitates a finding of equivalence. Instead, equivalence is effectively replaced by other concepts, such as 'clear and transparent rules', rules which ensure that securities can be 'traded in a fair, orderly and efficient manner' and requirements that ensure 'a high level of investor protection'. In fact, however, the four conditions merely reflect core requirements of MiFID, the TD and the MAD. The directives' requirements are therefore likely to serve as a benchmark. Note, however, that the four requirements are only minimum requirements. Even if the conditions were met, the wording of Article 4(1)(e) implies that a finding of equivalence may be subject to additional requirements. Other factors are, consequently, likely to enter the assessment process, including some form of reciprocity obligation.

Recognition of equivalence As in the case of third country GAAP, the power to decide on equivalence is in the hands of the European Commission.[95] Competent authorities are not completely sidestepped, however. They play a two-fold role. First, they are empowered to ask the Commission to issue a decision on equivalence.[96] Although competent authorities do not have the power to decide on equivalence, they can, by requesting the Commission to decide on equivalence, effectively launch the assessment process. Second, competent authorities play a role in assessing equivalence. Article 4(1)(e) requires competent authorities to provide, in the first instance, an assessment of equivalence, i.e., they must state why they believe that a finding of equivalence is justified and provide the Commission with any relevant information. This approach, which puts the burden of assessing equivalence on the applicant, looks familiar. Recall that in relation to third country GAAP, CESR proposed that third country authorities should assess equivalence of third country GAAP first. But note that under Article 4(1)(e), it is the EU competent authority that is required to provide 'relevant information', as opposed to the authority of the third country in which the regulated market is situated.

V Third country prospectuses

So far, I have examined equivalence-based regulation in relation to third country GAAP and employment share schemes. In each case, we have seen that the European Commission plays a crucial role. When

[95] Art 4(1)(e). [96] *Ibid.*

examining equivalence-based regulation in relation to third country GAAP, I dwelled on the operation of the assessment process in order to identify the issues at stake, but also because of the contrast that it offers with the PD's arrangements under Article 20, the final equivalence provision which this chapter seeks to discuss and assess. For a directive whose motto was meant to be maximum harmonisation and which sought to level the playing field by imposing uniform rules and standards, Article 20 certainly strikes one as a peculiar provision. This has to do with its subject matter, third country prospectus disclosure, and the fact that, while maximum harmonisation is the rule for prospectus disclosure, the purpose of Article 20 is to allow third country issuers to rely on domestic disclosure requirements. But it has also to do with the fact that Article 20 enacts a complex interplay of EU and Member State competence. Indeed, Article 20 is different from the type of arrangements that we have examined so far. It does not single out the European Commission as exclusive equivalence assessor or decision-maker, but gives a greater say to national authorities which are empowered to approve, under certain conditions, a prospectus prepared according to third country legislation. Prior approval is thus the answer of the European legislature to preserving decision-making powers for Member State authorities in this field (A). To be sure, this discretion is not open-ended. It is circumscribed by the wording of Article 20(1) and by Article 20(3) which grants the European Commission the power to lay down criteria for assessing equivalence and to take equivalence decisions (B). But the Commission has not yet made use of its powers. Member States, meanwhile, have implemented Article 20 in fairly different ways (C). Ultimately, the question arises whether it is time to reform Article 20 (D).

A Prior approval as a means to recognise equivalence

Nature and effects Article 20(1) empowers the home competent authority of a third country issuer – i.e., an issuer whose registered office is located in a third country – to approve a prospectus which was prepared according to third country legislation. By approving a third country prospectus, the home competent authority recognises that the third country disclosure requirements are equivalent to the common European requirements. Once approved, a third country issuer can rely on domestic documentation for the purposes of an admission of securities to trading on a regulated market or a public offer in the EU. Prior approval is hence the means through which a decision on equivalence is put into effect.

For the avoidance of doubt, the home competent authority which is empowered to approve prospectuses under Article 20 is the authority of the EU Member State which the PD designates as the 'home Member State' of the third country issuer.[97] Like the directive as a whole, Article 20 is based on the home state principle which overwhelmingly locates regulatory and enforcement competence with the issuer's home Member State, as opposed to other Member States which are treated as 'host Member States' under the directive. Crucially, however, Article 20(1) only creates an optional arrangement. It enables, but does not require, the home state authority to approve a third country prospectus. If it decides not to exercise its powers under Article 20(1), third country issuers will be subject to the PR disclosure requirements that are also applicable to EU issuers.[98] But if the home state authority wishes to exercise its powers, the directive requires two conditions be met. First, the prospectus prepared according to third country legislation must satisfy international standards 'set by international securities commission organisations, including the IOSCO disclosure standards'.[99] Second, the third country disclosure requirements – financial and non-financial – must be considered equivalent to those of the directive and, although not specified explicitly, the Level 2 PR which gives flesh to the requirements of the PD.[100] The requirement of equivalence is thus *sensu stricto* only one part of a two-pronged test. Yet, it is likely to emerge as the core test. Unfortunately, the directive leaves some crucial questions unanswered.

[97] As opposed to the state of the place where the third country issuer's registered office is located. The directive lays down the rules that allow defining the home Member State of a third country issuer. Like EU issuers, third country issuers can benefit from a choice of competent authority for non-equity securities with a denomination of at least EUR 1,000 and for certain assimilated instruments (e.g., exchangeables). See for details, Chapter 3, section IV. For equity securities and any other type of securities that does not fall under the choice-of-competent-authority regime, Article 2(1)(m)(iii) lays down separate rules. Indeed, absent a registered office in the EU, the directive provides that the third country issuer (or offeror or person asking for admission to trading) must elect a home Member State. This state may either be the Member State in which securities are meant to be offered to the public for the first time following the entry into force of the PD, or the Member State in which 'the first application for admission to trading on a regulated market is made'. If the third country issuer did not make this choice on its own, the directive allows it to make a subsequent election.

[98] But recall that separate equivalence arrangements are applicable to historical financial information. See section III, above on third country GAAP. A third country issuer may still benefit from these arrangements even if the home state authority does not exercise its powers under PD Art 20(1).

[99] PD Art 20(1)(a). [100] PD Art 20(1)(b).

It is apparent that there is no definition of 'equivalence' in the PD or in its implementing legislation. Unresolved questions also concern the manner in which equivalence should be measured or the scope of the assessment be determined (e.g., whether equivalence presupposes that so-called 'filters' are in place). There is also a question mark over whether Member State authorities should be allowed to make recognition of a third country prospectus subject to additional conditions not provided for under the PD (e.g., by requiring additional information disclosure), thereby giving effect to a form of 'conditional equivalence' which, in this form, is not envisaged by the directive, but not explicitly prohibited either. Resolving these questions is especially important because of the effects of prior approval: once a third country prospectus has been approved, prior approval will produce the same effects as approval of an EU prospectus. That is to say, the third country prospectus can be published and be used for a public offer or an admission to trading on a regulated market in the issuer's designated home Member State. But the prospectus will also benefit from the same cross-border access rights as EU prospectuses, provided that the PD's language requirements are complied with and that the host Member State authority and ESMA are duly notified in accordance with the ordinary procedure set out in the directive.[101] Thus, a third country issuer wishing to make a public offer or seek admission to trading on a regulated market can 'passport' its third country prospectus to any other Member State under the same conditions as EU issuers and without having to draw up new prospectus documentation in accordance with the disclosure schedules of the Level 2 PR. Pursuant to the terms of the directive, the host state authority will not be allowed to carry out any approval or administrative procedures of its own.[102] As with EU prospectuses, the host state authority will be left with little discretion to question the validity of the third country prospectus. Indeed, given that the PD's passport provisions are fully applicable and in the absence of any provision stating otherwise, that must be so even if the host state authority would not approve third country prospectuses under Article 20(1) *when acting itself as the home state authority of a third country issuer.* A finding of equivalence by the home state authority will therefore produce substantial benefits for third country issuers and, because of the passport rights, be of direct interest to all competent authorities.

[101] PD Art 20(2), referring to Arts 17, 18 and 19.

[102] PD Art 17(1).

B Limits to prior approval

I assess next the limits to the scope of the powers of home state authorities. Article 20(1) is examined first, after which I will focus on the relationship between the powers of competent authorities and those of the Commission.

Endogeneous limits It is useful to begin by briefly considering the ordinary purpose of prior approval under the PD. Prior approval is an individual decision that concerns a single prospectus. For better or worse, it performs mainly an enforcement function under the Directive.[103] That is to say, prior approval is meant to be a means for a competent authority to check whether a prospectus is complete and its information is consistent and comprehensible before it is published.[104] The completeness, consistency and comprehensibility of the disclosure can be described as different disclosure *quality* characteristics.[105] They concern the substance of the prospectus, the disclosure that is therein contained. Under Article 20(1), however, approval is not primarily conceived as an enforcement instrument. It performs a different or, at least, an additional function. It is a means for a national authority to recognise a prospectus that was prepared according to third country disclosure legislation. Whilst the latter decision also entails a quality assessment, it is an assessment of the quality of third country disclosure *rules/standards* – about whether they measure up to international and EU disclosure rules/standards – rather than a decision about the quality of the disclosure contained in the prospectus. Under Article 20(1), approval therefore primarily means that an authority is satisfied with the third country disclosure requirements themselves. For the avoidance of doubt, a third country prospectus will also be subject to an ordinary review of its content prior to its approval and subsequent publication.[106] Moreover, given that the prospectus approval system is a means to exercise individual decision-making power as opposed to

[103] Undoubtedly, competent authorities face important limitations when carrying out their approval tasks. For details, see P. Schammo, 'The prospectus approval system' (2006) 7 *European Business Organization Law Review* 501.

[104] PD Arts 2(1)(q) and 13(1).

[105] For a more detailed discussion, see Chapter 6, section III, B. See also, Schammo, 'The prospectus approval system'.

[106] In accordance with Art 2(1)(q) which defines the meaning of approval, read together with Art 13(1) which provides that the home state authority must approve a prospectus before its publication.

general decision-making power, approval will still be a decision that is specific to a single prospectus. It will give effect to, *inter alia*, a finding of equivalence,[107] but which is limited to a specific prospectus. Thus, the home competent authority will be required to decide on equivalence on an individual, case-by-case, basis.[108] By implication, this suggests that competent authorities do not have the power to rule in abstract or general terms on whether third country legislation is equivalent to relevant EU legislation.[109] This reading is faithful to the wording of Article 20(1) which states that the home state authority 'may approve a prospectus … drawn up in accordance with the legislation of a third country', as opposed to, say, a home state authority may recognise the legislation or standards of a third country. To be sure, as with all things European, there are complications, for the powers left to competent authorities also depend on whether Article 20 states the division of powers between competent authorities (Member States) and the Commission (under Article 20(3)) exhaustively. But, arguably, by laying down the powers of both the home competent authority and the Commission and by specifying their distinct scope, Article 20 does precisely that. The implication is, however, that the distribution of competence between Member States and the EU is not symmetrical.

Exogenous limits Whatever the precise scope of Article 20(1), the power of the home state authority to recognise third country prospectuses will be affected by the Commission's powers under Article 20(3). These powers are two-fold. Article 20(3) first creates EU competence by empowering the Commission to adopt measures 'to establish general equivalence criteria' by way of delegated acts. These equivalence criteria are meant to

[107] For the sake of completeness, recall that the home authority will also have to come to a conclusion about whether the prospectus has been prepared according to international standards.

[108] In this sense, see also FSA, 'The listing review and implementation of the Prospectus Directive – draft rules and feedback on CP203' (Consultation Paper 04/16***, October 2004) 18 with a suggestion to transpose Article 20(1) 'by determining whether a prospectus meets those criteria on a case-by-case basis and judge each application on its merits'; FSA, 'Implementation of the Prospectus Directive' (Policy Statement 05/7, June 2005) 8 (noting that the PD 'does not give us the power to determine that the law of a third country ensures the equivalence of prospectuses'). See also CESR, 'Summary of the answers to the questionnaire on factual information on the legislation and practices of Member States regarding the treatment of third country issuers with respect to the drawing up and approval of prospectuses (Article 20 of the Prospectus Directive)' (CESR/03-496, December 2003) para. 2, referring to Art 20(1) as dealing with 'ad hoc, one-off cases'.

[109] In this sense, see also FSA, 'Implementation of the Prospectus Directive' 8.

guide the assessment of equivalence and must comply with Articles 5 and 7 of the directive.[110] The former provision provides, *inter alia*, in broad and general terms, for the prospectus to include all necessary information for investors to make 'an informed assessment'. The latter lays down the framework principles upon which the Level 2 PR is based and provides, *inter alia*, for the Level 2 information items to be based on international standards.[111] The adoption of equivalence criteria under Article 20(3) will therefore be informed by the same framework principles which guided the adoption of information items under the Level 2 PR. The second power under Article 20(3) concerns recognition of equivalence. According to the directive, the Commission has the power, on the basis of the equivalence criteria which it has adopted, to take measures 'stating that a third country ensures the equivalence of prospectuses drawn up in that country with this directive by reason of its national law or of practices or procedures based on international standards set by international organisations, including the IOSCO disclosure standards'.[112] The directive thus essentially empowers the Commission to decide on whether the rules of a third country are deemed to be equivalent. This power is unlike that of national authorities. It is general in nature, in the sense that the Commission can, in effect, recognise the rules of a specific third country as being equivalent. It is part of a multi-stage procedure under which the Commission is delegated competence to lay down general equivalence criteria and empowered to decide, in relation to a given third country, on the recognition of equivalence. Were the Commission to exercise these powers, the principle of supremacy would come into play and the powers reserved to home competent authorities would necessarily be affected. But the Commission has yet to exercise its powers. The issue was raised in May 2008 at the level of the European Securities Committee, the Lamfalussy Level 2 comitology committee.[113] The Commission's decision to refrain from taking action appears to have been a conscious decision.[114] However, that is not the end of the matter, for the European Commission has made use of its powers to adopt equivalence decisions in relation to third country GAAP. Although these measures were not adopted on the basis of Article 20(3), they should nevertheless, as a consequence, pre-empt

[110] PD Art 20(3), para. 1. [111] PD Art 7(3). [112] PD Art 20(3), para. 2.

[113] ESC, 'Draft summary record of the 59th Meeting of the European Securities Committee (alternates)' (21 May 2008) 5–7, http://ec.europa.eu/internal_market/securities/esc/index_en.htm.

[114] *Ibid.*

competent authorities from departing, on the basis of Article 20(1), from the Commission's decisions.[115] Member State authorities should therefore have lost their discretion to assess unilaterally whether financial disclosure requirements of third countries are equivalent, notwithstanding the text of Article 20(1).[116]

C *Equivalence-based regulation in Member States*

It was shown above that Article 20 envisages two paths for assessing equivalence: first, recognition of third country prospectuses by way of approval under Article 20(1) and second, recognition of equivalence as a result of the adoption of implementing measures under Article 20(3). The division of competence between Member States and the EU was also highlighted. National authorities have the power to approve a third country prospectus and the Commission has the power to lay down common equivalence criteria and to decide, in relation to a given third country, on the recognition of equivalence. The purpose of the present section is to discuss the implementation and application of Article 20 at national level. This is by no means an easy task. Little information is available on the actual application or use of Article 20 (as transposed) by competent authorities. If we dig deeper, it is also apparent that, in fact, we know little about, *inter alia*, any methods of assessment used by competent authorities and how generally they see the scope of their powers. But the fact is that Member States have implemented Article 20 differently. The UK Prospectus Rules, for example, are faithful to Article 20 and state that the FSA may approve a prospectus of a third country issuer if the UK is the designated home Member State.[117] In France, the

[115] The adoption of implementing measures by the Commission would be rendered meaningless if authorities were not fully pre-empted from departing from the Commission's decisions on third country GAAP. Note that the exercise by the Commission of its power to decide on whether third country GAAP is equivalent has resulted in the Level 2 PR being amended (Art 35(5) and (5a) PR). See also the specific disclosure items annexed to the PR (e.g., Annex I Item 20.1., Annex IV Item 13.1). According to the provisions of the PR, the home state authority cannot generally ask for disclosure items, which are not found in the regulation, to be included in a prospectus (Arts 3, second para., and 22(1), second sub-para.). Allowing competent authorities to depart from the requirements that apply with respect to accounting standards would effectively undermine the goals of these provisions.

[116] Cf., CESR, 'CESR work to date in relation to the European Commission's measures on the use of third countries' GAAP in the EU' (CESR/07-022b, April 2007) 4 (adopting a somewhat different line of reasoning, but effectively coming to the same conclusion).

[117] UK FSA Prospectus Rules, PR [4.2].

AMF's *Règlement Général* – the French equivalent of the FSA's handbook – states, in broad and general terms, that third country issuers 'may draw up a prospectus meeting the standards of the International Organisation of Securities Commissions and containing information equivalent to that required under [the relevant legislation]'.[118] More generally, equivalence-based regulation is being used in somewhat different ways in Member States. Euronext regulators, such as the AMF or the Dutch AFM, have, for example, sought to facilitate cross-listings of third country issuers on Euronext markets in Paris and Amsterdam by accepting for the purposes of their approval procedures certain SEC filings from SEC registered issuers that are listed, or will shortly be listed, on NYSE.[119] These decisions must be seen in the light of the merger between NYSE and Euronext in April 2007 and the subsequent efforts of NYSE Euronext to develop its listing activities on a global basis and to compete with the London Stock Exchange as an international venue.[120] The precise substance, scope and operation of this procedure are not entirely clear given a dearth of publicly available information.[121] Moreover, there is also a question mark over whether the AMF draws authority from Article 20, as implemented into national law, in order to recognise SEC filings. There is better evidence of the legal basis – Article 20, as transposed – in the case of the Dutch arrangements.[122]

118 AMF *Règlement Général*, Art 212-36.

119 See NYSE Euronext, 'Fast path listing using SEC filings' (International Listing Guide 2008) 13, www.euronext.com/fic/000/033/111/331110.pdf; AMF, 'Décision de l'AMF en matière de reconnaissance des standards américains pour une admission à la négociation sur un marché réglementé' (Communiqué de presse, 1 Octobre 2007), www.amf-france.org/documents/general/7940_1.pdf. *A priori*, fast-path listing holds out two benefits for third country issuers. First, it promises cost savings because certain documents drawn up in accordance with US securities legislation will be accepted by Euronext regulators. The second potential benefit are time savings. While all SEC registered documents remain subject to prior approval, the approval procedure should nevertheless be lighter for documents that have been subject to prior review by the SEC (see NYSE Euronext, 'Fast path listing using SEC filings', 13 noting that '... under the regime, the European regulatory prospectus review period has been reduced to an absolute minimum').

120 J. Grant, 'NYSE set to challenge LSE in Europe' (FT online, 14 April 2008).

121 Note that 'fast path' issuers are not allowed to make a public offer in the EU (NYSE Euronext, 'Fast path listing using SEC filings' 5). The procedure is currently only available for technical listings or a listing which follows a private placement (see *ibid*., 5). Issuers that seek to cross-list on Euronext Paris can only do so on a 'professional segment'. In Amsterdam, they will be listed on 'the main board' (*ibid*., 13).

122 See J. Hoevers and D. Busch, 'Dutch securities regulator AFM grants non-EU SEC registered companies fast track access to European equity capital markets' (2007) 22 *Journal of International Banking Law and Regulation* 621, 621 (noting that '[t]he legal basis for the fast track regime may be found in Art.5:9(2) of the Dutch Financial Supervision Act

In January 2008, the French AMF adopted another noteworthy arrangement which required the signing of a Memorandum of Understanding ('MOU') with the Securities Authority of Israel ('ISA').[123] Like its decision to accept SEC filings, the AMF's decision to enter into a MOU with ISA is a response to the merger and the efforts of NYSE Euronext to develop its international activities.[124] But the MOU is particular, for it puts in place a mutual recognition system between the AMF and the securities authority of a third country. What is more, the MOU declares explicitly that it is intended 'to comply with the letter and spirit of Article 20 of the Prospectus Directive'.[125]

The MOU seeks to facilitate cross-listings of equity securities (excluding convertible securities).[126] The procedure which it lays down is meant to benefit French and Israeli issuers that are admitted to trading, or are seeking admission to trading, in their home jurisdiction[127] and that following a first approval by their home state authority, would like to cross-list securities abroad – i.e., on a French regulated market for Israeli issuers and the Tel Aviv stock exchange for French issuers.[128] For this purpose, the MOU records the AMF's and ISA's decision to consider prospectus regulation in each other's jurisdiction as being equivalent.[129] Equivalence is, however, not perfect.[130] Under the terms of the MOU, Israeli issuers must provide a number of additional disclosures in order to be able to cross-list on a French regulated market.[131] Given that national authorities are no longer competent to decide unilaterally on the equivalence of third country GAAP, the MOU also requires Israeli issuers to provide historical financial information that complies with the relevant PR disclosure

… Article 5:9(2) [of the Dutch Financial Supervision Act] is based on Art.20(1) of the Prospectus Directive').

123 'Memorandum of Understanding between the Autorité des marchés financiers and the Israel Securities Authority concerning the regulatory equivalence with regards to the cross-listing of securities' (28 January 2008), www.amf-france.org/documents/general/8145_1.pdf.

124 AMF, 'Financial regulation newsletter' (Issue No. 8, 4th Quarter 2007) 2, www.amf-france.org/documents/general/7992_1.pdf.

125 MOU preamble.

126 *Ibid.* and para. 3.1.

127 That is on a regulated market in France in the case of a French issuer and on the Tel Aviv Stock Exchange in the case of an Israeli issuer (see para. 2.1.3).

128 MOU, para. 2.1.

129 MOU, paras 1.1 and 1.2.

130 *Ibid.*

131 MOU, paras 4.3.1, 4.3.2 and 4.3.3. Additional requirements may be set by amending the MOU (para. 4.3, *in fine*).

item.[132] There are currently, under the MOU, no additional requirements to be met by French issuers seeking to cross-list on the Tel Aviv exchange, but the MOU states that such requirements may be specified by amending the MOU.[133] The MOU then goes on to lay down a procedure for cross listing.[134] It states that issuers that intend to cross-list simultaneously must first get their prospectus approved by their home authority.[135] For issuers that are already admitted to trading at home, prospectuses must be submitted to the home authority together with all information which was published subsequently about the issuer and the securities for which admission to trading is being sought abroad.[136] In each case, the home authority will, upon the request of the issuer, issue a 'Home Notice',[137] after making sure that any additional disclosure requirements have been met.[138] Upon receipt of the home notice, the host state authority 'will automatically accept the filing of the Prospectus for the purpose of its national approval procedure'.[139] In other words, the MOU does not exempt issuers from submitting their prospectus for approval to the host authority. Prospectuses remain subject to approval in the host state.[140] But the review and approval procedure for issuers should be lighter as a result of the recognition of equivalence and the preliminary review of the prospectus by the home authority.

The MOU's arrangements are also meant to apply in the context of an admission of securities to trading on a regulated market which follows an offer to qualified investors or is made in connection with a public offer.[141] The MOU adds some safeguards here. Additional requirements (e.g., language requirements) may be applicable where a public offer is made in the host state.[142] Moreover, if an Israeli issuer wishes to take advantage of the PD's single passport in order to make a 'pan-European offer', the MOU reverts back to the PR and provides that in such a case an Israeli issuer must provide the AMF 'with the list of any information items that have not been provided in the Prospectus in compliance with [the PR's annexes]'.[143] In order to ensure the smooth operation of all these arrangements, the MOU also lays down provisions on cooperation between both

[132] MOU, para. 4.3.1. [133] MOU, para. 4.5.

[134] The precise procedure is set out in MOU para. 4.

[135] MOU, para. 4.1. [136] MOU, paras 4.2.1 and 4.2.2.

[137] MOU, paras 4.1 and 4.2.1. [138] MOU, paras 4.3 and 4.5.

[139] MOU, para. 4.7. Note however that language or other specific obligations may have to be met if a public offer is made in the host state.

[140] MOU, para. 4.6. [141] MOU preamble. [142] MOU, para. 4.7. [143] MOU, para. 4.11.

authorities.[144] It states that the AMF and ISA 'shall cooperate, render mutual assistance and exchange information with each other'.[145] Indeed, the MOU provides for the establishment of a 'standing joint committee' which is entrusted with ensuring coordination and communication between the authorities.[146] Finally, it is worth noting that the MOU is not intended to be legally binding or to replace domestic law, but the adoption of regulations may be required to implement it in France or Israel.[147] It thus also states that the AMF and ISA must inform each other when the implementation of the provisions of the MOU can commence.[148]

A number of observations regarding Article 20 and equivalence-based regulation are warranted by way of conclusion. It might first of all be worth repeating that we know little about the practical operation and use of Article 20. It is probably fair to say that it has not (yet) attracted widespread interest among third country issuers or, for that matter, competent authorities. Nevertheless, it is apparent that currently two actors are effectively shaping the Article 20 regime: Member States, including their competent authorities, which have implemented Article 20 into national law, but also the European Commission which has chosen not to exercise its powers under Article 20(3) and thereby to leave Member State actions uncoordinated. Member States, including their securities authorities, appear to have a different understanding of the scope of their powers under the directive. Recall, for example, the text of the provisions implementing Article 20 in France and the UK,[149] or compare the position of the FSA which has stressed that Article 20(1) 'does not give [it] the power to determine that the law of a third country ensures the equivalence of prospectuses'[150] with the provisions of the MOU which, having stated that it was 'intended to comply with the letter and spirit of Article 20', goes on to declare, albeit conditionally, that 'Israeli laws and regulations are equivalent to the parallel regulation administered by the AMF and satisfy the regulatory requirements of French law'.[151] Adding to this diversity is the fact that competent authorities make their decisions to recognise third country prospectuses subject to additional conditions or restrictions. It is also apparent that the arrangements which were examined here are

144 MOU preamble. 145 MOU, para. 6.1.

146 MOU, paras 6.2 and 6.3. 147 MOU, para. 7.1.

148 *Ibid.* The MOU adds that the authorities will need to subsequently agree between them a start date.

149 See above.

150 FSA, 'Implementation of the Prospectus Directive' 8.

151 MOU, para. 1.1.

examples of regulatory competition. While regulatory competition is no longer a generic phenomenon – too dense is the regulatory environment – there is still space for it. My final observation is of a general nature and regards the competence of Member States or, for that matter, competent authorities, to enter into agreements with third countries regarding the recognition of equivalence or mutual recognition with respect to matters covered by the PD. The exercise by a Member State of this power would have to square perfectly with the Court of Justice's case law and the new Lisbon provisions on external relations. The Court's decisions are especially complex, but it has repeatedly held in its pre-Lisbon case law that the Community can benefit from an implied power to conclude international agreements.[152] Crucially, the Court has held that if the Community determines in an internal act the treatment to be given to third country nationals or if it fully harmonises a particular field, it acquires *exclusive external* competence in the field covered by the European act.[153] These rulings gave flesh to the Court's AETR decision, its earlier seminal ruling, in which it held that once the Community had adopted common rules, Member States could not enter into obligations with third countries which affected the Community's (common) rules.[154] The Lisbon Treaty codified, more or less successfully, the Court's case law in this field.[155] As far as the PD is concerned, recall that securities of third country issuers, which are meant to be admitted to trading on a regulated market or offered to the public in a Member State, are within the scope of the directive. A finding of exclusivity would mean that a Member State or a competent authority would act in contravention to EU law if it were to enter into an international agreement regarding recognition of equivalence of third country prospectus disclosure requirements. That said, a finding of exclusivity is not obvious because of a number of complicating factors. First, the Commission has not yet exercised its own powers to decide on equivalence under Article

[152] Case 22/70 *Commission v Council* [1971] ECR 263, paras 15–16; Case C-476/98 *Commission v Germany* [2002] ECR I-9855, para. 103; *Opinion 1/03* [2006] ECR I-1145, para. 114. See also Girard, 'Les méthodes de suppression des frontières au plan mondial dans le domaine bancaire et financier' 370.

[153] Opinion *1/94* [1994] ECR I-05267, paras 95–96; C-476/98 *Commission v Germany*, paras 109–110; *Opinion 1/03*, para. 122.

[154] Case 22/70 *Commission v Council*, para. 17.

[155] See TFEU Art 216(1) with respect to the competence of the EU to enter into international agreements. On exclusivity, see TFEU Art 3(2) which draws on the Court's AETR judgment when stating that '[t]he Union shall also have exclusive competence for the conclusion of an international agreement ... insofar as its conclusion may affect common rules or alter their scope'.

20(3). The point is noteworthy because, according to the Court's reasoning in AETR, exclusivity presupposes that common rules are adopted.[156] In the absence of the adoption of 'Article 20(3) measures' by the Commission, the conclusion should therefore be that Member States are not pre-empted from entering into agreements with third countries.[157] But this finding has unattractive consequences. The fact is that the PD's provisions apply to third country securities which are to be admitted to trading on a regulated market or offered to the public. This is regardless of the exercise by the Commission of its powers under Article 20(3). Thus, even in the absence of 'Article 20(3) measures', equivalence agreements with a third country on prospectus disclosure affect the PD's rules in the sense that each time a Member State enters into such an arrangement with a third country, third country issuers, that fall under the jurisdiction of this Member State, will effectively no longer be required to comply with the PD's 'ordinary' maximum harmonisation disclosure requirements which would be applicable in the absence of a decision on equivalence. The uniform application of the directive will be undermined given that third country issuers with a different home Member State will continue being subject to the PD's ordinary disclosure requirements. What is more, recall that, pursuant to Article 20(2), a third country issuer will benefit from the PD's passport system. Admittedly, there are other complicating factors. Recall that the directive creates explicitly Member State competence by granting national authorities the power to approve a third country prospectus. But earlier, it was suggested that these powers were rather more limited.[158] Other grounds, such as the duty of cooperation, which in the field of external relations has been shaped by the Court of Justice, would also be worthy of consideration.[159] Ultimately, it is for the European Court to provide clarification on the scope of competence of Member States and the EU. While no action has been initiated,[160] it is apparent, as it will be shown next, that the current state of affairs has not gone unnoticed by regulators and Member States.

[156] Case 22/70 *Commission v Council*, paras 17–18. See also now Art 3(2) TFEU.

[157] See, in this sense, on implied exclusive competence in the securities field, Girard, 'Les méthodes de suppression des frontières au plan mondial dans le domaine bancaire et financier' 370–1.

[158] What is more, the PD does not entrust Member States with powers to enter into negotiations with third countries.

[159] I am indebted to Panos Koutrakos for this comment.

[160] I have not sought to assess the validity of the MOU. Additional problems would have to be considered such as, for example, the fact that the MOU is not legally binding. See MOU, para. 7.1. Note that the European Commission does not appear to consider that

D *The merits of Article 20 PD: a shadow regime in need of reform?*

I examine next whether Article 20 ought to be reformed. I start by identifying actual or potential issues, after which I consider solutions.

1 Pathology

From the point of view of third country issuers, the main rationale for taking advantage of equivalence-based regulation lies in the fact that it promises to reduce compliance costs with EU legislation, to avoid over-regulation and facilitate access to markets or investors in the EU.[161] But from the point of view of the EU, the use of equivalence provisions by Member States raises distinct questions and problems. Three types of problems are identified hereinafter: maintaining mutual trust among national authorities; ensuring transparency; and safeguarding a common EU position vis-à-vis third countries. The next section will examine how these concerns are being, or should be, addressed and will, by the same token, map out alternative solutions.

a Mutual trust and the functioning of the internal market It has been shown that the application of Article 20 by competent authorities is currently left uncoordinated. Competent authorities are free to adopt distinct positions albeit within the limits set by Article 20(1). From a European policy perspective, this is potentially a source of concern in terms of ensuring a uniform application of the directive, but also, more generally, in terms of ensuring mutual trust between competent authorities. This is all the more so as approval of third country prospectuses under Article 20(1) produces effects beyond the domestic market of the home state authority. Once approved, a third country prospectus can be 'passported' in any Member State. A third country issuer will benefit from the same market access rights as EU issuers. The implementation of Article 20(1) by one Member State authority is therefore of direct interest to all other authorities. That is also to say that the implementation of Article 20 may, potentially, turn into a source of tension between home and host authorities and potentially affect the practical operation of the passport system. Concerns have already been voiced. Following the adoption of the

the MOU falls foul of EU law provisions (see ESC, 'Draft summary record of the 59th meeting' 5).

161 The benefits and costs of equivalence-based regulation are examined in Wei, 'The equivalence approach to securities regulation' 282–298.

fast-path procedure by Euronext regulators and the signing of the MOU with ISA, concerns were raised in the European Securities Committee.[162] Among comments about transparency and the need to prevent fragmentation, the risk that host state authorities would simply refuse recognition in response to the unilateral actions of home state authorities was highlighted.[163] Admittedly, this concern might be exaggerated, as host state authorities are given few powers to oppose the 'passporting' of prospectuses into their jurisdiction.[164] But in more practical terms, the point is nevertheless worth noting. Market integration is an ongoing process. Mutual trust feeds positively into the rule-making process at EU level and the enforcement process at national level. In any event, if competent authorities lack trust, they may not be deterred from refusing recognition in practice, notwithstanding their legal position under the terms of the directive.

b Transparency and legal certainty Another reason for being concerned about the application of equivalence provisions concerns the lack of transparency that surrounds them.[165] The transparency issues which are recorded here are really only specific manifestations of the general lack of information that surrounds the application of Article 20(1). There is no definition of equivalence which applies to Article 20 and, notwithstanding the two conditions of Article 20(1), the precise manner in which national authorities are required to assess equivalence before deciding to approve third country prospectus documents remains unclear.[166] The full range of legal and extra-legal considerations that is likely to influence the evaluation of third country legislation is therefore also unclear.

For equivalence-based regulation to work effectively, transparency is arguably especially important. This is because, unlike ordinary forms of regulation, equivalence-based regulation involves a comparison of different rules or standards, a process which is complex and may require making approximate judgments. The lack of transparency which characterises

[162] ESC, 'Draft summary record of the 59th meeting' 5–7.

[163] *Ibid.*, 5.

[164] They have limited powers under PD Art 23(2).

[165] Cf., Wei, 'The equivalence approach to securities regulation' 292–3 (asking questions about the transparency of equivalence decisions that are taken in the field of auditing and the regulation of financial conglomerates).

[166] The MOU that the French authority signed with ISA did little to improve transparency, as it does not disclose any details on how equivalence was assessed or how it was defined.

the assessment process is also in marked contrast with the transparency requirements that apply to decision-making at Level 2 or indeed at Level 1 of the Lamfalussy process. Arguably, it also makes decisions a source of legal uncertainty for third country issuers. These problems are worsened by the very fact that Article 20(1) ties the assessment of equivalence to the approval process. During the consultation phase preceding the implementation of the PD in the UK, the FSA acknowledged the problem of certainty. But it noted that it would essentially resolve itself after a number of third country prospectuses had been approved since 'sufficient precedent would have been set to provide issuers with a degree of certainty on which third country prospectuses are broadly judged to be equivalent'.[167] That may be so, but this approach is hardly satisfactory. A more standardised approach would appear to provide a better solution if considered in this light. But, as noted, such an approach would need to square with the scope of the powers of competent authorities under the directive. Moreover, the fact that competent authorities do not seem to have the same understanding of the type of actions allowed for by Article 20(1), does not promote legal certainty either.

c Safeguarding the EU's 'unity of action' Equivalence-based regulation is also potentially a source of tension between Member States (competent authorities) and the EU (especially, the European Commission). When approaching this point, it is important to bear in mind that recognition of equivalence might be preceded by bilateral or multilateral negotiations with third countries with a view to securing equal advantages for all actors concerned.[168] It should be clear by now that this type of negotiation raises questions of competence in the EU context which had, prior to the entry into force of the Lisbon Treaty, by and large to be resolved on the basis of the Court's case law. As noted, the European Court ruled that the Community could benefit from implied powers to conclude international agreements. Indeed, the Court admitted, under generous conditions, that the Community could benefit from exclusive competence in external matters. These rulings ultimately inspired the provisions on exclusive external competence of the Lisbon Treaty. While drastic in terms of its consequences for Member States, exclusivity can be justified on the

[167] FSA, 'Implementation of the Prospectus Directive' 8.

[168] Cf., Girard, 'Les méthodes de suppression des frontières au plan mondial dans le domaine bancaire et financier' 363.

grounds that it is necessary, as AG Tizzano put it, in order to 'prevent, for the sake of "the defence of the common interests of the Community", the Community's unity of action being compromised by potential divergences between the internal measures and those subsequently adopted externally'.[169] The actions which Member States take on the basis of Article 20 therefore also directly interest the Commission seeking to preserve the interests of the EU – the EU's 'unity of action' as Tizzano put it – as well as its very own institutional interests to see its competence safeguarded or extended. Any type of external action which does not square with the division of competences under Article 20 is thus likely to be a source of friction which pitches Member States and their competent authorities against the European Commission. Admittedly, there is a question mark over whether these are actual or potential tensions. So far, the Commission seems to be quite content with the actions undertaken by Member State authorities, although it has previously expressed concerns over the practices of the French authority and other Euronext regulators.[170]

2 Remedies

Among the problems identified in the previous section, it is the lack of transparency that strikes one as the most pressing concern. The potential problems caused by horizontal or vertical frictions between actors are probably best seen as second-order concerns. This is all the more so as it is difficult to assess their true importance. Moreover, it is not clear whether Article 20 (as transposed) has so far attracted much interest among third country issuers. But, in any event, transparency is also a key ingredient for fostering mutual trust. With that in mind, I examine next alternative solutions – whether or not currently available – to the application of Article 20. I begin by outlining strategies, after which I consider those actors that are, or could be, entrusted with their implementation.

a Strategies In attempting to improve the functioning of the Article 20 shadow regime, three possible strategies can be envisaged: (i) improving transparency; (ii) ensuring process uniformity; or (iii) ensuring substantive uniformity. The aim of the first strategy, improving transparency, is fairly obvious. By requiring greater transparency, one lifts the veil on the application of Article 20(1) and brings light to bear on practices,

[169] Opinion of AG Tizzano in Case C-466/98 *Commission v United Kingdom* [2002] ECR I-09427, para. 64.

[170] ESC, 'Draft summary record of the 59th meeting' 5.

assessment methods and considerations that enter the judgments of equivalence assessors. The meanings of process uniformity and substantive uniformity require some explaining. Process uniformity requires equivalence assessments to be conducted in the same manner, according to the same method and criteria. Currently, process uniformity is limited because the meaning of equivalence is unclear, because equivalence can be measured in different ways, and because there is uncertainty about the precise elements that should factor into an equivalence assessment. Substantive uniformity, as applied in the context of equivalence-based regulation, takes this logic a step further by requiring that a single position be adopted on the recognition of equivalence across all Member States. Thus, to ensure strict substantive uniformity requires equivalence assessments to be conducted, and decisions be taken, by a single equivalence assessor. But it does not require third country disclosure rules to be identical to EU disclosure rules. Indeed, equivalence-based regulation, as it is understood here, rejects this type of uniformity for the reason that the difference between equivalence-based regulation and (maximum) harmonisation is precisely that standards or rules do not need to be identical under the former regime for issuers to gain access to EU investors or EU markets. Substantive uniformity, in other words, concerns the *decisions* on the recognition of equivalence, rather than the disclosure rules that are the subject matter of these decisions. Allowing for variation among different sets of disclosure rules is thus entirely in the spirit of equivalence-based regulation. Having clarified the meaning of each of these strategies, I turn next to the actors that are involved in equivalence assessments and, on this basis, seek to identify the most appropriate strategy.

b Actors Three actors have been, or could potentially be, involved in equivalence assessments: the Commission, CESR and its successor ESMA, and competent authorities.

The Commission The PD's response to ensuring process and substantive uniformity is the exercise by the Commission of its powers under Article 20(3). Recall that Article 20(3) lays down two types of powers: (i) the power to decide on general equivalence criteria; and (ii) the power to, essentially, recognise third country rules as being equivalent. I consider these solutions in turn.

Defining general equivalence criteria is the PD's first line of response to ensuring process uniformity. In its pre-Lisbon wording, Article 20(3), sub-paragraph 1 required the Commission to 'adopt implementing measures' in order to 'ensure the uniform application of the Directive'. Following the 2010 revisions to the PD, the directive now provides for the Commission to lay down equivalence criteria by way of delegated acts. If the Commission were to exercise its delegated powers, the assessment of equivalence would still be carried out by multiple equivalence assessors (i.e., the relevant home state authority of each third country issuer). In addition, the home state authority would continue carrying out its ordinary prospectus review and approval tasks. But each home state authority would be required to decide on equivalence in accordance with the Commission's criteria. Before the directive was amended in 2010, this reading found support in the language of Article 20(3) which provided for the adoption of implementing measures in order 'to ensure the uniform application of the Directive'. Although the text of the directive no longer refers explicitly to this goal, it does not necessarily follow that the purpose of Article 20(3), sub-paragraph 1 has changed.[171] Indeed, the very fact that Article 20(3), sub-paragraph 1 makes provision for the adoption of delegated acts supports this reading as the adoption of delegated measures would be rendered meaningless if national authorities were not pre-empted from defining unilaterally separate criteria.

The adoption by the Commission of general equivalence criteria could improve transparency by clarifying the meaning of equivalence as well as the scope and content of the assessment. Admittedly, under Article 20(1), recognition by a home state authority of a third country prospectus is subject to two separate requirements which are that the third country prospectus is drawn up according to international standards and that the information requirements are equivalent to EU requirements. But compliance with the Commission's measures would be an unlikely source of conflict. This is because the adoption of implementing measures must be

[171] If the reference to ensuring a 'uniform application' of the directive had been left unchanged in the text of Article 20(3), sub-para. 1, it might have created confusion for two reasons. First, the wording would not have squared easily with the new provisions on binding technical standards. Thus, when authorising ESMA to prepare technical standards, the EU legislature often refers to the need to ensure uniform conditions of application of a directive (see e.g., PD Arts 5(2), 13(5), 18(4), etc.). Second, it could, possibly, also have created confusion with Art 291(2) of the TFEU. According to this article, the EU legislature must grant the Commission implementing powers (instead of delegated powers) if 'uniform conditions for implementing legally binding Union acts are needed'. Hence, my point is that the choice of wording in Art 20(3) was not neutral as regards the procedures for taking subordinate measures. This arguably explains why the legislature deleted the reference to ensuring a 'uniform application' of the directive. Recall that sub-para. 1 makes provision for measures to be adopted by way of delegated acts.

based on Articles 5 and 7 of the directive. Article 7 provides, *inter alia*, for EU disclosure standards to comply with international standards.

The exercise by the Commission of its powers to decide, pursuant to Article 20(3), sub-paragraph 2, that a 'third country ensures the equivalence of prospectuses', would further clarify the interplay between EU competence and Member State competence. The Commission would exhaustively occupy the decision-making field with respect to the recognition of equivalence. Besides clarifying the limits of the powers of competent authorities and ensuring uniformity in the application of the directive, the adoption by the Commission of equivalence decisions would also clarify and strengthen the case for exclusivity in external relations, thereby safeguarding the EU's common negotiation position. For the avoidance of doubt, the power of the home state authority to approve or to refuse approval of a third country prospectus on the grounds that the quality of the information is deficient (e.g., because there is a lack of consistency in the information provided) would be fully unaffected. This is because the exercise of this power is part of the enforcement prerogatives of national authorities.

Hence, the exercise by the Commission of its powers would lead to either process or substantive uniformity. There are reasons, however, for reserving the exercise of these powers. Indeed, the choice in favour of transparency, process uniformity or substantive uniformity, as different types of strategies for dealing with equivalence-based regulation, should first and foremost be a function of the severity of the issues that Article 20 raises. The more severe the policy issues, the greater the case for substantive uniformity. It was noted earlier that save for the lack of transparency which strikes one as a paramount concern, it is difficult to assess in the abstract whether Article 20 is currently causing actual meaningful tensions or is undermining mutual trust. Given this state of affairs, some caution may be warranted when contemplating action. Moreover, it must be remembered that from the point of view of the EU, recognition of equivalence of third country legislation is not only a means for facilitating access to EU markets or investors, but also likely to be a means of negotiation with third countries to secure equal advantages for EU actors in third country markets. Unless third countries enter into negotiations with the EU, for instance over the adoption of a mutual recognition agreement, the Commission is unlikely to make use of its powers.[172] Viewed in this light,

[172] Girard makes a similar point when noting that in the field of securities regulation work on mutual recognition 'is also made more complex by the fact that a partner willing to

the exercise by the Commission of its powers under Article 20(3), sub-paragraph 2 is arguably not only premature as a normative matter, but in positive terms also improbable until third countries are prepared to enter into negotiations with the EU. Note in this context that the wording used in the directive in relation to the adoption of equivalence decisions under Article 20(3), sub-paragraph 2 is enabling rather than mandatory (i.e., the Commission '*may* adopt implementing measures' (emphasis added)).

CESR/ESMA The next candidate for addressing actual or potential concerns with Article 20 is ESMA. But since we have as yet no experience with ESMA, I will first focus on CESR, given that we can learn from its experience when assessing the role of ESMA. If we ignore for a moment the realities of decision-making at Level 3 before the establishment of the European System of Financial Supervision and if we also leave aside for a moment the question of whether there is a case for strict process uniformity or substantive uniformity, CESR would *a priori* have been a good candidate for coordinating the actions of competent authorities. CESR could have improved transparency. If a need for additional measures was felt, it could also have contributed to addressing process and substantive uniformity. For example, one could have imagined CESR providing national authorities with an assessment of equivalence. Uniformity would have been improved by designating CESR as single equivalence assessor (unless, and until, the Commission decided to exercise its powers under Article 20(3)). National authorities would no longer have to bear the cost of unilateral assessments. Any possible lack of expertise among competent authorities would also have been redressed. Recall that CESR was in charge, in an advisory capacity, of much of the work on equivalence of third country GAAP. But to cut the story short, if we do take account of the realities of Level 3 decision-making prior to the establishment of the European System of Financial Supervision, it is apparent that CESR would not have been able to ensure process or substantive uniformity. The most obvious reason is that CESR had no legal powers to impose uniformity, or for that matter, greater transparency among its members. Besides, there were also reasons for being somewhat sceptical about what CESR had to offer. CESR announced in December 2008, after the European Commission voiced its wish for CESR members 'to agree on a common procedure for determining equivalence', that it had 'decided to work on

achieve the same results is required from the outset'. See Girard, 'Les méthodes de suppression des frontières au plan mondial dans le domaine bancaire et financier' 370.

a common assessment of the prospectus requirements of certain third country [sic] vis-à-vis the EU requirements'.[173] Perhaps unsurprisingly given the actions of Euronext regulators and especially the AMF, CESR stated that it would examine US and Israeli requirements first.[174] In its 2009 annual report, it reported that it had 'worked on a common assessment of the prospectus requirements of certain third countries … focusing to begin with on the requirements of Israel'.[175] But by the end of 2010, CESR had still not presented its findings.[176] To be sure, CESR took other initiatives. For example, it announced that it would adopt a procedure to ensure that CESR members are informed about decisions on equivalence taken by their peers.[177] But what is striking is that in contrast with the work on equivalence of third country GAAP, the Article 20 regime remained opaque, with CESR members seemingly preferring to address matters behind closed doors. This state of affairs appears out of step with common expectations over transparency in regulatory and supervisory practices in the wake of a painful financial crisis.[178]

[173] CESR, 'Assessment on the equivalence of prospectuses from non-EEA jurisdictions (Article 20.1 Prospectus Directive)' (CESR/08-972 December 2008).

[174] *Ibid.*

[175] CESR, 'CESR annual report 2009' (undated) 89.

[176] In its 2008 statement, CESR noted, *inter alia*, that '[a]s of today, no Member State has taken any blanket or unconditional decision with respect to the equivalence of the standards of a third country'. See CESR, 'Assessment on the equivalence of prospectuses from non-EEA jurisdictions. See also CESR, 'Report on CESR members' powers under the Prospectus Directive and its implementing measures' (CESR/07-383, June 2007) 22 (hereinafter, 'Report on CESR members' powers under the PD') noting that '[a]ll the countries accept prospectuses from third countries issuers provided that their prospectuses are set up under the conditions of article 20 of the PD'. CESR also conducted a 'short fact finding exercise' in December 2003 (i.e., before the entry into force of the PD). CESR did not publish the detail of its findings. See CESR, 'Summary of the answers to the questionnaire on factual information on the legislation and practices of Member States regarding the treatment of third country issuers with respect to the drawing up and approval of prospectuses (Article 20 of the Prospectus Directive)'.

[177] ESC, 'Draft summary record of the 59th meeting' 5.

[178] Some information on the use of the Euronext fast-path listing procedure is available from NYSE Euronext press releases. The first company having made use of the facility was Satyam Computer Services which cross-listed on Euronext Amsterdam, thereby falling under the jurisdiction of the Dutch financial markets authority, the *Autoriteit Financiële Markten*. See NYSE Euronext, 'NYSE Euronext welcomes NYSE-listed Satyam Computer Services to its European market. First issuer to seek cross-listing on NYSE Euronext in Europe using fast-path' (Press Release, 23 January 2008), www.euronext.com/news/press_release/press_release-1731-EN.html?docid=491514. Note that Satyam made subsequently headlines because of extensive frauds. See J. Grant, 'NYSE Euronext moves swiftly to suspend Satyam listing' (FT online, London, 7 January 2009). Overall, the interest in fast-path cross-listing appears to have been rather muted.

In comparison to CESR, ESMA has more to offer. Recall that ESMA has greater powers to take decisions and police its members. Its voting requirements will facilitate decision-making. Moreover, as an expertise provider, ESMA will have an important role to play in assisting the Commission.[179] But 'assisting' does not mean deciding. The realities of EU decision-making are such that the Commission will not relinquish its very own role of deciding on equivalence of third country legislation. Moreover, because of EU constitutional constraints, the new securities authority cannot, in any event, be vested with legislative powers.[180] ESMA has to rely on the Commission for any measures to have force of law. That being so, any potential benefits which may flow from letting a European Securities Authority deal with process uniformity seem to be rather redundant. One might just as well decide to rely directly on Article 20(3) and on the Commission.

Competent authorities So far, the role of competent authorities has been described as part of the problem, as it were, rather than as part of a solution to improving the implementation of Article 20. It might simply be the case that the scope of their powers needs to be clarified by the Court of Justice either as a result of a direct action or by way of a reference for a preliminary ruling. At any rate, the current state of affairs, especially as far as transparency or legal certainty is concerned, must also be ascribed to the very wording of Article 20(1). There is something inherently artificial about relying on prospectus approval as a means of giving effect to a finding of equivalence. But an instinctive thought is that it would be difficult to undo this relationship given that it is tangled up in the distribution of competence between EU and national actors. But not all is doom and gloom. Improvements can be made without upsetting the scope of the powers reserved to the Commission and national authorities. My bottom line continues to be that greater transparency in the current or future practices of Member State authorities is paramount while efforts aimed at process uniformity or substantive uniformity should, for the time being, be reserved. A minimum improvement would be to mandate competent authorities to disclose and justify the criteria, conditions and restrictions that they impose, as well as the considerations that underpin their

179 But note that Article 33(2) of ESMA's founding regulation only provides that ESMA should help the Commission to draw up equivalence decisions that concern 'supervisory regimes in third countries'. See Regulation (EU) No 1095/2010 [2010] OJ L331/84.

180 Case 98/80 *Romano v Institut national d'assurance maladie-invalidité* [1981] ECR 1241; Case 9/56 *Meroni v High Authority* [1958] ECR 133.

decisions. As part of this process, competent authorities should also clarify their understanding of the meaning of equivalence and the scope of their powers under Article 20(1), as implemented into national law. What is more, competent authorities should be required to disclose publicly the number of third country prospectuses or documents that have been approved.[181] The conditions, criteria and considerations on which assessments of third country prospectuses are based should be open to scrutiny by fellow regulators, but also by issuers, market participants and indeed the public at large. There may very well be advantages in terms of learning of having some degree of diversity in assessment methods among competent authorities. By disclosing technical criteria and considerations, a competent authority would not be at risk of being found to act outside the scope of its Article 20(1) powers, even if we admit a narrower, literal, reading of the powers reserved to competent authorities, provided a competent authority would not tie its assessment to a finding of equivalence of third country standards.

Arguing in favour of the above course of action, as opposed to arguing in favour of process or substantive uniformity, is choosing the path of least resistance. But choosing this path does not rule out any other type of action. Moreover, ESMA's contribution would not necessarily be essential, although it would be best placed to act as a forum of debate, collect information among decentralised national authorities, prepare recommendations and convey this information to its members, the markets and the public at large.

VI Conclusion

This chapter looked at prospectus regulation from the perspective of third country issuers. It focused on equivalence-based regulation in relation to third country GAAP, employee share schemes and third country disclosure standards. Article 20 emerged as a provision, which in marked contrast to equivalence decision-making for third country GAAP or employee share schemes, reserves greater competence to Member State authorities. This fact prompted me to examine Article 20 in greater detail. A few final observations about Article 20 are warranted by way of conclusion. From the perspective of third country issuers, what is striking about Article 20 is that it opens a path for them to gain access to EU markets

[181] Such a requirement was initially provided for in the Commission's proposal for a prospectus directive. See 'Initial Commission Proposal' 31.

and EU investors on disclosure terms that differ from the common 'maximum harmonisation' disclosure requirements that apply to EU issuers. In this sense, Article 20 is the legal basis of a 'shadow disclosure regime', whether embryonic or not. But painting the picture of a 'shadow disclosure regime' is not meant to convey a message about the level or quality of third country disclosure rules; just as drawing the picture of a 'maximum harmonisation' regime is not meant to convey a message about the quality of the EU's harmonised standards. The chapter identified, nonetheless, a number of concerns with Article 20, but which mainly arose from the interplay of national and EU competence and from the need to ensure transparency. In response, it advocated greater transparency, but in the same breath insisted that strategy choices be dictated by the actual severity of the policy issues raised: the greater the salience, the greater the case for strict process uniformity. An imperfect proxy for measuring saliency is the number of third country prospectuses or documents which are approved on the basis of Article 20 and 'passported' into other Member State(s). The advantage of this approach is that the number of prospectuses can be monitored objectively. Granted, it may well be that in the current economic climate, issuers have little appetite for cross-listing. Indeed, given that most markets in the EU have predominantly domestic orientations, most competent authorities might have limited incentives to apply Article 20(1), as transposed. While such a finding would matter for gauging the salience of the issues that Article 20 raises, it is not such as to undermine the conclusions which this chapter sought to draw on the need for greater transparency. Transparency should be an absolute standard except in the most extraordinary circumstances. It is an appropriate strategy for addressing current practices, but equally to prevent any future issues from arising. At any rate, transparency should not be a function of varying market trends or preferences of issuers and competent authorities.

PART III

Prospectus disclosure enforcement

5

Introduction

Part II examined prospectus disclosure regulation. Part III deals with prospectus disclosure enforcement. This chapter introduces the subject matter and presents the issues that will be discussed in the next chapters.

From an enforcement perspective, the problem with disclosure regulation can be described as follows. If we examine specific disclosure items, as they are found in the Level 2 PR, it is possible to make a rough distinction between (i) information items that essentially require issuers to provide standardised information and that, therefore, leave issuers comparatively little discretion, and (ii) items which require issuers to provide a description of their business or situation in more general terms (e.g., 'research and development', 'risk factors' or 'trend information').[1] As far as this second type of items is concerned, issuers are, at the outset, left with a good deal of discretion. They may decide to 'gloss over'[2] material facts. Of course, they may also simply 'lie outright'[3] with respect to any type of disclosure item. Hence, the point is that even under a mandatory disclosure regime, the *quality* of disclosure – e.g., the truthfulness and completeness of the information – may still vary significantly.

Strategies In order to deal with quality problems, a number of strategies can be envisaged. It is useful to differentiate between *ex ante* and *ex post* strategies.[4] Licensing and certification are both *ex ante* strategies. Both can be means for dealing with uncertainties regarding the quality of products.[5]

[1] Schammo, 'The prospectus approval system' 512–13.

[2] L. Loss and J. Seligman, *Fundamentals of Securities Regulation* (Aspen, New York, 2004) 129.

[3] Hertig, Kraakman and Rock, 'Issuers and investor protection', 204.

[4] See generally, A. Bhagwat, 'Modes of regulatory enforcement and the problem of administrative discretion' (1999) 50 *Hastings Law Journal* 1275 (discussing *ex ante* and *ex post* enforcement strategies).

[5] See generally J. Beales III, 'Licensing and certification systems' in P. Newman (ed.), *The New Palgrave Dictionary of Economics and the Law*, Volume 2 (New York, Palgrave Macmillan, 2002) 578.

Certification 'reveals information';[6] it tries to make the 'unobservable observable'.[7] In the securities field, certification is commonly offered by private market actors, so-called gatekeepers (e.g., auditors or possibly investment banks), who carry out verification or 'due diligence' tasks. Licensing, on the other hand, goes a step further. Its purpose is to prevent products that do not meet a certain standard from entering the market in the first place.[8] The difference between certification and licensing is, therefore, that a licensing system is typically a prior approval system: a product, or for that matter, a person needs to secure prior approval to enter a market.[9]

Ex post strategies deal with the consequences of low quality disclosure for issuers and investors once the failure to comply with the set standards or rules has emerged or begun emerging. These strategies can be divided into public or private enforcement actions. The former can take the form of administrative or criminal sanctions and involve administrative authorities (e.g., securities authorities), public prosecutors and the Courts. Private enforcement, meanwhile, describes generally redress actions in front of civil courts on the basis of civil liability provisions. The distinction between *ex ante* and *ex post* strategies then intersects with the distinction between public and private enforcement.[10] This is the case for *ex post* enforcement, but also for *ex ante* enforcement. We will see that prior approval of prospectuses is a matter for public (administrative) authorities, while certification is typically a service provided for by private market actors.

The problem with these strategies is that they are all likely to be, to some (albeit different) degrees, flawed. *Ex ante* enforcement, in the form of prior approval raises questions about the capacity and willingness of securities authorities to exercise their tasks effectively. Common arguments are that securities authorities find themselves constrained by finite resources or by a lack of expertise. They may have limited incentives to carry out their tasks diligently. Possibly, they may even be corrupt.[11] What is more,

[6] *Ibid.*, 579. [7] *Ibid.*

[8] *Ibid.*, noting that '[l]icensing systems ... seek to make information irrelevant by prohibiting trade in goods or services that do not meet the licensing standard'.

[9] On prior approval as *ex ante* enforcement, see Bhagwat, 'Modes of regulatory enforcement' 1282–3. See also A. Ogus, *Regulation – Legal Form and Economic Theory* (Hart Publishing, Oxford, 2004) 214–44.

[10] Cf., Bhagwat, 'Modes of regulatory enforcement' 1281.

[11] On the relation between entry regulation and corruption, see S. Djankov, R. La Porta, F. Lopez-de-Silanes and A. Shleifer, 'The regulation of entry' (2002) 1 *The Quarterly Journal of Economics* 1.

ex ante enforcement might be used for paternalistic reasons. If so, there are questions to be asked about whether such an approach is justified.[12] Gatekeeping by private actors has also shown its limits in the securities field.[13] Meant to provide the market or securities authorities with assurances regarding the quality of an issuer's disclosure that the latter cannot credibly provide on its own,[14] it was traditionally thought that it was the gatekeeper's reputational capital which ensured that it acted honestly and diligently.[15] But reputational capital has proven to be an insufficient behavioural constraint,[16] as financial scandals such as Enron, but also the recent financial crisis, have shown.[17] *Ex post* enforcement is not without its critics either. As noted, public authorities may lack resources, expertise or incentives to carry out their activities diligently. Meanwhile, private enforcement through court action has been criticised for there being both too little and too much of it. In Europe, critics have highlighted outdated civil procedures as presenting obstacles to effective private enforcement.[18] In the US, on the other hand, forceful private enforcement and the securities class action have been seen by some as a mixed blessing for the competitiveness of US capital markets.[19]

[12] The question of paternalism as a motivation for regulation is examined in Ogus, *Regulation – Legal Form and Economic Theory* 51–53.

[13] See generally on gatekeepers, J. Coffee, *Gatekeepers – The Professions and Corporate Governance* (Oxford University Press, 2006).

[14] J. Coffee, 'Gatekeeper failure and reform: the challenge of fashioning relevant reforms' (2004) 84 *Boston University Law Review*, 301, 309 (noting that '... the professional gatekeeper essentially assesses or vouches for the corporate client's own statements about itself or a specific transaction. This duplication is desired because the market recognises that the gatekeeper has a lesser incentive to deceive').

[15] See for a more detailed analysis, *ibid.*

[16] Behavioural law and economics scholarship has also questioned the rationality assumption underlying the 'reputational capital' argument. See e.g., R. Prentice, 'The case of the irrational auditor: a behavioral insight into securities fraud litigation' (2000) 95 *Northwestern University Law Review* 133.

[17] Coffee has examined the causes for failure in both cases. In the case of auditors, see Coffee, 'Gatekeeper failure and reform' 310. For rating agencies, see J. Coffee, 'What went wrong? An initial inquiry into the causes of the 2008 financial crisis' (2009) 9 *Journal of Corporate Law Studies* 1, 7–10.

[18] G. Ferrarini and P. Guidici, 'Financial scandals and the role of private enforcement: the *Parmalat* case' in J. Armour and J. McCahery (eds.), *After Enron: Improving Corporate Law and Modernising Securities Regulation in Europe and the US* (Hart Publishing, Oxford, 2006) 159.

[19] See e.g., Interim Report of the Committee on Capital Markets Regulation (November 2006), www.capmktsreg.org/pdfs/11.30Committee_Interim_ReportREV2.pdf. For a contrasting view, see J. Coffee, 'Law and the market: the impact of enforcement' (2007)

Empirical turn in enforcement studies In recent years, the debate on enforcement has taken a noticeable empirical turn. Among the most cited empirical contributions in the field of securities regulation, is the work of Rafael La Porta, Florencio Lopez-de-Silanes and Andrei Shleifer ('LLS') who in 'What works in Securities Laws?' set out to assess the impact of securities laws on the development of stock markets by way of a large-scale survey.[20] Among other things, the authors reported that based on their findings, public enforcement did not by and large matter; on the other hand, extensive disclosure requirements and proper liability standards were judged important.[21]

LLS's work forms part of a broader debate on legal origins for which LLS, together with Robert Vishny (hereinafter, 'LLSV'), have become best known in academic and policy circles.[22] 'Legal origin' appears to be a rather fluid concept.[23] In a 2008 paper, LLSV defined it in very broad terms as 'a style of social control of economic life'.[24] It is not necessarily obvious that the label 'legal origins' is best suited for describing the type of differences that LLSV have in mind when speaking about a style of social control. It might be more fitting to stress the difference between a more *dirigiste* style and a more liberal style of decision-making when examining how states intervene.[25] For my part, I prefer thinking of legal origins

156 *University of Pennsylvania Law Review* 229. But note that Coffee has not uncritically embraced the class action. For reform proposals, see J. Coffee, 'Reforming the securities class action: an essay on deterrence and its implementation' (2006) 106 *Columbia Law Review* 1534. See also on reforming civil liability, Fox, 'Civil liability and mandatory disclosure'.

[20] R. La Porta, F. Lopez-de-Silanes and A. Shleifer, 'What works in securities laws?' (2006) 61 *Journal of Finance* 1.

[21] *Ibid.*, 27–8.

[22] R. La Porta, F. Lopez-de-Silanes, A. Shleifer and R. Vishny, 'Legal determinants of external finance' (1997) 52 *Journal of Finance* 1131; R. La Porta, F. Lopez-de-Silanes, A. Shleifer and R. Vishny, 'Law and finance' (1998) 106 *Journal of Political Economy* 1113; R. La Porta, F. Lopez-de-Silanes and A. Shleifer, 'The economic consequences of legal origins' (2008) 46 *Journal of Economic Literature* 285.

[23] Criticising the concept and meaning of 'legal origins', see J. Armour, S. Deakin, P. Lele and M. Siems, 'How do legal rules evolve? Evidence from a cross-country comparison of shareholder, creditor, and worker protection' (2009) 57 *American Journal of Comparative Law* 579, 589.

[24] La Porta *et. al* 'The economic consequences of legal origins' 286.

[25] Inspiration could, possibly, also be sought elsewhere; for example, from Schmidt's classification of 'ideal-typical models' of capitalism, which include market capitalism, managed capitalism and state capitalism, and seek to establish how the civil and common law dichotomy maps onto these models. See V. Schmidt, *The Futures of European Capitalism* (Oxford University Press, 2002). Note that one would need to make these ideal-type models fit with today's reality. But, as Schmidt notes, differences between national

as having a narrower meaning; as referring to a system of rules, principles, and institutions necessary to ensure enforcement, and think of countries as having different policy and institutional legacies or traditions of which their legal legacies (i.e., common law or civil law) are a specific aspect.[26] In any event, LLSV claim that 'common law stands for the strategy of social control that seeks to support private market outcomes, whereas civil law seeks to replace such outcomes with state-desired allocations',[27] the underlying argument being that legal origins have 'significant consequences for the legal and regulatory framework of the society, as well as for economic outcomes'[28] with common law seemingly trumping civil law systems.[29]

Enforcement in the EU – problematic Many have taken exception to the above claims.[30] With respect to LLS, it is worth noting that certainly by the time that their paper ('What works in Securities Laws?') was published in the Journal of Finance, their data was, at least as far as the surveyed EU jurisdictions were concerned, no longer fully up-to-date.[31] LLS did not report that substantial institutional reforms had taken place in France during 2003 which had culminated in the creation of a new French securities authority, the *Autorité des marchés financiers*. In addition, by 2006 the PD, which had been adopted in 2003 and which Member States were required to implement by July 2005, had revamped securities laws in Member States. LLS's rejection of public enforcement has also attracted strong criticism. Among prominent critics are Howell Jackson and Marc

models continue persisting (see *ibid.*, 109), even if they are less pronounced. See also Pistor who has linked LLSV's insights to the related literature on varieties of capitalism (K. Pistor, 'Legal ground rules in coordinated and liberal market economies' in K. Hopt, E. Wymeersch, H. Kanda and H. Baum (eds.), *Corporate Governance in Context – Corporations, States, and Markets in Europe, Japan, and the US* (Oxford University Press, 2005) 249).

26 Cf., J. Armour, S. Deakin, P. Lele and M. Siems, 'How do legal rules evolve?' 589 (noting that '… classification by legal origin is really no more than a proxy for underlying differences. In order to avoid problems of classification, therefore, it would be better to seek to code these differences directly' (reference omitted)).

27 La Porta *et. al*, 'The economic consequences of legal origins' 286.

28 *Ibid.*, 326. 29 *Ibid.*, 298.

30 For a summary of various criticisms see La Porta *et. al.*, 'The economic consequences of legal origins'. For a recent contribution taking issue with LLSV's claims, see J. Armour, S. Deakin, P. Sarkar, M. Siems and A. Singh, 'Shareholder protection and stock market development: an empirical test of the legal origins hypothesis' (2009) 6 *Journal of Empirical Studies* 343. With respect to LLS's claims in 'What works in securities laws', see also M. Siems, 'What does not work in comparing securities laws: a critique on La Porta *et al.*'s methodology' (2005) 16 *International Company and Commercial Law Review* 300.

31 The dataset can be found at www.economics.harvard.edu/faculty/shleifer/dataset.

Roe as well as John Coffee (in a separate article) who have all found fault with LLS's assessment of public enforcement.[32] Like LLS, they seek to measure enforcement across jurisdictions.[33] As important measures of public enforcement, they highlight the budget and staff of regulatory authorities, as well as the number of enforcement actions and sanctions that are being applied. In his article, Coffee reflects on the proposition that civil law and common law countries display differences which can be associated with an *ex-ante/ex-post* divide.[34] That is to say, he discusses the idea that in civil law jurisdictions, *ex ante* regulation in the form of prior approval is more common than in common law jurisdictions in which regulators are 'less intrusive on an ex ante basis' but heavier handed in terms of *ex post* enforcement.[35] The meaning of *ex ante* regulation appears in Coffee's account to be somewhat tangled up between (i) approval of the activities of securities markets authorities by governmental authorities and (ii) prior approval of the activities of market actors by securities markets authorities.[36] In addition, Coffee adds later that among common law jurisdictions, the US and the SEC stand apart in terms of enforcement intensity.[37] But he concludes that it is at least conceivable that 'outside the United States, more is done through ex ante regulation than through ex post enforcement'.[38]

Whilst extending their research to European states, these authors, however, largely fail to take the interplay between European and national levels of decision-making seriously.[39] The point is not trivial, for in the European context there is a constant interaction between both levels

[32] H. Jackson and M. Roe, 'Public and private enforcement of securities laws: resource-based evidence' (2009) 93 *Journal of Financial Economics* 207; H. Jackson, 'Variation in the intensity of financial regulation: preliminary evidence and potential implications' (2007) 24 *Yale Journal on Regulation* 253; Coffee 'Law and the market'.

[33] On the methodological difficulties associated with this research strand, see H. Jackson, 'The impact of enforcement: a reflection' (2008) 156 *University of Pennsylvania Law Review PENNumbra* 400.

[34] Coffee 'Law and the market'. [35] *Ibid.*, 254.

[36] I, for my part, prefer referring to the latter type of measures as *ex ante* enforcement rather than *ex ante* regulation.

[37] Coffee 'Law and the market', 309. [38] *Ibid.*

[39] The importance of the EU for the legal origins debate has not, however, gone unnoticed in the European literature. See J. Armour *et al.*, 'How do legal rules evolve?' 628; S. Deakin, P. Lele and M. Siems, 'The evolution of labour law: calibrating and comparing regulatory regimes' (2007) 146 *International Labour Review* 133, 154; Siems, 'What does not work in comparing securities laws' 304. See also M. Siems and S. Deakin, 'Comparative law and finance: past, present and future research' (2010) 166 *Journal of Institutional and Theoretical Economics* 120, 136 suggesting that there is potential for future research on, *inter alia*, how harmonisation affects cross-country legal diversity.

which exert upward and downward pressures for change. Moreover, while enforcement remains a matter for Member States, national arrangements are by no means unaffected by EU influences. If this interaction is factored in, two questions move to the forefront of the debate on enforcement. First, the question of the factors that shape or influence the choice of enforcement arrangements at EU level. They include institutional factors, as well as Member State preferences for different enforcement arrangements.[40] The second question worth examining is how, once EU enforcement arrangements are adopted, enforcement patterns in Member States change, adapt or adjust to European law influences. Both questions deserve more attention. They will be under investigation in the next chapters. Chapter 6 begins by examining the first question; Chapter 7 will address the second question.

[40] Chapter 6 will begin examining the question by identifying salient institutional factors, leaving actor-based accounts for later in Chapter 10.

6

Prospectus disclosure enforcement: strategy and arrangements

I Introduction

Chapter 5 reviewed the literature on enforcement and the law and finance influences on the debate about the most appropriate enforcement measures. It concluded by highlighting the need to take EU decision-making and the interplay between EU and national levels of decision-making more seriously in this field. The next two chapters work towards this aim in my area of interest. Chapter 7 will examine how enforcement choices made at EU level are translated into national enforcement arrangements. This chapter, however, begins by identifying and assessing the EU's choice of enforcement measures in the prospectus disclosure field, the factors that have affected it, and the general orientations and effectiveness of the chosen strategy.

While regulatory policies have been at the heart of the EU's activities,[1] day-to-day enforcement of EU law against natural or legal persons has traditionally been a matter for Member States. Although the EU's regulatory policy output is significant, the EU relies, by and large, on national actors – national courts and administrative authorities – to enforce its regulatory policies against persons. Yet, as noted in Chapter 5, that is not to say that enforcement choices at national level, whether substantive or organisational, are unaffected by EU policy and regulatory output. Indeed, it is apparent that the EU has steadily increased its influence over enforcement in the prospectus disclosure, or for that matter, securities regulation field. But very much in contrast to the preferences of the normatively driven literature on enforcement, the EU's enforcement strategy for prospectus disclosure is biased towards *ex ante* administrative enforcement. This strategy, which relies importantly on prior approval of prospectuses, is supported by the ESFS network and ESMA under whose supposedly watchful eye, authorities are meant to exercise their enforcement tasks.

[1] See generally, G. Majone, 'The rise of the regulatory state in Europe' (1994) 17 *West European Politics* 77.

In trying to make sense of the EU's choices, a number of factors are worth highlighting. They include the EU's formal constitutional framework, the Treaties, but also, I will suggest hereunder, the passport system of the Prospectus Directive ('PD'). [2]

This chapter proceeds as follows. Section II begins by highlighting the factors that have affected the EU's enforcement choices in the prospectus disclosure field. Section III examines the PD's provisions dealing with administrative enforcement and, especially, those that deal with prior approval of prospectuses. Section IV turns to the role of collective securities authorities, i.e., the (former) CESR and ESMA. Section V examines the PD's provisions dealing with prospectus liability. Finally, section VI, concludes by highlighting the evolutionary or incremental trend that we have witnessed in the enforcement field and which, notwithstanding the fact that national authorities are still the primary enforcement actors in Europe, is consistent with a continuous centralisation and consolidation of competence at EU level.

II Enforcement and prospectus disclosure

In the literature, enforcement choices are generally justified by putting forward two broad objectives. The first sees the primary *raison d'être* of enforcement as that of deterring wrongdoing.[3] The second associates enforcement primarily with the compensation of victims of wrongdoing. Other distinctions too have proven prominent among scholars, for example, *ex ante* vs. *ex post* enforcement or public vs. private enforcement, with authors taking different views on how effective these measures may prove to be. But from a positive perspective, these objectives and enforcement arrangements only reflect broad normative preferences which in an EU context need, in order to materialise, to be translated into outcomes by means of a policy process which is populated by actors who may not only have differing normative (and cognitive) dispositions, but also different interests to defend. What is more, to achieve their aims, these actors will need to satisfy the Treaties which not only define the rules regarding the decision-making procedure by way of which common agreement

[2] Directive 2003/71/EC [2003] OJ L345/64.

[3] Deterrence, as opposed to compensation, has been a prominent rationale for enforcement in the law and economics literature. For a representative contribution, see Coffee, 'Reforming the securities class action'. For a critical discussion of the deterrence rationale, see G. Schwartz, 'Reality in the economic analysis of tort law: does tort law really deter?' (1994) 42 *UCLA Law Review* 377.

must be found, but which also only support certain types of enforcement arrangements. Thus, within an EU context, choices regarding enforcement arrangements must first of all be related to the broader EU Treaty framework that governs the competence of the EU and its institutions.

Fuzzy edges on enforcement choices The limits set on the menu of available enforcement choices in the prospectus disclosure field can be related to a number of principles found in the Treaties. These include the principle of conferral of competence, subsidiarity (albeit in a legally looser sense) and proportionality.[4] These constitutional principles are given for the adoption of secondary legislation and must, therefore, be respected by the EU legislature. To be sure, the need to respect the Treaties does, by no means, exclude altogether EU competence in respect of matters which pertain to enforcement. As far as *substantive* legislative enforcement choices are concerned, the absence of an explicit competence in tort law, for example, has not in the past prevented the EC legislature from making inroads into national tort law since the functional needs of market integration may justify harmonisation measures in this field.[5] There are also ready examples of EU law influences on public (administrative) enforcement. Adding to legislative acts provisions on administrative measures or sanctions has been a common practice at EU level. On the other hand, adopting criminal law provisions has, in the past, been more problematic, given that the European Community did not, as a matter of principle, enjoy competence with respect to criminal law.[6] Before the entry into force of the Lisbon Treaty, EU action in the field of criminal law was dealt with under the third pillar.[7] The latter had more distinctive intergovernmental orientations than the first, Community, pillar. Yet, even in this field, inroads were eventually made by the EC. In the environmental field, the ECJ thus ruled that the Community legislature had competence to adopt measures which concerned criminal law, if criminal penalties were judged an 'essential measure for combating serious environmental offences' and the measures in question were necessary for

[4] See TEU Art 5.

[5] E.g., Council Directive 85/374/EEC of 25 July 1985 on the approximation of the laws, regulations and administrative provisions of the Member States concerning liability for defective products [1985] OJ L210/29, as amended.

[6] Case C-176/03 *Commission v Council* [2005] ECR I-7879, para. 47; Case 203/80 *Criminal proceedings against Casati* [1981] ECR 2595, para. 27; Case C-226/97 *Criminal proceedings against Lemmens* [1998] ECR I-3711, para. 19.

[7] See, esp., ex Art 31(1) EU.

making sure that Community rules on environmental protection were 'fully effective'.[8] The entry into force of the Lisbon Treaty introduced new important amendments to the Treaties with respect to criminal law. The abolition of the pillar system by the Lisbon Treaty has indeed brought criminal law matters, previously dealt with under the third pillar, into the mainstream of EU decision-making, that is the ordinary legislative procedure (previously, the co-decision procedure).[9] What is more, the Court's pre-Lisbon case law is now reflected in Article 83(2) TFEU which provides, in general terms, that directives may lay down common minimum rules with respect to the definitions of criminal offences and sanctions where the harmonisation of national criminal law is 'essential to ensure the effective implementation of a Union policy in an area which has been subject to harmonisation measures'.[10]

Hence, the effects which European primary law, as interpreted by the Court, has on substantive legislative enforcement choices are best described as constraints or limits, but which do not exclude European competence altogether. However, as far as institutional or organisational enforcement choices are concerned – think of the establishment of an autonomous single European securities authority with vigorous discretionary powers to fulfil its tasks – EU primary law, as interpreted by the CJEU, continues to be a very effective obstacle. The Treaties do not support

[8] Case C-176/03 *Commission v Council* [2005] ECR I-7879, para. 48. In Case C-440/05 *Commission v Council* [2007] ECR I-9097, para 70, the Court, however, made clear that Community competence did not extend to the 'type and level of the criminal penalties to be applied'. Note that the Court has also limited the discretion of Member States to decide on enforcement matters which concern European law in various ways. Thus, in Case 68/88 *Commission v Greece* [1989] ECR 2965, para. 24, the ECJ held that 'whilst the choice of penalties remains within their discretion, [Member States] must ensure in particular that infringements of Community law are penalized under conditions, both procedural and substantive, which are analogous to those applicable to infringements of national law of a similar nature and importance and which, in any event, make the penalty effective, proportionate and dissuasive. The Court has also held that Member States must make sure that penalties, meant to sanction non-compliance with an obligation stemming from Community law, are not 'so disproportionate' to the seriousness of the alleged infringement that the constitutionally protected Treaty freedoms would be frustrated (e.g., Case C-193/94 *Criminal proceedings against Skanavi and Chryssanthakopoulos* [1996] ECR I-929, para. 36. In relation to CARD, see Case C-430/05 *Dionik and others* [2007] ECR I-05835, para. 54).

[9] See, in particular, TFEU Art 83(1). But see also Art 83(3), para. 1, which sets out an 'emergency brake' procedure.

[10] These measures are either adopted in accordance with the ordinary or special legislative procedure, depending on the procedure that applies in relation to the harmonisation measures. Note that the emergency brake procedure of Art 83(3), para. 1 also applies for Art 83(2) measures.

the establishment of an authority of such a stature in the securities field. Furthermore, as we have seen in Chapter 1, any powers that are granted to European agencies will need to respect the principles established in *Meroni* which, for better or worse, continue shaping a delegation to agencies following the entry into force of the Lisbon Treaty. As a reminder, in *Meroni*, the Court held, *inter alia*, that a delegation of power could not involve a 'discretionary power, implying a wide margin discretion', but only 'clearly defined executive powers'.[11]

Hence to sum up, constitutional obstacles are important to account for when seeking to explain why the EU legislature relies on decentralised enforcement. But they do not explain conclusively the PD's preference for *ex ante* administrative enforcement, especially since the Treaties do not exclude EU competence in the field of tort law or criminal law. We must therefore look elsewhere for explanations and here, I suggest, that another rule must be accounted for, that is mutual recognition.

Enforcement choices in the light of mutual recognition Another institutional arrangement that affects enforcement choices in the prospectus disclosure field is, it is suggested, mutual recognition.[12] As an arrangement that is meant to facilitate market integration, mutual recognition is common in internal market law. Depending on the terms of recognition, it applies with respect to rules or with respect to the control or enforcement of such rules.[13] Commonly, mutual recognition in internal market legislation is based on the home-host country principle. The effect of mutual recognition is then to create a sort of benign form of extra-territoriality[14] in which the host Member State is required to allow products or market actors who are regulated or supervised by another Member State – the home state – access to its territory. Depending on the terms of recognition, it thereby contributes to avoiding the multiplication of rule-making, supervisory or enforcement efforts. But it also erodes the territorial competences of Member States in which recognition is being sought. The point then is that, in practice, for mutual recognition to be acceptable to

[11] Case 9/56 *Meroni v High Authority* [1958] ECR 133 at 150, 152.

[12] For a more stylised assessment of mutual recognition, as an institutional rule, in different EU policy areas, see A. Héritier, 'Mutual recognition: comparing policy areas' (2007) 14 *Journal of European Public Policy* 800.

[13] See generally M. Ortino, 'The role and functioning of mutual recognition in the European market of financial services' (2007) 56 *International and Comparative Law Quarterly* 309; P. Slot, 'Harmonisation' 1996 (21) *European Law Review* 378, 386–7.

[14] K. Nicolaïdis and G. Shaffer, 'Transnational mutual recognition regimes: governance without global government' (2005) 68 *Law and Contemporary Problems* 263, 267.

Member States,[15] it is made subject to a number of safeguards or conditions that allow states to 'manage' mutual recognition.[16] The managed nature of mutual recognition has been identified and examined extensively by Kalypso Nicolaïdis. She identifies four ways in which mutual recognition is managed: (a) by setting 'prior conditions for equivalence'; (b) by altering the degree of 'automaticity' of recognition; (c) by setting limits to the scope of market access and, finally; (d) by putting in place '*ex-post* guarantees'.[17] While the first type of measures may entail some form of harmonisation of rules or standards, the second type typically includes measures which make sure that recognition is not granted automatically.[18] Under the third set of measures, recognition may, for instance, be restricted to specific types of activities or products.[19] Finally, the fourth set of measures may require putting in place regulatory networks in order, for example, to deal with monitoring or enforcement tasks.[20]

Nicolaïdis's findings allow framing a basic proposal with respect to the factors that affect the choice of enforcement arrangements in our field of interest. Recall that from a normative point of view, deterrence and compensation are the basic rationales for choosing among enforcement arrangements. But from the present point of view, it can be suggested that enforcement choices are affected by the practical need to manage mutual recognition (that is, the single passport). As a reminder, Article 17 of the

[15] Admittedly, Member States' willingness to enact mutual recognition arrangements may vary between policy sectors. Their readiness may, for example, depend on how hard the ECJ has promoted mutual recognition through its case law in a given policy sector (see Héritier, 'Mutual recognition: comparing policy areas'). The Court has been especially bullish in the field of goods, but less so in the financial services area (see Ortino, 'The role and functioning of mutual recognition' 323). In the prospectus field, it is worth noting that, even prior to the adoption of a proposal for a prospectus directive by the Commission, there were strong expectations among all stakeholders that a new mutual recognition arrangement was needed. See FESCO, 'A "European Passport" for issuers' (FESCO/00138b, 20 December 2000), www.cesr.eu; European Commission, 'Financial services: building a framework for action – communication of the Commission' (undated) 9 and 12, http://ec.europa.eu/internal_market/finances/docs/actionplan/index/fs_en.pdf; 'Lamfalussy Report', 92; European Council, 'Presidency Conclusions' (Lisbon, 23 and 24 March 2000) para 21, www.consilium.europa.eu/ueDocs/cms_Data/docs/pressData/en/ec/00100-r1.en0.htm.

[16] On managed mutual recognition, see Nicolaïdis, 'Regulatory cooperation and managed mutual recognition'; Nicolaïdis and Shaffer, 'Transnational mutual recognition regimes'.

[17] Nicolaïdis, 'Regulatory cooperation and managed mutual recognition' 595–7; Nicolaïdis and Shaffer, 'Transnational mutual recognition regimes' 290–1.

[18] Nicolaïdis, 'Regulatory cooperation and managed mutual recognition' 595.

[19] *Ibid.*, 597. [20] *Ibid.*

PD requires host state authorities to recognise prospectuses as being valid for cross-border capital-raising activities in the host Member State following a simple notification procedure provided for under Article 18. It prohibits, in particular, host state authorities from carrying out any 'approval or administrative procedures relating to prospectuses'. Because host Member States are, in order to facilitate market access, prevented from questioning the validity of a prospectus upon reception, one would expect Member States/policy actors to be concerned about ensuring effective enforcement by home competent authorities. What is more, one would also expect Member States/policy actors to be especially concerned about ensuring *ex ante* enforcement by the home state authority, if host authorities are explicitly prohibited from vetting prospectuses in an effort to facilitate cross-border movements. On the other hand, in the absence of any provision of the directive seeking to coordinate civil liability and civil litigation actions in cross-border situations, one would also, on this account, expect Member States/policy actors to be comparatively less concerned about private enforcement. There is support for these proposals. A number of measures were specifically included in the Commission proposal in an effort to manage a more aggressive passport system, seen as crucial for dealing with the failings of mutual recognition under the LPD and POD. 'Prior conditions of equivalence' (or, in the language of the European Commission, 'similarities in performing regulatory and supervisory functions') were viewed as paramount for introducing a new passport system.[21] New provisions requiring Member States to entrust competent authorities with a range of powers for them to carry out their enforcement tasks, were proposed and subsequently adopted. More generally, breaking with the past, enforcement was also meant to be entrusted to independent administrative authorities.[22] The emphasis which the PD places on prior approval of prospectuses by the home state authority appears also, at least partly, motivated by an effort to manage mutual recognition. In fact, the role of prior vetting of prospectuses, as a means to manage mutual recognition, was apparent well before the adoption of

[21] European Commission, 'Proposal for a Directive of the European Parliament and of the Council on the prospectus to be published when securities are offered to the public or admitted to trading' (COM (2001) 280 final, 30 May 2001) 13, stating that '[t]he introduction of a notification system [i.e., the single passport] requires mutual trust among competent authorities and similarities in performing regulatory and supervisory functions' (hereinafter, the 'Prospectus Proposal').

[22] Note that this requirement was subsequently watered down. See section III. A, for details.

the PD. In Nicolaïdis's classification, prior approval systems contribute to managing 'automaticity of recognition'.[23] Thus, even prior to the entry into force of the PD, issuers were, under the old disclosure directives, only allowed to take advantage of mutual recognition for disclosure documents that had been vetted by the relevant authorities.[24] For prospectuses that were not subject to prior approval, such as 'POD-Article-11 prospectuses' for public offers of securities which were not meant to be admitted to official stock exchange listing, mutual recognition was simply not available.[25] The PD's single passport system improves on these past arrangements, notably by making mutual recognition more widely available. But as a corollary, the obligation to seek approval was also extended. Moreover, the PD now also defines the scope of the vetting procedure which must be carried out by competent authorities. All in all, it is thus apparent that, in terms of enforcement choices, the PD is most comprehensive with respect to administrative enforcement, especially *ex ante* enforcement. It does not deal with criminal law and devotes little attention to private enforcement actions which remain uncoordinated under the terms of the directive.

Hence, seen in the above light, it can be suggested that the PD's preference for *ex ante* administrative enforcement must also be seen in light of a more aggressive mutual recognition system. To be sure, there is a risk of overemphasising the role of mutual recognition in shaping the PD's enforcement orientations. Broader trends were, admittedly, at work too. Because of the demutalisation of exchanges, the case for entrusting oversight of securities markets to administrative authorities was, for example, considerably strengthened at the outset. In addition, the Lamfalussy Committee had earlier advocated greater convergence of 'regulatory and supervisory structures'.[26] But these considerations only take us so far. In particular, they do not explain the specific factors motivating actors to translate them into legally binding provisions in the context of the PD. Without then accounting for actors, their preferences and their

[23] Nicolaïdis, 'Regulatory cooperation and managed mutual recognition' 595 (noting that '[a]t a minimum, parties will have to provide proof of licensing in their home country').

[24] 'Prospectus Proposal' 11.

[25] Council Directive (EEC) 89/298 [1989] OJ L124/8. There was an exception. If Member States granted issuers the possibility of drawing up a public offer prospectus in accordance with the requirements of the LPD, the prospectus was also subject to prior approval even if no admission to official listing was being sought (POD Art 12(1) and (2)). In such a case, the public offer prospectus could also benefit from mutual recognition (POD Art 21(1)). This point also underlines that prior approval contributed to managing mutual recognition.

[26] 'Lamfalussy Report' 15–6.

interactions, the picture remains incomplete and too simplistic. The fact that the PD neglects private enforcement must also, for example, be seen in light of the greater resistance of Member States to actions in the field of tort law. Likewise, the fact that the directive allows for a carefully limited exception to administrative enforcement[27] can only be made sense of after providing a more interaction-based account of the negotiations of the directive. In Chapter 10, this omission will be rectified. But far from undermining the findings regarding the role of mutual recognition, a more actor-based account will in fact underline the importance of accounting for mutual recognition and the issues that it raises for Member States in order to make sense of the PD's distinct approach to home-country based administrative enforcement.

III Administrative enforcement of prospectus disclosure

It is helpful to differentiate between actors involved in enforcement activities (A), instruments of enforcement (B) and powers of enforcement (C).

A Actors

Enforcement by independent administrative authorities The PD entrusts prospectus disclosure enforcement to administrative authorities.[28] The directive adds two precisions. First, in order to avoid unnecessary cost and overlapping responsibilities between authorities,[29] each Member State is meant to entrust enforcement tasks to a *central* administrative authority.[30] The directive allows for some flexibility by permitting Member States to designate other administrative authorities in order to perform certain tasks which are found in Chapter III of the directive (i.e., tasks regarding the approval of prospectuses or prospectus supplements, the control of advertising material, the filing of a prospectus and its online publication).[31] But it prevents this option from being used for the approval of prospectuses where a public offer is made, or an admission of securities is sought, abroad (i.e., in another Member State).[32] Moreover, following the adoption of the ESFS, the directive was amended in 2010 and now also requires competent authorities to cooperate with ESMA and share information whenever necessary.[33]

27 PD Art 21(2). 28 PD Art 21(1). 29 Rec (37).
30 Art 21(1). 31 *Ibid.* 32 *Ibid.*
33 Art 21(1a) and (1b).

The second requirement of the directive is that administrative authorities must be fully independent from market actors.[34] There is no definition of 'independence', but the fact is that the PD breaks with the past, since neither the LPD nor the POD required authorities to have administrative status. During the negotiations of the directive, the requirement to entrust enforcement to administrative authorities proved to be a contentious issue for some Member States which used to entrust the vetting of prospectuses to stock exchanges.[35] As part of a compromise, Member States finally agreed to include a provision that allows competent authorities to delegate tasks, including prior approval of prospectuses, to non-administrative authorities until the end of 2011.[36] After 2011, authorities will only be able to delegate two minor operational tasks, that is, the web-based publication of approved prospectuses and the filing of prospectuses, to non-administrative bodies.[37] For the avoidance of doubt, the transfer of prospectus approval tasks between competent authorities (i.e., *administrative* authorities) of different Member States is not affected by these provisions. Indeed, the directive expressly provides for such a transfer between the home state authority and another competent authority, provided that the latter agrees to this transfer and ESMA is duly notified.[38]

Enforcement by the administrative authority of the issuer's home Member State The PD is based on the home country control principle. Enforcement of prospectus disclosure, mostly under the directive by way of prior approval of prospectuses, is entrusted to the administrative authority of the issuer's home Member State.[39] The competence of the home state authority is cemented by the provisions on the passport system, which explicitly foreclose host state authorities from carrying out 'any approval or administrative procedures' in relation to prospectuses,[40] and especially by the PD's provisions on precautionary measures under

[34] Art 21(1). [35] For details, see Chapter 10.
[36] Art 21(2). [37] *Ibid.* [38] Art 13(5).
[39] Home country control is expressly provided for in the PD, for the approval of prospectuses and for advertising activities where the directive states that the home state authority ensures that the directive's provisions dealing with advertising are complied with (see Arts 13(1) and 15(6)). Home state competence also applies in relation to the rules governing the publication of a prospectus (Art 14). The directive also entrusts the home state authority with different administrative or operational tasks (see Art 14(1) and (4) and Art 18). Note that Member States do not always agree on the scope of home country control. For instance, they have had different views on whether the control of advertising activities is exclusively governed by home state control (see below for details).
[40] Art 17(1).

Article 23. The latter provides in essence that, if the host state authority discovers breaches or irregularities, it has, in the first place, to communicate its observations to the home state authority and ESMA.[41] The host state authority can only take appropriate precautionary measures[42] if, essentially, the measures taken by the competent authority of the home Member State are insufficient or inadequate to deal with the breaches and after it informed the home state authority and ESMA.[43] For the avoidance of doubt, these provisions, which testify to the subordinate role of the host state authority, only affect the allocation of competences between home and host state authorities insofar as the alleged breaches or irregularities concern requirements that arise, under the home country control principle, from the provisions of the PD. Accordingly, a host state authority is not prevented from taking action when irregularities or breaches to its legislation do not concern the PD's provisions, as implemented into its national law.[44] The point is not necessarily obvious on the face of Article 23, given that it does not expressly relate irregularities/breaches to obligations arising from the PD. But on a proper reading, the competence of the home state authority must be limited to matters which arise under the terms of the directive. Otherwise one would, in effect, extend home country control beyond the directive's purpose and scope.

Home country control vs territorial jurisdiction Notwithstanding the importance of home country control under the directive, home state competence is not absolute.[45] Certain matters remain outside its realm and continue being governed by ordinary principles of territorial jurisdiction. Competence to check compliance with Article 3(2), which exempts

41 Art 23(1), as amended.

42 The directive does not define which measures qualify as precautionary measures. It only states that measures, which a host state may (exceptionally) adopt, must be 'appropriate' and be taken 'in order to protect investors' (Art 23(2)). CESR (CESR, 'Report on CESR members' powers under the PD' 64–5) identified the position of various authorities on the subject matter. Among the measures which (some) authorities consider to qualify as precautionary measures are, *inter alia*, the suspension of the public offer or the admission of securities to trading, naming and shaming, replacing the 'management entities', administrative sanctions, or the referral of the matter to the national criminal courts.

43 Art 23(2).

44 'CESR Q&A, July 2010', Question 35 (noting that Art 23 only concerns obligations found in the PD, as implemented into host state law).

45 Where home country control applies, the directive generally refers expressly to the competence of the 'competent authority of the home Member State' (see e.g., Art 13(1)). In this sense, see also '3rd Transposition Meeting' 6.

issuers from publishing a prospectus in certain cases (e.g., offers to qualified investors or to less than 150 persons in each Member State),[46] is, for example, governed by ordinary territorial rules.[47] Competence to check compliance with Article 4(1) and (2) which includes another set of exemptions (e.g., for securities issued at the occasion of a takeover, merger or division)[48] is not based on the home country control principle either, but is again governed by territorial principles.[49] Where territorial jurisdiction applies, the competent authority will be the authority of the Member State in which an issuer seeks to raise capital by either making a public offer or seeking admission to trading on a regulated market. This may be the home state authority, but not necessarily. Think, for example, of the case where capital is raised exclusively in a host Member State.

An arguably more controversial application of the territorial principle concerns advertising. Article 15(6) provides for home country control: the home state authority is expected to 'exercise control over the compliance of advertising activity' with the principles laid down in the directive. Some authorities, however, have not fully embraced home country control and continue exercising control over advertising material when acting as a host state authority.[50] Practices have included prior endorsement of advertising material – a measure envisaged by the Commission in its proposal for the home competent authority, but which was later dropped[51] – or the addition of specific risk warnings to advertising material.[52] The Level 2 Prospectus Regulation ('PR')[53] missed an opportunity to clarify competences between home and host state authorities.[54]

[46] See Chapter 3, section V, A.3.a, for details.

[47] In this sense, '3rd Transposition Meeting' 4. There is no requirement for an *ex ante* decision that Art 3(2) applies (see '3rd Transposition Meeting' 4, noting that Art 3 provides for 'automatic exemptions' which are 'not related to any formal approval or decision by the competent authority'). Authorities can check compliance with Art 3(2) on an *ex post* basis. See '3rd Transposition Meeting' 4. See also, '4th Transposition Meeting' 2.

[48] See Chapter 3, section V, A.3.b for details.

[49] In this sense, '3rd Transposition Meeting' 4 and 6; '4th Transposition Meeting' 3. Note that, according to the Commission, where an issuer is exempted from publishing a prospectus under Art 4, but is instead required to prepare a document which includes information 'regarded by the competent authority as being equivalent', the competent authority of the host state must take a view on the equivalence of the alternative document on an *ex ante* basis (see '3rd Transposition Meeting' 4).

[50] See on this practice, 'CESR's Report on the PD' 32–3 .

[51] Art 13(1), Prospectus Proposal.

[52] 'CESR's Report on the PD' 32.

[53] Commission Regulation (EC) No 809/2004 [2004] OJ L149/3.

[54] PR Rec (35) simply states that 'Member States should ensure effective compliance of advertising rules concerning public offers and admission to trading on a regulated market.

CESR also missed an opportunity to find a solution at Level 3. It noted, rightly so, that the directive did not extend the passport system to advertising activities.[55] Host state authorities cannot, therefore, be required to automatically accept advertising material. On the other hand, CESR has also stressed that the appropriate solution for dealing with advertising in cross-border situations is greater coordination between authorities.[56] That being so, CESR could arguably have found a solution that is more in line with the home country control principle of Article 15(6). In other fields, national regulators have, for example, in the past used 'proxy passports' as a means to facilitate cross-border activities which did not benefit from mutual recognition provisions. To be sure, advertising raises particular problems, not least because of the language issues which are involved. But, arguably, there are ways to overcome such practical problems whilst respecting the home country control principle. Cooperation and delegation between authorities could, for example, have offered a way forward.

B *Instruments of enforcement*

We have seen that home state authorities are required to carry out various tasks under the directive. They include minor tasks, but also enforcement tasks. The main instrument for home state authorities to carry out the latter tasks is, for better or worse, prior approval of prospectuses. It is the lynchpin of the EU's enforcement strategy in the prospectus field. The approval system is a form of entry regulation.[57] More specifically, it is an *ex ante* enforcement instrument which is akin to a licensing system. But it also suffers from various limitations and, not surprisingly, raises questions regarding its merit.

Proper co-ordination between competent authorities should be achieved in cross-border offerings or cross-border admission to trading'.

[55] 'CESR's Report on the PD' 33.

[56] 'CESR's advice on Level 2 implementing measures for the Prospectus Directive' (CESR/03-399, December 2003), para. 66.

[57] This part was originally published as P. Schammo, 'The prospectus approval system' (2006) *European Business Organization Law Review* 501. It is reproduced, with permission of T. M. C. Asser Press, in an edited form. On prior approval of prospectuses and the scope of the prospectus review, I gratefully acknowledge the insight and helpful comments of Hubert Grignon Dumoulin and Georges Carton de Tournai. On prior approval, see also Ogus, *Regulation – Legal Form and Economic Theory* 214–44.

1 The prospectus approval, an *ex ante* enforcement instrument

Characteristics An *ex ante* enforcement system can be described as a system in which compliance with a set of requirements is reviewed by a competent authority *before* a product or a person is given access to a market or a regulated activity.[58] The compliance technique consists in denying access if the product or the person in question fails to meet the set regulatory requirements.[59] Prior approval of prospectuses has similar characteristics. Under the directive, it is the *sine qua non* for the publication of a prospectus and a subsequent public offer or an admission of securities to trading on a regulated market. Thus, Article 13(1) provides that '[n]o prospectus shall be published until it has been approved by the competent authority of the home Member State', a requirement which applies equally to prospectus supplements.[60] Meanwhile, Article 3(1) states that 'Member States shall not allow any offer of securities to be made to the public within their territories without prior publication of a prospectus', while paragraph (3) provides that 'Member States shall ensure that any admission of securities on a regulated market situated or operating within their territories is subject to the publication of a prospectus'.

The obligation to seek approval of a prospectus is more or less comprehensive. It extends to transactions that were previously not subject to this requirement. 'POD-Art-11 prospectuses' for securities intended for public offers, but for which no admission to official stock exchange listing was being sought, were not, for instance, subject to prior approval under Community law prior to the entry into force of the PD. But the obligation to seek approval is not all encompassing either. Base prospectuses, for instance, may, but do not need to, include the actual final terms of an offer.[61]

[58] See Bhagwat, 'Modes of regulatory enforcement' (discussing *ex ante* and *ex post* enforcement systems).

[59] See *ibid.*, 1283.

[60] PD Art 16(1). For the avoidance of doubt, the requirement for prior approval also applies with respect to tripartite prospectuses. Art 12 envisages the situation in which a registration document has either been approved previously by the competent authority or has only been filed with the competent authority, but without being approved. In the former case, the securities and summary notes are subject to a separate approval (Art 12(2)). In the latter case, the reference document is approved together with the securities and summaries notes (Art 12(3)).

[61] Art 2(1)(r). The base prospectus may include '"pro-forma" final terms' that will set out various information headings, but not yet the actual information. See L. Burn and

If they are not included, the directive does not require the final terms to be formally approved by the competent authority.[62]

The PD also sets time limits for the approval of prospectuses. It requires a decision regarding approval to be given within ten working days of the submission of the draft prospectus or within seven working days in the case of a prospectus supplement.[63] The ten-day limit is extended to twenty working days for a public offer of securities issued by an issuer which has no securities admitted to trading on a regulated market and has not yet made a public offer.[64] In all cases, the obligation to obtain the authority's approval is a positive requirement. The absence of a decision in the specified time frame is not tantamount to approval.[65] If a competent authority has 'reasonable grounds' for thinking that the submitted documents are incomplete or that additional information is required, it can disable the time limits by requesting new information.[66] In this case, the time limits will only apply once the relevant information has been provided.[67] Note that the meaning of 'reasonable grounds' is not defined by the PD. The importance of the time limits must, therefore, not be exaggerated. [68]

Scope of the review The approval procedure can be described as a two-stage process. The first stage consists in a review of the documents submitted to a competent authority by an applicant. Depending on the type and complexity of an operation, the review process can give rise to more or less lengthy discussions between the competent authority and the parties involved in the operation. The former may request documents and information, ask for clarification or for supplementary information. Besides their own investigations, competent authorities may also rely on third parties (e.g., auditors, financial professionals carrying out due diligence)

B. Wells, 'The pan-European retail market – are we there yet?' (2007) 2 *Capital Markets Law Journal* 263, 271. See also PR Rec (26) suggesting, *inter alia*, that a base prospectus leave 'blanks for any information to be inserted in the final terms'.

[62] PR Rec (21) (noting that '... where the final terms are not included in the base prospectus they do not have to be approved by the competent authority'). While the final terms do not need to be formally approved, the Commission has taken the view that competent authorities should nevertheless check them (see '4th Transposition Meeting' 4). Note that according to Art 5(4), final sub-para., the final terms can also be included in a supplement. In the past, national authorities have adopted different practices with respect to the final terms. See for details, 'CESR's Report on the PD' 27.

[63] Arts 13(2) and 16(1). [64] Art 13(3).

[65] Art 13(2). [66] Art 13(4). [67] *Ibid.*

[68] The fact that the definition of time limits has not led to consistency across Member States was, *inter alia*, highlighted by CESR in its 2007 Report on the functioning of the PD. See 'CESR's Report on the PD' 31.

who may be required to provide explanations or statements concerning the quality of the disclosure. The second stage of the process consists in the decision to approve a prospectus. It closes the review period and is followed by the filing of the prospectus with the relevant authority and the publication of the prospectus. Approval will mark the start of the period of validity of the prospectus[69] and will make it possible for prospectuses to benefit from passport rights.[70]

In an effort to improve the consistency of the approval process throughout Member States, the PD sought to streamline the scope of the prospectus review. Before the adoption of the directive, review processes differed markedly between Member State authorities. Practices included 'box-ticking' (i.e., a formal review of whether each information *item* was included in the prospectus),[71] but also thorough and lengthy reviews of the substance of the information disclosed under each information item. Different practices made cross-border operations more burdensome.[72] The PD is now defining the scope of the prospectus review. According to Article 2(1)(q), approval means 'the positive act at the outcome of the scrutiny of the *completeness* of the prospectus by the home Member State's competent authority including the *consistency* of the information given and its *comprehensibility*' (emphasis added). But the compromise wording of Article 2(1)(q) is ambiguous and is still leaving competent authorities with discretion to define unilaterally their standard of review. Consider, for example, the meaning of information 'consistency'. The extent of an authority's obligation to verify the consistency of the information is not specified under Article 2(1)(q). Hence, it is not clear whether authorities are only required to verify that the prospectus is internally consistent, or whether authorities are required to check that the information given in a prospectus is consistent with information which is not included in the prospectus (e.g., information provided previously by an issuer or supplied by third parties). *A priori*, similar questions can be raised in respect of methods of evaluation. Adopting a wide reading, one could thus talk of the review of the internal consistency of the information (instead of the internal consistency of the prospectus) and discuss whether authorities are required to examine the consistency of the issuer's evaluation methods over time, or whether these methods are consistent with those used by issuers in the same sector of activity. The obligation to verify the 'comprehensibility' of the

69 Art 9(1), as amended. 70 Art 17.

71 Recall that these items are found in the Level 2 PR.

72 PD Rec (30).

information is equally vague. The perspective which a competent authority adopts with regard to investor protection (e.g., an ordinary investor or professional investor perspective) seems to be a likely determining factor in this context. Finally, the meaning of the 'completeness' of the prospectus is also ambiguous, as it can be interpreted differently depending on whether one adopts a literal reading or rather a principle-based reading. For instance, there is no doubt that, as part of an authority's obligation to scrutinise the completeness of a prospectus, it has to examine whether all the disclosure requirements have been complied with. But what is the precise extent of this requirement? Some omissions may be apparent on the face of the documents and an authority will have no difficulty in identifying such omissions. Other omissions, however, may only be detected after a more thorough examination. Indeed, some omissions can simply not be detected, unless an investigation akin to a due diligence is undertaken. The directive leaves these questions unresolved. To be sure, the Level 2 and Level 3 measures are important to consider in this context. The Level 2 PR, for instance, provides guidance on the content of each information item, but only in summary form. The impact of the Level 3 measures deserves separate attention and will be examined below. Suffice it to say here that, Level 2 and Level 3 measures notwithstanding, the decision to approve, or to refuse to approve, will in each case still be a matter of judgment. As part of its assessment, each home state authority will need to make a judgement on the extent of its investigations within the broad parameters set by the PD and by the Level 2 measures. In the past, competent authorities appear to have been undeterred from adopting differing review practices during this process.[73] The Commission may, in the future, decide to clarify the scope of the prospectus review. It is empowered to adopt delegated acts with respect to the definitions found in Article 2(1) and, as such, also with respect to the definition of prospectus approval.[74] ESMA is also likely to contribute to promoting consistency among Member State practices over time.[75] How best to monitor whether an authority carries out its tasks diligently in practice, will be one of the challenges that ESMA is likely to face in this context.

[73] CESR, for example, reported observations by various market actors who experienced differing practices. See 'CESR's Report on the PD' 31.

[74] PD Art 2(4), as amended.

[75] ESMA is expected to play a greater role in bringing about convergence of prospectus vetting and approval practices (Directive 2010/73/EU [2010] OJ L327/1, Rec (8) (hereinafter, the 'PAD')).

2 Limits of a prior approval system

So far, the PD's prior approval system has been described as an *ex ante* enforcement system. Compliance with the prospectus disclosure requirements is determined by scrutinising the *content* of a prospectus and more specifically the completeness of the prospectus, including the consistency and comprehensibility of the information. This section identifies the limits of prior approval and highlights practices that fall foul of the PD's provisions.

Legal limits Notwithstanding the fact that the language used in Article 2(1)(q) is ambiguous, the PD rules out some review practices which clearly do not satisfy the set criteria. This is the case of a practice known as 'box-ticking'. In other words, it is not enough for a home state authority to simply check that all the relevant information *items* are included in the prospectus. Likewise, reviewing prospectuses selectively – in other words, reviewing only certain selected prospectuses following, for example, a predetermined method (e.g., risk-based, rotation or sampling) – is also ruled out. A number of other practices go beyond the requirements of Article 2(1)(q) and should therefore also be ruled out. Prior approval is, for instance, not meant to be a means for a competent authority to review the truthfulness of the disclosed information.[76] Nor is the prior approval system a means for a competent authority to pass judgment on whether a transaction is economically or financially desirable.[77] To assess the desirability of a securities transaction, an authority would first have to examine and decide upon the quality of a transaction, including the financial or economic situation of an issuer. The scrutiny of the quality of the proposed transaction is, however, different in nature from the examination that an authority has to perform prior to approving a prospectus.

[76] For the avoidance of doubt, it is submitted, that an authority cannot, *systematically*, verify the truthfulness of the disclosed information when exercising its prospectus vetting tasks. This would be tantamount to redefining the scope of the prospectus review, as defined by the PD. Obviously that is not to say that an authority is prevented, in a specific case, from taking additional steps in order to check whether the information provided is true. Indeed, it may have reasonable grounds for questioning the veracity of the information. If so, this practice seems hardly objectionable. In any event, the question may well, in practice, be of little importance given that there is scope for overlap between disclosure quality characteristics. Thus, if information in the prospectus is not true and sincere it may also be inconsistent with other sources of information.

[77] In the literature, this form of assessment is also referred to as 'merit regulation'. See, for instance, G. Hertig, R. Kraakman and E. Rock, 'Issuers and investor protection'193, 207–208.

Approval is thus the act which follows an assessment of the quality of the disclosure – or to be more specific, an assessment of different disclosure *quality aspects* which are the completeness of the prospectus, including the consistency and comprehensibility of the information – whereas to determine whether a transaction is opportune, an authority has not only to examine the quality of the disclosure, but also the quality of the proposed transaction. Prior approval is, therefore, not meant to be a 'hard' paternalistic regulatory instrument.

While Article 2(1)(q) defines the scope of the prospectus review and, thereby, also its boundaries, the Level 2 PR sets certain limits on the information which a competent authority can ask to be added to a prospectus during the approval process. Admittedly, the point is not necessarily obvious. The directive expressly grants competent authorities the power to ask for additional information to be added to a prospectus.[78] But because of the provisions of the Level 2 PR, this power is more limited than it appears at first sight. As a reminder, the Level 2 PR lays down specific information items which issuers have to comply with. One of the distinctive features of the PR is that it applies maximum harmonisation vigorously. It provides, as a general rule, that competent authorities cannot ask for information items, other than those that are found in the PR, to be included in the prospectus.[79] Given this requirement, it is submitted that the home state authority cannot, in the course of the approval process, ask for information to be included in a prospectus, if this would, in effect, be tantamount to a new information *item* being added to the prospectus. In other words, the home state authority can only ask for prospectus information to be completed 'for each of the information items, on a case by case basis'.[80]

Operational (practical) limits Prior approval also suffers from various practical limitations which severely affect its effectiveness. When reviewing prospectuses, competent authorities arguably face a dilemma between trying to prevent wrongdoing by a low-quality issuer and ensuring that transactions by high-quality issuers are not hampered by excessive delays. Even under the assumption that competent authorities are genuinely motivated by public interest objectives, what is problematic at

[78] Art 21(3)(a). [79] Arts 3 and 22(1).

[80] *Ibid.* Admittedly, the PR makes some adjustments and exceptions to the maximum harmonisation principle (see PR Arts 4a and 23). But these provisions are not such as to call into question the general maximum harmonisation principle.

the *ex ante* stage is to detect inaccuracies or material omissions within a limited period of time and on the basis of documents that an authority is provided with (save, of course, for apparent inaccuracies which an authority may detect on the face of the documents). *Ex post*, once the harm is done, or bad news that was not expected by the market emerges, the issuer is singled out and authorities are in a position to use their investigative powers to identify possible inaccuracies or material omissions in the issuer's documentation. Likewise, if an authority has a suspicion (e.g., because of rumours circulating in the market), a low-quality issuer can also be singled out at the approval stage. In other cases, however, detecting material issues in the documents which an authority is required to review is likely to require considerable skill, resources, efforts and time and may indeed prove impossible, or at least difficult, without performing exceptional investigations which may hamper market operations. Note that the directive does not require a competent authority to satisfy a particular standard of diligence, as may be the case for market professionals (gatekeepers) under applicable national law. The question of the appropriate standard of diligence is therefore likely to be determined according to national law governing the liability of authorities.[81]

3 The merits of a prior approval system

I examine next the merits of the prospectus approval system. When attempting to assess this point, simply assuming that authorities are inexperienced or necessarily under-resourced does not take us very far. What is needed is a meaningful and consistent approach that allows a critical assessment of the prior approval system. In order to make progress, it is helpful to begin by defining a set of premises. The first premise is that, in order for *ex ante* enforcement to be justified, it must contribute to improving the quality of disclosure. The quality of disclosure is understood as a function of a number of different, more or less important, and to some extent overlapping disclosure quality characteristics. The most important quality characteristic is the accuracy of the disclosure. The latter depends on the information being correct/true. Besides its accuracy, the quality of disclosure is also a function of the completeness of the information. The comprehensibility or indeed the presentation of the information may also

[81] The directive states that it does not affect the liability of competent authorities which continues being determined according to national law (Art 13(6)). But the PD adds that each Member State must restrict the application of national liability provisions to the approval of prospectuses by its own, national, competent authority/authorities (*ibid.*).

be important, as comprehensible and orderly presented information makes disclosure easier to analyse and to compare with information disclosed across a sector. The second premise is that any quality improvement must matter to those actors that are directly affected by it. In essence, issuers or investors must not be indifferent to quality improvements. Finally, the merit of prior approval must be assessed only in light of those disclosure quality characteristics which a national authority is legally held to review. Thus, given the scope of the prospectus review, issuers and investors can only be confident that, prior to approving a prospectus, a national authority has verified that the prospectus is complete and that the information is consistent and comprehensible. With that in mind, the merit of prior approval is examined next for investors and issuers.

a Prior approval and investors The prior approval system may benefit investors if it reduces verification costs or facilitates the processing of information,[82] or simply if the prior review and approval strengthens investor confidence, a concern underpinning the PD.[83] Investors have different degrees of expertise, means and resources. It accordingly makes sense to examine the merit of prior approval separately for professional and retail investors.

Professional investors It is common to observe that professional investors have comparatively greater expertise, resources and means to appreciate and process information.[84] For professional investors, a competent authority's efforts to review quality disclosure characteristics such as the comprehensibility or (internal) consistency of the disclosure have, accordingly, little added value.[85] Admittedly, the financial crisis has driven the

[82] The relation between verification and processing costs, and market efficiency is discussed in Gilson and Kraakman, 'The mechanisms of market efficiency', 592–614. There is no need to deal here with the limitations of the efficient market hypothesis (see Chapter 2 for details). See for a sobering assessment, Gilson's and Kraakman's follow-up paper, 'The mechanisms of market efficiency twenty years later: the hindsight bias'.

[83] PD Rec (18).

[84] Cf., Romano, 'Empowering investors: a market approach to securities regulation', 2378 (noting that '[t]he institutional investors who dominate today's markets have far greater ability, as well as financial incentives, to process information and price securities than does the SEC staff.').

[85] I assume here that a narrower view of an authority's own role in establishing quality characteristics such as the consistency of the information or the completeness of the prospectus is adopted. In fact, this assumption is reasonable because of the difficulty of assessing disclosure characteristics such as the completeness of the information without an examination which is akin to a due diligence.

point home that professional investors are fallible experts. They may not have the capacity or indeed the will to assess disclosure quality characteristics if more intense or complex investigations are required. They may thus be unwilling or unable to establish whether a prospectus is without material omissions or inaccuracies which are not obvious on the face of the document.[86] What is more, even professional investors may be unable to comprehend the transactions behind the disclosures.[87] Their assessment may also be affected by cognitive biases, clouding their judgment with respect to the quality of the investment, or they may come to rely excessively on third parties entrusted with assessing the quality of the information or the securities, but who themselves fail to live up to expectations, as shown by scandals such as Enron or, more recently, by the financial crisis.[88] Coffee, for instance, reported a drop in due diligence standards in markets in the years prior to the financial crisis.[89] But whatever the failures of professional investment, my point is that prior approval is not a remedy for these failings. Thus, even under the highly unlikely assumption that competent authorities have superior expertise and knowledge,[90] prior approval is not meant to address the financial desirability of securities transactions. Moreover, even within the permissible scope of the prospectus review, professional investors cannot, because of the limited scope of an authority's investigations, be confident that, following approval, there will be no omissions or inaccuracies in the disclosure. The approval system does not contribute to making gatekeepers more effective either. In fact, securities authorities bought just as much into the gatekeeper system as market actors.[91]

86 See also Easterbrook andFischel, 'Mandatory disclosure and the protection of investors', 675 (noting that '[i]nvestors do not even want to inspect; they seek to be passive recipients of an income stream, not to be private investigators'); H. Scott, 'Internationalization of primary public securities markets' (2000) 63 *Law and Contemporary Problems* 71, 75 (noting that '… there is generally no way for an investor, sophisticated or otherwise, to know that he is missing information and to attach an appropriate discount to that risk').

87 See, in the financial crisis context, Schwarcz, 'Disclosure's failure in the subprime mortgage crisis'.

88 See generally, Coffee, 'Gatekeeper failure and reform'; Coffee, 'What went wrong?'.

89 Coffee, 'What went wrong?' 3–4.

90 Cf., Schwarcz 'Disclosure's failure in the subprime mortgage crisis' 1120, noting with respect to the capacity of governmental actors to judge the quality of securities that '[i]t is doubtful that government employees would do a better job than private-sector analysts, who already perform this function for investors').

91 Cf., R. Mendales, 'Collaterized explosive devices: why securities regulation failed to prevent the CDO meltdown, and how to fix it' (2009) 5 *University of Illinois Law Review* 1359,

Arguably, the approval system could still benefit professional investors if a competent authority were able to contribute to a greater information standardisation. When reviewing documents, an authority could, for instance, request issuers, applying for approval, to further detail the disclosed information. By requesting all issuers to provide the same information complements, an authority could, in theory, work towards a greater standardisation of the content of prospectuses across sectors of activities. This, in turn, could make it easier to compare disclosure among issuers in, say, the same sector of activity. Ultimately, this could benefit investors.[92] But this argument is problematic in our context. First, it is worth repeating that the Level 2 PR specifies information requirements in greater detail and, as such, contributes *at the outset* to a greater level of standardisation. More fundamentally, the need for greater information standardisation hardly justifies the setting up of a prior approval system. Standardisation efforts are best addressed by exercising general decision-making power (e.g., by regulation or issuing recommendations). Prior approval, on the other hand, is an individual decision specific to each prospectus. Moreover, standardisation efforts are, more or less, ruled out because of the Level 2 PR. Recall that authorities cannot generally ask for information *items*, which are not provided for under the PR, to be added to a prospectus. Admittedly, the regulation allows a competent authority to ask for information to be complemented 'for each of the information items, on a case by case basis'.[93] But even if an authority's standardisation efforts did not lead to new items being added, questions would have to be asked about whether an authority would be truly acting on a 'case by case basis' when requesting information complements with a view to standardising information among issuers in such a manner.

Ordinary investors Unlike professional investors, ordinary or retail investors can be assumed to lack financial expertise. Moreover, their investment behaviour is also likely to be less sophisticated. Possibly, it is also more likely to be affected by cognitive biases. The obligation for competent authorities to review that the information is comprehensible

1362 (noting in the asset-backed securities field, that the SEC 'bears part of the blame for the reliance on ratings' having encouraged ratings 'as a surrogate for the full disclosure that securities law normally mandates').

92 Hertig *et al.*, 'Issuers and investor protection' 206 (noting that '[s]tandardization improves comprehensibility and comparability, thus increasing the value of information to investors').

93 Art 3, para. 3 and Art 22(1), sub-para. 3.

could therefore *a priori* be justified on retail investor protection grounds. If retail investors have difficulties comprehending 'legalese' writing and, as such, fail to appreciate the risks involved with a transaction, even the fullest and most accurate disclosure is unlikely to be useful. Given that ordinary investors are also likely to lack the expertise and skills necessary to appreciate whether a prospectus is even on its face complete, the obligation placed on authorities to review the completeness of a prospectus may also contribute to protecting retail investors. But ordinary investors will only benefit from these efforts if they are able to appreciate for themselves, on the basis of the prospectus disclosure, the quality of the securities transaction at offer. At the outset, this presupposes that investors fully read the prospectus.[94] Moreover, even if retail investors do read prospectuses, prospectus disclosure will always require a certain technical understanding and a level of financial literacy. Hence, even if carried out with the best intentions, an authority's efforts to improve upon the quality of the disclosure, is likely to be ineffective in the absence of measures which are aimed at educating retail investors.[95] These efforts, however, are independent of the prospectus approval process. In fact, it is possible to suggest that prior approval may have perverse effects if ordinary investors fail to appreciate the precise scope of an authority's *ex ante* review and think of prior approval as a statement about the quality of an investment, as opposed to a statement about specific and limited disclosure quality characteristics. Prior approval may thus contribute to making investors over-confident. Competent authorities should, accordingly, find ways to make the limits to their review plain to retail investors. Neither the directive, nor the PR, makes provision for this, but some authorities, such as the French AMF or its predecessor the Cob, have long insisted on the limitations of prior approval. They have thus added a specific statement onto approved prospectuses in an effort to draw attention to the limited

[94] See Scott 'Internationalization' 73 (noting that 'most individual investors do not read prospectuses').

[95] Admittedly, the literature has, in the past, argued that ordinary investors might be protected by professional trading in the market. The point seems somewhat overgeneralised and should not be overrated. See, e.g., Hertig *et al.*, 'Issuers and investor protection' 206, noting that '(…) the empirical literature suggests that liquid share markets mitigate this problem of unsophisticated investors, since professional trading efficiently reflects public information into share prices, and so (inadvertently) protects poorly informed traders. Yet there is no such protection when markets are thin and illiquid because, for example, they lack clientele of professional traders dealing in the shares of small and mid-sized issuers' (citations omitted).

scope of their review tasks. It might be worth considering whether such a requirement should be extended to authorities elsewhere as well.

b Prior approval and issuers The requirement to seek approval involves costs for issuers. Think, for example, of direct costs such as approval fees, but also other costs such as opportunity costs caused by an unduly inefficient approval process.[96] But, arguably, issuers may also benefit from prior approval. Central to this argument is that legal risk is a concern for issuers which they will seek to evaluate and mitigate.[97] Issuers should be interested in determining the extent of this type of risk before the securities are admitted to trading or offered to the public. The question is whether the approval system, as provided for under the PD, can be envisaged as an *ex ante* 'risk reduction' strategy.[98] As for investors, this line of enquiry takes as a starting point the definition of prospectus approval in Article 2(1)(q). Issuers can thus only be confident that, prior to deciding upon approval, a competent authority will scrutinise the completeness of the prospectus, the consistency of the information and its comprehensibility. While prior approval does not protect the issuer from subsequent actions by the authority or from subsequent court proceedings, it can be argued that issuers benefit from the fact that an authority checks, as part of its obligation to examine the completeness of the prospectus, the technical compliance with the disclosure requirements set out in the PD and the Commission Regulation. In theory, approval should thus provide the issuer with certainty that the regulatory authority is satisfied with the disclosure.[99] Hence, it should give issuers comfort that the competent authority will not, once the securities are admitted to trading or offered to the public, take action against it. But the strength of this argument depends on the efficiency of the approval system. If prior approval leads to undue delays, the costs for issuers may ultimately outweigh the potential benefits.[100]

[96] See generally Ogus, *Regulation – Legal Form and Economic Theory* 214 (with respect to opportunity costs caused by delayed approval).

[97] See also Easterbrook and Fischel, 'Mandatory disclosure' 699 (who note that '[f]irms that disclose what they think appropriate for investors may be surprised to learn, a few years later, that they did not disclose enough things or the right things. This is needless risk, and greater risk increases the firm's cost of capital').

[98] See *ibid.*, 704–5 (discussing the 'risk reduction' benefits of prior review of disclosure documents in a US context).

[99] Cf., *ibid.*, noting in relation to the SEC that '[a]lthough the process of review created no formal legal immunity, it did so as a practical matter because the administrative process ensured compliance with all formalities and created precautionary overdisclosure'.

[100] Admittedly, the PD provides for time limits. For details, see text to nn. 63–8, above.

C Powers

Prior to the entry into force of the directive, the powers of enforcement bodies in Member States differed considerably. Some of the differences were caused by the fact that the powers of private bodies such as stock exchanges, which could be entrusted with enforcement tasks under the LPD and POD, were naturally more limited than those of public administrative authorities with public prerogatives. The PD set out to change this state of affairs by making provision for independent administrative authorities to carry out enforcement tasks, but also by introducing specific provisions requiring Member States to entrust competent authorities with various powers. As finally adopted, the directive includes a broad rule-based principle which states that competent authorities should possess all the powers that are necessary for them to perform their tasks.[101] It adds thereto a list of specific powers which authorities can exercise on an *ex ante* or *ex post* basis. Article 21(3) deals with the powers that each authority must *at a minimum* possess if it exercises approval tasks. They include the power to request information or documents to be *provided* to the competent authority, or the power to request information to be *published* in a prospectus.[102] Article 21(3) also mandates the competent authority to have various sanctioning powers – that is, the power to suspend for a ten-day period a public offer or an admission to trading, or the power to prohibit trading or a public offer.[103] Each competent authority must also be empowered to prohibit advertising or suspend it for a ten-day period.[104] Finally, competent authorities must have the power to 'name and shame' an issuer by making its failures to comply with relevant requirements publicly known.[105] Additional powers are found in Article 21(4). They include the power to ask for additional disclosure, to require the suspension of the securities from trading or to conduct on-site inspections.[106] According to the directive, each competent authority must be able to exercise these powers once the securities are admitted to trading.[107] The final provision, which underlines the importance that the PD attaches to administrative enforcement, is found in the directive's chapter on implementing measures. While the directive makes plain that it does not affect national criminal laws, it provides that Member States shall make sure that administrative measures or sanctions are in place for dealing with non-compliance.[108] In line with the Court's case law, it states

[101] Art 21(3). [102] Art 21(3)(a), (b) and (c).
[103] Art 21(3)(d), (f), (g) and (h). [104] Art 21(3)(e).
[105] Art 21(3)(i). [106] Art 21(4)(a), (b) and (d).
[107] Art 21(4). [108] Art 25(1).

that the measures must be 'effective, proportionate and dissuasive'.[109] It also empowers competent authorities to make any measure and sanction public, provided that such publication does not 'seriously jeopardise' financial markets or cause 'disproportionate damage' to those involved.[110]

IV Prospectus disclosure enforcement and collective securities actors

The role of collective securities actors is examined next. I will start with CESR (A), after which I will turn to ESMA (B). As in Chapter 1, I proceed on the premise that we can learn lessons from CESR and that, accordingly, it is worth examining what it achieved with respect to prospectus enforcement.

A CESR

I begin by examining some of CESR's tasks at Level 3 (1), after which I will assess their merit (2).

1 CESR's tasks

CESR's actions with respect to prospectus disclosure can be divided roughly in five categories: (i) reviews; (ii) coordinated implementation; (iii) coordinated enforcement; (iv) operational cooperation; and (v) mediation. CESR's reviews – i.e., its reports on the functioning and operation of the prospectus disclosure framework – provide only a snapshot of the functioning of the prospectus regime at a particular moment in time and accordingly do not require separate attention.[111] 'Coordinated implementation' describes activities which concerned the application and interpretation of EU prospectus law in the day-to-day activities of competent authorities. I think, for example, of CESR's questions and answers on prospectuses.[112] These measures were not, strictly speaking, about enforcement and can be safely left aside. Improving operational (day-to-day)

[109] Art 25(1) *in fine*. On the Court's case law, see n. 8, above.

[110] Art 25(2).

[111] See e.g., CESR, 'Report on CESR members' powers under the PD'; CESR, 'An evaluation of equivalence of supervisory powers in the EU under the Market Abuse Directive and the Prospectus Directive. A report to the Financial Services Committee (FSC)' (CESR/07-334, June 2007).

[112] 'CESR Q&A, July 2010'. Strictly speaking, the Q&As were addressed to market actors. But they were also of obvious importance to competent authorities.

cooperation was, on the other hand, certainly important for enforcement. Suffice it to say that CESR sought to improve cooperation through its various activities, but also by developing procedures whose purpose was to facilitate actual contacts between Member State authorities. The last two types of activities – coordinated enforcement and mediation – are worth examining in more detail.

a Coordinated enforcement Although CESR did not have direct enforcement powers, it sought to coordinate enforcement practices among its members. With respect to the enforcement of financial information for instance, CESR issued two sets of Level 3 standards, known as Standard No. 1 and Standard No. 2.[113] The standards take the form of general principles which national enforcers were supposed to observe.[114]

Standard No. 1 Standard No. 1 deals with various aspects of the enforcement process. It includes broadly worded principles which *inter alia*: address the purpose of enforcement; clarify who is responsible for enforcing financial disclosure; address the question of the delegation of enforcement powers; highlight the importance for administrative authorities to be sufficiently independent and have adequate powers/resources; and underline the role of competent authorities in ensuring due process.[115] The principles also deal with methods of enforcement and enforcement actions.[116] In addition, they insist on transparency by requiring enforcers to report on their activities, and stress the need for enforcers to coordinate their enforcement decisions.[117]

Principles 9 and 10 deal with the scope of application of the standards. According to the former, the standards apply to financial information supplied by issuers that have securities admitted to trading on a regulated market or to issuers that have applied for such an admission. Principle 10 adds that the standards apply to 'financial information provided by all harmonized documents, including annual and interim financial statements and reports, prepared on individual and consolidated basis as well as prospectuses and equivalent documents'.

The scope of application of the standards prompts a number of observations. First, although Principle 10 identifies prospectuses as a type of

[113] CESR, 'Standard No. 1'; CESR, 'Standard No. 2'.
[114] Standard No. 1, Principle 5. [115] Principles 1–4, 6 and 8.
[116] Principles 11–19. [117] Principles 20–21.

document to which the standards apply, it is worth repeating that the standards only apply to financial information. What is more, because of the PD, CESR's (and indeed ESMA's) discretion to lay down separately enforcement standards is, in fact, rather more circumscribed than it appears at first. Recall that, unlike periodic financial information, prospectus disclosure is subject to *ex ante* enforcement. Accordingly, while Principle 11 of Standard No. 1 provides that the enforcement of financial information is based on *ex post* control, Principle 12 concedes that:

> [f]or prospectuses ex-ante approval is the normal procedure as specified by the EU directives, which also identify the nature of the approval. Ex-post enforcement of financial information provided by prospectuses is possible as a supplementary measure.

Hence, the standards reinforce the point that the EU's enforcement strategy for prospectus disclosure is built on *ex ante* enforcement. To be sure, *ex post* control is still possible, but only as a complementary measure pursuant to Principle 12. Because *ex ante* control is so dominant under the PD, the directive also affects other principles of enforcement, but in a less obvious manner. Principle 13, for instance, provides that 'enforcement of *all* financial information is normally based on selection of issuers and documents to be examined' (emphasis added). But the PD's provisions rule out a selective review of prospectuses. All prospectuses are subject to approval which involves, in each case, an *ex ante* review of various disclosure quality characteristics. Likewise, the PD's provisions affect the scope of Principle 15. The latter provides that methods of enforcement on selected information may include 'pure formal checks to in-depth substantive in-nature checking'. But as we have seen earlier, formal checks such as 'box-ticking' are also ruled out by the directive. Overall, therefore, it is fair to say that Standard No. 1 has more to offer for the enforcement of periodic financial information than for prospectus disclosure.

Standard No. 2 Like Standard No. 1, Standard No. 2 is only concerned with financial information. Its main thrust is to define shared principles, but also practical arrangements for fostering convergence. For this purpose, it provides that, subject to 'timing and feasibility constraints', enforcers should coordinate their decisions by taking existing 'precedents' into account when making *ex ante* or *ex post* enforcement decisions.[118] The term 'precedent' was arguably not especially well chosen.

[118] Standard No. 2, Principle 1.

CESR's precedent system had no footing in the EU legal order. As such, it did not benefit from EU constitutional principles such as supremacy. Nor, *a priori*, did it have any foundation in national legal orders which determine the competence and authority of enforcers, as well as the hierarchy of legal rules that enforcers must abide by. Be that as it may, Standard No. 2 seeks to facilitate convergence by a number of arrangements. Principle 1 states that, if feasible, important decisions should be preceded by peer discussions. Principle 2 provides that enforcers should be ready to share their decisions with other enforcers. Principle 4 provides for enforcement coordination sessions – known as 'European Enforcers Coordination Sessions' or EECS – to be organised during which enforcement decisions are discussed and experiences exchanged between national enforcers. Although the EECS was not a venue for decision-making,[119] the establishment of the EECS database is a good example of how CESR could contribute to facilitating the dissemination of expertise across territorial borders. Extracts from the decisions discussed during the EECS were made public. They were presented in anonymous form and typically concerned the application of specific reporting or accounting standards to a factual issue.

b Mediation Mediation is the second task that is worth examining in a bit more detail, as there are lessons to be learned from CESR's experience with mediation. Recall that ESMA can also play the role of a mediator. The use and functioning of CESR's mediation mechanism was governed by a protocol (the 'MP').[120] *Inter alia*, it determined the persons that could be involved in mediation and the range of matters that could be considered. CESR's mediation system had three core characteristics. First of all, the mediation mechanism was supposed to be 'one between peers'.[121] Parties to mediation could be CESR members and exceptionally other 'non-CESR competent authorities' if they were involved in the range of matters that could be subject to mediation.[122] Second, the matters that could be considered included disputes regarding legal obligations to exchange information or to cooperate, but also disputes arising in the context of

[119] CESR, '6th extract from EECS's database of enforcement decisions' (CESR/09-720 August 2009) 3.

[120] CESR, 'Protocol on mediation mechanism of the Committee of European Securities Regulators' (CESR/06-286b, August 2006).

[121] CESR, 'CESR mediation mechanism – feedback statement and protocol' (CESR/06-287b, August 2006), para. 88 (hereinafter 'Mediation Feedback').

[122] MP Art 2.

the enforcement of financial information obligations.[123] Disagreements concerning mutual recognition arrangements could be subject to mediation, as well as other cases where competent authorities were meant to find agreement.[124] In all cases, the matters referred to for mediation could only give rise to mediation if a number of conditions were met.[125] *Inter alia*, the disputed issue was supposed to have a cross-border dimension.[126] Prior to seeking mediation, parties had also to make 'reasonable bilateral efforts' to resolve the dispute or have decided to resort to mediation by common agreement.[127] The third distinguishing feature of the mediation system was that its outcomes did not produce legal effects.[128] They were neither legally binding, nor enforceable.[129] The only obligation for a party, who failed to observe the recommendations, was to explain its reasons.[130] Likewise, once a request for mediation had been admitted, a party could simply decide not to participate in the mediation procedure. If so, it was only required to make its reasons known.[131]

The PD itself did not make provision for mediation between home and host competent authorities until it was amended in 2010. It is apparent, however, that given the scope of the matters that were covered by the protocol, disputes arising in the context of the enforcement of prospectus disclosure would have qualified for mediation, subject to a noteworthy exception: it would not have been permissible to challenge a mutual recognition decision.[132] As a decision recognising individual rights, the decision recognising prospectus passport rights was excluded from mediation.[133] But disputes between home and host competent authorities on the appropriate methods, used in general for reviewing a prospectus, could have been subject to mediation.[134] CESR's mediation mechanism had, accordingly, something to offer, especially in order to deal with inconsistent prospectus approval practices. If it had been used, that is. The point is discussed next.

2 The merits of CESR's Level 3 tasks

As Level 3 measures, CESR's standards on financial information or its mediation mechanism had obvious limitations. Standard No. 1 and

123 Art 1(2).

124 *Ibid.* Such cases, however, had to originate from EU legislation, or Commission or CESR soft-law.

125 Art 1(3). 126 Art 1(3)(a). 127 Art 1(3)(b).

128 Art 5(3). 129 *Ibid.* 130 Art 5(4).

131 Art 5(2). 132 'Mediation Feedback', paras 27–28.

133 MP Art 1(3)(f). 134 'Mediation Feedback', para. 28.

Standard No. 2 were not legally binding and mediation did not produce binding effects. Hereunder, I will highlight another problem with CESR's Level 3 actions which has to do with the behaviour of its members. Recall that in Chapter 1, I identified two types of adverse behaviour which were coined 'no action' and 'defection'. In this part, I will attempt to elaborate on both types of behaviour.

No action I spoke of 'no action' behaviour in Chapter 1 in order to describe situations where CESR members resolved not to act or simply agreed to disagree, whether formally or informally. Chapter 1 illustrated this type of behaviour by referring to CESR's comments on the Commission's pre-consultation on amending the PD or on its comments on the *de Larosière* report. In both cases, CESR members simply agreed to disagree between themselves. But of more immediate interest is CESR's lack of action with respect to mediation. In its 2007 report on the future of supervision, CESR noted that the mediation procedure had not been 'in operation thus far'.[135] The Commission noted, meanwhile, in 2008 that the use of mediation had been 'too limited'.[136] In fact, by the end of 2009 there still had not been a single mediation case in front of CESR.[137] Nor has any case been reported thereafter. Mediation simply remained unused and untested. CESR also failed to carry out a review of its mediation mechanism.[138] It is this apparent lack of interest for mediation between CESR members that represented the Achilles heel of the mediation system. It is regrettable, given that there did not seem to be a shortage of issues on which competent authorities begged to differ.[139]

Defection The second type of behaviour worth highlighting is coined 'defection'. To illustrate this type of behaviour, it is necessary to return to CESR's Standard No. 1 and Standard No. 2 on financial information. As part of its peer review activities, CESR reviewed the application of the standards at Member State level. By 2009, it had completed

[135] CESR, 'A proposed evolution of EU securities supervision beyond 2007' (CESR/07-783, November 2007) 2.

[136] European Commission, 'Public consultation paper on amendments to Commission Decisions establishing CESR, CEBS & CEIOPS' (23 May 2008) 4, http://ec.europa.eu/internal_market/finances/docs/committees/consultation_en.pdf.

[137] Personal communication with CESR (5th January 2010, on file).

[138] *Ibid.* This review was announced in the recitals to its MP.

[139] See, generally, 'CESR's Report on the PD'. Among other issues, market actors reported that competent authorities adopted different prospectus vetting procedures (*ibid.*, 31).

two review exercises. The peer review was based on a self-assessment by national enforcers. On the basis of this assessment, CESR concluded in 2009 with respect to Standard No. 1 that, whilst progress had been made since its 2006 assessment, by the end of September 2008 still 'less than half of the 29 Member States fully applied Standard No. 1 on financial information, and 6 percent of the membership either did not apply this standard or did not contribute to the review'.[140] As far as Standard No. 2 is concerned, CESR reported that by August 2008, only nine CESR member jurisdictions fully applied Standard No. 2.[141] Sixteen jurisdictions simply did not apply Standard No. 2.[142] These results are well worth highlighting, for the standards were *agreed* Level 3 measures which members were supposed to apply. To be sure, Level 3 measures were not legally binding. But that is not so much the point, given that the purpose of Level 3 was precisely to foster sincere cooperation between competent authorities through the power of argument, persuasion and reputation. The failure of Member States or competent authorities to apply the standards is, accordingly, worth highlighting, for it testifies to the limits of Level 3 actions. Indeed, the practice of defecting from agreed courses of action at Member State level was sustained enough for CESR's former chairman to highlight it, in a more general fashion, in front of the European Union Committee of the House of Lords when giving evidence in March 2009.[143]

B ESMA

I begin by briefly introducing ESMA's tasks (1), after which I will attempt to assess the questions that they are likely to raise in the future (2).

[140] CESR, 'Final report of the review panel concerning the updated self assessment and peer review of CESR's Standard No. 1 on financial information' (CESR/09-374, September 2009) 7.

[141] CESR, 'Final report on CESR's peer review of the implementation of Standard No. 2 on financial information – coordination of enforcement activities' (CESR/09-188, July 2009) 5.

[142] *Ibid.*, 6.

[143] See the testimony of E. Wymeersch in front of the House of Lords, European Union Committee (HL European Union Committee, 'The future of EU financial regulation and supervision – Volume II: Evidence' (14th Report of Session 2008–09) 144 and 145 (stating at 145 that '[t]he difficulty is that some of the members may have afterthoughts and then not apply the rule or change it'), www.publications.parliament.uk/pa/ld200809/ldselect/ldeucom/106/106ii.pdf.

1 ESMA's tasks

Before beginning it is worth repeating that for ESMA to take action, it must act in accordance with its founding regulation which sets out its tasks and powers, and within the scope of various sectoral legislative acts and subordinate measures (together, the 'Framing Acts'). Among these acts is also the PD and, as an act based on the PD, the PR.

As far as ESMA's founding act is concerned, I examined ESMA's powers and tasks in Chapter 1.[144] As a result, I will move fairly swiftly and only mention those powers which underline that, in terms of its powers, ESMA is clearly superior to CESR. Recall that ESMA has a critical role to play in developing binding technical standards which, once endorsed by the Commission, will be legal acts.[145] ESMA can also, in certain circumstances, decide disputes between competent authorities and, if certain conditions are met, take a direct decision against a market actor.[146] Moreover, it has a role to play in policing the behaviour of competent authorities that fail to apply ESMA's Framing Acts or apply them in a manner that contravenes EU law.[147] In certain circumstances, ESMA will, in this context, have the power to issue a decision against a market actor.[148] Finally, ESMA will have direct supervisory powers over credit agencies, and an important role to play in crisis situations when it will be entitled, in certain circumstances, to take individual decisions against a competent authority or a market actor.[149]

As one of the Framing Acts, the PD was amended in 2010 in order to put into law certain of ESMA's powers in the prospectus field.[150] These amendments make miscellaneous changes to the PD; I have already mentioned some of them earlier. As amended, the PD requires, *inter alia*, competent authorities to cooperate with ESMA for matters that are within the scope of the directive.[151] They must share all the information that ESMA requires to fulfill its tasks.[152] ESMA can also join on-site inspections where they are carried out by, at least, two competent

144 See Chapter 1, section III, B. 4.

145 ESMAReg, Arts 10 and 15.

146 Art 19. 147 Art 17. 148 Art 17(6). 149 Art 18.

150 Directive 2010/78/EU of the European Parliament and of the Council of 24 November 2010 … in respect of the powers of the European Supervisory Authority (European Banking Authority), the European Supervisory Authority (European Insurance and Occupational Pensions Authority) and the European Supervisory Authority (European Securities and Markets Authority) [2010] OJ L 331/120 (hereinafter, the 'Omnibus Directive').

151 PD Art 21(1a), as amended by the 'Omnibus directive'.

152 Art 21(1b).

authorities.[153] Various other provisions require competent authorities to inform, notify or share documents with ESMA. For example, when a competent authority seeks to transfer the power to approve a prospectus to another competent authority, ESMA must be informed.[154] Likewise, it must be notified each time a prospectus (or a supplement) is approved.[155] Other notification or information obligations apply when a person seeks to use the passport system;[156] when a competent authority has agreed to delegate tasks;[157] or when a host authority finds that an issuer or market actor was involved in irregularities or breaches and if it wishes to take precautionary measures in this context.[158]

The PD now also includes the necessary legal authorisation for ESMA to prepare draft technical standards in the prospectus field. In essence, under the PD, it can make use of this power in relation to, *inter alia*, matters pertaining to the transfer of the prospectus approval; in relation to the passport system; or in relation to cooperation and exchange of information.[159] What is more, the directive now also enacts the necessary sectoral provisions for ESMA to play its role as mediator and dispute settler under Article 19 of its regulation. Note that the power is specifically reserved to cases where a competent authority fails to fulfill its cooperation obligations, especially with regard to exchange of information.[160]

2 The merits of ESMA's tasks

Introduction It is too early to judge ESMA or to prejudge the impact of its actions. At the time of writing, ESMA has not yet taken any action in the prospectus enforcement field. But the fact is that ESMA was designed to be a regulatory agency with teeth. 'On paper', so to speak, ESMA has a lot to offer. But it is already plain that ESMA's actions will depend a great deal on two broad factors: first, the behaviour of ESMA's members; and second, the constitutionality of the delegation of powers to ESMA.

As far as the first point is concerned, recall that just like CESR, ESMA is a collective securities actor.[161] Although this is, by no means, without advantages, it nevertheless brought, in the past, limits to bear on what CESR was able to achieve. The question of whether ESMA will succeed

153 Art 21(4). 154 Art 13(5).

155 Art 13(2). It must also receive a copy of the prospectus including any supplements.

156 Art 18(3). ESMA must be notified the certificate of approval.

157 Art 21(2). 158 Art 23.

159 Arts 13(5); 18(4) and 22(4).

160 Art 22. 161 Chapter 1, section III, A.

where its predecessor failed will hence also depend on the behaviour of ESMA's members and, when necessary, their willingness to challenge each other; for instance, by asking ESMA to act as a mediator or dispute settler.

The second point, the question of the constitutionality of the delegation of powers, is worth examining in more detail. In Chapter 1, I highlighted the importance of case law such as *Meroni* and *Romano*, but when examining ESMA's tasks, I did not examine them fully through the prism of *Meroni*, or for that matter, EU primary law.[162] Hereunder, I will expand on the questions of the constitutionality of ESMA's delegation, but mainly focus on ESMA's power to settle disagreements. I will examine the issues involved with this power by raising questions and making arguments (instead of providing conclusive answers) and with the caveat that many details about how ESMA's powers will be structured, and how precisely they will be put into operation, are still unknown. Some of the problems that a delegation of powers to ESMA may possibly raise can, *a priori*, be prevented if the delegation is properly structured. Until we know more about these precise procedures and arrangements, it is difficult to formulate conclusive answers. On the other hand, however, the points that I will make can also be transferred into other contexts; e.g., ESMA's power to police breaches.

Structuring the delegation I will first examine how the legislature has sought to address the problems involved with a delegation of powers with the example of a dispute settlement system such as the one found in ESMA's regulation.[163] The dilemma that the establishment of an effective dispute settlement system involves can be put as follows. On the one hand, it must be ensured that lessons are learned from the experience with CESR's mediation mechanism. Recall that CESR members lacked interest in mediation; they were seemingly unwilling to challenge each other. To address this problem, the most effective means is to distribute the right to initiate mediation widely, i.e., among a wide population of actors. One of the flaws of CESR's mediation system was arguably that only CESR members could launch it. But allowing third parties (e.g., market actors) to trigger mediation does not seem to be very compatible with the nature of mediation. A compromise solution might be to broaden the

162 See Chapter 1, section III, B.2.
163 ESMAReg Art 19.

right of initiative among peers. In our case, the most likely candidate is ESMA itself as it speaks with the collective authority of its members.

Delegating the power to decide disputes to an EU agency in the case where Member State authorities disagree about whether EU law obligations have been satisfied, raises, however, problematic questions. Deciding a disagreement might involve making choices involving the exercise of a wide margin of discretion which falls foul of *Meroni*.[164] It is also conceivable that it might require an agency taking a position on the interpretation of a rule (as opposed to merely making simple factual observations). Problems are arguably further aggravated if the delegatee has, in addition, the power to decide to intervene at its own will. In this case, it is a short step to conclude that the delegatee has a real power of appreciation over what can constitute a possible disagreement which deserves to be addressed. In other words, the delegatee might have a wide margin of discretion when deciding which case to follow up. What is more, inaction, just as much as action, can involve an active choice. In deciding whether to follow up a case, the delegatee might need to adjudicate between different objectives or interests. The delegatee might develop an active strategy to guide its choice to initiate the mechanism. That said, *Meroni* also suggested that one way in which such problems could be mitigated was by properly structuring the delegation in order to make sure that the *Meroni* principles were respected.

Turning back to ESMA, its right to intervene in a disagreement can be seen as raising similar issues. In Chapter 1, we saw that ESMA's provisions on dispute settlement provide for two distinct scenarios: a first scenario in which ESMA has no right to intervene in a disagreement on its own initiative and a second scenario where it has such a right.[165] Once ESMA gets involved, it can, in both cases, act as a mediator. In addition, it can, if certain conditions are met, also take individual decisions against a competent authority or a market actor.[166] ESMA's power is structured by additional requirements set out in sectoral legislation such as the PD. The latter only provides for conciliation and dispute settlement (pursuant to Article 19 of ESMA's Regulation) if a request for cooperation or to exchange information between competent authorities is ignored or not satisfactorily addressed.[167] Furthermore under ESMA's founding text

[164] Case 9/56 *Meroni* [1958] ECR 133. See also Case 98/80 Romano [1981] ECR 3715.

[165] See Chapter 1, section III, B.4.

[166] ESMAReg Art 19(3) and (4).

[167] PD Art 22. The directive adds explicitly that a competent authority may bring this to the attention of ESMA. It is not entirely clear whether this is supposed to be a condition for ESMA to take action.

it is apparent that additional conditions apply in the case where ESMA would seek to intervene in a disagreement on its own initiative. Thus, for ESMA to intervene on its own, it must be possible to determine the disagreement on the basis of 'objective criteria'.[168] As already noted earlier, this appears to be a direct reference to the requirements found in *Meroni* and an attempt to make sure that the exercise of delegated powers is non-discretionary.[169]

Questions over the permissible scope of a delegation of power It is this effort to structure the delegation in a way that makes it *Meroni* compliant and politically acceptable that explains much of the reasoning behind the requirements which are found in ESMA's Regulation and in sectoral legislation. The problematic issue is whether these conditions and requirements, including the provisions on appeals in ESMA's Regulation, are sufficient to make the delegation permissible. First of all, it is, at this juncture, not clear whether deciding disagreements over an action or inaction by a competent authority will always be strictly limited to evaluating and deciding factual matters which do not involve a wide margin of discretion. If interpretations of EU law were involved, the delegation would not be permissible in light of *Meroni* and *Romano* for that matter. Moreover, it is not obvious either that an individual decision taken by ESMA against a competent authority will not, in effect, have wider consequences. Once ESMA has taken position on an issue and addressed a legally binding individual decision to a competent authority, it seems unlikely that other competent authorities will ignore ESMA's decision. It could thus be argued that ESMA's power to take individual decisions is, in effect, akin to the exercise of general decision-making powers.

The delegation raises many other questions. The Financial Services Committee ('FSC') – a group of legal experts in the City of London – has expressed doubts about whether ESMA can be delegated powers to take binding individual decisions against competent authorities.[170] It has pointed out that the relevant procedures for dealing with failures by Member States to fulfil their EU obligations are set out in the Treaties.[171]

[168] ESMAReg Art 19(1).

[169] The ESMAReg also includes a recital which clarifies that ESMA cannot take decisions against a competent authority if the latter acts within its permissible discretionary scope of action (see Rec (32)).

[170] Financial Markets Law Committee, 'European financial supervision: legal risks' (Issue 152, August 2010) 9, www.fmlc.org/papers/Issue152Aug10.pdf.

[171] TFEU Arts 258 and 259.

The fact that the Treaties do not foresee ESMA's role and intervention could accordingly be problematic.[172]

The power to take a decision against a market actor raises questions as well. As a reminder, if a competent authority fails to comply with ESMA's decision and, in turn, a market actor fails to comply with obligations that are directly applicable to him by reason of ESMA's Framing Acts, ESMA can take an individual decision against the market actor.[173] ESMA's Regulation envisages this type of action in the context of the dispute settlement system, but also where ESMA is policing breaches of EU law.[174] The goal is to require compliance with directly applicable obligations. But how does this power accord with the formal hierarchy of legal acts which the Treaties lay down? Thus, the FSC has noted that ESMA's power to take individual decisions does not fit in well with the exercise of implementing powers under the Treaties.[175] But arguably there is another issue with the power to take individual decisions against market actors. It is an enforcement power. The subject matter of ESMA's decisions is to request a market actor to take an action or end a practice in order to comply with its obligations under EU law. This type of power is generally part of the enforcement toolkit of competent authorities. The problem with enforcement against individuals or firms is that the EU has generally no such competence in the internal market field. That seems all the more so for sanctioning powers, such as the power to impose fines on individuals or firms. It is a prerogative of Member States, closely linked to statehood, and an essential aspect of the vertical division of competences between Member States and the EU.[176] To be sure, there are exceptions. Competition law is one field that comes to my mind. But absent an express conferral, the EU relies on national enforcers to impose sanctions. Hence, if the EU has no such express power in the internal market field, it is hard to see how an EU institution can delegate an enforcement power to an agency. It would not act within the limits of its powers conferred upon it by the Treaties[177] and the delegation would infringe the Treaties. Admittedly, if this argument were accepted, it could, in practice, have some fairly unattractive consequences for the EU. There might indeed be good reasons for centralising

[172] Financial Markets Law Committee, 'European financial supervision: legal risks' 9.

[173] ESMAReg Art 19(4).

[174] Art 17(6). See also in relation to crisis situations, Art 18(4).

[175] Financial Markets Law Committee, 'European financial supervision: legal risks' 10.

[176] See also A. Dashwood, 'States in the European Union' [1998] 23 *European Law Review* 201, 213 (noting that coercion is the 'hallmark of statehood').

[177] TEU Art 13(2).

some enforcement powers. It might be more efficient to have a single body levying fines and policing the application of technical regulations. Different enforcement strategies at Member State level can undermine the effectiveness of harmonisation. The question of delegating sanctioning powers is not merely of academic interest. Recall that ESMA will be entrusted with the supervision of credit rating agencies. At the time of writing, discussions are still ongoing, but it is likely that ESMA will have the power to levy fines against market actors.

Effet utile and the delegation of powers The answers to all the questions that the delegation of powers raises depend, of course, on a correct legal understanding of the constitutional rules, principles and decisions which together form the framework in which the EU and ultimately ESMA must operate. In the final instance, it is a matter for the Court of Justice to provide answers. It is, however, fair to say that fitting the delegation of powers into an established set of rules, principles and decisions presupposes some inventive readings and interpretations. And yet – as a final argument – that is often what the Court of Justice does when it uses teleological or contextual interpretations. Indeed, the Court has traditionally been rather inventive, so to speak, when the question of the effectiveness of EU law was at stake. Seminal cases such as *Van Gend* or *Francovich* testify to the fact that the Court has been receptive to arguments which strengthen enforcement against non-complying Member States.[178] Thus, in *Van Gend* the Court was quick to rebut the argument that enforcement actions against a Member State had to be brought in front of the Court of Justice in accordance with the Treaty provisions. It did not matter that national courts were effectively enforcing EU law; nor did it matter that the Commission, the guardian of the Treaties, did not initiate the action. In fact, it was just as well. It amounted to 'an effective supervision in addition to the supervision entrusted by Articles 169 [Article 258 TFEU] and 170 [Article 259 TFEU] to the diligence of the Commission and of the Member States'.[179]

The fact that the Court was open-minded about the way in which EU law is enforced in order to ensure the full effectiveness of EU law arguably augurs well for ESMA. Indeed, the Court's notion of *effet utile* might

[178] Case 26/62 *Van Gend en Loos* [1963] ECR 1; Joined Cases C-6/90 and C-9/90 *Francovich* [1991] ECR I-5357.

[179] *Ibid.*

ultimately prove to be a potent argument in favour of the delegation of powers.

V Private enforcement and prospectus liability

So far, the EU's strategy for prospectus disclosure enforcement has been shown to be based on decentralised administrative enforcement and cooperation between competent authorities under the watchful eye of ESMA. The final aspect to consider is the PD's approach to private enforcement. The directive is emphatically minimalist with respect to private enforcement. Given the investor protection and market access ambitions of the PD, this lack of attention is not unproblematic. Liability or litigation risk may reduce the attractiveness of cross-border capital raising and may, as such, undermine the very aim of the single passport.[180] In contrast to *ex ante* administrative enforcement, effective liability standards are the principal guarantors of disclosure quality characteristics such as the accuracy of the disclosure including its truthfulness, and the completeness of the information. But the directive did not aspire to attempt to coordinate or harmonise liability regimes. The task would, no doubt, have been immense. The substantive and procedural aspects of civil liability are thus left to be decided by national law, with conflict of laws provisions addressing problems of Court jurisdiction and applicable law.[181]

[180] Note that the Commission has suggested that differing national liability regimes may not, in actual practice, create a significant obstacle for issuers. See 'Commission Background Document' 15.

[181] Ferran (E. Ferran, 'Cross-border offers of securities in the EU: the standard life flotation' (2007) 4 *European Company and Financial Law Review* 461–490, 482–84) has examined these questions in the light of the provisions of Council Regulation (EC) No 44/2001 of 22 December 2000 on jurisdiction and the recognition and enforcement of judgments in civil and commercial matters [2001] OJ 12/1 (the 'Brussels I Regulation') and Regulation (EC) No 864/2007 of the European Parliament and of the Council of 11 July 2007 on the law applicable to non-contractual obligations (Rome II) [2007] OJ L199/40 (the 'Rome II Regulation'). Art 2(1) of the Brussels I Regulation grants jurisdiction to the Member State in which the defendant is domiciled. For legal persons, domicile is determined on the basis of the place where the statutory seat, central administration or principal place of business is located (Art 60(1)). Art 2(1) knows a number of derogations. Thus, Art 5(3) grants 'in matters relating to tort, *delict* or *quasi-delict*', special jurisdiction to the courts of 'the place where the harmful event occurred or may occur'. According to the ECJ, the 'place where the harmful event occurred' can cover both 'the place where the damage occurred and the place of the event giving rise to it' (see Case C-189/08 *Zuid-Chemie v Mineralenfabriek* [2009] ECR I-06917, para. 23; Case 21/76 *Bier* ('*Mines de potasse d'Alsace*)' [1976] ECR 1735, para. 24). Meanwhile, the Rome II Regulation provides that, as a general rule, the law applicable to a 'non-contractual obligation arising out of a tort/

The greater resistance among Member States for common action in the field of tort law undoubtedly significantly reinforced their lack of interest in harmonising private enforcement. During the negotiations of the PD, the German government proposed to harmonise civil liability regimes on the grounds that civil liability was indispensable for ensuring accurate and reliable information and an 'essential element' for achieving the objective of a level playing field.[182] However, the German proposal did not rally much support among national governments.

In its final version, the directive only devotes a single article to private enforcement matters. It provides that Member States must make civil liability provisions applicable to those who are responsible for the prospectus disclosure.[183] As noted earlier, the directive does not deal with criminal liability.

Article 6(1) identifies the persons or bodies which may be held responsible for the information disclosed in the prospectus. Pursuant to the provision, shall, at least, be responsible for the disclosure: 'the issuer or its administrative, management or supervisory bodies, the offeror, the person asking for the admission to trading on a regulated market or the guarantor, as the case may be'. Some of these terms are fairly open-ended. For instance, Article 6(1), or the directive for that matter, does not specify the meaning of guarantor. The Level 2 PR only mentions that guarantees include arrangements such as sureties, mono-line insurance policies or keep well agreements.[184] At any rate, it is apparent that Article 6(1) is a minimum harmonisation provision. Responsibility may be extended under national law to persons other than those mentioned in the directive,

delict' is the law of the state 'in which the damage occurs irrespective of the country in which the event giving rise to the damage occurred and irrespective of the country or countries in which the indirect consequences of that event occur' (Art 4(1)). As far as prospectus liability is concerned, this is, according to Arons, likely to be the place where the financial loss was suffered and, more precisely, reasoning by reference to the Court's case law on the Brussels convention, the place where an investor's investment account is located. See T. Arons, "'All roads lead to Rome': Beware of the consequences! The law applicable to prospectus liability claims under the Rome II Regulation" (2008) 4 *Nederlands Internationaal Privaatrecht* 481. Note that Art 4(1) can be displaced in certain cases, such as when a tort/delict is 'manifestly more closely connected' with another state (Art 4(3)).

182 Council Document, 'Letter from Mr Hans Eichel to Mr Rodrigo de Rato i Figaredo dated 30 May 2002' (ref. 9505/02, 31 May 2002, on file).

183 Art 6(2).

184 Annex VI (1), PR. The Commission has stated that Art 6(1) does not require the guarantor to be made responsible for the full prospectus. Provided that the limits of responsibility are made plain, the guarantor's liability can be restricted to the disclosure found in Annex VI of the Level 2 PR. See '3rd Transposition Meeting' 8.

as long as Member States satisfy EU primary law (e.g., the freedom of movement) and the general principles of EU law (e.g., proportionality).[185] Moreover, at least one of the persons that Article 6(1) identifies must be responsible for the prospectus as a whole.[186] The directive adds that the persons who bear responsibility for the disclosure must be identified in the prospectus.[187] They must provide statements that 'to the best of their knowledge' the disclosure is factually correct and that the prospectus does not omit any information that is likely 'to affect its import'.[188]

The question of who is liable for the prospectus when securities are placed or resold to retail investors by financial intermediaries is briefly addressed in a recital to the directive that amended the PD in 2010 (the 'PAD').[189] The controversy over retail cascades was examined in more detail in Chapter 3.[190] Recall that retail cascades involve the resale of securities by financial intermediaries to retail investors.[191] The directive, as amended, allows resales or final placements of securities to be made through intermediaries without requiring another prospectus to be prepared, if a valid prospectus is available and written consent has been given for the use of the prospectus by the issuer or the person who is responsible for drafting the prospectus.[192] The (legally binding) text of the directive does not, however, explicitly address the question of who bears liability in such a scenario. To prevent uncertainty, a recital to the PAD adds that if the issuer (or the person responsible for drafting the prospectus) consents to the use of the prospectus, he should be liable for its information and for any final terms which may need to be prepared and filed in the case of a base prospectus.[193] If no such consent is given, the recital states that financial intermediaries should be asked to prepare a new prospectus and be liable for its disclosure, including any information incorporated by reference or added through the final terms.[194]

In order to address concerns that the prospectus summary, which by definition is incomplete, may be the sole basis for liability claims, the directive lays down special rules for summaries. These rules make a noteworthy inroad into national law, but they create only a certain carve-out

185 Cf., Case C-430/05 *Dionik*, paras 53–54 (in relation to penalties).
186 '4th Transposition Meeting' 4.
187 Art 6(1). 188 *Ibid.*
189 Directive (EU) 2010/73 [2010] OJ L327/1.
190 See Chapter 3, section V, A.3.
191 See, e.g., European Commission, 'Proposal for a Directive of the European Parliament and of the Council amending Directives 2003/71/EC ...' 7.
192 Art 3(2), as amended. 193 PAD Rec (10). 194 *Ibid.*

from national rules governing *civil* liability. Thus, the summary, or its translation, may give rise to liability if it is 'misleading, inaccurate or inconsistent, when read together with the other parts of the prospectus' or if 'it does not provide, when read together with the other parts of the prospectus, key information in order to aid investors when considering whether to invest in such securities'.[195] This second limb was added during the revisions of the directive in 2010 after much discussions and negotiations. In sum, the directive, as amended, allows a person to avoid liability – that is, civil liability – if the summary is not, when read together with other parts of the prospectus, misleading, inconsistent, inaccurate or fails to include key information.

To conclude, save for the provision on the prospectus summary, the PD does not make any significant inroads into national laws governing civil liability. While the PD establishes a more or less comprehensive *ex ante* administrative enforcement system, the directive refers mainly to national law with respect to prospectus liability. There are no provisions on the nature of the liability regime. Critical questions regarding the time limits for taking action, the burden and standard of proof or possible defences to liability are left untouched. The rules governing causation, as well as the nature and type of remedy, are unaddressed. And, of course, the personal scope of application of the relevant provisions will continue to differ given the minimum nature of Article 6(1). Undoubtedly, harmonising the content of national liability regimes would have represented an impossible challenge to achieve within the FSAP time deadlines. But ignoring private enforcement has meant that the EU's prospectus enforcement strategy is far from comprehensive and, given the preeminent position of *ex ante* enforcement, certainly overly one-dimensional.

VI Conclusion: evolutionary or revolutionary change?

This chapter examined the EU's prospectus disclosure enforcement strategy. By way of conclusion, it is worth making a few final points on the pattern of institutional change in the prospectus enforcement field. First, it is worth repeating that given its administrative enforcement orientations, the EU's prospectus enforcement strategy is overly one-dimensional. It is evident that patterns of legal integration in relation to disclosure

[195] Art 6(2), as amended. A warning will need to be added to the summary to this effect (*ibid.*). 'Key information' is a defined concept under the (amended) directive. It was examined in Chapter 3, section III, B.2.b.

regulation and disclosure enforcement have been developing at different paces. European disclosure regulation is based on internationally sanctioned disclosure standards. But these standards are enforced pursuant to distinct national law provisions and by separate national competent authorities. Nevertheless, the PD, in comparison to the LPD (as consolidated) and POD, made progress with respect to prospectus disclosure enforcement. It established a more comprehensive approval system and added provisions on the nature and powers of competent authorities. And even though the PD, by and large, avoided making inroads into national civil liability regimes, the addition of Article 6 represented an improvement on the LPD and POD. So also did the PD's provisions on administrative measures/sanctions. The establishment of CESR did, of course, also represent a noteworthy improvement on the pre-Lamfalussy situation. ESMA promises to mark a significant leap forward.

Overall, however, it is safe to say that the pattern of change with respect to substantive enforcement arrangements under the PD is consistent with the same form of 'incremental activism' which was shown to dominate institutional changes in Chapter 1. In comparison to disclosure regulation, there are obvious differences in the extent of harmonisation. But the direction of change is similarly consistent with an evolutionary trend towards greater centralisation and consolidation of competence at EU level.

7

Enforcement: national implementation

I Introduction

Chapter 6 examined the EU's approach to prospectus disclosure enforcement and discussed the different measures and powers which the PD introduced in order to ensure that its provisions and its implementing legislation were properly enforced and applied. The PD's preference for administrative *ex ante* enforcement was seen as part of an effort to 'manage' mutual recognition, in the sense suggested by Nicolaïdis.[1] I will return to the managed nature of the passport system in Chapter 10, but for now, it is worth turning the page and moving to enforcement at Member State level. I begin this chapter with an obvious observation. Because European and national levels of decision-making are interlocked, choices made at EU level with respect to enforcement affect enforcement patterns at Member State level. Although obvious, the point is important given that, as was noted in Chapter 5, there is a rich debate on enforcement in the law and economics, and law and finance, literature. This literature is, *inter alia*, interested in questions such as what are the most effective enforcement arrangements or what factors account for differences in enforcement patterns. Yet, what is missing from this debate is how enforcement patterns change, adapt or adjust to European law influences. This chapter seeks to fill this gap in the prospectus disclosure field. As elsewhere in this book,[2] I am interested in evaluating change, adjustment or adaption. To be sure, this chapter has limited ambitions. It only deals with the implementation of the PD's provisions in two Member States, albeit in two Member States with distinct legal systems. But the matter seems interesting enough, not least because the EU's enforcement strategy for prospectus disclosure places great emphasis on *ex ante* enforcement. Questions about whether civil law jurisdictions put more emphasis on prior approval, or for that matter, licensing (as a form of *ex ante* enforcement) cannot,

[1] Nicolaïdis, 'Regulatory cooperation and managed mutual recognition'.

[2] See the conclusions to Chapters 1, 3 and 6.

therefore, be fully answered without having regard to EU influences.[3] To carry out this assessment, inspiration can be drawn from the vast literature on Europeanisation.[4] This literature examines, in essence, how the EU affects 'domestic policy, politics and polity structures'[5] at Member State level.[6] In order to gain ground and chart the impact of European decisions, Europeanisation scholarship uses distinctions and classifications. Lenschow, for instance, identifies five different outcomes which are coined 'inertia', 'retrenchment', 'absorption', 'accommodation' and 'fundamental transformation'.[7] She notes:

> In the case of *inertia* member states resist adaptations; *retrenchment* implies the fortification rather than adaption of existing structures; in the case of *absorption* member states incorporate European requirements or inputs without modifying existing structures; *accommodation* implies the adaptation of existing structures without challenging their core features; and finally, *transformation* points to a fundamental shift of national practices.[8]

I will use these concepts in this chapter in order to capture both the size and direction of change[9] and, by the same token, to evaluate changes in enforcement patterns in France and the UK. The main instruments transposing the provisions of the PD in France are the *loi Breton* amending the French *code monétaire et financier* ('CMF') and the *règlement général* ('RG') of the French *Autorité des marchés financiers* ('AMF').[10] The Financial Services and Markets Act 2000 ('FSMA') and the Prospectus

[3] See Chapter 5 for details of this debate.

[4] E.g., K. Featherstone and C. Radaelli (eds.), *The Politics of Europeanization* (Oxford University Press, 2003); P. Graziano and M. Vink (eds.), *Europeanization – New Research Agendas* (Palgrave Macmillan, Basingstoke, 2008); S. Saurugger and C. Radaelli, 'The Europeanization of public policies: introduction' (2008) 10 *Journal of Comparative Policy Analysis* 213.

[5] A. Lenschow, 'Europeanisation of public policy' in J. Richardson (ed.), *European Union – Power and Policy-making* (Routledge, Abingdon, 2006) 55, 63.

[6] Implementation studies are part of the Europeanisation literature, but they do not define the scope of this literature exhaustively.

[7] Lenschow, 'Europeanisation of public policy' 62. Classifications are also provided in C. Radaelli, 'The Europeanization of public policy' in Featherstone and Radaelli (eds.), *The Politics of Europeanization* 27, 37; T. Börzel and T. Risse, 'When Europe hits home: Europeanization and domestic change' (2000) 4 *European Integration Online Papers* 1, 10.

[8] Lenschow, 'Europeanisation of public policy' 62.

[9] See on this, Radaelli, 'The Europeanization of public policy' 37.

[10] Loi n° 2005–842 du 26 juillet 2005 pour la confiance et la modernisation de l'économie (JO n° 173, 27 juillet 2005, p. 12160); AMF 'Règlement Général de l'Autorité des Marchés Financiers', www.amf-france.org.

Rules ('FSA-PR') transpose the directive in the UK. The FSA-PR are a separate set of rules in the Handbook of the Financial Services Authority ('FSA').[11] They co-exist, *inter alia*, with: (i) the FSA's Listing Rules, which are based on the old (yet reviewed and amended) UK listing rules, and certain provisions of the Consolidated Admissions and Reporting Directive ('CARD');[12] (ii) the Disclosure Rules and Transparency Rules which transpose provisions of the Market Abuse Directive ('MAD') and the Transparency Directive ('TD').[13] Note that the FSA, when acting as the competent authority for the purposes of the PD, will act as the UK Listing Authority ('UKLA').[14]

This chapter proceeds as follows. I begin in section II by examining administrative enforcement, after which I will turn, in section III, to private enforcement. Because of the PD's enforcement orientations, most of this chapter will be about administrative enforcement. Given that the directive does not address public enforcement in front of criminal Courts, I will only discuss it marginally when examining the power of competent authorities to bring criminal proceedings. Section IV concludes by returning a final time to the Europeanisation literature and the legal origins literature in order to examine whether the findings of this chapter add anything useful to the questions that are examined in the legal origins literature.

II Administrative enforcement in France and the UK

Neither in France nor in the UK did the implementation of the PD's provisions require changes in organisational structure. While the PD provides that competent authorities must be fully independent from market actors,[15] the meaning of independence is nowhere defined. Given that independent financial markets authorities – i.e., the FSA and the AMF – were already in place in the UK and in France prior to the entry into force of the PD, the directive's requirement was easily absorbed in both Member

[11] The FSA's Handbook is available at http://fsahandbook.info/FSA/html/handbook.

[12] Directive 2001/34/EC [2001] OJ L184/1.

[13] Directive 2003/6/EC [2003] OJ L96/16; Directive 2004/109/EC [2004] L390/38.

[14] It is also worth noting that the FSA's fate appears to be sealed for good. The British government decided in 2010 to replace the FSA by a set of new authorities. At the time of writing, detailed proposals are yet to be drawn up.

[15] PD Art 21(1). Art 21(2) allows for a limited delegation of tasks to non-administrative authorities.

States.[16] It is useful to begin this comparative study by differentiating between the existence of enforcement powers (A) and their exercise (B).

A *Existence of powers*

As we have seen in Chapter 6, the PD includes various rules and requirements whose purpose is to make sure that prospectus regulation is properly applied and enforced. The directive does not, however, define a uniform level of prescription with respect to these rules and requirements. The directive is most prescriptive with respect to the power to approve prospectuses. For other powers, it adopts a less specified approach, concentrating, for instance, on a core set of minimum powers or adopting open-ended language such as with respect to administrative sanctions/measures. Recall that the PD does not prescribe criminal sanctions.

1 Power to approve: *ex ante* enforcement

a Power to approve in France *Approval and scope of review: absorption.* As a reminder, the PD requires home state competent authorities to approve prospectuses before their publication and, therefore, before securities can be admitted to trading on a regulated market or offered to the public. As far as France is concerned, this requirement is laid down in the CMF and the AMF's RG.[17] Prior approval has been a familiar practice in France for many years.[18] Long before the PD was adopted, French courts had already ruled on the scope of the prospectus review by holding that when approving a prospectus, the regulatory authority certified that it had examined the consistency (*cohérence*) and relevance (*pertinence*) of the information.[19] The PD adopts a similar approach when providing that approval requires a home state authority to verify that the prospectus

[16] The statutory framework establishing the FSA is FSMA. The AMF was set up pursuant to the law on financial security (*loi de sécurité financière*) of 1 August 2003 (Loi n° 2003–706 du 1er août de sécurité financière (JO n°177, 2 août 2003, p. 13220)).

[17] C. monét. fin. Art L. 621-8; RG Art 212-1.

[18] The decision to approve a prospectus is known as 'visa' in France.

[19] E.g., CA Paris, 7 juill 1995, D. aff. 1995 p. 61; D.98, Som. 72, obs. Isabelle Bon-Garcin; CA Paris 19 mai 1998 RJDA 11/98 n° 1235. Although the review had to go beyond a mere formal check, French Courts held that approval was not meant to be an approval of the opportuneness of the transaction or represent an authentification of accounting and financial aspects. See also P-H. Conac, *La Régulation des Marchés Financiers par la Commission des Opérations de Bourse (COB) et la Securities and Exchange Commission (SEC)* (L.G.D.J., Paris, 2002) 49.

is complete and the information consistent and comprehensible.[20] The relevant provision of the directive was, accordingly, easily absorbed into French law.[21]

Approval and risk warnings: accommodation A noteworthy change, which followed the implementation of the PD, concerns the French authority's practice of adding risk warnings to prospectuses. The practice goes back to the *Commission des opérations de bourse* or Cob, one of the predecessors of the AMF. These warnings, which were distinct from the 'risk factor' item typically found in prospectuses, were, in essence, meant to alert the public to certain hazards of the investment for investors.[22] French courts had previously validated the practice,[23] but following the adoption of the PD, the AMF decided to reassess it.[24] It did not drop it altogether, but chose the path of accommodation. The AMF thus no longer adds risk warnings to prospectuses. Instead, it may decide to add a warning to advertising material. The RG states that advertising material relating to an offer to the public or admission to trading must be communicated to the AMF before being distributed.[25] Pursuant to the RG, such material shall, *inter alia*, make reference to the 'risk factor' item of the prospectus.[26] But, in addition, it provides that the AMF may, if necessary, ask that an additional warning be added to advertising material which regards 'certain exceptional characteristics of the issuer or the guarantors, if any, or the securities being offered to the public or admitted to trading on a regulated market'.[27]

Hence, the changes that the RG introduced are best seen as an attempt to reconcile previous practices with the new realities of regulation following the adoption of the PD and its more 'aggressive' single passport system. The AMF merely changed the way in which it conveys warnings to investors, but it did not call into question the need for such warnings. Crucially, by adjusting to the new realities of disclosure regulation, the AMF can address real or perceived regulatory arbitrage. Thus, it can ensure that issuers cannot circumvent potential risk warnings, which the AMF might see fit to add, by seeking approval of a prospectus abroad

[20] PD Art 2(1)(q).

[21] C. monét. fin. L. 621-8-1. I.

[22] See H. de Vauplane and J. Bornet, *Droit des Marchés Financiers* (Litec, Paris, 2001) 154.

[23] See *ibid.*, Conac, *La Régulation des Marchés Financiers* 50 (fn 3).

[24] For details, see D. Gewinner and C. Uzan, 'La transposition de la directive "prospectus" en droit français' (Juillet-Août 2005) *Bulletin Joly Bourse* 375, 385–6.

[25] RG Art 212-28. [26] Art 212-28 5°. [27] Art 212-28 6°.

(in accordance with the PD) and by subsequently taking advantage of the passport system in order to 'passport' the prospectus into France without having to seek approval with the French authority.[28] But the AMF's implementation is not without causing frictions with the text of the directive. This is because the RG does not differentiate between the situation where the AMF acts as an issuer's home state authority *or* as a host state authority. Specifically, the AMF's power to add risk warnings when acting as the host state authority seems to flatly contradict Article 15(6) of the PD which deals with advertising and provides for home country control: '[t]he competent authority of the home Member State shall have the power to exercise control over the compliance of advertising activity'.[29] In order to justify the AMF's competence to take action when acting as a host state authority, some have argued that Article 15 is not a maximum harmonisation provision.[30] The underlying reasoning is simply that in the absence of exhaustive harmonisation, Member States cannot be prevented from adopting stricter standards. But this argument is not convincing given that the wording of Article 15(6), which provides for home country control, does not state that home country control is without prejudice to the actions of host state authorities. A better argument for resolving the conundrum, but one which is not free of criticism either, was made by CESR which noted that advertising activities did not have the benefit of the single passport.[31] Host Member States cannot, as a result, be obliged to accept advertising material originating from elsewhere, even though they must accept prospectuses which have been approved in another Member State. For CESR, no further action was, therefore, required;[32] the intervention of host Member States was permissible. Accordingly, the changes that the AMF introduced can be described as examples of accommodation, although, admittedly, the case in favour of host state competence under Article 15 of the directive is by no means clear-cut.

Approval of a tripartite document (ex post approval for registration documents): inertia While prior approval of prospectuses has been part and parcel of the French approach to prospectus regulation, the AMF and its predecessor, the Cob, have nevertheless over time sought to facilitate

[28] See for details, Gewinner and Uzan, 'La transposition de la directive "prospectus"' 385–6.
[29] Art 15(6).
[30] Gewinner and Uzan, 'La transposition de la directive "prospectus"' 385.
[31] CESR, 'CESR's report on the PD' 33.
[32] *Ibid.*

approval requirements for certain types of issuers by adopting a number of special procedures. We have already seen in Chapter 4 that, in 2007, the AMF adopted special arrangements for the review and approval of documents submitted by SEC registered companies that intend to cross-list on a regulated market in France.[33] In January 2008, it also signed a memorandum of understanding ('MOU') with the Israel Securities Authority in order to facilitate cross-listings.[34] However, of special interest for the present purposes is another, separate, arrangement for issuers using shelf-registration. Recall that the PD provides for shelf-registration. A prospectus may be drawn up as a tripartite document consisting of a registration document, a securities note and a summary note.[35] The directive's rules on tripartite prospectuses were easily absorbed into French law. Shelf-registration has been in place in France for many years. Under the RG, a registration document is known as either a *document de référence* or, in the case of a first admission to trading of equity securities, a *document de base*.[36] Registration documents can benefit from a special approval procedure. Thus, the RG includes specific arrangements for issuers having submitted three registration documents in succession.[37] These issuers can make their registration document available to the public the day that follows the filing of the document with the AMF.[38] The registration document will, as a result, be available to the public before the AMF has reviewed it. In essence, therefore, the AMF uses an *ex post* procedure for the review of certain registration documents. The procedure goes back to the Cob which first introduced it. It survived the PD's provisions on *ex ante* approval.

The fact that the AMF continues approving certain documents on an *ex post* basis is somewhat suspect. The PD does not provide for an *ex post* control. It only knows one type of control: *prior* approval of prospectuses. CESR has also made this point plain in its standards on financial

[33] AMF, 'Décision de l'AMF en matière de reconnaissance des standards américains pour une admission à la négociation sur un marché réglementé'. See also NYSE Euronext, 'Fast path listing using SEC filings' 13.

[34] 'Memorandum of understanding between the Autorité des marchés financiers and the Israel Securities Authority concerning the regulatory equivalence with regards to the cross listing of securities' (28 January 2008), www.amf-france.org/documents/general/8145_1.pdf.

[35] PD Art 5(3). [36] RG Art 212-9. [37] Art 212-13.

[38] Art 212-13 III. If an issuer has not yet submitted three consecutive registration documents, the AMF will register the registration document first (Art 212-13 II.). Registration will be preceded by an *ex ante* control of the document. See AMF, 'Le prospectus' (March 2007) Annexe 1, www.amf-france.org/documents/general/7709_1.pdf.

information which I examined in Chapter 6. Recall that Principle 12 of Standard No. 1 stresses that for prospectuses 'ex-ante approval is the normal procedure'.[39] *Ex post* control is still possible, but only as a complementary measure pursuant to Principle 12. Admittedly, the point about the AMF's *ex post* review procedure is rather academic given that an offer to the public or an admission to trading on a regulated market cannot take place in France before all parts of the prospectus have been reviewed and approved.[40] But it is nevertheless the case that the directive treats a registration document as a constituent part of a prospectus[41] and that accordingly, in the absence of an express provision, a registration document should not be treated as making exception to the arrangements that apply for the approval of prospectuses.[42] Under the directive, approval is a condition for the publication of a prospectus. Given that the registration document is a constituent part of a prospectus, an *ex post* procedure for the approval of a registration document does not seem to be consistent with the PD. The AMF's implementation of the relevant provisions can accordingly be seen as an instance of inertia. The AMF does, evidently, not share this view.[43] It remains committed to its *ex post* procedure.[44]

Approval and third party investigations: accommodation Before deciding to approve a prospectus, the AMF, like other competent authorities, typically relies on the investigations and declarations of third parties. Statutory auditors (*contrôleurs légaux des comptes*) and investment services providers (so-called *prestataires de services d'investissement*) provide the AMF

[39] CESR, 'Standard No. 1'. [40] RG Art 212-10. [41] See PD Art 5(3).

[42] The PD envisages the situation where a reference document has been *filed* with an authority, but has not been approved (Art 12(3)). But note that the filing of a prospectus and the publication of a prospectus are separate requirements under the directive.

[43] Nor did the Cob share this view. When the Cob consulted on the introduction of an *ex post* procedure in 2001, market actors drew its attention to the fact that the adoption of an *ex post* control procedure was not in line with developments at EC level, notably with propositions made in the context of a Commission proposal for a prospectus directive (see COB, 'Bulletin mensuel d'information de la Commission des opérations de bourse' (n° 362, November 2001) 47, www.amf-france.org/affiche.asp?id=5715). The Cob responded by noting that an *ex ante* procedure was envisaged only for prospectuses, but not foreseen for registration documents (*ibid.*).

[44] In fact, it made new adjustments to its approval procedures in 2008. For issuers that are subject to *ex post* control, the AMF put in place a simplified and lightened approval procedure for the securities and summaries notes (see Instruction n° 2005-11 du 13 décembre 2005, Art 5 II). Provided a number of conditions are met, the AMF reviews the securities and summaries notes within a three-day period (Instruction n° 2005-11, Art 5 II. 5°).

with assurances regarding the quality of the disclosure.[45] The role of the former has been especially noteworthy in France, as the French regulator has insisted that statutory auditors not only examine financial statements, but also proceed to an overall review (*lecture d'ensemble*) of all other information included in a prospectus, or for that matter, a registration document.[46] On the completion of these extended review tasks a written statement is produced. But following the adoption of the PD and especially the Level 2 PR, the AMF re-assessed these arrangements. They were indeed potentially at risk of falling foul of the PR which leaves Member States very little room to define unilaterally additional requirements and, as such, to ask statutory auditors to make additional statements in a prospectus, on top of those required by the regulation.[47] Given that the AMF considered its practice to be important for investor protection,[48] it finally adopted Article 212–15 II. which specifies that the auditor, following his overall review, addresses a letter (*lettre de fin de travaux*) to the issuer in which he records, *inter alia*, his possible observations. Importantly, a copy of this letter must be addressed by the issuer to the AMF prior to the AMF deciding to approve the prospectus or prior to the registration document being filed or registered.[49] Article 212–5 II. states that it is for the AMF, when examining the prospectus, to draw the necessary conclusions from the auditor's observations. For the present purposes, this procedural change provides yet another example of how the AMF has sought to accommodate EU arrangements without having to make any fundamental changes to its existing and long-established practices. It is thus by adjusting the way in which the auditor communicates her observations that the AMF was able to maintain its practice. As a result, the extended role of the auditor as a quality gatekeeper could also be maintained under the RG.

b Power to approve in the UK *Approval of public offer prospectuses: transformation.* The requirement for prior approval of prospectuses

[45] RG Arts 212-15 and 212–16.

[46] RG Art 212-15 I. and II. See also on this practice and the implementation of the PD, Gewinner and Uzan, 'La transposition de la directive "prospectus"' 381–2.

[47] See Gewinner and Uzan, 'La transposition de la directive "prospectus"' 381–2.

[48] AMF, 'Transposition de la directive "prospectus" dans le règlement général de l'AMF: consultation publique jusqu'au 10 juin 2005' (Consultation Document, undated) 37, www.amf-france.org/documents/general/6074_1.pdf.

[49] RG Art. 212-15 II.

is found in the FSA's Prospectus Rules and FSMA.[50] On a closer look, it is apparent that the transposition of the PD's provisions on prior approval led to a major extension of the approval mechanism – or as the Treasury put it, a 'fundamental change from the existing regime'[51] – in the UK. Prospectus Rule 3.1.10 R implements Article 13(1) of the PD. It provides that '[a] prospectus must not be published until it has been approved by the FSA'. The adoption of this rule broke with the past. Prior to the PD, prospectuses for public offers of unlisted securities only had to be filed with the Companies House.[52] The obligation to seek prior approval now extends to these offers. The faithful implementation of Article 13(1) of the directive is, therefore, consistent with transformation as described in the introductory section of this chapter.

Approval of tripartite documents: absorption The FSA's Prospectus Rules also transpose the provisions of the directive regarding the format of a prospectus.[53] Shelf-registration was not unknown in the UK before the transposition of the PD. But it was not, unlike in France, particularly popular with issuers.[54] Moreover, unlike in France where certain issuers benefit of an *ex post* procedure, registration documents are approved on an *ex ante* basis in the UK.[55]

Approval and scope of review: inertia? Section 87A of FSMA sets out the criteria which the FSA – the UKLA, to be more precise – is held to consider before deciding whether to approve a prospectus. *Inter alia*, it provides that the UKLA must make sure that the prospectus contains the 'necessary information' and that the relevant regulatory requirements

[50] FSA-PR 3.1.10 R, FSMA s 85(1) and (2).

[51] HM Treasury, 'UK implementation of the Prospectus Directive 2003/71/EC – a consultation document' (HM Treasury, October 2004) 21 (noting that '[u]nder the Prospectus Directive regime all prospectuses in relation to public offers will need to be approved by the FSA. This is a fundamental change from the existing regime which requires that for all non-listed securities, prospectuses needed to be filed at Companies House but did not require approval'), http://webarchive.nationalarchives.gov.uk/+/www.hm-treasury.gov.uk/d/DFE27339-BCDC-D4B3–16FD311B308ABF54.pdf.

[52] *Ibid.* [53] FSA-PR 2.2.1 R.

[54] PricewaterhouseCoopers, 'Primary market comparative regulation study – Key themes' (April 2002) in FSA, 'Review of the listing regime' (Discussion Paper 14, July 2002) 39, www.fsa.gov.uk/pubs/discussion/dp14.pdf.

[55] The FSA-PR include an interpretative provision that allows drawing this conclusion. See FSA-PR 3.1.11 R (2), stating that 'a reference in this section to a prospectus is, unless the context otherwise requires, to be taken to be a reference to the document or documents to which the application relates'.

have been complied with. Necessary information is information which is necessary for investors to make an 'informed assessment' on, in essence, the financial situation of the issuer and the rights attached to the securities.[56] Moreover, this information is to be presented in comprehensible form and must be easy to analyse.[57] Section 87A draws (essentially) on Article 5 of the directive, especially Article 5(1), which, *inter alia*, sets out a general disclosure principle. However, neither FSMA nor the FSA's Prospectus Rules transpose Article 2(1)(q) of the directive which defines the scope of the prospectus review.[58]

Prior to the transposition of the PD, the FSA insisted on the scope of its review and approval procedures in the guidance manual to its old listing rules. The manual stated that the FSA did

> not itself investigate or verify the accuracy or completeness of the information set out in such documents, nor does it check the sources of, or verify, the information.[59]

During the consultation phase preceding the adoption of the Prospectus Rules, the FSA noted that, as far as the rules regarding approval procedures were concerned, no substantial modifications were planned, except for the adoption of the PD's rules governing tripartite prospectuses.[60] The extent to which the FSA revised its approval and review procedures following the transposition of the directive is, thus, not entirely clear. Admittedly, the failure to transpose Article 2(1)(q) might, in practice, make little difference given the vague language of the rule in question. But from a legal point of view, Articles 5(1) and 2(1)(q) of the PD are nevertheless distinct in nature. The former sets out a general disclosure principle. It is the latter which creates a specific obligation incumbent upon competent authorities.

Approval and third party investigations: accommodation/transformation
Before the PD was adopted, prospectus enforcement was a field that testified to deep-rooted differences between Member States such as France or the UK. Under the old UK listing rules, it was mainly a market professional,

[56] FSMA s 87A(2). [57] FSMA s 87A(3).

[58] It defines approval as 'the positive act at the outcome of the scrutiny of the completeness of the prospectus ... including the consistency of the information given and its comprehensibility'.

[59] FSA, 'UKLA Guidance Manual' (update June 2003, on file), para. 1.3.14.

[60] FSA, 'The listing review and implementation of the Prospectus Directive' 15.

the so-called sponsor, who was entrusted with the task of making sure that issuers complied with their listing requirements.[61] The tasks of sponsors were diverse.[62] They advised issuers, but also acted as intermediaries between issuers and the FSA.[63] Moreover, sponsors were meant to assure the FSA that the relevant regulatory requirements were satisfied.[64]

During the consultation phase preceding the implementation of the PD, the FSA noted that the PD did not contain an express provision that dealt with the role of sponsors.[65] It later took the view that, because the PD was a maximum harmonisation directive, it could not make provision for issuers to appoint a sponsor if they sought admission to trading on a regulated market.[66] But the FSA did not drop the sponsor requirement altogether. For issuers admitted, or seeking admission, to the UK Official List, the FSA considered that the sponsor regime could be maintained in areas that were outside the scope of the PD.[67] As a result the FSA's Prospectus Rules did not enact the requirement to appoint a sponsor. Instead, the provisions governing sponsors were included in a separate set of rules, the FSA's Listing Rules ('FSA-LR'), which deal with admissions to the Official List.[68] Under these rules, the sponsor requirement applies to issuers with, or which seek, a premium listing of equity securities in the UK.[69] Previously known as a primary listing, a premium listing is considered to be the "'premium brand' of the Official List".[70] The latter requires issuers to comply with a number of super-equivalent requirements, i.e., requirements on top of those set by EU legislation (e.g., the sponsor regime).[71] It is different from a standard listing. A standard listing only presupposes that issuers comply with EU requirements.[72]

61 Sponsors did not need to be appointed for each and every transaction. A sponsor was, for instance, not required for so-called 'specialist debt securities' bought and traded by professional investors.

62 FSA, 'Review of the listing regime' (CP 203, October 2003) Annex H (summarising the main tasks and obligations of the sponsor under the old listing rules), www.fsa.gov.uk/pubs/cp/cp203.pdf.

63 *Ibid.*, 70. 64 See also now FSA-LR 8.3.1 R.

65 FSA, 'Review of the listing regime' (DP 14) 29.

66 FSA, 'Review of the listing regime' (CP 203) 70.

67 *Ibid.* 68 FSA-LR 8. See also FSMA s 88.

69 For details, see FSA-LR 8.2.

70 FSA, 'A review of the structure of the listing regime' (DP 08/1, January 2008) 11, www.fsa.gov.uk/pubs/discussion/dp08_01.pdf. See also on the listing regime, FSA, 'Listing regime review – policy statement for CP08/21 and further minor consultation' (CP09/24**, October 2009), www.fsa.gov.uk/pubs/cp/cp09_24.pdf.

71 FSA, 'Listing regime – FAQs' (Issue 2, June 2010) 1, www.fsa.gov.uk/pages/Doing/UKLA/pdf/listing_regime_faqs.pdf.

72 *Ibid.*

In the past, the FSA's rules meant that UK issuers would often have to appoint a sponsor. Specifically, UK issuers were obliged, for equity securities, to seek a primary listing if they wished to access the Official List.[73] What is more, these issuers were obliged to seek a primary listing if they wished equity securities to be admitted to certain types of markets, including – importantly – regulated markets in relation to which the provisions of the PD apply.[74] As a consequence, UK issuers, wishing to have equity securities admitted to, say, the main market of the London Stock Exchange, were effectively required to appoint a sponsor, notwithstanding the FSA's earlier conclusion that the PD did not support a sponsor regime.

To be sure, following the FSA's recent review of the listing regime which introduced the new segmentation into premium and standard listing, the FSA no longer requires UK issuers, which seek admission to the Official list, to choose a premium listing for their equity securities.[75] The latter may now decide to list on the standard segment where the sponsor requirement does not apply. The adoption of these rules has brought the UK closer to a pattern of change that is more consistent with transformation than accommodation. But it postdates the implementation of the PD and is mainly due to the FSA's view that it should no longer discriminate between UK and overseas issuers listing in the UK.[76] What is more, UK companies will, in practice, continue having some incentives to choose the premium segment over the standard segment. This is because only companies with a premium listing are eligible for inclusion in the FTSE UK index series.[77]

2 Power to request information, investigate and sanction

Absorption or accommodation Besides the power to approve a prospectus, the PD requires competent authorities to have a range of additional powers to carry out their duties[78] and makes provision for administrative sanctions to be put in place.[79] But, as already noted, the directive took a modest approach with respect to these powers and

[73] FSA, 'A review of the structure of the listing regime' 21.

[74] For example, the main market of the London Stock Exchange. See London Stock Exchange, 'A guide to the main market' (February 2007) 12, www.londonstockexchange.com/companies-and-advisors/main-market/main/guide-main-market.pdf.

[75] FSA, 'Listing regime review' (CP09/24**) 11.

[76] See *ibid.*, 11 (noting that '[o]ur view remains that UK companies should have the same choice as overseas companies').

[77] *Ibid.* [78] PD Art 21(3) and (4). [79] Art 25.

sanctions. It concentrated on a *minimum* set of core powers. In relation to administrative sanctions, it failed to identify any particular measures or sanctions and only provided, in line with the Court's case law, for measures to be 'effective, proportionate and dissuasive'.[80] The implementation of these provisions seems to have been fairly painless.[81] This might, in turn, have to do with the fact that the directive is not prescriptive with respect to these powers and sanctions. Overall, any adjustments or changes, which ensued in France or the UK in order to implement the relevant provisions, appear to be consistent with either 'absorption' or 'accommodation'. Below, I will concentrate on three types of powers, i.e., the power of an authority to request information, the power to investigate and the power to sanction, each of which is crucial to the functioning of the regime.

Powers to request information In order for authorities to carry out their review and approval tasks, the EU legislature decided that competent authorities should have the power to request information or documents to be *provided* to them or to be *published* in a prospectus.[82] Both the FSA and AMF have such powers. When reviewing an application for approval, the FSA is thus empowered to ask a person applying for approval to provide documents and information.[83] Likewise, it may request documents and information from a person controlled by the applicant or controlling it, from an auditor, a manager of the applicant, or a commissioned financial intermediary.[84] The AMF, on the other hand, is empowered in

[80] Art 25(1).

[81] That is not to say that the PD did not require the adoption of new provisions in both Member States. But these changes or adjustments do not appear to have led to fundamental shifts. Having said this, specific changes were more difficult to identify, not least because of the fact that changes were given less prominence in policy documents. Arguably, this supports the view that there were no fundamental changes in relation to *ex post* enforcement. Nevertheless, some hesitations remain. Note that in order to gain ground, I also used information made available by CESR (see CESR, 'An evaluation of equivalence of supervisory powers in the EU under the Market Abuse Directive and the Prospectus Directive – a report to the Financial Services Committee').

[82] Art 21(3).

[83] FSMA s 87C(4). FSMA s 87C(6) specifies that the information/documents must be 'reasonably required in connection with the exercise by the competent authority of its functions in relation to the application'. See also FSMA s 87C(7) which states that '[t]he competent authority may require any information provided under this section to be provided in such a form as it may reasonably require'.

[84] FSMA s 87J(1)(b), (c) and (d).

broad and general terms to ask for any explanation or justification[85] and to request documents and information from the issuer, from the persons controlled by the issuer or controlling it, as well as from the issuer's auditors or its statutory auditors.[86]

With respect to the power to require information to be published in the prospectus, FSMA states that 'as a condition of approving a prospectus' the FSA may ask for supplementary information to be added to the prospectus.[87] The AMF is given similar powers under the CMF. It may request information to be added to the prospectus or may ask for statements to be changed before approving a prospectus.[88]

Powers to investigate The AMF and FSA are also granted various powers of investigation. The AMF is, for example, empowered to ask for additional investigations to be carried out by the issuer's statutory auditors or, if it considers that the statutory auditors have not exercised their tasks with sufficient care, for an audit to be carried out by an external specialist.[89] In addition, the AMF has the power to carry out inspections or open an investigation procedure if it deems it necessary for performing its tasks.[90] FSMA, meanwhile, requires the FSA 'to maintain arrangements designed to enable it to determine whether persons on whom requirements are imposed by or under [FSMA] ... are complying with them.[91] In order to satisfy its obligations, Part VI of FSMA grants the FSA various specific powers when acting as the UK Listing Authority. Thus, when it considers an application for approval of a prospectus, the FSA can ask for any information to be verified in such manner as it 'may reasonably require' – whether this information is provided in a document or in some other form.[92] It may also ask for any document to be authenticated 'in such manner, as it may reasonably require'.[93] Moreover, like the AMF, the FSA can launch a formal investigation procedure if there are circumstances that appear to suggest that there has been a breach of relevant provisions.[94]

[85] C. monét. fin. Art L. 621-8-1 I. In particular, the AMF may request explanations/justifications about the issuer's situation, its activities, its results or about any guarantor (*ibid.*).

[86] C. monét. fin. Article L. 621-18.

[87] FSMA s 87J(1)(a).

[88] C. monét. fin. L. 621-8-1. See also Art L. 621-18 in relation to published documents.

[89] RG Art 212-20. [90] C. monét. fin. Art L. 621-9 I.

[91] FSMA Schedule 1, para 6(1). [92] FSMA s 87C(8). [93] *Ibid.*

[94] FSMA s 97(1). A course of action which is open to the FSA is to appoint a person to conduct investigations on its behalf. See FSMA s 97(2) and the FSA's Enforcement Guide, FSA-EG 3.10.

Powers to sanction (administrative sanctions)[95] The PD positively identified a number of sanctioning powers.[96] In the UK, these powers were mainly implemented in FSMA. Thus, in accordance with the directive, FSMA states that the FSA has the power to require an offeror to suspend, on the basis of reasonable grounds, an offer to the public for up to ten working days.[97] With respect to advertising material relating to an offer, it may require that no advertisement is made, or that existing advertisement is suspended, for up to ten working days.[98] In case of a breach, or if the FSA reasonably believes that a relevant provision is likely to be breached, it has the power to require the offer to be withdrawn.[99] Similar powers are accorded to the FSA in the case of an admission of securities (or an application for admission) to trading on a UK regulated market.[100] The FSA may ask that a request to be admitted to trading be suspended for up to ten working days if it has 'reasonable grounds for suspecting that an applicable provision has been infringed'.[101] If the securities have already been admitted to trading, it can ask that trading be suspended for up to ten working days.[102] In case of an actual finding of an infringement, the FSA is empowered to ask that trading in the securities be prohibited.[103] As with public offers, the FSA's powers also extend to advertising material relating to the securities.[104]

The UK authority has also various other powers to carry out its duties. It can 'name and shame' by making public the fact that an issuer, a person offering securities to the public or seeking admission to trading on a regulated market has failed to comply with applicable provisions.[105] It may, of course, also impose financial penalties for the infringement of relevant provisions.[106] Note that FSMA does not prescribe a maximum amount for such penalties. It merely states that the penalty may be 'of such amount as [the FSA] considers appropriate.[107] The precise amount is, therefore, a matter for the FSA to decide.[108]

[95] Given our interest in the PD, I will pay attention to those enforcement powers that apply either in relation to an admission of securities to trading on a regulated market or a public offer. Injunction powers are not specifically examined here. In the case of the FSA, see FSMA ss 380 and 381. In the case of the AMF, see C. monét. fin. Art L. 621-14.

[96] PD Art 21(3) and (4), Art 25.

[97] FSMA s 87K(2).

[98] *Ibid.* [99] FSMA ss 87K(3) and 87K(4).

[100] FSMA s 87L. [101] FSMA s 87L(2). [102] FSMA s 87L(3).

[103] FSMA s 87L(4). [104] FSMA s 87L(2)(b) and (3)(b).

[105] FSMA s 87M. [106] FSMA s 91(1A). [107] *Ibid.*

[108] The FSA has recently reviewed the manner in which it calculates penalties. See FSA, 'Enforcement financial penalties – feedback on CP09/19' (PS10/4, March 2010), www.fsa.gov.uk/pubs/policy/ps10_04.pdf.

The AMF too is granted various sanctioning powers in order to enforce prospectus requirements. Like the FSA, it is empowered to suspend an offer to the public or an admission to trading on a regulated market for up to ten trading days if it has reasonable grounds for suspecting that a transaction does not comply with applicable laws and regulations.[109] It may prohibit a transaction if it has reasonable grounds for suspecting that a public offer does not comply with applicable laws and regulations, or if a proposed admission to trading on a regulated market does not comply with applicable laws and regulations.[110] Like the FSA, the AMF's powers extend to advertising material which it may prohibit or suspend for ten trading days if it has reasonable grounds for suspecting that they do not comply with relevant requirements.[111] It can make any observation, which it made to an issuer, known to the public.[112] Indeed, it can make public any other information that it considers necessary.[113] Finally, the AMF has also the power to impose financial sanctions. In relation to securities admitted to trading on a regulated market (or for which admission to trading is sought), the *code* provides that the AMF may sanction any person who, in France or abroad, has engaged, or has attempted to engage in, *inter alia*, the dissemination of false information in relation to the securities, or whose actions with respect to the securities harm investor protection or the proper functioning of markets.[114] The power to sanction a person for the dissemination of false information in France or from abroad, also applies with respect to public offers.[115] As far as penalty amounts are concerned, the CMF sets, however, a cap on the amounts that can be claimed. According to the French *code*, financial penalties cannot be greater than EUR 100 million or ten times the amount of profit which may have been made.[116] Note that the AMF's sanctions can also be made public unless the publication would risk seriously disrupting markets or causing a disproportionate harm to the parties involved.[117]

[109] RG Art 213-1. See also C. monét. fin. L. 621-8-1 II.

[110] RG Art 213-2. See also C. monét. fin. L. 621-8-1 II.

[111] C. monét. fin. L. 621-8-2.

[112] C. monét. fin. L. 621-18. [113] *Ibid.*

[114] C. monét. fin. L. 621-15 II. c). The CMF adds that the AMF may also sanction a person if these actions were committed on French soil, but concerned financial instruments admitted to trading, or for which admission to trading on a regulated market has been sought, abroad (i.e., in another Member State or in a State of the EEA). See C. monét. fin. L. 621-15 II. d).

[115] C. monét. fin. L. 621-15 II. e).

[116] C. monét. fin. L. 621-15 III. c).

[117] C. monét. fin. L. 621-15 V.

3 Power to bring criminal proceedings

The PD did not make provision for criminal sanctions. It merely stated that Member States were not prevented from imposing criminal sanctions.[118] It is apparent that considerable differences persist in this area between Member States. In France, for instance, the AMF cannot take criminal action. Instead, a public prosecutor (*procureur de la République*) will decide on beginning criminal proceedings for, for example, breach of Article L. 465-2 of the CMF which sanctions, *inter alia*, the dissemination by any person of 'false or deceptive information'.[119] The division of tasks between judicial authorities and the AMF has, in the past, been criticised for the lack of effective coordination between authorities.[120] Besides, it appears that, in practice, the office of the public prosecutor has used its (limited) resources only to prosecute the 'most reprehensible' cases.[121]

In the UK, on the other hand, the FSA is empowered to prosecute offences. FSMA authorises the FSA to bring criminal proceedings for offences which are set out in FSMA or in subordinate legislation[122] and for offences under various other acts.[123] In addition, as a corporate body, the FSA also enjoys a right of private prosecution.[124] The Court of Appeal held that FSMA does not exhaustively specify the FSA's powers to bring criminal proceedings. It concluded that 'the FSA does have the power to prosecute offences beyond those referred to in sections 401 and 402 of

[118] PD Art 25(1).

[119] Note that Art L. 621-15-1 requires the AMF to inform the public prosecutor if it finds that a possible offence under Art L. 465-1 or L. 465-2 may have been committed. If the public prosecutor decides to take action, it is required to inform the AMF 'without delay' (*ibid.*). See also Art L. 621-20-1 which requires the AMF to inform the public prosecutor if it notices that an offence (*crime* or *délit*) has been committed.

[120] E. Rosenfeld and J. Veil, 'Sanctions administratives, sanction pénales' *Pouvoirs* 2009/1 n° 128, p. 61, 68.

[121] E. Bouretz and J-L. Emery, *Autorité des marchés financiers et Commission bancaire – Pouvoirs de Sanction et Recours* (Revue Banque, Paris, 2008) 45.

[122] FSMA s 401(1). For offences, see, for example, FSMA s 397 (misleading statements and practices) or s 85 which makes it an offence for a person to make a public offer in the UK or seek admission to trading on a UK regulated market unless an approved prospectus is made available to the public. For a detailed examination of offences, see A. Hudson, *Securities Law* (Sweet & Maxwell, London, 2008).

[123] See FSMA s 402(1) enacting a right to institute proceedings for the FSA under Part V of the Criminal Justice Act 1993 (insider dealing), under 'prescribed regulations' concerning money laundering and under Schedule 7 to the Counter-Terrorism Act 2008 (terrorist financing or money laundering).

[124] *R v Neil Rollins*; *R v Michael McInerney* [2009] EWCA Crim 1941.

FSMA 2000'.[125] The Supreme Court recently confirmed the decision on appeal.[126]

B Exercise of powers

Weak EU influences We have seen so far that the FSA and the AMF hold various enforcement powers, but we have said little about the exercise of these powers. The question of the manner in which securities authorities exercise their powers has become central to the debate on enforcement in the law and economics literature.[127] Roe, Jackson and Coffee have all sought to draw conclusions on this subject by relying on measures such as the budget or staff of regulatory authorities, or the number of enforcement actions brought by them.[128] For the present purposes, the relevant point is that the EU legislature has taken a hands-off approach to these matters. While Ecofin ministers have stressed the importance of ensuring adequate funding and staffing and invited Member States to make sure that sufficient resources are available for competent authorities to be able to carry out their tasks,[129] the fact is that the budget and staff levels of competent authorities remain ultimately matters to be decided by national actors. The EU has had modest influences on other matters too: for example, the statutory (or institutional) objectives of national authorities. Arguably, these objectives can contribute to influencing an authority's behaviour in the enforcement field. Ecofin ministers have previously agreed to amend the mandates of competent authorities at national level in order for them to be able to take an 'EU dimension' into account when carrying out their tasks.[130] But CESR has, rightly, been sceptical of the prospect of seeing

[125] *Ibid*. According to the Court, the decision made 'practical good sense'. It noted: '[w]here offences form part of the same criminality as offences that the FSA has undoubted power to prosecute under FSMA 2000, it is sensible that they should be capable of being included in the same indictment and that the FSA should be able to act as the single prosecutor instead of having to bring in another prosecuting authority'.

[126] *R v Rollins* [2010] UKSC 39.

[127] See Chapter 5 for details.

[128] Jackson and Roe, 'Public and private enforcement of securities laws'; Jackson, 'Variation in the intensity of financial regulation'; Coffee, 'Law and the market'.

[129] Council of the European Union (Ecofin), 'The EU supervisory framework and financial stability arrangements – Council conclusions' (8515/3/08, Brussels 15 May 2008) 6, http://register.consilium.europa.eu/pdf/en/08/st08/st08515-re03.en08.pdf.

[130] *Ibid*., 3. See also Council of the European Union (Ecofin), 'Press Release' (4 December 2007) 17, http://register.consilium.europa.eu/pdf/en/07/st15/st15698.en07.pdf, stating that the Council underlines 'the importance of considering including in the mandates of national supervisors a task to cooperate within the EU and to work towards European

consistent changes being introduced at national level without the support of a specific legislative measure at EU level.[131] Ecofin ministers have also endorsed efforts to foster supervisory convergence and cooperation and for some time have been supportive of developing a common supervisory culture among authorities.[132] But the main influence on the exercise of enforcement powers was always meant to come from elsewhere, that is, from CESR and its successor, ESMA.

In Chapter 1, I was somewhat critical of CESR and its capacity for effective collective action when its members beg to differ. In Chapter 6, I highlighted, for instance, the fact that many of its members have preferred not to fully apply CESR's Level 3 standards on financial information.[133] I also stressed that mediation had remained unused. Indeed, it is apparent that many questions and issues which day-to-day enforcement raises in the prospectus disclosure field are still ultimately decided at national level. For instance, how diligent will a national authority be when verifying compliance with the PD's rules? Will it, for example, be proactive in checking compliance with, say, the obligation to publish a prospectus or with the PD's exemptions? How far will it delve into the detail of the information which it is supposed to review before approving a prospectus?[134] How will it respond to breaches of prospectus rules? Will it prefer a soft approach to enforcement; in other words, will it prefer dialogue with non-compliant issuers to administrative penalties or judicial actions? At this ultimate level of decision-making, choices are also influenced by the degree of expertise or diligence of a competent authority, as well as its financial and human resources. Unlike the harmonisation of enforcement and oversight powers which can be achieved by way of legislative action, the harmonisation of the day-to-day exercise of these powers is more laborious in a decentralised enforcement and oversight structure. To be sure, ESMA can be expected to make a more significant contribution to day-to-day enforcement. As already noted, ESMA has greater powers to deal with disputes between its members and to police their actions. Moreover, it

supervisory convergence and to take into account the financial stability concerns in all Member States'.

131 CESR, 'Re: The EU Mandate' (CESR/08-210, March 2008) 3.

132 E.g., Council Conclusions, 'The EU supervisory framework and financial stability arrangements' (Brussels, 15 May 2008, 8515/3/08).

133 CESR, 'Standard No. 1'; CESR, 'Standard No. 2'.

134 Admittedly, when reviewing prospectuses, competent authorities face important limitations. But the point is that each national authority is required to assess certain disclosure quality characteristics and that, therefore, opinions about adequate quality levels may also differ across jurisdictions.

is expected to play a greater role in bringing about convergence of prospectus vetting and approval practices.[135] It also continues working on developing a common supervisory culture. Whether ESMA will be successful in completing these tasks will only become apparent in the years following its institutional creation. For the time being, however, the fact is that the EU has not been a key influence on enforcement styles. As will be shown next, factors that have had a major impact on enforcement styles in the recent past have had quite different origins. The point is especially evident in the case of the FSA.

Styles of enforcement – the FSA and AMF Consider the FSA's approach to the day-to-day exercise of its various enforcement powers. Until the banking crisis erupted and the FSA was singled out for its inadequate handling of markets and market actors, the FSA was emphatic that it was not, unlike other regulatory authorities – notably the SEC – 'enforcement-led'.[136] The FSA has also long prided itself on a so-called 'risk-based' approach that has, *inter alia*, guided its approach to enforcement.[137] According to this methodology, breaches to prospectus rules are more likely to be pursued if they fall within an area that the FSA has, at a strategic level, determined to be a priority area.[138] The determination of priority areas will influence the way in which the FSA decides to allocate its finite resources.[139] One of the implications of the FSA's approach is that certain breaches cannot and will not be subject to enforcement action.[140] The UK authority has also formalised the way in which it handles the review (or vetting) of prospectuses. The level of scrutiny and the

135 PAD, Rec (8).

136 M. Cole, 'The UK FSA: nobody does it better?' (Fordham Law School, New York, 17 October 2006) reprinted in (2007) 2 *Fordham Journal of Corporate and Financial Law* 266, 273. See also Ferran, 'Cross-border offers of securities in the EU', 480 (noting that '... when compared to the US, the FSA does not rely heavily on its enforcement powers').

137 FSA-EG 2.3 noting that '[a]s a risk based regulator with limited resources, throughout its work the FSA prioritises its resources in the areas which pose the biggest threat to its *regulatory objectives*. This applies as much to the enforcement tool as it does to any other tool available to it'. On risk-based regulation and enforcement, see also E. Ferran, 'Principles-based, risk-based regulation and effective enforcement' in M. Tison, H. de Wulf, C. Van der Elst and R. Steennot (eds.), *Perspectives in Company Law and Financial Regulation* (Cambridge University Press, 2009) 427.

138 FSA-EG 2.6 and 2.7. 139 FSA-EG 2.6.

140 FSA-EG 2.9. That is not to say that there is no scope for *ad hoc* flexibility; for example, in order to deal with especially serious cases (see FSA-EG 2.8).

amount of resources that it allocates to the review of prospectuses will thus depend on a prior risk assessment.[141]

The FSA's methodology has long been a distinguishing feature of the FSA. To be sure, all authorities are likely to adopt some form of risk-based approach at the operational level, in the sense that they are likely to focus comparatively more attention on cases which are seen as posing particular risks, or on issuers which have a particular risk profile.[142] But the FSA's methodology has arguably been more sophisticated and has had greater strategic implications for the allocation of its resources and, as such, for the manner in which it has exercised its powers. CESR, for example, has, in the past, singled out the FSA's risk-based approach when reporting on the powers of competent authorities.[143]

Yet, as noted in Chapter 1, while not abandoning its risk-based approach, much else has changed for the FSA since the banking crisis. Especially, its 'not enforcement-led' motto has fallen from grace in the wake of the crisis. 'Credible deterrence' is the new enforcement mantra of the FSA.[144] According to the FSA:

> [c]entral to this philosophy is the realisation that the FSA should use all of the powers available to it to stop and deter those in the financial services industry who break the law or flout FSA rules.[145]

The FSA had also to step up its recruitment efforts[146] and crucially its enforcement activities as a result. Financial penalties rose to a total

[141] C. McCarthy, 'Risk based regulation: the FSA's experience' (FSA speech, 13 February 2006), noting that '[o]ur assessment of risk is based on a broad range of easily understood factors that focus on the type and complexity of the transaction, the size and profile of the issuer and other relevant factors. The risk level that results then determines the depth of our document review and the amount of resource we commit to the vetting process. The result is that we focus our resources on genuine areas of risk', www.fsa.gov.uk/pages/Library/Communication/Speeches/2006/0213_cm.shtml. See also the FSA's response to CESR's survey on the implementation of Principle 15 of CESR's Standard No. 1 on financial information: '[t]he FSA's risk assessment of prospectuses is formalised and focuses on market impact, complexity, compliance history and thematic risk which is assessed at the outset of the prospectus vetting process', www.cesr.eu.

[142] The AMF is now too paying greater attention to risk evaluation. See, e.g., AMF, 'Cartographie 2009 des risques et des tendances sur les marchés financiers et pour l'épargne' (Risques et tendances n° 8, Juin 2009), www.amf-france.org/documents/general/8979_1.pdf.

[143] E.g., CESR, 'Report on CESR members' powers under the PD', paras 6 and 41.

[144] FSA, 'A regulatory response to the global banking crisis' (DP 09/2) 191.

[145] *Ibid.*

[146] See FSA, 'A regulatory response to the global banking crisis – feedback on the Turner review and DP09/2' (Feedback Statement 09/3 September 2009) 21, www.fsa.gov.uk/pubs/discussion/fs09_03.pdf.

of £27.3 million during 2008/09.[147] This compares to an average of just £14 million over the preceding five years.[148] To support its new enforcement paradigm, it introduced changes to the manner in which it decides on financial penalties[149] and began pursuing with unprecedented vigour criminal proceedings. In 2009, it secured its first criminal conviction for insider dealing.[150]

In France, the financial crisis led to reflections and new initiatives as well.[151] Moreover, like the FSA, the AMF decided to step up its recruitment efforts.[152] But in the case of the AMF, it is hard to detect any rethink of a magnitude similar to the one which we witnessed in the case of the FSA. The French authority has historically been a rather different type of organisation, more concerned about retail investor protection and often seen as embracing the role of a *gendarme de la bourse*.[153] Admittedly, this image of a retail investor champion is most often associated with the Cob, one of the AMF's predecessors which was also dubbed by some as being administrative or bureaucratic.[154] But, as argued in Chapter 1, the AMF is not the mirror image of the Cob. Its internal organisation gives a greater say to market actors and it is also probably fair to say that the AMF pays greater attention to the competitiveness of the Paris market.[155] The important point, however, which needs repeating is that any development or change in enforcement styles was not driven or prompted by European law influences or, indeed, by CESR which did not have a major impact on the general orientations of competent authorities. The proximate causes were national factors, including, in the case of the FSA, a change in public expectations about the role of the regulator.[156] Indeed, a similar conclusion is warranted for the final episode in the fallout from the banking crisis which is the abolition of the FSA. A change in government in the UK

147 FSA, 'Enforcement annual performance account 2008/09' para. 8, www.fsa.gov.uk/pubs/annual/ar08_09/Enforcement_report.pdf.

148 *Ibid.*

149 FSA, 'Enforcement financial penalties'; FSA, 'Enforcement financial penalties – feedback on CP09/19' (PS 10/4, March 2010) www.fsa.gov.uk/pubs/policy/ps10_04.pdf.

150 FSA, 'Enforcement annual performance account 2008/09', para. 18.

151 See, e.g., AMF, 'Plan stratégique de l'Autorité des marchés financiers' (29 juin 2009), www.amf-france.org/documents/general/8983_1.pdf.

152 AMF, 'L'Autorité des marchés financiers précise la déclination opérationnelle de son plan stratégique' (Communiqué de presse, Paris, 16 december 2009), www.amf-france.org/documents/general/9251_1.pdf.

153 See Chapter 1, section IV, for details.

154 *Ibid.*

155 *Ibid.* See also Chapter 4, section V, C, on equivalence-based regulation.

156 FSA, 'A regulatory response to the global banking crisis' (DP 09/2) 186.

in 2010 sealed its fate. The FSA is expected to be replaced by new authorities.[157] New statutory objectives will be enacted and new enforcement styles are likely to emerge. But at the time of writing, formal proposals have yet to be adopted.

III Private enforcement in France and the UK

Weak European influences The PD's contribution to private enforcement – that is, for our purposes prospectus liability – was modest. Absorption of the relevant requirements at Member State level appears, accordingly, to have been mostly a non-issue. Recall that the PD does not exhaustively determine who is responsible for the disclosure and only requires Member States to ensure that their national laws governing civil liability are applicable.[158] The only noteworthy inroad into national tort law concerns the prospectus summary. According to the directive, civil liability can be avoided if the summary is not, when read together with other parts of the prospectus, misleading, inconsistent, inaccurate or fails to include key information.[159] With that in mind, I will begin by examining the PD's impact on the personal scope of national liability regimes (A), after which I will examine the content of these regimes (B). All in all, the transposition of the directive's requirements has not caused any fundamental changes in France or the UK, notwithstanding that amendments to statutory instruments were required.[160]

A Personal scope

The impact that the PD has had on the personal scope of prospectus liability regimes in France and the UK is fairly minor given the minimum nature and limited scope of the directive's requirements. Both Member States continue therefore to adopt distinct solutions to the question of who should be held responsible for faulty disclosure and under which conditions.

157 See the consultation by HM Treasury, 'A new approach to financial regulation: judgement, focus and stability' (July 2010), www.hm-treasury.gov.uk/d/consult_financial_regulation_condoc.pdf.

158 PD Art 6(1) and (2). 159 PD Art 6(2).

160 See also HM Treasury, 'UK Implementation of the Prospectus Directive 2003/71/EC' 24 noting that '[o]ur proposed implementation of the Directive leaves the structure and identification of responsibility for the prospectus unchanged compared to the existing regime'.

In France, Article 212–14 of the RG transposes Article 6(1) of the directive. It provides, in line with the text of the directive, that the prospectus shall identify the persons who are responsible for it.[161] It also states, in accordance with the text of the directive, that the persons responsible must certify that 'to the best of their knowledge' the disclosure 'is in accordance with the facts and makes no omission likely to affect its import'.[162] To identify the persons responsible for faulty disclosure, one needs, however, to look elsewhere, especially to the case law of the French courts. Indeed, it is the French judiciary which has played a key role in shaping the personal scope of the civil liability regime in France. Its decisions have not been without controversy, particularly as far as its case law on the liability of a company's directors is concerned.[163] French courts have held that proof of a separate fault was required – that is, 'a fault separate from [the director's] functions' – in order for a third party to bring a successful civil liability claim against a director in front of civil courts.[164] Indeed, for the commercial chamber of the *Cour de Cassation*, the highest court of the judicial order in France, directors must have 'intentionally committed a fault of a particular seriousness incompatible with the normal exercise of [the director's] functions' (*fonctions sociales*).[165] As a result, bringing proceedings in front of civil courts has not been popular with third parties in France, especially if they can gain compensation by using another route, i.e., by joining proceedings in front of criminal courts (which is known as '*constitution de partie civile*').[166] Note that the commercial chamber of

[161] RG Art 212-14.

[162] *Ibid.* Art 212-14 also makes provision for the issuer to certify that he has been given a 'completion letter' (*lettre de fin de travaux*) from its statutory auditors and, where applicable, to disclose any material observation made by the auditors.

[163] See Art L. 225–251 of the French *code de commerce* which states that '[t]he directors and managing director shall be individually or jointly and severally liable to the company or third parties either for infringements of the laws or regulations applicable to public limited companies, or for breaches of the memorandum and articles of association, or for tortious or negligent acts of management'. For details on the civil liability of directors, see A. Couret, H. Le Nabasque, M-L. Coquelet, T. Granier, D. Poracchia, A. Raynouard, A. Reygrobellet and D. Robine, *Droit financier* (Dalloz, Paris, 2008) 912–15; J. Méadal, *Les Marchés Financiers et l'Ordre Public* (L.G.D.J., Paris, 2007).

[164] Couret *et al.*, *Droit financier* 912 (own translation).

[165] Cass. Com. 20 mai 2003, n° 99–17092 (own translation).

[166] The criminal chamber of the *Cour de Cassation* has accepted that a director who has 'intentionally committed an offence having caused harm to a third party' – e.g., by disseminating false or misleading information which is a criminal offence under Art L. 465-2 of the CMF – can expose himself to a civil liability claim brought by a third party (Cass. Crim. 20 mai 2003, n° 02–84307 (own translation)). For details, see Couret *et al.*, *Droit financier* 913–4. Note that a director can also expose himself to administrative

the *Cour de Cassation* has recently clarified that the requirement for an intentional fault of a particular severity which is not compatible with the normal exercise of the director's functions does not apply when civil proceedings are brought against directors by shareholders who have suffered personnel losses.[167]

Whatever the twists in the case law of the *Cour de Cassation*, the important point for our purposes is that the PD does not as such require directors to be held personally responsible. It only requires that the issuer *or* its administrative, management or supervisory bodies be responsible for the disclosure. Hence, there was no room for tension between the EU and Member State requirements.

In the UK, Article 6 of the directive was implemented by adopting very detailed provisions. They not only identify who can be held responsible for the prospectus disclosure, but also determine the conditions under which a person can be exempted from responsibility.[168] At the outset, the personal scope of the responsibility regime will vary depending on the type of securities that are issued. Thus, under the FSA's prospectus rules, the personal scope is more extensive for (i) equity shares, (ii) warrants or options which give a right to subscribe for equity shares and are issued by the issuer of the equity shares, and (iii) transferable securities which are similar to these two categories.[169] For these types of securities, liability will, in addition to the issuer,[170] extend to (i) any director of the issuer who is a director at the time when the prospectus is published[171] and (ii) any person who has 'authorised himself' to be identified in the prospectus as a director and is identified therein as such[172] or as a person who is bound to become a director of the issuer,[173] and finally (iii) any person who has agreed to bear responsibility for the prospectus, provided that this information is set out in the prospectus.[174] In the case of a public offer, the prospectus rules add that responsibility lies with the offeror (if the latter is different from the issuer) and any person who is a director of the offeror at the time when the prospectus is published.[175] Likewise, in the case of an admission to trading, the person asking for admission (if different from the issuer) and any person who is a director of the (legal)

sanctions, without there being a need to establish a fault separate from the director's functions. See Cass. Com. 31 mars 2004 n° 03–14.991. For details, see Bouretz and Emery, *Autorité des marchés financiers* 63; Couret *et al.*, *Droit financier* 896.

167 Cass. com. 9 mars 2010 n° M 08–21.547 and n° D 08–21.793.

168 FSA-PR 5.5. 169 FSA-PR 5.5.3 R (1). 170 FSA-PR 5.5.3 R (2)(a).

171 FSA-PR 5.5.3 R (2)(b)(i). 172 FSA-PR 5.5.3 R (2)(b)(ii).

173 *Ibid.* 174 FSA-PR 5.5.3 R (2)(c).

175 FSA-PR 5.5.3 R (2)(d).

person asking for admission at the time when the prospectus is published, are responsible for the prospectus.[176] Any other person, who has given authorisation for the prospectus content, but who is not caught by any of the above provisions, can also be made responsible.[177]

For securities other than those mentioned above – for example, bonds or exchangeables – the responsibility of the issuer's directors is not required. According to the FSA's prospectus rules, responsibility lies with: (i) the issuer; (ii) any person who has accepted to be responsible for the prospectus, provided that this information is set out in the prospectus; (iii) the offeror (if the latter is different from the issuer); (iv) the person seeking admission to trading (if the latter is different from the issuer); (v) any guarantor but only 'in relation to information in the prospectus that relates to the guarantor and the guarantee'; and (vi) any other person who has given authorisation for the prospectus content.[178]

The prospectus rules also lay down an exemption regime: for example, where an issuer has not made or approved an offer, or an application for admission to trading.[179] If so, an issuer or its directors cannot be held responsible.[180] Likewise, where a prospectus is published without a director being aware of it, or without having approved it, the latter cannot be held responsible.[181] Nor can an offeror or its directors be held responsible if responsibility for the prospectus (i) lies with the issuer, (ii) where the prospectus was prepared mainly by the issuer or by persons acting on the issuer's behalf, or (iii) where the offeror makes an offer 'in association with the issuer'.[182] What is more, the rules allow persons to limit their responsibility to 'specified parts' of the prospectus or in 'specified respects'.[183] Finally, the rules also include a rule of construction which states that the provisions regarding responsibility cannot be construed in a way that would make a person responsible only because he or she provided professional advice about the prospectus content.[184]

[176] FSA-PR 5.5.3 R (2)(e). [177] FSA-PR 5.5.3 R (2)(f).

[178] FSA-PR 5.5.4 R. [179] FSA-PR 5.5.5 R.

[180] More precisely, FSA-PR 5.5.5 R exempts the persons mentioned under FSA-PR 5.5.3 R (2)(a); 5.5.3 R (2)(b); 5.5.4 R (2)(a).

[181] FSA-PR 5.5.6 R (applying to 5.5.3 R(2)(b)(i)). The director will not be responsible provided that 'on becoming aware of its publication he, as soon as practicable, gives reasonable public notice that it was published without his knowledge or consent'.

[182] FSA-PR 5.5.7 R. More specifically FSA-PR 5.5.7 R applies with respect to FSA-PR 5.5.3 R (2)(d) and 5.5.4 R (2)(c).

[183] FSA-PR 5.5.8 R. Rule 5.5.8 R applies to the persons mentioned in FSA-PR 5.5.3 R (2)(c); 5.5.4 R (2)(b); 5.5.3 R (2)(f) and 5.5.4 R (2)(f).

[184] FSA-PR 5.5.9 R.

B Common vs special statutory regimes

In France, prospectus liability is based on the general tort law provisions of the French Code Civil, especially Article 1382 which provides that 'any act whatever of man, which causes damage to another, obliges the one by whose fault it occurred, to compensate it'.[185] In order to seek redress against a person who has failed to comply with disclosure obligations, the common tort law requirements of a wrong (*faute*), harm (*dommage*) and a causal link between the wrong and the harm must therefore be established.[186]

In accordance with the requirements of Article 6(2) of the directive, the CMF limits civil liability for prospectus summaries. Art L. 412-1 of the CMF provides that no civil liability action can be brought in front of the courts solely on the basis of the summary or its translation 'unless the content of the summary or its translation is misleading, inaccurate or inconsistent when read together with information found in other parts [of the prospectus]'.[187] Except for this rule, the implementation of the PD's provisions, which mandate the application in Member States of national civil liability regimes, did not require any action by the French legislator. As noted earlier, the task of fleshing out civil liability has, by and large, been left to the courts.

Like in France, civil liability for the prospectus summary and its translation is expressly limited in the UK.[188] In contrast to France, however, liability for faulty prospectus disclosure can ensue on the basis of a special statutory regime which also includes a range of defences to compensation claims.[189] Specifically, section 90(1) of FSMA allows a person who has acquired securities and who has suffered loss because of wrong or misleading prospectus disclosure or because of omitted information, to claim

[185] See generally for a more detailed assessment, H-J. Puttfarken and A. Schrader 'Frankreich' in K. Hopt and H-C. Voigt (eds.) *Prospekt- und Kapitalmarktinformationshaftung* (Mohr Siebeck, Tübingen, 2005) 595.

[186] For a detailed assessment of each of these elements, see Couret *et al.*, *Droit financier* 905–910. See also C. Clerc, 'La réparation du préjudice subi par un actionnaire du fait de la diffusion de fausses informations' RTDF N° 1 – 2007 p. 31.

[187] Note that, in the future, the text of the CMF will have to be brought into line with the revised text of Art 6(2) (on the limitation of liability for summaries) which was agreed during 2010. For details, see Chapter 6, section V.

[188] FSMA s 90(12).

[189] Admittedly, there are various other means for seeking redress (for example, common law torts). For a detailed examination of alternative routes including the FSMA regime, see Hudson, *Securities Law* 571–80. Ferran notes that it is FSMA's statutory regime under s 90 which provides the most promising route. See E. Ferran, *Principles of Corporate*

compensation.[190] FSMA thereby not only offers a compensatory route to those who have acquired securities, but also to persons who have committed themselves contractually to acquire securities or have any interest in the securities.[191] Causation must be established between the loss suffered and the faulty prospectus disclosure,[192] but FSMA does not go as far as requiring an aggrieved party to show that he was 'specifically aware' of the faulty disclosure and that he relied on it when deciding to invest.[193] The extent of financial compensation which may be given is not specified under the Act, but Ferran suggests that compensation may be determined on the basis of deceit rules.[194]

Defences to compensation claims FSMA also sets out a number of defences to compensation claims.[195] The rules are detailed and set out in a separate schedule.[196] The schedule, essentially, differentiates between seven scenarios.

The first scenario addresses the situation where a prospectus statement was untrue or misleading or where a matter, which should have been included in the prospectus, was omitted.[197] In such a case, FSMA provides that a person can escape liability under section 90(1) if the person 'reasonably believed' when the prospectus was submitted to the FSA that the statement was truthful and not misleading or, in the case of omissions, that the information was 'properly omitted'.[198]

The second scenario deals with statements which are ostensibly made by an expert and described as being included in the prospectus with the

Finance Law (Oxford University Press, 2008) 450 (if compared to remedies available for 'deceit, misrepresentation, or breach of a duty of care').

190 Note that s 90(1) applies to prospectuses pursuant to s 90(11). Section 90(4) extends liability to supplementary prospectuses.

191 FSMA s 90(7). 192 Ferran, *Corporate Finance Law* 456.

193 *Ibid.* 194 *Ibid.*, 458.

195 FSMA s 90(2) and (5) cross-referring to FSMA Sch 10.

196 FSMA Sch 10 which applies to prospectuses pursuant to FSMA s 90(11).

197 FSMA Sch 10, para 1(1).

198 FSMA Sch 10, para 1(2). To benefit from this defence, at least one of the following, additional, conditions must be met under FSMA Sch 10, para 1(3): (i) the person's belief perdured 'until the time when the securities in question were acquired', (ii) the securities were bought 'before it was reasonably practicable to bring a correction to the attention of persons likely to acquire them', (iii) the person in question sought prior to the securities being bought, to take 'all such steps as it was reasonably for him to have taken' to ensure that the persons concerned were made aware of the correction, or finally (iv) where the person's belief perdured 'until after the commencement of dealings in the securities following their admission [to trading on a regulated market] and they were acquired after such a lapse of time that he ought in the circumstances to be reasonably excused'.

(so-called) expert's consent.[199] FSMA provides that a person can escape liability if he 'reasonably believed' that, when the prospectus was submitted to the FSA, the so-called expert 'was competent to make or authorise the statement' and the expert had agreed to the statement being included in the prospectus.[200]

The third scenario deals with the correction of statements and allows a person to escape liability where prior to the securities being bought, a statement (which was untrue, misleading or was omitted) has been corrected and published 'in a manner calculated to bring it to the attention of persons likely to acquire securities',[201] or where a person who faces liability has taken 'all such steps as it was reasonable for him to take to secure such publication', provided that he 'reasonably believed' that the publication 'had taken place before the securities were acquired'.[202]

The fourth scenario also deals with expert statements and allows a person to escape liability if he can establish either that prior to the securities being bought, the lack of competence of the expert or its failure to agree to the publication had been published 'in a manner calculated to bring it to the attention of persons likely to acquire securities',[203] or that all reasonable steps had been taken by him to make sure that such facts were published provided that he 'reasonably believed that it had taken place before the securities were acquired'.[204]

The fifth scenario concerns official statements which were included in a prospectus and have caused losses. FSMA provides that a person will escape liability under section 90(1) if such a statement was made by an official person or was included in a 'public official document' added to the prospectus, provided that the statement is 'accurately and fairly reproduced' in the prospectus.[205]

[199] Sch 10, para 2(1).

[200] Sch 10, para 2(2). One of the following additional conditions must nevertheless be met under FSMA Sch 10, para 2(3): (i) the person who seeks to escape liability must have had such belief 'until the time when the securities were acquired', (ii) the securities were bought 'before it was reasonably practicable to bring the fact that the expert was not competent, or had not consented, to the attention of persons likely to acquire the securities in question', (iii) the person had before the securities were bought taken 'all such steps as it was reasonable for him to have taken' to make sure that persons were informed of this fact or (iv) the person's belief perdured 'until after the commencement of dealings in the securities following their admission [to trading on a regulated market] and they were acquired after such a lapse of time that he ought in the circumstances to be reasonably excused'.

[201] Sch 10, para 3(2)(a).

[202] Sch 10, para 3(2)(b).

[203] Sch 10, para 4(2)(a).

[204] Sch 10, para 4(2)(b).

[205] Sch 10, para 5.

The sixth scenario allows a person to escape liability under FSMA if the aggrieved party who suffered a loss bought the securities in the knowledge that the statement was 'false or misleading' or knew of the 'omitted matter' or 'of the change or new matter'.[206]

The final, seventh scenario, deals exclusively with supplementary prospectuses and allows a person to escape liability if the person 'reasonably believed' that a supplementary prospectus was not required in order to deal with a change or a new matter.[207]

IV Conclusion: lessons for the legal origins literature

This chapter examined prospectus disclosure enforcement in the UK and in France. By assessing changes in enforcement patterns in each Member State, the purpose of the chapter was to examine the influence of EU prospectus disclosure regulation on national laws governing enforcement in this field. Because of the PD's enforcement orientations, much of the chapter was about *ex ante* enforcement. I used concepts found in the Europeanisation literature in order to designate and catalogue changes and in order to evaluate them in terms of their 'magnitude' or 'direction'.[208] Some changes were consistent with absorption. But there were also instances of accommodation. Thus, national practices that were judged important by the French and UK competent authorities, but not supported by the provisions of the PD, were not necessarily abandoned. Instead, competent authorities sought ways to accommodate EU requirements whilst maintaining the gist of their practices. Think, for instance, of the changes which the AMF introduced to the way in which statutory auditors are meant to communicate their observations about an issuer. Other instances were consistent with transformation or inertia. The FSA extended the scope of prior approval to prospectuses that were previously not subject to FSA vetting. France, meanwhile, decided to continue approving certain documents on an *ex post* basis which, on a strict reading of the provisions of the directive appears at least suspect. In areas where the PD only made minimal or marginal contributions, the implementation of its provisions did not raise particular issues. As a result, differences remain noticeable at Member State level. Think, for example of private enforcement. Moreover, as far as the actual exercise of enforcement

[206] Sch 10, para 6. [207] Sch 10, para 7.

[208] I borrow the terms from Radaelli, 'The Europeanization of Public Policy' 37.

powers is concerned, EU influences remain weak, CESR's contribution tenuous and ESMA's contribution as yet unspecified.

Before drawing this chapter to a close, it is worth returning to the legal origins literature to examine whether this chapter's conclusions have anything to add to the debate on legal origins. Specifically, the question is whether legal origins can be said to have influenced the manner in which the UK and France transposed the provisions of the PD. As noted in Chapter 5, legal origins, as described by LLSV, is a somewhat fluid concept. In a 2008 paper, LLSV defined it in very broad terms as 'a style of social control of economic life'.[209] For LLSV, 'common law stands for the strategy of social control that seeks to support private market outcomes, whereas civil law seeks to replace such outcomes with state-desired allocations'.[210] For the authors, when rules and regulations change in a given country, change takes place in a manner which is 'consistent with broad strategies of how the state intervenes'.[211] The type of empirical research that LLSV has pioneered is beyond the reach of this chapter. But it is, nevertheless, fair to say that LLSV's description of legal origins is fairly abstract, making it difficult to pin down precisely what we are meant to look for in a concrete situation. In any event, it seems reasonable enough to suggest that national legacies exert influences on the way in which a country deals with change. But that is not to say that policy actors' responses to social or economic problems are determined mechanistically by a pre-established set of ideas about legal origins. Moreover, given the interplay between EU and national levels of decision-making in the field of securities regulation, the influence of the EU on the evolution of rules, regulations or enforcement patterns at Member State level must be factored into the equation. Hence, my starting point for identifying the factors that affect national enforcement patterns is the EU. Changes in enforcement patterns at national level must, first of all, be related to the type of arrangements which the EU legislature lays down. Specifically, attention must be paid to the more or less prescriptive nature of these arrangements.[212] As Schmidt notes, different arrangements create

[209] R. La Porta, F. Lopez-de-Silanes and A. Shleifer, 'The economic consequences of legal origins', 286.

[210] *Ibid.* [211] *Ibid.*, 308.

[212] Cf. V. Schmidt, 'Europeanization and the mechanics of economic policy adjustment' (2002) 9 *Journal of European Public Policy* 894, 897 (noting that adjustment pressures will depend on 'how constraining the decisions taken at the EU level are in their implementation at the national level').

different 'adjustment pressures' at national level.[213] In our context, adjustment pressures are *prima facie* highest for maximum harmonisation measures which leave Member States no room for discretion.[214] They are weaker for minimum harmonisation measures or measures which reflect outcomes at the lowest common denominator. They are weakest when EU decisions do not prescribe palpable requirements, for example, when EU policies seek to prompt adjustments to European objectives at national level only indirectly by attempting to affect 'beliefs and expectations' of national actors; a strategy which Knill and Lehmkuhl describe as often 'prepar[ing] the ground' for more challenging policies.[215] As an example, think of the rules on civil liability. Given that the PD had only a few things to say on civil liability, its rules requiring the application of civil liability provisions were easily absorbed in France and the UK. On the other hand, where the PD was more prescriptive such as with respect to *ex ante* administrative enforcement, potential adjustment pressures were higher.

The above factors are, however, not sufficient to account for Member State responses to the implementation of these arrangements. National factors matter too. Among these national or 'mediating factors' are, according to Schmidt: economic pressures which a state might suffer (e.g., because of competition from abroad); the capacity of a state's political institutions to translate change; the fit between existing national policy legacies and the new arrangements; and the fit with existing preferences of policy actors and the public.[216] The premise is that the greater the fit with existing policy arrangements or policy preferences at national level, the better the chances that change will be absorbed easily. The lower the fit, the lower the chances to absorb the changes without tensions. Moreover, it is here – among these mediating factors – that legal legacies fit in. As a factor among others.

[213] *Ibid.*, 897.

[214] Schmidt (*ibid.*, 898) reminds us that adjustment pressures are at the outset best seen as potential rather than actual for the reason that the extent to which pressures will crystallise will depend on other factors such as the fit between national preferences or institutions and the new European arrangements. See also J. Caporaso, 'The three worlds of regional integration theory' in P. Graziano and M. Vink, *Europeanization – New Research Agendas* (Palgrave Macmillan, Basingstoke, 2008) 23, 29.

[215] C. Knill and D. Lehmkuhl, 'The national impact of European Union regulatory policy: three Europeanization mechanisms' (2002) 41 *European Journal of Political Research* 255, 258.

[216] Schmidt, 'Europeanization' 898–900. Schmidt also mentions the importance of discourse as a factor that affects preferences (*ibid.*, 900).

With that in mind it is worth returning a final time to the chapter's findings. They teach us a few lessons. First of all, it is apparent that even long-held traditions with respect to enforcement can be subject to revolutionary change in the face of prescriptive EU requirements. Thus, before the PD was implemented in France and the UK, there were clear differences in terms of the scope of *ex ante* enforcement in these Member States. The obligation to seek prior approval used to be less extensive in the UK where public offer prospectuses of unlisted securities were simply not subject to approval. This appears, *prima facie*, consistent with the findings of the law and finance literature, examined in Chapter 5, which has pointed out that entry regulation – recall that prior approval is a form of entry regulation – is predominantly part of the toolkit of civil law countries, especially of French legal origin.[217] But the important point for the legal origins literature is that the PD extended the obligation to seek prior approval. The implementation of the PD's provisions on prior approval led to transformation in the UK, notwithstanding legal origins.

But possibly, if we think of legal origins as a sort of mediating factor, one can see its influence elsewhere. Recall that LLSV gives legal origins a very broad meaning as 'a style of social control'. The fact that the FSA used to rely greatly on market actors such as sponsors in order to ensure *ex ante* compliance with its disclosure requirements arguably testifies to a more market-reliant approach to enforcement. Recall also that the FSA, when initially implementing the PD, sought to maintain the role of the sponsor for certain operations. The AMF, on the other hand, maintained its control over advertising activities, a practice that arguably testifies to a more interventionist approach to enforcement. The problem is that these are all fairly approximate statements. The point then is that at a macroscopic level, legal origins *if defined in sufficiently generous terms* might be satisfactory enough to explain variations. But the closer we look for explanations, the greater the number of factors that appear to play a role in the implementation equation. Thus, other factors would also deserve to be highlighted in their own right. For example, in the case of the AMF, one factor that appears to explain why the AMF extended its grip on advertisement is the threat of regulatory arbitrage from issuers circumventing the AMF's risk warnings by using the passport system. What is more, stating that the FSA prefers a more market-reliant approach to enforcement

[217] E.g., La Porta *et al.*, 'The economic consequences of legal origins' 294 (noting that '[r]elative to common law countries, French legal origin countries have more entry and labor regulation').

also ignores the recent changes that it introduced to its enforcement style, following changes in governmental and public expectations. The risk is that by focusing on a generously defined concept of legal origins, we no longer pay attention to these other factors. Hence, the bottom line is that more attention needs to be paid to EU arrangements and their implementation process. Whilst country specific legacies are worth accounting for in the field of prospectus disclosure, specific enforcement patterns among common law or civil law countries, including preferences for *ex ante* or *ex post* enforcement, cannot be made sense of without having regard to EU influences.

PART IV

Prospectus disclosure and regulatory competition

8

Introduction

Regulatory competition has been a topic in law, economics and political science for many years. In law and economics it has proven to be of enduring interest, especially in the literature on company law and securities regulation'.[1] Regulatory competition describes a fairly simple idea. States compete (in an effort to attract capital, investment, revenue-generating business, and so on) by attempting to offer legal regimes which a given regulated population is likely to prefer. This process is meant to lead to better laws, rules or regulations. To kick off this process, proponents of regulatory competition, turn to regulatory arbitrage which, in essence, describes the action of picking and choosing between different regulatory regimes. Regulatory arbitrage presupposes that actors can 'exit' a regulatory regime either by relocating to another jurisdiction or better, by taking advantage of some kind of legal mechanism that allows them to choose between different legal regimes. Whatever the precise arrangements, regulatory arbitrage is seen as the 'engine'[2] of regulatory competition. That is in essence the thrust of the argument.

A flawed theory Yet, despite the interest in the subject matter, the heydays of regulatory competition as a *normative* proposition in the securities field are over. The reason for this can arguably be traced back to a number of factors. One factor is that the so-called theory of regulatory competition has shaky theoretical foundations. It derived initially from

[1] For representative contributions, see R. Romano, *The Advantage of Competitive Federalism for Securities Regulation* (AEI Press, Washington D.C., 2002); Fox, 'Retaining mandatory securities disclosure'; R. Romano, *The Genius of American Corporate Law* (AEI Press, Washington D.C., 1993); L. Bebchuk, 'Federalism and the corporation: the desirable limits on state competition in corporate law' (1992) 105 *Harvard Law Review* 1435; W. Bratton, J. McCahery, S. Picciotto and C. Scott (eds.), *International Regulatory Competition and Coordination: Perspectives on Economic Regulation in Europe and the United States* (Clarendon Press, Oxford, 1996).

[2] W. Bratton, J. McCahery, S. Picciotto and C. Scott, 'Introduction' in Bratton, *et al.*, *International Regulatory Competition and Coordination* 1, 38.

Charles Tiebout's pure theory of local expenditures.[3] But Tiebout's findings quickly became overinterpreted and overblown in the literature on regulatory competition.[4] In order to salvage regulatory competition, Tiebout was by and large abandoned and law and economics scholars began to make more qualified claims.[5] But in the process, the findings became increasingly approximate and much of the initial insight was lost. Other theories or concepts came to the rescue of the literature, such as public choice or capture theories. Regulatory competition was presented as a means to keep self-interested regulators/bureaucrats in check or to prevent regulatory capture.[6] But claims were overgeneralised and soon the argument was turned on its head. Regulatory competition was found to reinforce the type of capture that it was supposed to prevent.[7] Some sought to gain ground by insisting on an altogether different vision of competition, a Hayekian conception of competition.[8] Hayek thought of competition as being a discovery process, a process meant to uncover information which would otherwise be unknown or unused.[9] Seen from this perspective, regulatory competition was first and foremost a means to stimulate regulatory learning. But on the flipside, it left regulatory competition theorists with a somewhat unattractive vision of competition that makes predictions difficult.[10] Others finally sought to resolve the

[3] C. Tiebout, 'A pure theory of local expenditures' (1956) 64 *Journal of Political Economy* 416. For an excellent critique of the Tiebout model, see T. Bewley, 'A critique of Tiebout's theory of local public expenditures' (1981) 49 *Econometrica* 713.

[4] For an excellent critique see W. Bratton and J. McCahery, 'The new economics of jurisdictional competition: devolutionary federalism in a second-best world' (1997) 86 *Georgetown Law Journal* 201.

[5] See the so-called 'third generation literature', D. Esty and D. Gerardin (eds.), *Regulatory Competition and Economic Integration – Comparative Perspectives* (Oxford University Press, 2001).

[6] E.g., J-M. Sun and J. Pelkmans, 'Regulatory competition in the single market' (1995) 33 *Journal of Common Market Studies* 67, 82–3; W. Bratton *et al.*, 'Introduction' 13.

[7] W. Bratton and J. McCahery, 'The case of corporate law in the United States of America' in Bratton *et al.*, *International Regulatory Competition and Coordination* 207 (in relation to U.S. charter competition).

[8] Drawing on Hayek, see e.g., S. Deakin, 'Two types of regulatory competition: competitive federalism versus reflexive harmonisation. A law and economics perspective on Centros' (1999) 2 *Cambridge Yearbook of European Legal Studies* 231; S. Deakin, 'Legal diversity and regulatory competition: which model for Europe?' (2006) 12 *European Law Journal* 440; K. Heine and W. Kerber, 'European corporate laws, regulatory competition and path dependence' (2002) 13 *European Journal of Law and Economics* 47.

[9] F. Hayek, *New Studies in Philosophy, Politics, Economics and the History of Ideas* (Routledge & Kegan Paul, London, 1978), 179.

[10] E.g., M. Streit, 'Comment [on: R. Van den Bergh 'The subsidiarity principle and the EC competition rules: the costs and benefits of decentralisation']' in D. Schmidtchen and

dilemma with regulatory competition theory, by rooting their claims in empirical case studies. In US corporate law, these studies have drawn on an impressive amount of quantitative data.[11]

While US corporate law has been mostly the focal point for the literature, the debate on regulatory competition spilled over into US securities regulation at the end of the 1990s and the beginning of 2000. By far the most controversial propositions in this field came from scholars such as Stephen Choi, Andrew Guzman and especially Roberta Romano.[12] Romano's proposal, which eclipsed Choi and Guzman's earlier proposal, led to a contentious debate, pitching those who, like her, were in favour of regulatory competition in securities regulation against those who were opposed to it. This debate is nowadays merely of historical interest and I will not spend much time on assessing its twists and turns. Essentially, however, Romano proposed to make US federal securities laws elective and thereby let issuers choose a securities domicile that would determine which securities laws applied to the issuer's securities transactions.[13] Her main argument was a preference-matching argument. For Romano, if given choice, issuers would select a legal regime that investors favoured.[14] As a result, an issuer's cost of capital would be reduced.[15] But Romano's claim did not go unchallenged. Among her more vocal critics, Fox questioned her underlying economic reasoning.[16] Others questioned the need for issuer choice given that existing US securities laws already allowed

R. Cooter (eds.), *Constitutional Law and Economics of the European Union* (Edward Elgar, Cheltenham, 1997) 184, 187 noting that '[g]iven the properties of competition, it is difficult to establish its particular effects in advance'.

11 The empirical evidence too has been debated and discussed. See e.g., L. Bebchuk, A. Cohen and A. Ferrell, 'Does the evidence favor state competition in corporate law?' (2002) 90 *California Law Review* 1775; L. Bebchuk and A. Cohen, 'Firms' decision where to incorporate' (2003) 46 *Journal of Law and Economics* 383.

12 S. Choi and A. Guzman, 'Portable reciprocity: rethinking the international reach of securities regulation' (1998) 71 *Southern California Law Review* 903. Choi and Guzman recommended allowing issuers and investors to select the laws governing their securities transactions (*ibid.*, 907); Romano, *The Advantage of Competitive Federalism*. See also a related proposal by P. Mahoney, 'The exchange as regulator' (1997) 83 *Virginia Law Review* 1453 (arguing that exchanges should be given greater regulatory powers).

13 Romano, *The Advantage of Competitive Federalism* 112–24.

14 Romano, 'Empowering investors' 2366; Romano, *The Advantage of Competitive Federalism* 15–16.

15 *Ibid.*

16 Fox argued that the level of disclosure by issuers would likely be below the social optimum absent mandatory disclosure and, as far Romano's proposal was concerned, if issuers were allowed to choose among disclosure regimes. See Fox, 'Retaining mandatory securities disclosure' 1346; Fox, 'The issuer choice debate'.

for flexibility (e.g., in the form of exemptions), or noted that issuer choice would, in fact, deprive investors of the benefits of greater disclosure standardisation.[17] More generally, with hindsight, the faith which the mainstream regulatory competition literature put in conventional paradigms such as the efficient market hypothesis (EMH) and its underlying assumptions, was arguably also ill advised, especially as the behavioural literature gained ground in the law and economics debate at the turn of the century.[18]

Regulatory competition and EU policy-making – problematic Whilst normative scholarship on regulatory competition produced imaginative and innovative work, it is nevertheless the case that the proposals were seriously out of touch with the real world.[19] In the first place, market actors have not supported the type of full-fledged regulatory competition which Romano offered to implement.[20] Instead of adopting ideological preferences in favour of devolution (or subsidiarity in the European context) which are often at the heart of the regulatory competition debate, market actors are more likely to prefer pragmatic solutions that do not produce dramatic changes and legal uncertainty. In addition, the financial crisis has reinforced the feeling among actors that financial market integration requires greater coordination and a level playing field. Indeed, in Europe, where integration is part of the fabric of the EU, regulatory competition in the financial markets field, has been beaten for good, in the battle of regulatory paradigms, by its nemesis, its archrival, that is harmonisation. Hence, for those interested in real-world policy-making, it is the failure to take into account those factors and processes which ultimately influence policy outcomes in the real world which make the above issuer choice proposals look largely irrelevant.[21] That is not to say, however, that

[17] J. C. Coates, 'Private vs. political choice of securities regulation: a political cost/benefit analysis' (2001) 41 *Virginia Journal of International Law* 531, 542–53, J. Coffee, 'Law and regulatory competition: can they co-exist?' (2002) 80 *Texas Law Review* 1729, 1732.

[18] For details on the behavioural literature, see Chapter 2. For a behavioural law and economics contribution questioning proposals on regulatory competition in the securities field, see Prentice, 'Whither securities regulation?'.

[19] Cf., *ibid.*, 1510 (noting that '[i]t is a telling point that although many academics take these proposals seriously, virtually no one in the "real world" does'); E. Kitch, 'Proposals for reform of securities regulation: an overview' (2001) *41 Virginia Journal of International Law* 629, 630.

[20] In this sense, see also Kitch 'Proposals for reform of securities regulation' 630.

[21] For a contribution discussing the problematic question of the implementation of issuer choice proposals, see F. Tung, 'Lost in translation: from U.S. corporate charter competition to issuer choice in international securities regulation' (2005) 39 *Georgia Law Review* 525.

regulatory competition, as a subject of study, no longer deserves attention.[22] There is still space for regulatory arbitrage – and I use the term in its broadest sense – in European securities markets. And given that regulatory arbitrage is often a by-product of greater integration, there is still a need to explore the implications of regulatory arbitrage and *a fortiori* regulatory competition; but from a positive, empirical, perspective that focuses on regulatory decision-making at EU level.[23] Much has been written about the Court of Justice's case law and the implications of its rulings for regulatory arbitrage and competition. Less is known about how the EU policy-making process responds to the threat of regulatory arbitrage. This is the subject of the next two chapters which attempt to develop this line of enquiry in the prospectus disclosure field.

[22] Indeed, others continue advocating some form of regulatory competition. John Coffee, for example, has recently noted that a form of competition in the field of securities enforcement can be beneficial. See J. Coffee and H. Sale, 'Redesigning the SEC: does the Treasury have a better idea?' (2009) 95 *Virginia Law Review* 707, 764–6.

[23] See also H. Tjiong, 'Breaking the spell of regulatory competition: reframing the problem of regulatory exit' (2002) 66 *Rabels Zeitschrift für ausländisches und internationales Privatrecht* 66, 95–6 (calling for more positive research).

9

Regulatory competition and EU decision-making

I Introduction

Chapter 8 discussed the theory of regulatory competition critically. As a reminder, regulatory competition can be described, in optimistic terms, as an institutional arrangement which contributes to keeping self-interested regulators (or policy-makers) in check and which may fuel regulatory policy learning. But, as stressed in Chapter 8, there are good reasons for being critical of the theory. It not only suffers from flaws and weaknesses, but its message in favour of competitive regulatory decision-making is increasingly at odds with the real world. Against this background, Chapter 8 suggested abandoning normative theory for good and concentrating instead on empirical work, especially on how the threat of regulatory arbitrage affects EU decision-making. The aim of this chapter is to begin investigating these questions and, ultimately, to draw lessons for the literature interested in prospectus disclosure regulation.[1] This chapter contains the theoretical part. The next chapter will deal with the empirical part. As elsewhere in the book, I will use the term 'regulation' in its widest sense, as market regulation instead of simply rule-making. Section II begins by describing regulatory competition as a regulatory

[1] For earlier work on regulatory competition and EU decision-making, see J-M. Sun and J. Pelkmans, 'Regulatory competition in the single market'; P. Genschel and T. Plumber, 'Regulatory competition and international co-operation' (1997) 4 *Journal of European Public Policy* 626; Scharpf, *Governing in Europe – Effective and Democratic?* 84–120; P. Genschel, 'Why no mutual recognition of VAT? Regulation, taxation and the integration of the EU's internal market for goods' (2007) 14 *Journal of European Public Policy* 743. See also Simon Deakin's work on reflexive harmonisation, Deakin, 'Legal diversity and regulatory competition'; Deakin, 'Two types of regulatory competition'. Deakin is interested in harmonisation and regulatory competition, but ultimately he sees harmonisation as a rather stylized process. My own views fit better with Nicolaïdis's work on 'managed mutual recognition' to which I return hereinafter. See Nicolaïdis, 'Regulatory cooperation and managed mutual recognition'; K. Nicolaïdis and S. Schmidt, 'Mutual recognition on "trial": the long road to services liberalization' (2007) 14 *Journal of European Public Policy* 717.

problem that the EU legislature faces when attempting to support market integration and from there develops a research perspective. Section III turns to the political science literature for insights on the mechanics of EU decision-making and examines, in particular, the role of two broad sets of factors, actor preferences and institutions.

II Regulatory competition as a regulatory problem in the securities markets field

It is apparent that proposals in favour of regulatory competition as an institutional arrangement for the EU are vulnerable on theoretical grounds, but also because such proposals plainly ignore real-world institutional trends in the securities markets field. Shifting to regulatory competition as a new paradigm would indeed require a highly unlikely revolutionary move away from the current evolutionary pattern that has caused a gradual erosion of Member State competences through greater centralisation and harmonisation.[2] But that is not to say that the interest in the subject matter is exhausted, given that, for regulatory competition to happen, paradigmatic policy change is not required in an internal market context.

A Regulatory competition and market integration

It is commonly observed that regulatory competition and market integration are closely intertwined.[3] Decisions about market integration often also imply, intentionally or not, choices about regulatory arbitrage and regulatory competition. While the point may be especially apparent when the Court provides an impetus for regulatory arbitrage by facilitating mobility through its deregulatory case law on the freedom of movement,[4] harmonisation is not necessarily incompatible with regulatory competition either. For some, a level of harmonisation that underpins and supports

[2] See on the evolutionary nature of change in the securities regulation field, Chapter 1, section V; Chapter 3, section VII; and Chapter 6, section VI. See also the earlier work by Thatcher and Coen, 'Reshaping European regulatory space'.

[3] See generally on the topic, Sun and Pelkmans, 'Regulatory competition in the single market'; C. Barnard and S. Deakin, 'Market access and regulatory competition' in C. Barnard and J. Scott, *The Law of the Single European Market – Unpacking the Premises* (Hart Publishing, Oxford, 2002) 197; Scharpf, *Governing in Europe*; Tjiong, 'Breaking the spell of regulatory competition'.

[4] E.g., P. Schammo, 'Arbitrage and abuse of rights in the EC legal system' (2008) 14 *European Law Journal* 351; Barnard and Deakin, 'Market access and regulatory competition'.

mutual recognition is necessary for regulatory competition to work in the EU.[5] Others have pointed out, rightly so, that regulatory arbitrage may also occur as a result of differing approaches to the implementation, application or enforcement of EU rules.[6] Recall that some institutional choices – an autonomous European single securities authority – find no support in the Treaties. As a result, national securities authorities are in charge of ensuring that EU rules are properly applied and enforced, albeit under the supposedly watchful eye of collective securities actors such as CESR and more recently ESMA. But there are other reasons to pay attention to harmonisation, especially if we think of it as a *process* and not just see it as an outcome.[7] Harmonising means substituting distinct national legal regimes with a single European regime.[8] In this process, the EU legislature must choose, among a range of different rules and regulatory arrangements, those that will be common to all Member States. Crucially, in the internal market field, harmonisation is generally not meant to be an end in itself, but a means to facilitate cross-border mobility and market integration. As long as the EU legislature satisfies EU primary law and the Court's interpretation of it, the former enjoys considerable discretion

[5] E.g., S. Woolcock, 'Competition among rules in the single European market' in W. Bratton, J. McCahery, S. Picciotto and C. Scott (eds.), *International Regulatory Competition and Coordination: Perspectives on Economic Regulation in Europe and the United States* (Clarendon Press, Oxford, 1996) 289, 296. The argument that legislative mutual recognition supports regulatory competition seems to have been exaggerated in the past. In the field of disclosure regulation, for example, mutual recognition has not been the key to regulatory competition. See, prior to the adoption of the PD, the findings of H. Jackson and E. Pan, 'Regulatory competition in international securities markets: evidence from Europe in 1999 – Part I' (2001) 56 *Business Lawyer* 653, 676 who find that mutual recognition under the LPD and POD was not used frequently.

[6] Cf., S. Weatherill, 'Pre-emption, harmonisation and the distribution of competence to regulate the internal market' in Barnard and Scott, *The Law of the Single European Market* 41, 68; G. Ferrarini, 'Securities regulation and the rise of pan-European securities markets: an overview' in G. Ferrarini, K. Hopt, E. Wymeersch (eds.), *Capital Markets in the Age of the Euro – Cross-Border Transactions, Listed Companies and Regulation* (Kluwer Law International, The Hague, 2002) 241, 250; L. Enriques and T. Tröger, 'Issuer choice in Europe' (2008) 67 *Cambridge Law Journal* 521, 558.

[7] As a footnote, this way of thinking, which focuses on a process rather than an outcome, has long been advocated by Hayek, but in relation to private market competition. Deakin has built on these ideas and argued that regulatory competition should be described as a 'process of discovery', instead of simply a 'state of affairs'. See Deakin, 'Legal diversity and regulatory competition' 444.

[8] See generally on the topic of harmonisation, S. Weatherill, 'Why harmonise?' in P. Tridimas and P. Nebbia (eds) *European Union Law for the Twenty-First Century – Rethinking the New Legal Order Volume 2* (Hart Publishing, Oxford, 2004) 11; Slot, 'Harmonisation'.

in determining the substance of the legal arrangements which are meant to further market integration. As such, the EU legislature is entitled to determine the precise scope of mutual recognition and the distribution of competences between home and host Member States under the home country control principle.[9] Indeed, provided primary law is respected, there is no ground for preventing it from enacting rules and arrangements which together could considerably enhance legal mobility and thereby lay down the conditions for regulatory arbitrage. To be sure, claiming that harmonisation serves to facilitate regulatory competition appears somewhat counter-intuitive, if not plainly mistaken. The FSAP, for example, exemplifies that harmonisation is an exercise in re-regulation rather than deregulation.[10] But the relevant point here is that the EU legislature *needs to decide* over various rules and arrangements which, by promoting market integration, affect the scope for, or may indeed facilitate, regulatory arbitrage at Member State level. Ideally, these choices should be based on qualitative grounds. In practice, however, the decision process is typically not frictionless, for at a closer look, the EU legislature is made of both national governments in Council and supranational actors, whose preferences depend on their underlying interests and ideas, but who need to find common agreement under what is now known as the ordinary legislative procedure (formerly, the co-decision procedure).[11] If we focus only on the harmonisation outcome, we no longer pay attention to this process of selection and decision. Yet, if we are interested in regulatory competition there are good reasons to pay attention to it. I will next seek to elaborate on this idea by drawing on common concepts used in the regulatory competition literature and by building on the insights on regulatory competition or EU policy-making offered by authors such as Scharpf or Nicolaïdis.[12] The starting point, however, is Hirschman's conceptualisation of exit and

[9] In Case C-233/94 *Germany v Parliament and Council* [1997] ECR I-2405, para. 64, the ECJ held in relation to the EC Treaty, that home country supervision was not a principle set out in the Treaty. The EC legislature 'could depart from it, provided that it did not infringe the legitimate expectations of the persons concerned'.

[10] As Moloney points out, the FSAP was profoundly re-regulatory 'chang[ing] the character of EC securities regulation from a minimum harmonization/mutual recognition-based regime to a regime of unparalleled regulatory detail'. See Moloney, *EC Securities Regulation* 10.

[11] Arts 289(1) and 294 TFEU.

[12] F. Scharpf, *Games Real Actors Play*; Scharpf, *Governing in Europe*; Nicolaïdis and Schmidt, 'Mutual recognition "on trial"'; Nicolaïdis, 'Regulatory cooperation and managed mutual recognition'. See also Genschel and Plumber, 'Regulatory competition and international co-operation'.

voice which has been a reference point in much of the work on regulatory competition in the law and economics literature.[13]

B The 'threat of exit' and EU decision-making

> From a positive concern with examining the real world consequences of regulatory exit one is presented with the need more accurately to trace out the possible and plausible connections between (economic) regulatory exit and political response.[14]

The meaning of exit The literature on regulatory competition commonly discusses regulatory competition and arbitrage by referring to the concept of 'regulatory exit'.[15] As a reminder, the common claim is that regulatory arbitrage/competition will keep self-interested regulators in check and improve policy learning, if market actors are able to 'exit' a legal regime cheaply. The concept of 'exit' is borrowed from the seminal work of Albert Hirschman who sought to identify and conceptualise ways in which consumers or members of an organisation could react to the deteriorating performance of a producer or an organisation.[16] According to Hirschman, a dissatisfied consumer could raise her voice.[17] That is to say, she could manifest her dissatisfaction by simply letting people know. But she could also use the 'exit option' by no longer purchasing the goods or services or, in the case of an organisation, by leaving the latter, thus revealing her dissatisfaction by her very action.[18] Hirschman's ideas can easily be transposed into many settings. But in the regulatory competition context, the idea of an exit option is nevertheless more complex to conceptualise given that exit must be understood as a form of *regulatory* exit. It requires dissatisfied economic actors to be mobile, thus allowing them to move between legal regimes without incurring significant switching costs. Actors must also benefit from regulatory diversity, thus allowing them to choose between regulatory alternatives (meaning differences between rules, but also differences caused by variation in the implementation, application or enforcement of common rules). Hence, regulatory exit is in our context a type of *selective exit* when economic actors benefit from diversity at national level on the basis, or without foregoing the benefits, of increased mobility following regulatory action at EU level. This type of selective exit

[13] Hirschman, *Exit, Voice, and Loyalty.*
[14] Tjiong, 'Breaking the spell of regulatory competition' 95.
[15] E.g., *ibid.* [16] Hirschman, *Exit, Voice, and Loyalty.*
[17] *Ibid.*, 4. [18] *Ibid.*

can be opposed to total exit,[19] that is the complete withdrawal from an activity or market governed by EU securities regulation.[20]

EU policy-making under the threat of (selective) exit Besides claiming that the exit option keeps regulators in check, proponents of regulatory competition have also argued that a mere credible outlook of exit – in other words, if regulators appreciate that there is a credible threat of exit – could be sufficient to rein regulators in. The claim is similar to Hirschman's original argument. For the latter:

> [t]he chances for voice to function effectively as a recuperation mechanism are appreciably strengthened if voice is backed up by the *threat of exit*, whether it is made openly *or whether the possibility of exit is merely well understood to be an element in the situation by all concerned* (emphasis added on the latter part).[21]

Hirschman's claim then presupposes that the threat of exit is sufficiently credible.[22] If not – for example, because exit is not possible or especially hard – the sequence described by him seems to unravel: the threat of exit is no longer credible and the chances for voice to function effectively accordingly low(er). For our purposes, this point is significant. Recall that we are interested in regulatory decision-making at EU level. Once common rules are agreed, the scope of selective exit at national level will be determined, or at least affected, by the regulatory choices that were made at EU level. This has a number of implications for how we conceive of the relationship between exit and voice in the present context. First of all, if the EU legislature's choices regarding integration affect the scope of selective exit *ex post*, it is a short step to conclude that the outlook of selective exit (or regulatory arbitrage, to put it more simply) may also factor into the legislature's *ex ante* evaluation of the courses of action which it should pursue with respect to positive harmonisation. Indeed, a similar message

[19] The expressions 'selective exit' and 'total exit' are borrowed from Weiler who, however, ascribes them a different meaning and uses them in a different context. See J. Weiler, 'The transformation of Europe' (1991) 100 *Yale Law Journal* 2403.

[20] As an example, think of those issuers that have chosen to issue on a market which is not a regulated market under EU secondary law in order to avoid European rules/standards which are applicable to regulated markets. The price for total exit is paid in the form of a loss of benefits such as increased market access to other Member States by using the PD's passport system.

[21] Hirschman, *Exit, Voice, and Loyalty* 82.

[22] *Ibid.*, 85 noting that ('... if voice is to be at its most effective, the threat of exit must be credible, particularly when it most counts').

underpins Nicolaïdis's work on 'managed mutual recognition' in which the prospect of regulatory competition/arbitrage prompts states to insist on safeguards and conditions when determining the shape and form of mutual recognition.[23] The fact that the threat of selective exit factors into the legislature's *ex ante* evaluation is apparent in various fields of activity, including corporate law and financial markets regulation. Think of the negotiations over the 10th Company law directive which seeks to facilitate cross-border mergers of companies,[24] or the Commission's announcement of a proposal for a 14th Company law directive which was supposed to facilitate the transfer of a company's registered office, but which now appears to have been abandoned by the Commission.[25] The fear of seeing domestic companies taking the 'exit option' by way of a cross-border merger or a cross-border transfer of their registered office, in an attempt to avoid rules on worker participation that exist in some Continental Member States, appears to have figured prominently in 'behind-the-scenes' discussions at EU level.[26] In the financial markets field, concerns about selective exit and regulatory arbitrage have not been absent either.[27] Chapter 10 will examine the issues that the threat of selective exit has raised in the prospectus field. But for now the point is that the threat of selective exit, as a politically salient regulatory problem which affects the search for greater economic integration, can affect preferences for the choice of rules and institutional arrangements at EU level. Unless we pay attention to the harmonisation process, we are unlikely to fully appreciate its implications for the selection of rules and legal arrangements at

[23] Nicolaïdis, 'Regulatory cooperation and managed mutual recognition' 594.

[24] Directive 2005/56/EC of the European Parliament and of the Council of 26 October 2005 on cross-border mergers of limited liability companies [2005] OJ L310/1.

[25] See Commission Staff Working Document, 'Impact assessment on the directive on the cross-border transfer of registered office' (Part I, SEC (2007) 1707), http://ec.europa.eu/internal_market/company/docs/shareholders/ia_transfer_122007_part1_en.pdf.

[26] A number of interviews were conducted with company law experts such as Jaap Winter (former chairman of the High Level Group of Company Law Experts) and with Commission officials. While these interviews were mainly exploratory, it is nevertheless worth highlighting that these interviewees pointed to the fear that German companies could try to circumvent German co-determination rules, were they to benefit from greater mobility. See also European Commission, 'Proposal for a Directive of the European Parliament and of the Council on cross-border mergers of companies with share capital' (COM(2003) 703 final, 18 November 2003) 4 noting that '[e]mployee participation in a company created by cross-border merger … was the reason for the deadlock over the original proposal of 1984 … The overriding fear concerning cross-border mergers was that the process might be hijacked by companies which, faced with having to live with employee participation, might try to circumvent it by means of such a merger'.

[27] E.g., Rec (22) MiFID.

European level. What is more, recall that the notion of 'EU legislature' obscures the fact that legislative activity in the EU involves a complicated interplay between different institutions and actors. Under the ordinary legislative procedure, which is now the main decision-making procedure in the internal market, EU decision-making involves interactions between various actors, including those actors which regulatory competition theorists would like to see exposed to regulatory competition at national level: the Member States. Although Member States have proven to share a broad interest and commitment to the FSAP,[28] it is reasonable to assume that they may, nevertheless, have to gain and lose differently on specific issues. As economic actors exit for the most attractive legal regime, gains and losses can be economic (in terms of revenues or resources). They can also be decisional in the form of a *de facto* redistribution of regulatory or enforcement authority over mobile economic actors. Opposition to regulatory action may be especially severe where regulatory changes would affect the *status quo* and, thereby, jeopardise an existing distribution of economic resources or decisional power between Member States. Furthermore, recall that regulatory arbitrage is only incidental to greater economic integration promoted by way of legal integration. Preferences over selective exit (or regulatory arbitrage) may therefore only be incidental to preferences for greater integration and economic mobility. At the same time, agreement over substantive re-regulation may be further complicated by the fact that actors might be unwilling to suffer the necessary adjustment costs involved with managing the threat of selective exit through re-regulation.[29] To be sure, the point about preference diversity seems obvious enough. But in the present context, it leads to another twist in Hirschman's account of the benefits of the threat of exit. Recall that for Hirschman the chances that the 'voice' of consumers is heard are greatly improved if 'voice' is raised under the threat of exit. But in the present setting, market actors' voice is only second to the voice of those actors whose *ex ante* regulatory choices affect the scope of selective exit *ex post* and who risk gaining or losing unevenly from selective exit at national level. The latter's voices may then materialise in conflicting demands for the scope and shape of harmonisation, mutual recognition and home country

[28] The only measure which proved stubbornly resistant to progress was, in fact, the proposal for a 14th Company Law Directive, which, as mentioned earlier, the Commission appears to have abandoned for now. See text to nn. 25 and 26.

[29] Cf., A. Héritier, *Policy-Making and Diversity in Europe – Escape from Deadlock* (Cambridge University Press, 1999) 15 (citing adjustment costs, and distributional and decisional losses as factors that can cause actors to oppose action).

control and thus, for the horizontal and vertical allocation of regulatory competences.

It is now possible to state the final lesson which this shift in analysis from national to EU decision-making has to offer in a field such as prospectus regulation, where there has traditionally been a degree of regulatory competition between Member States and financial centres. Recall that for proponents of regulatory competition, exit and the threat of exit are a means to discipline 'competing' decision-makers and to stimulate regulatory policy learning between them. But in the present context, where the constitutionally protected objective of integration is meant to be promoted through *common* action, it is suggested that the threat of selective exit is worth examining, as an underlying regulatory problem, when turning to specific explanations of *conflict* between actors at EU level and accounting for factors that impede effective decision-making at EU level. To be sure, the extent of conflict and indeed its outcome cannot be prejudged. The former is likely to vary depending on the precise configuration of interests among actors and the latter is affected by the institutional setting in which they interact.[30] Both must be accounted empirically. But the concluding point for now is that, given our context and provided that we do not treat the analysis of regulatory problems as exogenous to the enquiry, it should be possible to identify situations where the threat of selective exit, as a specific, but politically salient regulatory problem, contributes to explaining conflict over the content of the prospectus regime among actors at EU level.[31]

The threat of (selective) exit under the Lamfalussy approach In examining the 'threat of exit' hypothesis, I have so far made abstraction of the peculiarities of the Lamfalussy decision-making process. While the Lamfalussy process did not radically change European policy-making, the creation of CESR at Level 3 was nevertheless a noteworthy development. ESMA replaced CESR in January 2010, but it is yet too early to assess its contribution. I will therefore focus on CESR. But note that the questions that I raise can just as well be asked with respect to ESMA.

CESR was meant to remedy common problems of European securities regulation: a lack of sustained and consistent cooperation between

[30] I am drawing on Scharpf's insights on policy-making (Scharpf, *Games Real Actors Play*). For details, see section III, below.

[31] See Scharpf's fuller analysis of regulatory competition and EU problem-solving (*Governing in Europe* 102–20) from which I greatly benefited.

national authorities; differing approaches to enforcement, supervision and the day-to-day application of EU rules by national authorities. In the past, these differences have given rise to regulatory arbitrage. From my vantage point, the establishment of CESR therefore held out two promises: first, to be a means to monitor, but also to manage, the threat of selective exit (or regulatory arbitrage) at the level of the application and enforcement of EU rules by ensuring cooperation, coordination and trust between securities authorities; second, by managing the threat of selective exit, to facilitate over the long-term agreement among actors at Levels 1 and 2. The latter point is based on Majone's claim that by abandoning authority to a delegate – CESR, in our case – a delegator can enhance the credibility of its policy commitments.[32] For Majone, this type of goal can be advanced if the relationship between delegator and delegate is akin to a fiduciary (trust) relationship as opposed to a principal-agent relationship.[33] The reason is the greater degree of independence of the delegate towards the delegator.[34] According to Majone, the trust relationship involves the transfer to the delegate (trustee) of what the author refers to as 'political property rights', that is 'the rights to exercise public authority in a given policy area'[35] – for example, the transfer of monetary policy competence to a central bank[36] or the delegation of powers, such as the right of legislative initiative or the right to take enforcement actions, to the European Commission.[37]

De Visscher, Maiscocq and Varone have examined Majone's claims in the context of the Lamfalussy process, assessing, *inter alia*, whether CESR was a trustee of Member States dealing with 'the assets that national regulatory competences constitute, for the benefit of market participants'.[38] However, after examination, de Visscher *et al.* found themselves unable to draw final conclusions given that the Lamfalussy process had not been in operation for long and that CESR's independence from Member States was contingent on various aspects including CESR's 'internal organisation and

[32] See Majone, *Dilemmas of European Integration* 64–82. See also G. Majone, 'Two logics of delegation – agency and fiduciary relations in EU governance' (2001) 2 *European Union Politics* 103; Majone, 'The credibility crisis of Community regulation'.

[33] For details, see Majone, *Dilemmas of European Integration* 64–82.

[34] *Ibid.* [35] *Ibid.*, 76. [36] *Ibid.*

[37] *Ibid.*, 78. According to Majone, the Commission wears both the hat of a trustee and that of an agent. See *ibid.*, 78–9.

[38] C. de Visscher, O. Maiscocq and F. Varone, 'The Lamfalussy reform in the EU securities markets', 31–2. Majone's findings have also been discussed in various other contexts, e.g., K. Alter, 'Delegation to international courts and the limits of re-contracting political power' in D. Hawkins, D. Lake, D. Nielson and M. Tierney (eds.), *Delegation and Agency in International Organizations* (Cambridge University Press, 2006) 312.

dynamics'.[39] In any event, given what was said about CESR in Chapter 1, it is not necessarily obvious that Majone's argument holds in the context of CESR. In particular, it is questionable whether CESR necessarily had the right incentives for playing the role of a trustee. As noted earlier, CESR was a collective actor (a 'club-like' body). It had no independent, overriding choice over its preferences.[40] The preferences that directed its Level 3 activities were those of its members – national competent authorities – which were ultimately accountable at national level. This suggests that for issues which are perceived as being salient at national level, it would be mistaken to assume that CESR managed 'the assets that national regulatory competences constitute'[41] without having the national interest or, for that matter, the separate organisational interests of its members in mind.[42] What is more, recall that in the disclosure field there are ready examples of CESR members defecting on commonly agreed, albeit not legally binding, CESR standards.[43] One should, therefore, approach with a degree of scepticism any argument that claims, without making space for qualifications, that the establishment of a collective securities actor such as CESR improves decision-making at Level 1 or 2, by feeding back its efforts to manage the threat of selective exit to decision-makers at EU level. That said, ultimately the matter must be examined empirically. I will thus return to the point in Chapter 10. Moreover, the point will need re-examining once ESMA comes of age. Its founding text makes it plain that ESMA is expected to prevent regulatory arbitrage.[44] Recall also that ESMA's Board of Supervisors is expected by law to 'think European' when fulfilling its duties.[45]

[39] de Visscher *et al.*, 'The Lamfalussy Reform' 38. Other relevant aspects that the authors mention are CESR's funding and 'external events (competition between financial centres)'.

[40] On the features of collective actors, see Scharpf, *Games Real Actors Play* 54–56.

[41] de Visscher *et al.*, 'The Lamfalussy Reform' 31.

[42] But cf., de Visscher *et al.*, 'The Lamfalussy Reform' 35 noting that '... CESR does not actively behave as a guardian of national interests, but takes its decisions by consensus for the benefit of market participants'. De Visscher *et al.*, however, do not take account of the problem of defection at national level. For a more balanced view, see Quaglia, 'Financial sector committee governance in the European Union', 575, arguing that although expertise and arguments have good currency within CESR most of the time, dynamics in Level 3 committees are contingent on the issues being examined and especially on their 'political salience'.

[43] See Chapter 6, section IV A.2.

[44] ESMAReg Art 1(5)(d). [45] Art 42.

III Actor preferences and institutions

So far, the threat of selective exit (or regulatory arbitrage) has been described as an underlying regulatory problem which actors confront when pursuing integration by way of common legal action. It was suggested that in the prospectus disclosure field, the threat of selective exit was worthy of examination when accounting for outcomes and indeed for conflict between actors at EU level.

By now, it should be apparent that I address EU decision-making in a somewhat oblique manner. Given the interest in regulatory competition, the assessment of the threat of selective exit for EU decision-making is an integral part of the analysis, in addition to the workings of the EU policy-making process. As far as the former is concerned, Nicolaïdis concept of 'managed' mutual recognition will provide a helpful reference point in Chapter 10. As far as the latter is concerned, my primary goal is not to make original theoretical propositions on the process of policy-making at EU level which is well understood, but rather to seek orientations and insight by building on existing literature, especially on Scharpf's work on policy-making. I do not aspire to generalise about my findings either. I am content with this approach because I merely aim to provide a meaningful discussion of the issues which regulatory competition raises in my field of interest, that is in the field of prospectus regulation.

With that in mind, I turn next to two basic concepts, actor preferences and institutions, which are relevant for my discussion on policy conflict. Accounting for conflict does indeed not yet tell us, in itself, anything about outcomes. Building on Scharpf, the extent of conflict among actors will depend importantly on the precise configuration of preferences among them and its outcome will be affected by the institutional setting in which actors interact.[46] To explain outcomes, we must therefore account for these two broad sets of factors.

A Actor preferences

Actor preferences can be described loosely as the 'wants and desires'[47] of actors. They:

> will be activated and specified by the stimulus provided by a particular policy problem or issue, and they will refer to the desirable or undesirable

[46] See Scharpf, *Games Real Actors Play*.

[47] Hix, *The Political System of the European Union* 13.

> nature of the status quo, to the causes of a perceived problem, to the efficacy and desirability of perceived courses of action, and to the outcomes associated with these.[48]

When explaining preferences and how they are formed, an actor's self-interest is generally seen as important. Thus, policy actors might have the prospect of distributive or competence losses in mind, or otherwise think of the cost of having to adjust national policies as a result of the adoption of common standards at EU level.[49] Moreover, the demands of powerful interest groups also enter the preference calculation of policy actors.[50] Other factors too may, however, contribute to the formation of preferences. There is a rich literature on the role of 'ideas'[51] in the political science and international relations literature.[52] For advocates of ideational approaches, ideas are important to account for when seeking to explain policy change or conflict. But precisely how much attention should be paid to ideas (as opposed to interests), as a factor which affects preferences and policies, has been a much-debated topic, with different views being taken on their meaning and their role. On the one hand, ideas can simply serve as normative frames (or 'hooks') which actors use in order 'to propagate and to legitimize their interests'.[53] In this sense, ideas can offer 'symbols and concepts with which to frame solutions to policy problems in normatively acceptable terms through transposition

[48] Scharpf, *Games Real Actors Play* 43. To be accurate, Scharpf refers, in this context, to the broader concept of actor orientations (instead of actor preferences) which are made of perceptions and preferences, with the latter being subdivided into different components, i.e., an actor's self-interest, normative orientations and identity (*ibid.* 62–6). In order to simplify the presentation, I will not consider the role of an actor's identity hereinafter.

[49] Héritier, *Policy-Making and Diversity in Europe* 15.

[50] See e.g., A. Moravcsik, *The Choice for Europe – Social Purpose and State Power from Messina to Maastricht* (UCL Press, London, 1998) 36–7 noting that governments will 'promote producer interests within broad constraints set by general demands for regulatory protection, economic efficiency, and fiscal responsibility'.

[51] The term 'ideas' is generally loosely defined by scholars interested in the role of ideas. Campbell, for instance, uses it to describe 'worldviews, norms, identities, values, intellectual paradigms, culture, and other beliefs'. See Campbell, *Institutional Change and Globalization* 90.

[52] E.g., J. Goldstein and R. Keohane (eds.), *Ideas and Foreign Policy – Beliefs, Institutions, and Political Change* (Cornell University Press, Ithaca New York, 1993); K. McNamara, *The Currency of Ideas: Monetary Politics in the European Union* (Cornell University Press, Ithaca New York, 1998); D. Braun and A. Busch (eds.), *Public Policy and Political Ideas* (Edward Elgar, Cheltenham, 1999).

[53] J. Goldstein and R. Keohane, 'Ideas and foreign policy: an analytical framework' in Goldstein and Keohane, *Ideas and Foreign Policy – Beliefs, Institutions, and Political Change* (Cornell University Press, Ithaca New York, 1993) 3, 4.

and bricolage'.[54] But ideas can also be conceptualised as more powerful influences that contribute to policy change or conflict.[55] Indeed, ideas may directly affect what actors think is in their interest.[56] In the policy frame literature, Schön and Rein, for instance, argue that while frames can be used to justify interests, frames also define what actors 'see as *being* in their interests'.[57] For them, policy frames provide 'a perspective from which an amorphous, ill-defined problematic situation can be made sense of and acted upon'.[58] Actors see and interpret situations differently and, as a result, 'support different courses of action concerning what shall be done, how it shall be done, and by whom'.[59] In short, in accounting for preferences a number of factors appear to deserve closer attention: interests, but also ideas (or frames) at a normative or cognitive level.[60] The literature on ideas then has obvious affinities with similar movements in the social sciences – think, for example, of the behavioural economics literature that I reviewed in Chapter 2. But although this literature brings us closer to a more realistic conception of actor preferences and prompts us not to simply infer preferences from an actor's revealed choices,[61] the addition of subjective factors also creates methodological difficulties.[62] I will therefore venture on the cautious side in the rest of the book. I will treat interest-based factors as having a 'special place in explanations of policy

[54] J. Campbell, 'Institutional analysis and the role of ideas in political economy' (1998) 27 *Theory and Society* 377, 394.

[55] See e.g., P. Hall, 'Policy paradigms, social learning, and the State – the case of economic policymaking in Britain' (1993) 25 *Comparative Politics* 275 (on policy change).

[56] E.g., S. Nahrath, 'The power of ideas in policy research: a critical assessment' in D. Braun and A. Busch (eds.), *Public Policy and Political Ideas* (Edward Elgar, Cheltenham, 1999) 41, 51 noting that '... the definition of interests depends on the inseparable relation between the objective material situation and the subjective perception (founded on values, beliefs, cognitive schemes, etc.) of this objective material structure' (citation omitted).

[57] D. Schön and M. Rein, *Frame Reflection – Toward the Resolution of Intractable Policy Controversies* (BasicBooks, New York, 1994) 29.

[58] M. Rein and D. Schön, 'Frame-reflective policy discourse' in P. Wagner, C. Hirschon Weiss, B. Wittrock and H. Wollmann (eds.), *Social Sciences and Modern States – National Experiences and Theoretical Crossroads* (Cambridge University Press, 1991) 262, 263.

[59] *Ibid.*, 264–5.

[60] On the distinction between cognitive and normative ideas, see Campbell, *Institutional Change and Globalization* 93.

[61] This conventional precept is also known as 'revealed preferences' which has been put to scrutiny by the behavioural literature. See in this context, e.g., D. Kahneman and A. Krueger, 'Developments in the measurement of subjective well-being' (2006) 20 *Journal of Economic Perspectives* 3.

[62] For criticism of the literature, see J. Jacobsen, 'Much ado about ideas: the cognitive factor in economic policy' (1995) 47 *World Politics* 283; A. Yee, 'The causal effects of ideas on policies' (1996) 50 *International Organization* 69.

interactions'.[63] As far as ideas are concerned, I start from the premise that 'ideas' also matter in real-world interactions. They have a role to play in explaining preferences of actors (think, for example, of shared norms or public sentiment which creates expectations)[64] and one must also, at all times, remain attentive to their potential impact for explaining policy change or conflict. But more often than not, ideas and interests are likely to be 'inextricably intertwined'.[65] Because of the methodological challenges involved in establishing their distinct impact and because of the limited scope of my enquiry, I therefore resist making a strong claim in favour of the independent role of ideas. As such, I also take the view that as long as interest-based explanations are good enough when accounting for preferences, then there is, for my purposes, less need for insisting on the distinct impact of ideas.[66]

B Institutions

The role of institutions The second broad factor which needs explaining when seeking to account for outcomes are institutions. The meaning of the term needs first specification, for scholars working in the main traditions of new institutionalism, which has dominated institutional analysis in political science, have come to understand it in different ways.[67] In rational choice institutionalism (which is closest to the new institutional movement in economics), the term 'institutions' is generally given a narrow meaning encompassing 'formal legalistic entities and sets of decision rules that impose obligations upon self-interested political actors'.[68] Voting rules within the Council would, for instance, qualify as an institutional rule under this definition.[69] In historical institutionalism, the definition is generally wider, referring, for example, to 'formal rules,

[63] Scharpf, *Games Real Actors Play* 64.

[64] On the role of public sentiment, see Campbell, *Institutional Change and Globalization* 96–8.

[65] J. Kindgon, 'Politicians, self-interest, and ideas' in G. Marcus and R. Hanson (eds.), *Reconsidering the Democratic Public* (Pennsylvania State University Press, University Park PA, 1993) 73, 75.

[66] Cf., Jacobsen, 'Much ado about ideas' 286 (arguing that going down this route leads to 'unnecessarily strained arguments').

[67] For good overviews of new institutionalist approaches, see P. Hall and R. Taylor 'Political science and the three new institutionalisms' (1996) 44 *Political Studies* 936; B. Rosamond, *Theories of European Integration* (Palgrave Macmillan, Basingstoke, 2000).

[68] Rosamond, *Theories of European Integration* 115.

[69] *Ibid.*

compliance procedures and standard operating practices that structure relationships between individual units of the polity and the economy'.[70] There is more scope under this definition to include besides legal arrangements, also informal arrangements such as, for instance 'codes of behaviour' or 'conventions'.[71] Finally, the third brand, sociological institutionalism, defines institutions in a very loose, if not peculiar, manner as 'not just formal rules, procedures or norms, but the symbol systems, cognitive scripts, and moral templates that provide the "frames of meaning" guiding human action'.[72] Whatever the precise definition, the reason why institutions matter and why they are examined here is because they affect the behaviour of actors.[73] But the different versions of new institutionalism have a different understanding of what this precisely means. For rational choice institutionalists, for instance, institutions matter, but they are seen as external forces 'structuring the purposeful choices of self-interested rational actors'.[74] Preferences of actors are assumed to be fixed and, as a result, actors are seen as behaving 'entirely instrumentally so as to maximize the attainment of [their fixed set of preferences], and do so in a highly strategic manner'.[75] On the other hand, in sociological institutionalism, preferences are not treated as exogenous and the looser concept of institutions will not only determine what actors 'can do, but also their perceptions and preferences – and thus what they will want to do'.[76] It is then obvious that the discussion on institutions intersects with the earlier discussion on preference formation.[77] But whereas in rational choice institutionalism, institutions matter because they affect the strategies that actors pursue, for scholars working in sociological institutionalism, institutions also impact on the formation of preferences and indeed on actors' identities.[78] It should not therefore come as a surprise that sociological institutionalism scholarship has been most receptive of the role

[70] P. Hall, *Governing the Economy – The Politics of State Intervention in Britain and France* (Polity Press, Cambridge, 1986) 19, cited in Rosamond, *Theories of European Integration* 115.

[71] Rosamond, *Theories of European Integration* 115.

[72] Hall and Taylor, 'Political science and the three new institutionalisms' 947.

[73] For details, see *ibid.*, 950–2.

[74] F. Scharpf, 'Institutions in comparative policy research' (2000) 33 *Comparative Political Studies* 762, 770.

[75] Hall and Taylor, 'Political science and the three new institutionalisms' 944–5.

[76] Scharpf, 'Institutions in comparative policy research' 770.

[77] Note that historical institutionalism allows accommodating both the postulates of rational choice and sociological institutionalism (Hall and Taylor, 'Political science and the three new institutionalisms' 950).

[78] *Ibid.*, 948.

of 'ideas'. Given that in rational choice institutionalism preferences are assumed to be fixed, the impact of ideas is naturally limited for rational choice scholars.

Inspiration can be drawn from all of these approaches. But to gain ground in a complex empirical world, a one-dimensional approach seems unnecessarily reductionist.[79] I will therefore keep an open mind with respect to the meaning of 'institutions' and think of institutions (or institutional rules) as potentially affecting actors (and thus outcomes) in various ways.[80] To begin with, institutional rules will affect the behaviour of actors by constraining or facilitating their choices.[81] They will, for instance, define the setting within which actors seek to reach agreement at EU level.[82] Thus, the ordinary legislative procedure, which before the entry into force of the Lisbon Treaty was known as the co-decision procedure, is the formal legal setting in an internal market context. It will determine the procedural steps that must be followed for the adoption of common rules, but also the parties to the legislative process and the voting requirements that actors must observe. Informal rules/norms or an institutional environment can affect behaviour too. One can think of the 'consensus norm'[83] which translates in the Council into efforts to 'pull as many members as possible into agreements'[84] or to 'accommodate the individual member which is isolated'.[85] Institutional rules can also affect perceptions and role orientations.[86] Think, for instance, of an

[79] Cf., Scharpf, 'Institutions in comparative policy research' 770 (noting that rational choice and sociological institutionalism are theoretically 'too deterministic').

[80] Cf., Scharpf's and Mayntz's own brand of actor-centered institutionalism where the institutional setting 'does not have the status of a theoretically defined set of variables'. See Scharpf, *Games Real Actors Play* 39.

[81] Héritier, *Policy-Making and Diversity in Europe* 13; Scharpf, *Games Real Actors Play* 39 (noting that 'sanctioned rules will reduce the range of potential behavior by specifying required, prohibited, or permitted actions' (citation omitted)).

[82] Scharpf, 'Institutions in comparative policy research' 775 (referring to 'modes of interaction').

[83] R. Eising, 'Policy learning in embedded negotiations: explaining EU electricity liberalization' (2002) 56 *International Organization* 85, 90. See also on the impact of an institutional environment, J. Lewis, 'Institutional environments and everyday EU decision making: rationalist or constructivist?' (2003) 36 *Comparative Political Studies* 97, 121 (noting that environments can affect the behaviour of actors by leading to a 'retooling of identities, attitudes, and roles').

[84] F. Hayes-Renshaw and H. Wallace, 'Executive power in the European Union: the functions and limits of the Council of Ministers' (1995) 2 *Journal of European Public Policy* 559, 566.

[85] *Ibid.* [86] Scharpf, *Games Real Actors Play.*

institutionally embedded set of objectives of a securities authority which defines the role of an authority and which acts as a lens through which it views and interprets a complex world.[87] Admittedly, this account is not nearly exhaustive. But the context of the enquiry (or the stage of the policy process under investigation) will later help sorting through institutions and institutional rules worth examining. Already worth mentioning is that from the present vantage point, the formal institutional setting will be especially important to account for. The point needs explaining.

Institutions and policy conflict As noted above, the ordinary legislative procedure (the former co-decision procedure) defines the basic institutional setting in which policy actors interact at Level 1 of the Lamfalussy process. The procedure corresponds to what Scharpf calls a 'joint decision mode', that is a mode of decision-making where decisions require both supranational institutions and Member States to participate.[88] This formal setting matters for the reason that the type of institutional setting affects the capability of actors to take decisions or, for that matter, to deal with policy conflict. Thus,

> [a]t a given level of policy conflict, the capacity to act is greatest if a single (corporate or collective) actor is able to adopt and enforce effective policy choices unilaterally, and it is reduced to the extent that effective action may be impeded by the requirement of negotiated agreement among the occupants of multiple veto positions.[89]

Admittedly, in an EU context, the shift from unanimity to qualified majority voting in the internal market field has facilitated decision-making under co-decision (and now the ordinary legislative procedure). But there are nevertheless a number of rules which can complicate agreement. Thus, Council members must still act unanimously at first reading where amendments to the Commission's proposed text are tabled which the Commission has failed to endorse.[90] Likewise at second reading, unanimity is required

[87] See e.g., Tafara and Peterson, 'A blueprint for cross-border access to US investors' 42 (noting that the SEC's founding legislation acts as a 'lens through which the SEC sees the world').

[88] F. Scharpf, 'Legitimate diversity: the new challenge of European integration' in T. Börzel and R. Chichowski (eds.), *The State of the European Union Vol. 6 – Law, Politics, and Society* (Oxford University Press, 2003) 79, 83.

[89] F. Scharpf, 'What have we learned? Problem solving capacity of the multilevel European polity' (MPIfG Working Paper 01/4, July 2001) para. 2.1, www.mpi-fg-koeln.mpg.de/pu/workpap/wp01-4/wp01-4.html.

[90] Art 293(1) TFEU.

where Council members vote on amendments introduced by the EP which have not been endorsed by the Commission.[91] What is more, even when acting by qualified majority the voting arrangements may not necessarily be sufficient to find effective solutions, either because of the distribution of preferences among Member States or because the Council prioritises the search for consensus over the search for effective policy solutions.[92] The empowerment of the European Parliament under the co-decision procedure and now the ordinary legislative procedure has not facilitated agreement either, notwithstanding the benefits of adding an institution with democratic credentials to the decision-making procedure. Moreover, if we sharpen our lens to take the micro-level functioning of Union institutions into account, it is apparent that they provide many entry points for organised interests groups to make their voices heard (e.g., at the level of the Parliament's committees or at the level of the Commission).[93] Thus, in sum, Scharpf argues with respect to joint decision-making that:

> [t]aken together, these institutional arrangements provide so many veto positions, and so many access points for interest groups, that the actual policies produced by joint decision processes are unlikely to violate status quo interests that have high political salience in member states or that are represented by well-organized interest groups.[94]

The tendency to favour the *status quo*, which the author describes, is well known in the literature. In its starkest form, its implications became known as the 'joint-decision trap',[95] causing EU policy-making to result

[91] Art 294(9) TFEU.

[92] See D. Heisenberg, 'The institution of "consensus" in the European Union: formal versus informal decision-making in the Council' (2005) 44 *European Journal of Political Research* 65, 66 noting in relation to the Council that '(...) on average from 1994 to 2002, 81 per cent of all decisions were made by consensus without voting. Thus even when the formal decision-making rule is voting (a qualified majority vote (QMV) of approximately 71 per cent), the Council bargains until there is consensus, setting a higher hurdle for itself than is mandated by the treaties'. See also Hayes-Renshaw and Wallace, 'Executive power in the European Union' 566, noting '[t]he price of accommodating the laggards and the reluctant is often paid in the appearance of ungainly compromise'.

[93] See generally S. Mazey and J. Richardson 'Interest groups and EU policy-making – organisational logic and venue shopping' in J. Richardson (ed.), *European Union – Power and Policy-making* (Routledge, London, 2006) 247; M. Pollack, 'Representing diffuse interests in EC policy-making' (1997) 4 *Journal of European Public Policy* 572, 577.

[94] Scharpf, 'Legitimate Diversity' 84.

[95] F. Scharpf, 'The joint-decision trap: lessons from German federalism and European integration' (1988) 66 *Public Administration* 239. Note that the generalisation of these findings proved problematic and the author, in its later work, insisted on the limited scope of application of its conclusions. See F. Scharpf, 'The joint decision trap revisited' (2006) 44 *Journal of Common Market Studies* 845, 846–7.

in less than effective outcomes in the form of blockages or lowest common denominator decisions. To be sure, resolving blockages or finding agreement that goes beyond the common minimum denominator is nowadays, by no means, out of reach under the ordinary legislative procedure. A politically astute Commission, for instance, can help resolving policy conflict among parties by proposing original and agreeable solutions in its role as an 'honest broker'.[96] As noted in Chapter 1, delegation (e.g., trilogues) and work in committees can also help overcoming obstacles. Lewis, for instance, points to the role of Coreper which he views as the 'place to do the deal'.[97] Comitology committees have, meanwhile, been associated with a 'culture of inter-administrative partnership which relies on persuasion, argument and discursive processes rather than on command, control and strategic interaction'.[98] Recall that the Lamfalussy process depends importantly on the input of committees such as the ESC. And, of course, blockages can be resolved by making solutions agreeable to actors through bargaining. Héritier describes specific ways: agreeing 'package deals', 'paying compensation', 'making concessions' or settling for vague framework decisions which leave actors sufficient room for interpretation.[99] Not all of these strategies might, however, be available in a given negotiation situation.[100] Moreover, as far as committees are concerned, Quaglia has shown that not even the ESC or CESR are insulated from political considerations.[101] Last but not least, the fact that agreement may be reached tells us little about the quality of the measures that are agreed upon. For instance, taking vague decisions in order to deal with conflict is unlikely to promote legal certainty and worse, may simply provide a handy justification for a Member State to subsequently depart from the common set of standards. This concludes my examination of the role and importance of actor preferences and institutions. It is fair to say that the above picture about the EU's ability to deal with conflict is somewhat diffuse, with each observation seemingly triggering a counterclaim. Ultimately, however, this also drives the point home that we must account for the issues at stake for actors when examining how effective

96 Scharpf, 'The joint decision trap revisited' 850.

97 J. Lewis, 'Informal integration and the supranational construction of the Council' (2003) 10 *Journal of European Public Policy* 996, 1001.

98 C. Joerges and J. Neyer, 'Transforming strategic interaction into deliberative problem-solving: European comitology in the foodstuffs sector' (1997) 4 *Journal of European Public Policy* 609, 620.

99 Héritier, *Policy-Making and Diversity in Europe* 19.

100 Scharpf, 'The Joint Decision Trap Revisited' 851.

101 See Quaglia, 'Financial sector committee governance in the European Union'.

EU problem-solving is likely to be[102] and, in this context, I suggested earlier, that the threat of selective exit, as a politically salient regulatory problem, was worth examining in the prospectus disclosure field. I thus end this chapter intentionally without drawing a formal and final conclusion given that the issues and suggestions raised in this chapter still need to be examined empirically. This is something for the next chapter which will return a final time to the PD and its negotiations.

[102] F. Scharpf, 'Introduction: the problem-solving capacity of multi-level governance' (1997) 4 *Journal of European Public Policy* 520, 531.

10

Regulatory competition and the prospectus directive: the issuer choice policy dispute

I Introduction

In Chapter 9, I proposed that more attention should be paid to EU regulatory decision-making in the context of scholarly research on regulatory competition. Specifically, the chapter attempted to do this by exploring the implications which the concept of 'regulatory exit' has for collective decision-making at EU level in the securities field. It suggested, first, that the threat of selective exit was worth accounting for when attempting to explain legislative choices for specific regulatory arrangements at EU level. But the chapter went further. After turning for guidance to authors such as Nicolaïdis or Scharpf, it suggested that in the securities field, where there has traditionally been a degree of regulatory competition between Member States, the threat of selective exit was worth examining, as a substantive and specific regulatory problem, when attempting to explain policy conflict and when accounting for underlying factors that contribute to impeding effective decision-making and problem-solving at EU level. This chapter examines these propositions and turns, for that purpose, to the legislative history and the negotiations of the PD.

The PD was finally adopted in 2003 at second reading under the co-decision procedure. The negotiations are noteworthy, for they were marked by a dispute over the precise arrangements that should govern the horizontal allocation of competences between Member States. More precisely what was at issue was whether issuers should be allowed to choose a home Member State and, hence, a home competent authority (hereinafter, the 'issuer choice policy dispute'). Chapter 3 examined the relevant rules, as finally agreed upon. Recall that the PD is based on the home country control principle and requires issuers to seek approval of their prospectuses with the competent authority of their designated *home* Member State.[1] As

[1] In order to ease the discussion, I will generally use the term 'issuer' hereinafter, instead of differentiating between issuer, offeror or the person seeking admission to trading on a regulated market.

finally adopted, the rules governing the definition of home Member State allow issuers of certain types of securities to choose a home Member State (and hence a home competent authority) from among the Member States: (i) where the issuer's registered office is situated; (ii) where admission to trading on a regulated market is sought; or (iii) where a public offer is made. Issuers of other types of securities are denied such a choice and effectively tied to the Member State of their registered office. What explains this (horizontal) distribution of competence and the dispute that preceded it? Admittedly, the preferences of actors, their underlying interests and interactions, as well as institutional factors are important to consider in this context. But merely emphasising these factors without unpacking the regulatory problem underlying the policy dispute obfuscates the main lesson of this dispute for the literature on regulatory competition. The aim of this chapter is to draw these lessons. For that purpose, it relies on empirical (qualitative) research – especially primary sources such as interviews, but also written sources such as working documents or press releases – which was mainly carried out in the wake of the adoption of the PD.[2] While the chapter mainly

[2] Interviews (37 in total) mainly took place in 2004 and 2005 following the adoption of the directive. A few additional interviews took place at the European Commission and at the European Parliament in 2010 when the PD was revised. Interviews were divided into two sets and generally took a semi-structured form. The first set covered the negotiations of the PD. Interviewees were either involved in the decision-making process or were lobbyists. The second set of interviews was more inclusive and dealt with broader aspects of European securities regulation. Interviewees were typically officials from national securities authorities or from CESR, or lawyers with expertise in international capital markets. Interviewees were generally identified by an identification code (this is similar to Jackson and Pan, 'Regulatory competition in international securities markets'): 'EUNO' for 'EU National Official', 'EUO' for European Union Official, 'EUMAPA' for 'EU Market Participant', 'EUNR' for 'European National Regulator' and 'EUR' for members of CESR. A few interviewees chose to be identified by their names: e.g., Christopher Huhne, the original *rapporteur* of the PD in the European Parliament (EMAC); Wolf Klinz, the *rapporteur* of the directive in the European Parliament (EMAC) during 2009–10; and Clifford Dammers, former secretary general of the (former) International Primary Market Association ('IPMA'). Note that when compiling the interview material, I decided, for the sake of consistency, to amend and renumber the original identification codes. Besides interviews, a video recording of the Ecofin meeting during which political agreement over the PD was reached in November 2002 allowed collecting further observations. It records the opening statements of national governments as well as the formal vote in Council (first reading). Agreement between Member State delegations was reached during a break from the Council meeting. During this break, the broadcast was, however, interrupted. While best qualified as a 'soft primary source' (Moravcsik, *The Choice for Europe* 81) given that the videotape records the part of the Ecofin meeting which was transmitted to the press room, it proved useful for verifying the views expressed during confidential interviews. For a fuller description of the methodology, see P. Schammo, *The Prospectus*

focuses on the initial negotiations, the 2010 revisions of the directive are not altogether ignored. We will see that as far as the issuer choice problematic is concerned, not much has changed since 2003, notwithstanding the presence of actors such as CESR whose purpose was, *inter alia*, to keep a watchful eye over competent authorities.

The chapter proceeds as follows. Section II begins by introducing the issuer choice policy dispute. Section III explains and assesses the regulatory problem that was at the heart of this dispute. Section IV explains how the dispute was resolved. Section V, focuses on the recent revisions of the directive. Section VI concludes by examining the chapter's findings in the light of the propositions made in the previous chapter.

II Introducing the issuer choice policy dispute

This section introduces the issuer choice policy dispute. It begins by situating the dispute in its broader context (A). As mentioned in the introductory section, the subject of this dispute was the rules governing the distribution of competence between Member States. These rules also determine which national authority is competent to approve a prospectus. The second sub-section reveals the tensions that this distribution raised for actors (B). A somewhat unexpected finding of the empirical work on the negotiations of the directive was that actors with conflicting positions on the question of horizontal competence, appeared routinely to put forward competing claims on the merit of issuer choice and competition between regulators.[3] In other words, regulatory competition – I

Directive – New Perspectives on Issuer's Choice and Regulatory Competition (D.Phil. dissertation, unpublished, Oxford University, 2006) 9–14.

[3] The fact that these claims on issuer choice were at the foreground of the discussions on horizontal competence during the negotiations of the directive is also evidenced by the fact that major lobbying groups addressed them in press releases or other documents. See for instance the Common Press release by the FBE and IPMA (5 November 2002, on file) noting that '[t]he Directive will set detailed standards of disclosure and requirements for the review of prospectuses (maximum harmonization) and CESR will ensure harmonized implementation of the Directive and the Level Two legislation. Therefore, there is no chance of regulatory arbitrage or the so-called race to the bottom. On the contrary, choice of competent authority will ensure that prospectuses are reviewed by those authorities which have the expertise and proximity to the investors'. Similar points were made in a common letter dated 31 October 2002 (on file), addressed by fourteen business organisations to the Danish Presidency and national governments, in which the undersigned noted '[w]hat is asked for is then not "forum shopping," but a regime that maintains and builds on the efficiency and competitiveness of today's market practices while introducing a unified investor protection regime and an effective single passport'.

use the term 'regulation' in its broadest sense here – had an important discursive dimension at EU level. These competing claims or 'frames', which were at the foreground of the discussions,[4] are examined in more detail in the second sub-section.

A The context

The European Commission put forward its proposal for a directive on prospectuses in May 2001.[5] The proposal was meant, *inter alia*, to remedy the failings and flaws of the PD's predecessors, the Public Offers Directive (POD) and the (consolidated) Listing Particulars Directive (LPD).[6] *Inter alia*, the Commission proposed to replace the LPD and POD's defective mutual recognition system with a new single passport system. At the same time, it offered to introduce home country control and thereby entrust the approval of prospectuses to the administrative authority of the issuer's home Member State. Moreover, the Commission proposal addressed various loopholes which had hitherto allowed issuers to take advantage of differences between the (national) rules governing private placement exemptions, public offers, language requirements or the enforcement of disclosure requirements at national level. With respect to prior approval of prospectuses, for instance, Member State authorities adopted widely differing practices[7] and issuers made effective use of the disparities, especially in the debt market.[8] The Commission proposed to harmonise language requirements, to introduce a much needed definition of public offer

[4] Cf., Campbell, *Institutional Change and Globalization* 98 (suggesting that '[f]rames are normative concepts that reside in the foreground of decision-making debates').

[5] 'Initial Commission Proposal'.

[6] Council Directive 89/298/EEC [1989] OJ L124/8 (repealed); Council Directive 80/390/EEC [1980] OJ L100/1 (repealed). The LPD was consolidated in the Consolidated Admissions and Reporting Directive (CARD). See Directive 2001/34/EC [2001] OJ L184/1.

[7] Prospectus review practices ranged for example 'from a simple verification that a document has been sent to the competent authority, without reading the document, to an extensive verification of the clearness, the objectivity, accuracy and consistency of the prospectus on all items of information, including the financial statements'. Written Question E-1874/03 by Christopher Huhne to the Commission, [2004] OJ C 65E/97.

[8] For example, referring to practices *before* the adoption of the PD, see Interview Clifford Dammers noting that 'it takes an average three weeks for a plain vanilla deal to get approved in France, six weeks in Portugal, even though the regulation says ten days. (...) As a result all Portuguese issuers have MTN programs listed in Luxembourg'; Interview Christopher Huhne noting that 'the Euromarkets and bonds are very free and the way in which they worked and continue to work is that a company wanting to issue bonds will often get the prospectus approved by whichever of the main regulators happens not to have a queue (...)'.

and, with respect to approval practices, to issue Level 2 guidance in order to ensure equivalent review procedures in Member States. Further topics for reform included the delegation of powers at Member State level. Here the Commission sought to put an end to the practice of delegating approval tasks to stock exchanges. But the Commission's initial 2001 proposal was received with considerable criticism. In particular, it was criticised for adopting a stricter approach than FESCO – the Federation of European Securities Commissions, CESR's predecessor – with respect to the question of the distribution of competences between Member States.[9] The Commission offered to determine the issuer's home Member State and, hence, the national authority which would be competent to approve a securities prospectus, by reference to the location of the issuer's registered office.[10] The International Primary Market Association (IPMA),[11] a key lobbyist on the directive which feared for Eurobond market activities, was among the most vocal critics of the proposed text. In its August 2001 position paper, it expressed its discontent with what it saw as the most important flaw of the proposal: the rules which allowed determining the home state competent authority.[12] Meanwhile, the European Parliament, led by Christopher Huhne – a UK MEP (ELDR) who had previously worked in London's financial sector and, as *rapporteur* of the directive in the Committee on Economic and Monetary Affairs (EMAC) proved to be highly influential in defining the Parliament's position – tabled numerous amendments. Following Huhne's report, the Parliament's plenary voted an amendment the purpose of which was to give issuers a (limited) choice of competent authority. Thus, it defined the home Member State as either (i) the state where the issuer's registered office was situated, or (ii) the state where an issuer had first been admitted to trading or where the issuer sought to apply for admission, or (iii) the state where an issuer intended to offer its securities to the public.[13] Meanwhile, two opposing coalitions

[9] FESCO had suggested leaving issuers an option between the authority of the place of the issuer's registered office or where a primary listing was sought. See FESCO, 'A "European Passport" for issuers' 4.

[10] Separate rules applied for third country issuers. For these issuers, the Commission proposed to determine the home state by reference to the place where the third country issuer's securities were first admitted to trading.

[11] In July 2005, IPMA merged with the International Securities Market Association. This merger led to the creation of the International Capital Market Association (ICMA).

[12] IPMA, 'Good intentions and flawed execution – preliminary comments on the proposed Prospectus Directive' (10 August 2001, on file) 2.

[13] For third country issuers, the EP proposed that an issuer should be given a choice between the place where it intended to make a public offer or where it intended to apply for admission to trading.

formed at Council level. The first coalition was led by the UK and was in favour of a choice of competent authority for issuers, while the second was led by France and Italy and was opposed to such a choice.

B Policy frames on issuer choice

> Ideas provide actors with symbols and concepts with which to frame solutions to policy problems in normatively acceptable terms through transposition and bricolage.[14]

This section identifies two policy frames, the cost frame and the merit frame, which were held by opposing coalitions during the negotiations of the PD.[15] The frames reflected competing, indeed conflicting, 'problem-setting stories'[16] on the benefits and costs of a choice of competent authority and competition between authorities, and provided a narrative justifying and legitimising distinct positions on this issue.[17]

1 The cost frame

The cost frame offered, as its name suggests, a cost account of issuer choice and competition between national authorities. For cost frame holders, the competent authority of the Member State where the issuer's registered office was situated was best able to protect (retail) investors. Allowing

14 J. Campbell, 'Institutional analysis and the role of ideas in political economy' 394.

15 In order to help me identify the components of each frame, I turned for guidance to the literature on policy frames and ideas, discussed in Chapter 9, and to the analysis of the policy framing process in M. Rhinard, *Ideas, Interests, and Policy Change in the European Union: The Mobilization of Frames by Actors in the Agricultural and Biotechnical Policy Sectors* (D.Phil. dissertation, unpublished, Cambridge University, 2002).

16 I borrow the phrase from Rein and Schön, 'Frame-reflective policy discourse' 265.

17 It is worth noting that during interviews, concepts such as 'regulatory arbitrage', 'supervisory arbitrage' or 'shopping' were often cited. The common distinction between regulation (as rule-making), supervision and enforcement seemed to be of lesser significance, with interviewees talking in the same breath about regulatory arbitrage or supervisory arbitrage, or using expressions such as regulatory arbitrage in relation to enforcement. A source of confusion at first, the fact that policy actors used terms such as regulatory arbitrage loosely became even more obvious when I examined documentary material and the Ecofin video recording (see n. 2 above). In fact, the link between enforcement and regulatory arbitrage was also made in one of the core documents that proved influential in the phase leading up to a proposal for a prospectus directive. See FESCO, 'A "European Passport" for issuers' 10 (noting that '[h]aving the same rules is still, not sufficient to ensure the creation of a real pan-European securities market. If information is not properly controlled, issuers might exploit regulatory arbitrage and host competent authorities would be tempted to introduce local standards for the sake of investor protection').

issuers to choose an authority for approving prospectuses was seen as creating the conditions for undesirable arbitrage or legal shopping. Choice of competent authority thus not only meant that retail investor protection was at risk (e.g., by failing to improve clarity among investors or allowing issuers to seek approval with an authority with inadequate means or a lighter standard of review),[18] but also raised the outlook of authorities being 'incentivised' to 'downgrade standards of supervision'[19] or provide 'low cost regulation'. The following statement by a national official summarises, more or less, this line of argument:

> If you open up the choice you definitely have the possibility for all authorities to be incentivised to actually attract investors on the basis of – I would say – low cost regulation … And this was definitely a threat that we had identified quite quickly and that we tried to put forward when negotiating this directive.[20]

Besides highlighting the possibility of shopping or arbitrage,[21] cost frame holders also referred to the threat of a race-to-the-bottom.[22] According to the *rapporteur* of the PD within the European Parliament, '[t]here was a clear statement that there could be a race-to-the-bottom from certainly the Italians and the French'.[23] Evidence of the cost account can be found up to senior levels of decision-making. Thus, during a crucial Ecofin meeting in November 2002, the Italian Minister for Economy and Finance, Giulio Tremonti and the Belgium Minister for Finance, Didier Reynders both continued to underscore their respective positions by referring to the dangers of 'shopping' by issuers, while the French Minister, Franci Mer, referred (in more implicit terms) to the danger that retail investors would fail to benefit from proper prior verifications, if issuers were granted a choice of competent authority.[24]

[18] E.g., Interviews 08-EUNO; 09-EUNO; 13-EUNO.

[19] Interview 13-EUNO noting that 'there could be a competition to downgrade standards of supervision' or a competition 'to move standards down'.

[20] Interview 08-EUNO. The reference to 'low cost regulation' seemed at first puzzling, especially in the light of the maximum harmonisation approach of the directive. The point was followed up. See Interview 08-EUNO, noting that '[t]he cost of regulation depends essentially on the *level of quality* of requested information (…) Local regulators as well as professional best practices peculiar to each financial place are establishing these standards' (emphasis added).

[21] See Interviews 04-EUO; 12-EUNO; 13-EUNO; 02-EUO; 09-EUNO; 06-EUNO; Clifford Dammers (referring to their own views or the views expressed by cost frame holders).

[22] See Interviews Christopher Huhne; 05-EUNO; 04-EUO; 07-EUMAPA.

[23] Interview Christopher Huhne.

[24] Ecofin Meeting (Brussels 5 November 2002).

Hence, by focusing attention on (retail) investor protection and undesirable 'shopping', cost frame holders suggested that issuer choice was inappropriate. By the same token, cost frame holders were able to justify or legitimise their opposition to any proposal that would allow issuers to choose a competent authority. What is more, given that cost frame holders favoured concentrating competence with the Member State where the issuer's registered office was situated, they effectively benefited from the position that the Commission had adopted in its initial proposal, forcing advocates of issuer choice in a 'reactive mode'.[25] Once it became apparent that proponents of issuer choice were likely to win sufficient support from other Member States willing to offer issuers of non-equity securities a certain choice of competent authority, cost frame holders sought to restrict the scope of this choice as much as possible.[26] The cost account of issuer choice was commonly associated with France and Italy, the coalition leaders. The cost frame camp also included Belgium, Portugal, Spain and, initially, Greece.

2 The merit frame

The merit frame focused attention on the benefits of issuer choice and competition between competent authorities. Rather than stress the need to protect (retail) investors, it highlighted the benefits of a choice of competent authority for *issuers*. Indeed, unlike cost frame holders, merit frame holders saw a choice of regime as a means to ensure that issuers were able to have their prospectuses approved by those authorities which proved to have expertise or provided efficient regulatory practices.[27] This view was put across forcefully in relation to the international debt market. For merit frame holders, competent authorities in Member States that concentrated international debt market activities had expertise in dealing with specific financial products. Moreover, while a cost frame holder such as France felt that competition between national authorities was not desirable, a merit frame holder such as the UK saw a level of competition between national authorities as providing national authorities with the right incentives to remain responsive and to provide efficient services. Especially in relation to the review and approval of prospectuses, a degree of competition was

[25] I borrow the expression from A. Héritier, 'The accommodation of diversity in European policy-making and its outcomes' 150.

[26] See for details, section IV, B, below.

[27] Referring essentially to this line of argument, see Interviews 02-EUO; 06-EUNO; 11-EUNO; Christopher Huhne; 07-EUMAPA; Clifford Dammers; 04-EUO; 09-EUNO; 12-EUNO; 13-EUNO; 14-EUNO.

viewed as beneficial. Hence, in comparison to France and Italy, the UK had a fundamentally different appreciation of the benefits and costs of issuer choice and competition between authorities. The following statement by a national official summarises this line of argument:

> That was certainly a line of argument that the UK made, that on the basis that the content is exactly the same, then really issuers should have the ability to choose solely on things like efficiency, if a competent authority was more rapid in their response, for example. So in other words, that there should be a degree of regulatory competition because it keeps regulators on their toes, it means that they don't get the sort of fat bloated state monopolies, sort of feel about them, and that we are in a game where there is competition.[28]

Hence, merit frame holders thought that it was desirable for issuers to take advantage of different approaches or approval practices. During a November 2002 Ecofin meeting, the benefits of issuer choice were highlighted by Gordon Brown, the (former) British Chancellor of Exchequer, when stating that:

> This is not about weakening investor protection, nor is it about reducing disclosure of information for retail investors, but it's ensuring that issuers are able to choose the regulators with their expertise best able to deal with their prospectus.[29]

What is more, allowing issuers to choose a competent authority was viewed as essential for the functioning of an already well-integrated Eurobond market. Indeed, the merit frame's message echoed with the objective of facilitating the widest possible access to investment capital by means of the passport, as agreed by the Lisbon European Council. Hence, by focusing on the benefits of a choice of competent authority for issuers, merit frame holders suggested a course of action diametrically opposed to the preferred course of action of cost frame holders. Once it became apparent that only non-equity securities would benefit from a limited choice regime, merit frame holders sought to secure a broad scope of application of this regime. The most important advocate of the efficiency frame within the Council was the UK. Other merit frame holders were Ireland and Luxembourg. Initially small, the coalition won subsequently the support of (mainly) Northern Member States and especially Germany.[30] Outside the Council, the Economic and Social Committee and

[28] Interview 06-EUNO.

[29] Ecofin Meeting (Brussels 5 November 2002).

[30] See section IV, B, below, for details.

the European Parliament's Economic and Monetary Affairs Committee led by Christopher Huhne, also subscribed to the merit frame.[31] Finally, it was the frame put forward by the wholesale industry in their lobbying efforts at national level and at European level. In its submission to the Economic and Monetary Affairs Committee in October 2001, IPMA thus praised the expertise of competent authorities in Member States that concentrated the international debt market whilst emphasising the dangers of monopolistic regulatory authorities (in terms of the quality of their service).[32] Similar points had been made earlier by IPMA in its August 2001 position paper.[33]

III Unpacking the issuer choice policy dispute: the regulatory problem

In the previous section, we saw how cost and merit frame holders were able to frame the issuer choice problematic in very different terms by putting forward competing problem stories on the benefits and costs of a choice of competent authority and competition between authorities. This section concentrates on the core issues that underlay the issuer choice problematic. The preferences of cost and merit frame holders were not 'free-floating', as it were, but were rooted in an assessment of the costs and benefits of a specific regulatory problem that changes to the rules governing the distribution of competences was likely to cause. This regulatory problem can be conceptualised as having two dimensions: a substantive dimension and an institutional dimension (B). I will examine each dimension separately in a second subsection, but first, it is worth beginning by examining the factors that are likely to have motivated actors. As noted in Chapter 9, interest-based considerations are among these factors. But the more interesting question is whether underlying the cost and merit frames, was also

[31] Economic and Social Committee, 'Opinion of the Economic and Social Committee on the Proposal for a Directive of the European Parliament and of the Council on the prospectus to be published when securities are offered to the public or admitted to trading' [2002] C80/52, paras 4.3.3.4. and 4.3.7.; Committee on Economic and Monetary Affairs, 'Report on the proposal for a European Parliament and Council directive on the prospectus to be published when securities are offered to the public or admitted to trading' (Final A5-0072/2002, 27 February 2002), comments under amendments 2 and 16.

[32] IPMA, 'Submission to the Committee on Economic and Monetary Affairs on the Commission's Proposal for a Directive on the Single European Prospectus' (15 October 2001, on file), para. 6.

[33] IPMA, 'Good intentions and flawed execution – preliminary comments on the proposed Prospectus Directive' (10 August 2001, on file).

a more fundamental, never mind ideological, disagreement over the role of competent authorities in securities markets (A).

A *Differing interests and ideas?*

Cost and merit frame holders not only differed with respect to their immediate cost-benefit judgment of issuer choice, but also with respect to underlying goals, such as retail investor protection, when assessing the merit of issuer choice. Underlying the frames were, in this sense, more ingrained differences about the legitimate role and objectives of regulatory authorities. In the case of France, for instance, the strong attachment to the role of regulatory authorities in protecting retail investors contrasted with the UK's attachment to a more market-driven, pro-competitive authority, sensitive to the cost of regulation for issuers. Differences of this type, especially with respect to retail investor protection, have been identified elsewhere in the literature. Moloney, for example, has described retail investor protection as at the crossroads of different national traditions.[34] Recall also that differences emerged in earlier chapters when I contrasted the enforcement styles of the FSA/UKLA and the AMF.[35] In Chapter 1, the respective institutional mandates of the FSA and AMF seemed also to substantiate the point about different role orientations.[36] Thus, the preference of the UK for a competitively minded securities authority is also apparent in a set of statutory principles which informs the activities of the FSA/UKLA.[37] More precisely, the FSA's founding text, FSMA, states that, when acting as the UK listing authority, the FSA must, *inter alia*, have regard to the 'international character of capital markets and the desirability of maintaining the competitive position of the United Kingdom'.[38] On the other hand, the mission statement of the French AMF makes it

[34] See N. Moloney, 'Building a retail investment culture through law: the 2004 Markets in Financial Instruments Directive' (2005) 6 *European Business Organization Law Review* 341, 348.

[35] See Chapter 7, section II, B.

[36] As Goldstein notes, institutions may reflect '(…) a set of dominant ideas translated through legal mechanisms into formal government organizations' (see J. Goldstein, 'Ideas, institutions, and American trade policy' (1988) 42 *International Organization* 179, 181). In particular, the regulatory objectives or mission of a regulatory authority can reflect such dominant ideas (cf., Scharpf, *Games Real Actors Play* 64–5).

[37] The point is examined in greater detail in Schammo, *The Prospectus Directive* 186–95.

[38] FSMA s 73(1)(d). A similar requirement applies to the FSA in general (FSMA s 2(3)(e)).

plain that the AMF was established in order to safeguard and protect, and ensure the proper functioning of markets.[39]

While the founding texts of the FSA and AMF thus appear to lend support to the idea that the UK and France had fundamentally different conceptions of the role of competent authorities in an internal market context, one must be careful not to infer too much. Statutory objectives are only broad constraints on the activities of competent authorities. They leave competent authorities sufficient scope to define and justify specific courses of action. As we have seen, the FSA's ethos has been fundamentally rethought in the wake of the financial crisis, without first requiring changes to its underlying statutory objectives and principles. Moreover, the AMF, perhaps more than its predecessor, is nowadays concerned about promoting the competitiveness of the French market, notwithstanding its strong retail investor protection orientations. That being said, the point about different role orientations is simply that at the time when the directive was initially negotiated, they seem to have *reinforced the conflict* between merit and cost frame holders. They were, as it seems, closely intertwined with interest-based considerations, contributing to reinforcing, instead of reconciling, differences. Thus, the fact that the UK was comparatively less concerned about retail investor protection must, obviously, also be seen in the light of the UK's interests in maintaining its position as a centre for wholesale finance. Indeed, the precise horizontal distribution of competences between Member States raised simple economic and competence issues for them. For merit frame holders, a change to the existing distribution of competences threatened to disrupt the working and functioning of existing markets, in particular the international debt market which attracted issuers from all over Europe and beyond. For the UK, Luxembourg and Ireland in particular, the so-called 'registered-office' approach also raised the prospect of a loss of competences over the capital raising activities taking place on their markets, given that many issuers listing on these markets were not incorporated under domestic law.[40] On the other hand, for cost frame holders, which had typically more domestic securities markets, a choice of competent authority promised to lead to a loss of decisional powers over domestic

[39] C. monét. fin. Art L. 621-1 states that the AMF 'deals with protection of the savings invested in financial instruments and all other investments which give rise to public offerings, the information provided to investors, and the proper functioning of the financial instruments markets. It lends its support to the regulation of those markets at a European and an international level'.

[40] For details, see section III, B.2, below.

issuers and threatened to distort the level playing field that the directive set out to achieve.[41] Indeed, as will be shown in the next section, it also threatened specific safeguards that were built into the mutual recognition systems under the POD and (consolidated) LPD.

B The substantive and institutional dimensions of the regulatory problem

This part examines the regulatory problem underlying the issuer choice dispute. I continue to proceed on the premise that interest-based motivations must have a 'special place'[42] when accounting for preferences. As mentioned, the regulatory problem can be conceptualised as having two dimensions: a substantive dimension (1) and an institutional dimension (2). By describing the regulatory problem along these lines, the issuer choice policy dispute can be situated at the intersection of three types of concerns: (i) proper enforcement (and the proper implementation) of prospectus disclosure rules at Member State level; (ii) the precise distribution of competences; and (iii) the operation of the single passport system. It is the interplay between these three types of issues that, it is submitted, gave shape to the threat of selective exit and ultimately to the competence and economic issues which the distribution of competences raised for actors.

1 The substantive dimension of the regulatory problem

The substantive dimension of the regulatory problem was essentially made up of questions and concerns over the enforcement (and the implementation) of prospectus rules at Member State level.[43] But the precise nature

[41] E.g., FT online, 'Brussels agenda: bonds foreign and financial' (1 July 2003) (highlighting the fear of the so-called 'Club Med' countries that issuers would choose to be regulated in London or Luxembourg).

[42] Scharpf, *Games Real Actors Play* 64.

[43] Although the PD is a 'maximum harmonisation' directive, maximum harmonisation does not necessarily guarantee an entirely level playing field. Recall that the directive contains a number of options, transitional periods and minimum harmonisation provisions, as well as inevitable textual ambiguities. While, in practice, issues and concerns are likely to have been somewhat intertwined, the findings in this section point to enforcement issues, especially concerns over prior approval of prospectuses, as a primary concern of cost and merit frame holders. These issues seemed to be tangled up with implementation issues. As far as cost frame holders are concerned, see, in particular, interviews 08-EUNO, 09-EUNO, 13-EUNO. Further comments pointing towards questions over enforcement were made by Clifford Dammers, Chris Huhne, 02-EUO, 04-EUO, 05-EUNO, 06-EUNO, 07-EUMAPA, 12-EUNO, 14-EUNO; 27-EUNR. The Ecofin video-recording allowed comparing and contrasting these views.

of these concerns differed. Recall that in the absence of a single securities authority, the application and enforcement of the PD's disclosure requirements, especially the review and approval of prospectuses, is a matter for national authorities.[44] Thus, for cost frame holders, the fact that the PD was meant to be adopted as a maximum harmonisation directive was, quite simply, not sufficient to ensure a level playing field between Member States.[45] This was all the more so as Member States adopted strikingly different approaches to *ex ante* enforcement. Thus, Southern Member States (and also Belgium) commonly considered prior approval of listing particulars and public offer prospectuses a matter of public interest and, consequently, a matter to be dealt with by public authorities only. In contrast, Northern Member States were often more sympathetic to self-regulation. Indeed, it was not uncommon for private actors (e.g., stock exchanges) to approve listing particulars in these Member States. Besides having incentives to turn over documents in short time delays, especially as exchanges started to demutalise and competition intensified, private actors had presumably also more limited enforcement powers. 'Box-ticking' – a practice

[44] Admittedly, proper liability standards are crucial for ensuring the quality of disclosure. But as noted in Chapter 6, the EU's enforcement strategy is biased towards *ex ante* public (administrative) enforcement and relies on national authorities to review and approve prospectuses. While these national authorities face obvious limitations when attempting to assess disclosure quality characteristics, the relevant point is that they are, nevertheless, required to take a decision on such quality characteristics when approving a prospectus, either on the basis of their own review or by relying on the investigations of third parties. Because the enforcement strategy is decentralised, there is therefore also scope for variation at national level.

[45] E.g., Interviews 08-EUNO, 09-EUNO, 13-EUNO. Incidentally, the point was also made by FESCO in the period that preceded the adoption by the Commission of its proposal. See (n. 17) above. 26-EUMAPA summarised the point nicely when noting that '[t]here is no doubt that if you are trying to build a pan-European market, unless you have a single competent authority to approve all prospectuses, you will get different disclosure standards. Because you know, you can never write down the disclosure standards in ultimate detail. The best you can do… look at the level 2 Regulation under the Prospectus Directive, it has a lot of headings. It says "describe the plant machinery equipment". But actually for me when I write a prospectus, "plant machinery equipment" is the heading of the section which is about three pages long. What goes in that section will vary depending on who the issuer is. Every issuer has a different structure, different equipment and different pressure points. No one wants to know that you got fifteen cracking units. That is not interesting. What is interesting is that your cracking units are thirty years out of date or that they are state of the art. That they break down regularly and when they break down you lose three days of production. Those are the sorts of issues which are interesting. But the regulation can never set out that kind of detail. So inevitably, the advisers of the deal, the issuer, the investment bank, and the competent authority have to take a judgement on what you say'.

consisting in merely checking whether relevant information items were included in the prospectus without any further enquiry – appears to have been more common in some Northern Member States. The Commission sought to end self-regulatory practices when it proposed that only independent administrative authorities should be entrusted with the approval of prospectuses. But a number of Northern Member States were opposed to changing existing practices and resisted the Commission proposal. The prospect of seeing commercial actors being involved in the approval process only exacerbated the tensions with cost frame holders.[46] Interestingly, the establishment of CESR appears to have had no significant impact on this assessment. *A priori*, CESR could have contributed to alleviating defection fears, precipitated by the insistence of some Northern Member States on a delegation to non-administrative bodies, if it were seen as acting as a type of trustee, in the sense suggested by Majone.[47] But, as a senior national official noted, CESR's activities were only starting to unfold and the precise contribution that CESR could make at Level 3 was unclear.[48]

Merit frame holders, on the other hand, had an altogether different set of concerns. For them, a choice of competent authority was necessary to ensure that competent authorities adopted efficient approval practices, offered a quality service to issuers and approved prospectus documents on time. Recall that prior approval is akin to a licensing system, in the sense that under the PD it is a *sine qua non* for accessing regulated markets. But prior to the adoption of the PD, considerable differences existed in the manner and the time frame in which national authorities approved prospectuses.[49] This fact did not augur well for the Eurobond market, where market actors were used to accessing markets swiftly. What is more, for merit holders the concentration of Eurobonds and other 'niche' products in a number of jurisdictions (e.g., Eurobonds and Medium Term Note programmes in London and Luxembourg; asset-backed securities in Ireland; and covered warrants in Germany (Stuttgart)) meant that competent authorities in these jurisdictions had developed a great deal of expertise that other authorities simply lacked.

[46] E.g., Ecofin Meeting (Brussels, 5 November 2002). The defection fears were, probably, best expressed by the French minister during the 2002 Ecofin meeting who noted that '[s]ome countries, during the course of their history, may have been more lax or may have had more facilities than others. But one cannot conclude from that that these countries are absolutely right. We are not in favour of a system where it's only the market which dictates the rules'.

[47] See Chapter 9, section II.

[48] Interview 13-EUNO. [49] See e.g., n. 8 above.

2 The institutional dimension of the regulatory problem

The second dimension of the regulatory problem concerned the rules governing the horizontal allocation of competence and the passport system (mutual recognition). To appreciate the problems that these rules, and especially their interplay, created for cost and merit frame holders, it is helpful to take a step back for a moment. Thus, I will first examine mutual recognition and the rules governing competence under the LPD (as consolidated) and POD, whose provisions the PD replaced.[50] Specifically, I will begin by assessing the LPD and POD's arrangements in light of Nicolaïdis's insights on 'managed mutual recognition' which I examined earlier in Chapter 6.[51] As a reminder, Nicolaïdis identifies four ways in which parties, in practice, manage mutual recognition and – crucially – deal with the prospect of regulatory competition.[52] According to the author, parties may agree to set 'prior conditions for equivalence'; they may decide to alter the degree of 'automaticity' of recognition or set limits to the scope of market access. They may also seek to put in place '*ex-post* guarantees'.[53] In the case of the LPD and POD, it is possible to think of a number of measures which contributed to managing mutual recognition, in the sense described by Nicolaïdis:

- Limits to the degree of automaticity: Member States agreed to limit the degree of automaticity by requiring prospectuses/listing particulars to be first vetted by the relevant authorities and by recognising residual powers to host Member States (e.g., the power to ask for a translation of the prospectus/listing particulars or require certain additional information);[54]
- Limits to the scope of recognition: Member States agreed on limits to the scope of recognition by excluding POD-Article-11 prospectuses – i.e., prospectuses for public offers of securities that were not meant to be admitted to official stock exchange listing – from the mutual recognition system, and by making the recognition of listing particulars, which benefited from exemptions or derogations in a Member State, subject to conditions;[55]

[50] For the sake of accuracy, recall that the LPD had been consolidated in CARD. However, to ease the presentation, I will continue referring to the LPD hereinafter.
[51] See Chapter 6, section II.
[52] Nicolaïdis, 'Regulatory cooperation and managed mutual recognition' 594.
[53] *Ibid*. 595–7.
[54] POD Art 21(1); LPD Art 24(a) and (b) (CARD Arts 38 and 39).
[55] LPD 24(a)(2) (CARD 38(2)).

- *Ex post* guarantees: specific provisions on cooperation between authorities were agreed.[56]

What is more, the registered-office-primacy rule, which was examined in Chapter 3 and which governed the horizontal distribution of competences between Member States for the purposes of mutual recognition,[57] also contributed to managing mutual recognition.[58] As a reminder, prior to the adoption of the PD, competence depended, as a general rule, on the place where a public offer was made or admission to stock exchange listing was sought. But special rules applied when a person wished to benefit from mutual recognition. In this case, the registered-office-primacy rule could apply which made it more difficult for issuers to take advantage of mutual recognition in order to circumvent home authorities.[59] In other words, under the LPD and POD, the registered-office-primacy rule contributed to preventing regulatory arbitrage type of issues by foreclosing the possibility of a *domestic* company to use mutual recognition against its 'home' state. By 'home', I mean the state where the issuer's registered office was situated. Indeed, in the absence of a market for the transfer of corporate seats in Europe, the latter state has, for public limited liability companies, also tended to correspond to the state where a firm has its principal place of business or real head office; at least, in those Member States that have traditionally applied the *real seat* doctrine.[60] During the negotiations of the PD, these states were typically cost frame holders.

Returning to the negotiations of the PD, the European Commission set out to overhaul the LPD's and POD's defective mutual recognition arrangements by introducing the single passport for prospectuses and the home country control principle. It thus offered to facilitate the operation

[56] LPD 24(c); POD Art 22(1).

[57] Under POD Art 21(1) and LPD Art 24(a) (CARD Art 38)).

[58] See Chapter 3, section IV, for details.

[59] LPD Art 24 (CARD Art 37), POD Art 20(1).

[60] Private limited liability companies, on the other hand, benefit from a greater degree of mobility as a result of the Court of Justice's case law on the right of establishment. See Case C-212/97 *Centros Ltd v Erhvervs- og Selskabsstyrelsen* [1999] ECR I-1459; Case C-167/01 *Kamer van Koophandel en Fabrieken voor Amsterdam v Inspire Art Ltd* [2003] ECR I-10155 and Case C-208/00 *Überseering BV v Nordic Construction Company Baumanagement GmbH (NCC)* [2002] ECR I-9919. Some restrictions on corporate mobility remain. See Case 81/87 *R v HM Treasury and Commissioners of Inland Revenue, ex parte Daily Mail and General Trust plc* [1988] ECR 5483; Case C-210/06 *Cartesio Oktató és Szolgáltató bt* [2008] ECR I-09641. The practical effects of the Court's case law on company mobility are examined in M. Becht, C. Mayer and H. Wagner, 'Where do firms incorporate? Deregulation and the cost of entry' (2008) 14 *Journal of Corporate Finance* 241.

of mutual recognition by, *inter alia*, eliminating the residual powers of host Member States. Moreover, it proposed to extend the scope of mutual recognition. At the same time, a number of conditions and safeguards were meant to give the new passport system its managed character. Thus, in order 'to provide the degree of harmonisation and mutual confidence to allow Member State [sic] to recognise the home prospectus without requiring the inclusion of additional information',[61] detailed disclosure requirements were to be adopted at Lamfalussy Level 2. Given that the passport system was seen as 'requir[ing] mutual trust among competent authorities and similarities in performing regulatory and supervisory functions',[62] the Commission proposed to entrust *administrative* authorities with enforcement matters and to harmonise, to some extent, their powers. What is more, the Commission offered to streamline review and approval procedures by adopting Level 2 guidance.[63] Provisions regarding cooperation and precautionary measures were to be added and cooperation was also to be harnessed by CESR at Level 3. Finally, the Commission proposed, in essence, to safeguard the former registered-office-primacy rule. Indeed, it was supposed to be extended because the initial Commission proposal defined the issuer's home Member State as the state where the issuer's registered office was located. In other words, under the initial Commission proposal the registered-office-primacy rule was no longer tied to mutual recognition or subject to limitations. It was the sole rule governing competence, regardless of whether an issuer sought to raise capital in the Member State in which it was incorporated.

By extending the registered-office-primacy rule, the Commission proposal introduced a major change to the existing distribution of competences between Member States. This is because competence under the LPD and POD had so far essentially been divided along territorial lines,[64] save, of course, if a person sought to take advantage of mutual recognition.[65] As a result of this proposed change, the definition of the home Member State became itself a disputed *ex ante* condition for the acceptance of the passport system and the directive as a whole. Member States that had hitherto exercised competence over the capital raising activities taking place on their territory were suddenly at risk of becoming dependent on the control

[61] 'Initial Commission Proposal' 9.

[62] *Ibid.*, 13. [63] *Ibid.*, 11.

[64] In other words, the authority of the Member State on whose territory the issuer sought to raise capital, approved listing particulars or public offer prospectuses.

[65] In this case, the registered-office-primacy rule could apply, hence preserving the authority of the Member State in which an issuer was incorporated.

procedures of the Member State in which an issuer's registered office was situated. While of no particular significance for Member States in which *domestic* issuers (i.e., issuers incorporated under domestic law) dominated capital raising activities – typically, cost frame holders during the negotiations – it was a major issue for the international debt and Eurobond markets and for the Member States that hosted these markets – typically, merit frame holders. This is because issuers listing on these markets were from all over Europe and beyond. The adoption of the passport system under the registered office approach thus raised the prospect of a loss of decisional powers for merit frame holders, but also threatened the functioning of the international debt market (e.g., by driving away issuers unhappy with their new designated home state authorities). On the other hand, however, the suggested solution of a choice of competent authority was a major source of concern for cost frame holders because the adoption of additional criteria for determining competence (such as, for example, the place of trading, or the place where a public offer was made) meant that *domestic* issuers would benefit from additional mobility, thus allowing them to seek approval with an authority other than the domestic authority (i.e., the competent authority of the Member State in which an issuer was incorporated). What is more, the mobility of issuers promised to be greatly improved by the directive's proposed passport system. Indeed, because of the proposed passport system, which was seen by all actors as an essential measure for facilitating integration, even a limited choice of competent authority meant only departing further from the safeguards that had underpinned mutual recognition under the LPD and the POD, *including* the registered-office-primacy rule which the Commission's initial proposal sought to extend and which promised to provide a safeguard against regulatory arbitrage type of behaviour under the proposed passport system. To be more specific, the adoption of a choice of competent authority raised the prospect of a domestic issuer (say, e.g., France Télécom) seeking approval with an authority abroad (e.g., by seeking admission to trading on a regulated market in Luxembourg) and, subsequently, taking advantage of the passport system in order to raise capital in the Member State of the place of its registered office (e.g., France), thereby effectively circumventing the competent authority of the latter Member State.[66] Hence, for cost frame holders, issuer choice only promised to undermine their decision-making authority over

[66] E.g., Interview 06-EUNO noting that ('... they were really most concerned about the idea that companies of their jurisdiction would go somewhere else to have their prospectus

domestic issuers. Meanwhile, the demands of some states to adopt a more flexible regime governing the delegation of powers to entities other than independent administrative authorities risked unbundling even further the package of *ex ante* measures that was supposed to manage the single passport. Unsurprisingly, the policy dispute materialised most vividly over the adoption of a possible choice of competent authority and a possible delegation of prospectus approval powers to entities other than independent administrative authorities (e.g., stock exchanges). Both issues were the only remaining 'B' items – i.e., items on which no agreement had yet been reached at Coreper level – on the agenda of the November 2002 Ecofin meeting.

IV Reconstructing the policy outcome

The previous section examined the policy dispute over the horizontal distribution of competences between Member States and went on to unpack the regulatory problem underlying it. This part seeks to explain its resolution and the final outcome. It begins by identifying the *status quo* tendencies of the competence distribution as finally agreed upon (A), after which it returns to the negotiations of the directive in order to square the terms of the regulatory bargain and, by the same token, to stress the limited problem-solving effectiveness of the political compromise (B).

A The distribution of competences between Member States: a status quo *decision?*

While the adoption of the PD testifies to the fact that conflict among actors does, by no means, lead inevitably to deadlock, especially when actors share a broad primary interest in pursuing reform,[67] the issuer choice policy dispute illustrates, nevertheless, the difficulties of pursuing regulatory change when preferences among actors differ markedly. Resolution of the issuer choice dispute led to the adoption of Article 2(1)(m) and (n) which governs the allocation of competence between

approved but then that prospectus would then be passported back into their jurisdiction and sold to their investors').

[67] One contextual factor that improved the odds of the directive being adopted is the commitment of all actors to the FSAP and the single passport, viewed as essential for the completion of the single securities market, and the tight timetable which had been set for the adoption of the PD. The Commission also played its part in reaching a compromise by taking a 'middle-ground' position on the question of issuer choice in its revised proposal.

Member States and allows each issuer to determine its home competent authority. As a reminder, for non-equity securities which have a denomination per unit of at least EUR 1,000, including certain types of hybrid or derivative securities that are under the directive treated as non-equity securities (hereinafter, 'type-1 securities'), Article 2(1)(m)(ii) allows an issuer to choose a home Member State among the following Member States:

(i) the Member State where the issuer's registered office is located;
(ii) the Member State where the regulated market, on which securities are to be admitted to trading, is located; or
(iii) the Member State on whose territory securities are offered to the public.

For equity securities and any other types of securities that are not caught by the above provision (hereinafter, 'type-2 securities'), issuers are denied a choice of home Member State and are, therefore, subject to the sole competence of the Member State where their registered office is situated.[68] These arrangements are *de jure* not consistent with the rules governing competence under the LPD or POD. Recall that prior to the adoption of the PD, the allocation of competences was generally decided along territorial lines. What mattered was the place where an offer was made or where admission to listing was sought, unless an issuer sought to use mutual recognition. In the latter case, the registered-office-primacy rule could apply.[69] On the other hand, the PD's rules on competence allocation are not consistent with the rules governing home state competence of other directives (e.g., MiFID) either. Indeed, for legal persons, competence tends to be vested exclusively with the Member State in which a company's registered office is situated.[70] In fact, at closer look it is apparent that the main merit of the distribution of competence under the PD is simply to safeguard to a large extent the *status quo* interests of all parties concerned, subject to, admittedly, a number of noteworthy changes.

As adopted, the rules governing home state competence fully reflect the Commission's initial proposition, based on the location of the place of the issuer's registered office, for type-2 securities (mainly, equity securities). As a matter of law, the PD, therefore, broke with the past. However, in practice – and this is the crucial point – it only departed to some degree from the *status quo*. This is because for shares, issuers have long preferred

[68] Art 2(1)(m)(i).

[69] See section III, B.2, above for details.

[70] E.g., MiFID Art 4(20)(a)(ii).

to seek a primary listing, or make a public offer, in the jurisdiction where their registered office is situated. Indeed, in the absence of a market for the transfer of corporate seats for public limited liability companies, this state has also tended to be an issuer's 'true' home state – i.e., the state with which a firm has more than artificial ties. Thus, because of this 'home bias', issuers of shares were *de facto* already subject to the competence of the Member State in which their registered office was situated before the PD was adopted. In other words, as far as shares are concerned, the new rules governing competence did not, as a consequence, change existing practices. Moreover, because the place of the registered office is the sole criterion for determining the home Member State, the registered-office-primacy rule is safeguarded and, indeed, extended under the PD. The interests of cost frame holders were, as a result, safeguarded.

Consider next the case of non-equity securities as type-1 securities (i.e., non-equity securities with higher denominations). Here the Commission's initial proposal was significantly watered down; indeed so much so that the PD also safeguards the interests of merit frame holders. Recall that as far as debt securities are concerned, issuers from all over Europe and beyond commonly listed their securities outside the state in which their registered office was situated; for instance, in London or Luxembourg.[71] Article 2(1)(m)(ii) allows issuers to continue seeking approval of their prospectus with the competent authorities of these jurisdictions.

However, the interests of merit and cost frame holders were not fully respected. For example, because of the interplay between the 'choice element' of Article 2(1)(m)(ii) and the single passport system, the PD no longer prevents issuers, which benefit from Article 2(1)(m)(ii), from seeking approval 'abroad' (e.g., by applying for admission to trading on a regulated market situated there) and subsequently from 'passporting' their prospectus back to the Member State of their registered office. What is more, the passport system explicitly prevents the competent authority of the latter Member State from re-examining the prospectus.[72] In other words, for 'type-1 securities', the interests of cost-frame holders were not fully safeguarded, given that the PD effectively abandoned the registered-office-primacy rule for these types of securities.

On the other hand, issuers of low denomination non-equity securities and certain types of hybrid securities (e.g., convertible securities,

[71] See also J. Casey and K. Lannoo, *Europe's Hidden Capital Markets – Evolution, Architecture and Regulation of the European Bond Market* (CEPS, Brussels, 2005) 33.

[72] PD Art 17.

as opposed to exchangeables) that are very popular in the international debt market, do not benefit from a choice regime. These issuers are effectively tied to the Member State where their registered office is situated, notwithstanding the demands for more flexibility from merit frame holders, such as the UK, during the negotiations.

By way of summary, while the distribution of competences does not fully accommodate *status quo* interests, it is nevertheless fair to say that these *status quo* interests effectively shaped it.[73] As such, the distribution also drives home the point that pursuing regulatory change in the face of conflict is a difficult endeavour. The static comparison between the rules governing competence allocation prior and after the adoption of the PD does not, however, yet fully explain the resolution of the issuer choice policy dispute. It is, therefore, necessary to return to the negotiations of the directive.

B The distribution of competences between Member States: bargaining or problem-solving?

The static comparison between the distribution of competences before and after the adoption of the directive is fairly crude. Whether, for instance, agreement on the rules governing competence is (i) the overall outcome of an 'adversarial process to "divide up the pie"'[74] or (ii) the result of a reasoned consensus reflecting a problem-solving oriented debate, must be assessed empirically. It is, accordingly, necessary to return to the negotiations of the directive. But to cut a long story short, there is little evidence that is consistent with the second proposition.

First reading under the co-decision procedure Following endorsement of EMAC's opinion by the Parliament's plenary in March 2002 and the contentious debate between cost and merit frame holders in Council, the Commission came forward with an amended proposal for a prospectus directive in August 2002 in which it took on board a number of amendments put forward by Member States and the European Parliament's *rapporteur*, Christopher Huhne. In relation to the horizontal distribution of

[73] The fact that the final compromise was reached with an eye to the existing distribution was confirmed by Christopher Huhne when noting that 'in fact the reasoning behind that as a compromise was really that, in general, a company would tend to go to a domestic market in equity anyway, whereas a company issuing bonds is very likely to go to another market and free choice is even more important than it is in equity'.

[74] Héritier, *Policy-Making and Diversity in Europe* 20.

competences, the Commission amended its initial proposal by introducing an element of choice for issuers. It effectively took a 'middle-ground' position by proposing that issuers should have a limited choice for non-equity securities with a denomination of at least EUR 50,000, whilst continuing to insist on its initial registered office approach in relation to equity securities. But the Commission's efforts did not lay the dispute to rest. The Commission had failed to take into account existing figures in the wholesale market,[75] in which a majority of securities were issued with low denominations or, depending on the instrument, with no denomination at all.[76] The idea of a threshold found, accordingly, little support among merit frame holders which did not see any rationale for introducing a threshold amount. But given that merit frame holders had failed to find sufficient support for extending choice of competent authority to issuers of equity securities and placed in a position of having to negotiate over the Commission's revised proposal, merit frame holders began to concentrate their efforts on two specific issues: first, the threshold amount for non-equity securities; second, the fate of certain derivative or hybrid instruments. Hybrid or derivative instruments include a vast variety of instruments such as, for instance, covered warrants or convertible securities. In particular, the fate of convertibles seems to have created tensions between frame holders.[77] Depending on the contract, convertible securities allow their holders to exchange bonds for shares of the issuer

[75] Answer given by Mr Bolkestein on behalf of the Commission to the Written Question E-1876/03 by Christopher Huhne (ELDR) [2004] OJ C65E/98.

[76] Annexe 2 to a letter addressed by the industry to the Austrian Chancellor of the Exchequer, dated 31 October 2002 (on file).

[77] E.g., Interview 06-EUNO having noted that convertible bonds were 'a proxy for home/host': 'yes, this was a big one. There was the fear put forward that if you did a straight split – shares, your stock with where you are incorporated but everything else you can go wherever you like – then what companies would do is that they would issue some form of convertible debt that was convertible the day after an issue and so, therefore, at the instigation of the issuer, and so, therefore, in effect companies were issuing shares but using another jurisdiction to do it. (...) But this was the sort of fear; that there would be bucket loads of these sorts of securities issues, purely in order to avoid the home competent authority'; Interview 02-EUO noting that 'we discussed a lot on convertible issues. Whether or not they should be with the country of origin approach or freedom of choice (...) It's exactly the same story. It's all this kind of argument. It was regulatory arbitrage, a fear of delocalisation of issues from one Member State to another Member State, the fact that they want to keep control on some issues'; Interview Christopher Huhne noting that 'we [the Parliament] stated very much that we wanted to have convertibles treated as bonds and therefore to have choice. And the French delegation was particularly "anti". And I think there may have been some problems in France with convertibles which caused the French delegation to have a very strong view on them. They didn't want them to be elsewhere on the grounds that they would not be able to stop an issue which they

of the convertible, or a company of the same group as that of the issuer (parent or subsidiary), or a third company that is not part of the same group. In the latter case, the convertible is also known as an *exchangeable*, although, in practice, this terminological distinction is not often made.[78] Hereinafter, I will mainly focus on convertible securities (i.e., convertibles/exchangeables), bearing in mind that a number of instruments share similar characteristics and were, as a result, supposed to be treated in a similar manner during the negotiations.

Returning to the negotiations, proponents of issuer choice insisted on no, or on a low, threshold for non-equity securities. They also insisted on a broad definition of the term 'home Member State' for issuers of non-equity securities in order to extend the scope of the definition to instruments other than simple bonds. On the other hand, opponents sought to secure a higher threshold amount and a narrower definition. Moreover, the dispute about whether issuers of hybrid securities should benefit from a choice of competent authority also appears to have spilled over into the discussions on the definitions of equity and non-equity securities.[79] The scope of these definitions determines the type of instrument that is classified as equity or non-equity for the purposes of the directive. As a result,

might think would be unfavourable for French investors'; Interview Clifford Dammers (IPMA) noting that 'we had a graphic growth in the number of convertible bond issues and there had been some mandatory convertibles and some convertibles with some strange economic terms; strange in the sense that they were off-market in France. And the French regulator had stepped in to stop what they perceived as abusive. So France was highly sensitised on the issue and led the fight to have convertibles included in the non-freedom of choice'; Interview 08-EUNO (less conclusive) noting that 'the real reason was that through the convertible bonds you definitely give effect to equity. And today the market practice is to have convertible bonds of a maturity between three to five years and you can extend that if you want. So fine. In effect these instrument do not give you a right to equity quite soon. The mutive impact might very likely never happen. But if you open up that kind of possibility, you can imagine that you have a convertible bond maturing in one day after an issuance. And as a consequence it is pure equity. So you do not definitely want to open up a door for pure equity instruments not to be counted as – you know – real equity instruments in terms of investor protection'. See also Interview 13-EUNO confirming that the freedom of choice issue spilled over into the discussions on convertible securities; Interviews 12-EUNO and 14-EUNO confirming that some Member States feared that convertibles may be used to issue equity securities, without having to seek approval with the home (registered office) authority. At Ecofin level, the Italian Minister for Economy and Finance, Giulio Tremonti, having highlighted the danger of shopping, pressed against 'an extension of the list of securities which are subject to free choice of authority' (Ecofin Meeting, Brussels, 5 November 2002).

78 See Clifford Chance, 'The Prospectus Directive and its likely impact – Part 3: Convertible bonds and exchangeable bonds' (Newsletter February 2004, on file) 1.

79 Art 2(1)(b) and (c).

they also contribute importantly to determining whether a given instrument can benefit from the more flexible choice of competent authority regime. Under the Commission's revised proposal, hybrid instruments, such as convertible securities, were assimilated either to equity or non-equity securities depending on whether the issuer of the *underlying shares* was a third party or not. Thus, if the issuer of the convertible was also the issuer of the underlying shares or was part of the same group – in other words, the security was a convertible *stricto sensu*, as opposed to an exchangeable – the security was classified as an equity instrument for the purposes of the Commission proposal. If this was not the case, the security was not caught under the definition of equity securities and, consequently, classified as a non-equity instrument. Cost frame holders pressed for a broad definition of equity securities which, if adopted, would have captured *all* types of securities convertible in, or giving right to acquire, an underlying security (e.g., exchangeable bonds along convertible bonds *stricto sensu*). On the other hand, a merit frame holder such as the UK sought to curtail the definition of equity securities in order to exclude from its scope securities that were convertible at the option of the investor. If adopted, most types of convertible securities (i.e., convertibles *stricto sensu* besides exchangeables) would, as a result, have been excluded from the definition. In addition, before the Ecofin meeting in November 2002, the UK pressed for a new recital being added to the preamble of the proposed directive. It stated that securities convertible at the option of the investor fell within the definition of non-equity securities,[80] thus implying that all convertible securities (exchangeables *and* convertible bonds *stricto sensu*) are non-equity securities, as long as the conversion can be triggered by the investor.

The November 2002 Ecofin meeting While the idea of a split between equity and non-equity securities for the purposes of determining the home Member State and hence the home authority, did little to lay the dispute between cost and merit frame holders to rest, it nevertheless allowed the UK-led coalition to broaden to mainly Northern Member States (especially, Germany) which opposed a choice of competent authority for equity securities, but were prepared to support a possible choice for issuers of non-equity securities. Despite efforts to find agreement at Coreper

[80] E.g., Council Document dated 29 October 2002 (ref. 13593/02) 8; Council Document dated 31 October 2002 (ref. 13593/1/02 REV1) 5 ('Depositary receipts and convertible notes, e.g. securities convertible at the option of the investor, fall under the definition set out in this Directive of non-equity securities').

level, the controversy was still outstanding at the end of 2002. At the November 2002 Ecofin meeting, out of the many issues which national delegations had been discussing, two continued to hold up political agreement between Member States: (i) the question of the allocation of tasks to entities other than independent administrative bodies and (ii) the determination of the home state/competent authority which continued to be a scource of disagreement between the UK-led coalition and the coalition led by France and Italy. As far as the first issue is concerned, a number of Member States (Ireland, Luxembourg, Sweden and Denmark) continued insisting on allowing entities other than administrative authorities to be delegated powers. The Commission, supported by cost frame holders, especially France, sought to end this practice. But in the Presidency compromise submitted to Ecofin ministers as a basis for discussions, the Danish Presidency suggested that a permanent delegation of tasks to non-administrative bodies should be allowed. As far as the second issue is concerned – the main bone of contention between Member States – the Presidency compromise suggested a threshold of EUR 30,000 for non-equity securities. While improving on the EUR 50,000 figure proposed by the Commission, this figure was still greater than any of the amounts that were common in the Eurobond market and far greater than any of the amounts that the UK-led coalition and the wholesale industry considered acceptable. The UK-led coalition and the coalition led by France and Italy continued opposing each other. The latter continued to remain, by and large, united.[81] The former, as mentioned, broadened over the course of the negotiations to include mainly Northern Member States and, in particular, Germany, which was prepared to support a limited choice for issuers of non-equity securities. The reasons why these Member States decided to give their support to the UK appears to have to do with domestic matters, such as the demands of national market actors and the national banking industries which wished to continue accessing the international debt market under the same arrangements.[82] Crucially, Germany also wished to secure freedom of choice for issuers of derivative instruments (e.g.,

[81] There was one clear positional shift in the case of Greece. The motivations for Greece's shift remain somewhat obscure, but it is probably best explained as a consequence of the lobbying efforts of the wholesale industry.

[82] In relation to the Netherlands, see Interview 12-EUNO noting in relation to non-equity securities that 'banks wanted to have their choice'. In relation to Germany, see Interview 14-EUNO pointing to the demands of German banks as far as non-equity securities are concerned, but noting with respect to equity securities that 'German firms belong in Germany'. According to 05-EUNO, Denmark had no particular concern over a choice of competent authority and, instead, saw it as a 'bargaining chip'. The positions of Sweden, Finland and Austria could not be explored in detail with national officials.

covered warrants), given that Stuttgart had established itself as a major player in this market.[83] Recall that derivative instruments were under the proposal assimilated to either equity or non-equity securities.

At the 2002 Ecofin meeting, Member States continued to disagree over the problem definition of issuer choice.[84] France, for instance, continued framing its position by referring to retail investor protection, while the UK forcefully insisted on a choice of competent authority for issuers. Belgium continued stressing the dangers of 'shopping' for competent authorities.[85] Likewise, Italy referred to the dangers of shopping.[86] With both coalitions holding a blocking minority, deadlock threatened. It was only after first concessions and comprises were tabled that progress was finally made. France, the UK and Germany played the decisive roles.[87] The UK, for instance, was prepared to drop all of its earlier reservations in exchange for substantial progress on issuer choice.[88] Yet, it is only during a break that a EUR 5,000 threshold was finally agreed upon in relation to non-equity securities. There is no clear rationale for the choice of this figure, save for the fact that it neither met the earlier demands of cost frame holders, nor merit frame holders. However, while making a concession on the threshold, the demands of a cost frame holder such as France were, in return, largely met on the question of the delegation to non-administrative authorities, the second 'B' item on the agenda. During the Ecofin meeting France and Belgium insisted that a delegation of authority was acceptable only during a transitional period. Thus, by compromising on the minimum denomination for non-equity securities, these cost frame holders made sure that any delegation of the power to approve a prospectus to non-administrative bodies would only be temporary.[89] This practice, which was common in Northern Member States, is therefore bound to end.

[83] Interview 14-EUNO.

[84] Ecofin Meeting (Brussels, 5 November 2002).

[85] *Ibid.* [86] *Ibid.*

[87] See Interviews 13-EUNO, 02-EUO, 14-EUNO. According to one senior official who attended the Ecofin meeting (13-EUNO), it is only after France, Germany and the UK reached agreement during break time that the Franco-Italian coalition broke up.

[88] Ecofin Meeting (Brussels, 5 November 2002).

[89] This agreement was not reached without difficulties. The prospect of failing to secure a permanent delegation led Ireland to intervene during the Ecofin meeting when agreement already seemed to have been reached. The Irish attempt, which led the Presidency to re-open the debate, failed after the Belgium Minister protested vehemently against re-opening discussions.

As far as derivative and hybrid instruments are concerned, no further changes were made to the text of the Presidency compromise. Thus, convertible bonds, which can be exchanged into shares of the issuer of the convertible or any other entity that is part of the same group as the issuer (e.g., convertibles *stricto sensu* as opposed to exchangeables), are treated as equity instruments. Recital 12 of the preamble, however, essentially continues implying the opposite when saying that '... securities convertible at the option of the investor, fall within the definition of non-equity securities set out in this Directive'. The fact that this recital was added to the preamble of the directive is the final element to highlight in order to square the regulatory bargain. It was described by interviewees as 'an attempt to appease the UK delegation', an 'unfortunate result of the negotiations', a 'concession' in order to make progress on the text of the directive, or a necessary 'ambiguity' to get it through the Council.[90]

Second reading under the co-decision procedure The Council's common position was subsequently forwarded to the European Parliament for a second reading. Following Huhne's report in EMAC in which further amendments were tabled, the Council, the Commission and the European Parliament led by its *rapporteur* met subsequently during informal meetings. It is during these informal meetings – the so-called, trilogues – that actors finally agreed on a EUR 1,000 threshold for non-equity securities. However, it is fair to say that the initial EUR 5,000 threshold represented the breakthrough, as it represented a significant departure from the earlier EUR 50,000 or EUR 30,000 thresholds. Note that whilst the contradiction between Recital 12 and the definition of equity securities in the directive was identified in EMAC's final report,[91] no further changes were made to the recital or, for that matter, to the definition of equity securities

[90] Interviews 06-EUNO, 08-EUNO, 10-EUNO, Christopher Huhne. Similar comments were made by 09-EUNO; 13-EUNO; 14-EUNO. See also Interview 02-EUO noting that 'we discussed the convertible bond issue before the common position in November 2002 during nearly one month. Even you have a kind of contradiction between the article and the recital. Because in the article it is clear that convertible bonds are in the scope of equities, whereas the UK negotiated a recital saying that convertible bonds are debt securities. You see that was really the result of this kind of discussions'.

[91] Committee on Economic and Monetary Affairs, 'Recommendations for second reading' (Final A5–0218/2003, 13 June 2003) 35 noting that '[r]elated to the discussion on issuer choice is the lack of clarity regarding the definition of "equity securities" and "non-equity securities". There is a confusion in the Common Position concerning the categorisation of convertible bonds and warrants, since in Article 2.1(b) of the Common Position, convertible bonds and warrants where the underlying shares are shares of the issuer are defined as "equity securities", whereas Recital 12 refers to convertible bonds

during the second reading. The contradiction between Recital 12 and the text of the directive is thus reflected in the directive, as finally adopted.

V The 2010 revisions of the directive

Sections III and IV examined the problematic underlying the issuer choice policy dispute and how the dispute was finally resolved. This section turns briefly to the revisions of the PD that were announced by the Commission in 2009 and completed, at first reading, in 2010. What has changed since 2003? Is the issuer choice problematic no longer an issue? The short answer is that not much has changed since 2003, notwithstanding the fact that CESR was, by 2009, a firm fixture of the regulatory and supervisory landscape.[92] The 2009 and 2010 negotiations testify to the fact that the arguments, which underpinned the cost and merit frames, continue to be popular at political level. The fear that domestic issuers might turn to other authorities for approval of a prospectus and use the single passport to subsequently 'passport back' has not vanished either.[93]

In 2009, the European Commission came forward with a proposal to amend the PD and the TD.[94] The Commission proposed a number of amendments to the PD, mainly under the motto 'reducing administrative burdens'.[95] It also proposed to revisit Article 2(1)(m) governing the distribution of competences between Member States. Specifically, the Commission took the view that the threshold in Article 2(1)(m)(ii), whose purpose is to determine whether issuers of non-equity securities benefit from a choice of competent authority, should be abolished on the grounds that it caused 'practical problems to issuers'.[96] The Economic and Monetary Affairs Committee in the European Parliament led by its

as "non-equity securities". Convertible bonds and warrants should be classified as non-equity instruments in accordance with Recital 12'.

92 For practical reasons, having to do with the cut-off date for the submission of the book manuscript, it was not possible to conduct a fresh battery of interviews. But a couple of interviews took place at the European Commission and at the European Parliament that gave fairly consistent insight into the negotiations over the revisions of the directive. Among the interviewees was also the *rapporteur* of the directive in the European Parliament (EMAC), Wolf Klinz (ALDE).

93 Interview 01–2010-EUO (referring to the (hypothetical) case of a Spanish issuer seeking approval in Sweden and subsequently 'passporting' its prospectus back to Spain).

94 European Commission, 'Proposal for a directive of the European Parliament and of the Council amending Directives 2003/71/EC … and 2004/109/EC' (COM(2009) 491 final, 23 September 2009).

95 *Ibid.* 96 *Ibid.*, 6.

rapporteur, Wolf Klinz, a German MEP, supported the Commission's amendment.[97] But Member States in Council were divided on the issue. There were essentially three different positions among them: those in favour of abolishing the threshold; those in favour of the *status quo*; and those that insisted on the threshold being raised to EUR 100,000 or even EUR 150,000.[98] The arguments underpinning the different positions were familiar ones: 'regulatory arbitrage'; the view that 'local investors should be supervised by local supervisors'; the feeling that some authorities were more 'specialised' than others;[99] and the feeling that there were still differences in the way in which prospectuses were being approved in Member States.[100] It is an interesting fact that the prospect of establishing ESMA did not have an impact on this assessment. But given that ESMA had at the time of the negotiations not yet been established, the time for ESMA was, according to one official, 'not right yet ... from a political point of view'.[101] Likewise, for the *rapporteur* in EMAC, the argument that ESMA could address regulatory arbitrage, whilst 'unofficially' mentioned, did not gain currency.[102]

In light of the differences within the Council, Member States decided to make no further changes to Article 2(1)(m).[103] During the trilogues, which took place before the Parliament's plenary vote in June 2010, the European Commission, the Council and the Parliament's representatives compromised and agreed not to reopen the issue of the distribution of competences. Instead of making changes to Article 2(1)(m)(ii), a recital was added to the amending directive stating that the Commission should 'undertake a review of Article 2(1)(m)(ii)' and, at the outcome of this review, make a proposal on whether this article should be changed.[104] But the point seems fairly redundant given that the Commission had already

97 Committee on Economic and Monetary Affairs, 'Report on the proposal for a directive of the European Parliament and of the Council amending Directives 2003/71/EC ... and 2004/109/EC' (A7–0102/2010, 26 March 2010) 58.

98 Interview 01–2010-EUO.

99 *Ibid*. See also Interview Wolf Klinz (noting that some Member States stressed the dangers of 'regulatory arbitrage'); Interview Victoria Klein (EP) (confirming that some Member States referred to 'regulatory arbitrage').

100 Interview Wolf Klinz.

101 Interview 01–2010-EUO.

102 Interview Wolf Klinz.

103 See the Council's general approach to the Commission's proposal, Council of the European Union, 'Proposal for a Directive of the European Parliament and of the Council amending Directives 2003/71/EC ... and 2004/109/EC' (ref. 17451/1/09 REV1, 4 February 2010).

104 PAD Rec (8).

concluded that Article 2(1)(m) needed to be amended because it created 'practical problems to issuers'[105] when it came forward with its amending proposal in 2009. Incidentally, Recital (12) of the PD was not amended either. The contradiction between the recital and the text of the directive survived scrutiny.[106]

VI Conclusion

This chapter examined the negotiations of the PD and especially the dispute over issuer choice that marked these negotiations. What can we learn from the case study? First and foremost, the foregoing analysis offers support for the propositions of Chapter 9. That is to say, the empirical evidence examined in this chapter confirms the relevance of the 'threat of exit' explanation. Thus, the threat (or fear) of selective exit can be linked to the position of cost frame holders. Specifically, the outlook of seeing domestic issuers seeking approval with an authority abroad under a choice of competent authority regime and possibly 'passporting back' their prospectus to their home state by using a more aggressive passport system, is a crucial factor in explaining why cost frame holders opposed issuer choice. Meanwhile, the differing impact of this *ex post* outlook on cost and merit frame holders was well accounted for when examining the underlying interest-based motivations of actors. While selective exit risked ending in a loss of decisional powers over domestic issuers for cost frame holders, it raised no particular issues for those Member States which were described earlier as merit frame holders. The latter had a strong vested interest in making sure that the international debt market, on which issuers from all over Europe and beyond listed securities, remained unaffected by changes in EU regulatory arrangements and especially in the rules governing Member State competence. Indeed, for merit frame holders, selective exit only promised to safeguard their decisional powers and the benefits flowing from the operation of the international debt market, given that many issuers using these markets were incorporated under foreign law.

The study of the policy outcome contributed, meanwhile, to illustrating the problem of addressing effectively regulatory problems such as the threat of selective exit under the EU's existing institutional framework. If we are interested in the quality of legislation, the adoption of a

[105] See n. 95.

[106] Admittedly, the issue was not raised for consideration in the Commission proposal or, for that matter, in EMAC's report.

wholly arbitrary EUR 1,000 threshold for non-equity securities or even the contradiction between Recital 12 and the definition of equity securities points to the limitations which the EU decision-making process faces when attempting to respond effectively and creatively to regulatory problems. Admittedly, the alternative solution might well have been deadlock. Seen in this light, an arbitrary threshold might be a price worth paying. In any event, for our purposes, the main message is that, given the findings of this chapter, there are good reasons for starting to pay more attention to the question of how the prospect of selective exit (or regulatory arbitrage, to put it simply) affects decision-making at EU level. It may well be that the type of problematic which this chapter examined is more widespread. Regulatory arbitrage type of issues can take various forms. What they have in common is that they arise in the context of the pursuit of market integration by way of judicial or, indeed, legislative harmonisation.

PART V

Conclusions and suggestions for the future

11

Conclusions

The aim of this book was to examine EU prospectus law and shed fresh light on regulatory competition in the field of EU securities regulation by engaging in a more meaningful manner with EU decision-making. In this spirit, the chapters looked for insight and inspiration to the political science literature and, in this process, departed from law and economics, the conventional lens for interdisciplinary studies in the regulatory competition or the securities regulation literature. The result was a series of chapters with often distinctive positive orientations. This concluding chapter draws the final lessons and ends, in a conciliatory tone with convention, on a normative note.

Two lessons can be learned from previous chapters. The first lesson concerns the need to come to grips with the nuts and bolts of EU decision-making in the securities regulation field. Securities regulation is now the product of a multi-level system of governance. EU institutions are the main force shaping the regulatory framework governing regulated markets, while collective securities actors, such as ESMA, testify to a 'European way' of dealing with regulation and supervision within a constitutional and political setting that is preventing the establishment of an autonomous, single European securities markets authority.[1] Endless discussions about whether Europe would be better off with an independent EU securities regulator which would have its place along other EU institutions, have in my opinion little added value,[2] at least as long as they ignore the reality of EU decision-making and Treaty change. The more useful question is how best to arrange supervision between the EU and Member State levels within the constitutional limits set by the Treaties and the Court's case law on the delegation of powers.

[1] I.e., in the sense of a new EU institution.

[2] Moloney has made a similar point, noting that '[m]uch of the central securities-supervisor discussion is cast in terms of comparison with the SEC. Perhaps after the seismic regulatory, supervisory and institutional reforms of the FSAP period it is time to move on'. See Moloney, *EC Securities Regulation* 1166–7.

As far as regulatory competition is concerned, the thesis of this book was that it remains a topic of interest. To be sure, given the direction of institutional change, the opportunities for regulatory arbitrage[3] are nowadays restricted and issue specific. But the purpose of the book was to look at regulatory competition differently; that is, by focusing on decision-making at EU level in an effort to understand how regulatory competition, the threat of regulatory arbitrage and its discourse, affect harmonisation in the field of European prospectus disclosure. Thinking merely of harmonisation as an outcome, instead of treating it as a process involving actors with their own interests and ideas who are meant to find common agreement over sets of rules and arrangements, means ignoring this part of the European story of regulatory competition. Additional case studies would be useful to establish whether this type of empirical enquiry has something to offer in other fields. Studies which assess how ESMA addresses the real or perceived threat of selective exit would be especially interesting, given that ESMA is meant to contribute to preventing regulatory arbitrage.[4] As others before me, I therefore advocate a positive agenda.[5] Studies that claim that regulatory competition is a superior institutional arrangement and therefore ought to be preferred to harmonisation, should at least make their assumptions about the political feasibility of such proposals explicit.

The second lesson concerns ESMA. My argument with respect to ESMA began with the observation that like CESR, ESMA is a collective securities actor.[6] It has no preferences of its own, by which I mean that, in the final analysis, its preferences are those of national securities authorities, acting collectively, and who are the ultimate bearers of decision-making powers. As a matter of political and constitutional reality, this relationship with national actors is vital to appreciate when attempting to evaluate whether ESMA will successfully confront old challenges. These challenges have to do with issues that were discussed or touched upon in various chapters: a lack of trust between national securities authorities, the fact that there is competition between financial centres and the

[3] Note that I use the term 'regulation' in its widest sense; not just as rule-making, but as market regulation in general, including enforcement.

[4] ESMAReg, Art 1(5)(d).

[5] E.g., C. Radaelli 'The puzzle of regulatory competition' (2004) 24 *Journal of Public Policy* 1; Tjiong, 'Breaking the spell of regulatory competition' 95; Sun and Pelkmans 'Regulatory competition in the single market'.

[6] I drew on Scharpf's concept of collective actors. See F. Scharpf, *Games Real Actors Play* 54–6.

fact that securities authorities are national actors that are individually accountable at national level.[7]

But ESMA has also a lot to offer, especially if it comes to be seen at Lamfalussy Level 1 or Level 2 as a sort of trustee, in the sense imagined by Majone.[8] Thus, ESMA's future actions are worth watching closely for the reason that they might contribute importantly to improving trust among actors at Level 1 or Level 2. But, as noted in Chapters 1 and 6, the question of whether ESMA's actions will prove to be effective will depend importantly on two broad factors: (i) the behaviour of ESMA's members; and (ii) the Court's view on whether the delegation of powers to ESMA is permissible. As far as the first aspect is concerned, it is fair to say that ESMA has on paper the necessary powers to address adverse behaviour by individual competent authorities. The second aspect remains uncertain, not least because we are still, at this juncture, somewhat in the dark about the precise arrangements which will structure the delegation of powers.

Because ESMA is still in its infancy, so to speak, it also seems premature to make detailed proposals on how to improve ESMA. That said, given that ESMA is a collective securities actor and, therefore, not fundamentally different from CESR, it does not seem entirely premature to put forward for discussion a few suggestions on how ESMA might be strengthened in the future, drawing on the experience with CESR.[9] The proposals are two-fold. They concern ESMA's internal organisation and its internal environment.

The first proposal concerns the distribution of competence between ESMA's Board of Supervisors, the Management Board and the Executive Director. The essential idea is to strengthen ESMA's core in order to create a counterweight to the national influences which predominate within ESMA. Thus, one could imagine having a stronger Office of Executive Director as a counterweight to the Board of Supervisors, which is the main decision-making body and the main voice of ESMA's members. In this process, the role and need for a Management Board could also be reassessed. Recall that the Management Board 'sits', as it were, in between the Board of Supervisors and the Executive Director. It is composed of

[7] See Chapters 1, 4, 9 and 10.

[8] Majone, *Dilemmas of European Integration* 64–82. Chapter 9 discussed Majone's argument in more detail. See also de Visscher, Maiscocq and Varone, 'The Lamfalussy reform in the EU securities markets', who first applied Majone's ideas on fiduciary delegation to the Lamfalussy process.

[9] For details on CESR, see, in particular, Chapter 1.

ESMA's Chairperson who chairs the board's meetings,[10] and six members chosen by, and from among, the voting members of the Board of Supervisors for two and a half years.[11] The Commission and ESMA's Executive Director can also attend the meetings, but they have no voting rights, except that the Commission can vote on budgetary matters.[12] *Inter alia*, the Management Board proposes ESMA's annual and multi-annual work programmes, as well as its annual report, to the Board of Supervisors.[13] Although its members are meant to act in the EU's interests, it is apparent that the Management Board brings together voices that are already represented in ESMA's Board of Supervisors. Indeed, the members that are elected to the Management Board by the Board of Supervisors vote both in the Board of Supervisors and in the Management Board. Overall, it is therefore fair to say that 'national' influences permeate decision-making in ESMA.

ESMA's Executive Director ('ED') is, on the other hand, one of only two institutionalised positions that must, under ESMA's founding regulation, be held by a 'full-time independent professional'.[14] Currently the role of the ED is primarily that of an administrator and executor. In the future, thought could be given as to whether the ED's role should be strengthened in order to create a counterweight to national influences. As a starting point, one could consider putting the ED not only in charge of preparing ESMA's annual and multi-annual work programmes,[15] but also entrusting him with the task of proposing them to the Board of Supervisors after consulting relevant actors, including the Commission. As mentioned above, the task of proposing the work programmes to the Board of Supervisors is currently a matter for the Management Board. The intervention of national influences at this level is, arguably, not necessary given that the Board of Supervisors has, in any event, the final say on the matter. At the same time, as part of ESMA's commitment to transparency and in order to make sure that the ED fulfils his tasks, statutory obligations could be imposed on the ED to explain and justify ESMA's actions, and importantly, its inactions or delays in light of its work programmes.[16] One could also imagine giving the ED a greater say over ESMA's annual report. Under the current arrangements, the Board of Supervisors adopts the annual report on a proposal from the

[10] ESMAReg, Art 45(3). [11] Art 45(1).

[12] Art 45(2). The Commission representative can vote on budgetary matters under Art 63.

[13] Art 47(2); Art 47(6). [14] Art 51(1). [15] Art 53(4) and (5).

[16] For the time being, the Board of Supervisors is mainly in charge of assessing the Executive Director (Art 51(4)).

Management Board.[17] The role of the Executive Director is to prepare a 'draft report' which the Management Board will use as a basis to propose the report to the Board of Supervisors.[18] As an alternative arrangement, one could imagine that the ED proposes the annual report directly to the Board of Supervisors. The underlying reasoning is again that there is no need for the intervention of national influences at the level of the Management Board given that the Board of Supervisors has the final say. Of course, much will, in the final analysis, depend on the personality, attitude and resolve of the ED. Leadership is as much a question of powers vested in a position, as it is a question of personality and resolve. In the present case, personality is all the more important because, even under the above proposals, the ED would have few real, independent, powers. Thus, whoever assumed the role would need to show resolve and a willingness to take a leading role, whilst leaving representative tasks to the Chairperson.

My second proposal for the future concerns the organisational environment of ESMA.[19] Recall that the former Level 3 Committees were small bodies. Besides a number of permanent employees, CESR relied on the staff of its members. In order to strengthen staff allegiances, ESMA should be able to rely extensively on its own staff. Granted, the point seems needless to make. ESMA will inevitably have a larger number of staff given that it will have more extensive tasks. But even at the risk of making redundant proposals, the point is worth noting. Unlike remote or seconded staff, ESMA's own staff can be expected to view their individual self-interest, (in terms of career building, for example), as being closely intertwined with the fate of ESMA. The fact that ESMA will, and should, have its own staff does not mean that ESMA will not need to continue relying on staff delegated from national authorities. But as in other agencies, their number should be limited.[20] For seconded staff, it might, meanwhile, be worth

[17] Art 43(5). [18] *Ibid.* and Art 53(7).

[19] Organisational context has been of particular interest to scholars interested in organisational approaches which see such context as having a deeper impact on actors. See e.g., M. Egeberg, 'An organisational approach to European integration: Outline of a complementary perspective' (2004) 43 *European Journal of Political Research* 199.

[20] See e.g., Regulation (EC) No 216/2008 of the European Parliament and of the Council of 20 February 2008 on common rules in the field of civil aviation and establishing a European Aviation Safety Agency, and repealing Council Directive 91/670/EEC, Regulation (EC) No 1592/2002 and Directive 2004/36/EC [2008] OJ L79/1, Art 29(3) which states that '[t]he Agency's staff shall consist of a strictly limited number of officials assigned or seconded by the Commission or Member States to carry out management duties. The remaining staff shall consist of other employees recruited by the Agency as necessary to carry out its tasks'.

requiring longer periods of secondments. It appears at least conceivable that secondments might, over time, somewhat improve allegiance.[21]

By way of conclusion, it might be worth repeating that, at the time of writing, the internal organisation of ESMA is, save for the statutory division of competences, still very much unknown. The suggestions that I made on ESMA's internal organisation and its internal environment are, therefore, first thoughts only, inspired by the experience with CESR. In any event, ESMA will need to be given time to prove itself. As we were able to learn from CESR's experience, in time, we will also learn from ESMA's experience and be able to make more concrete suggestions on how to improve its functioning; if need be.

[21] M. Egeberg, 'Transcending intergovernmentalism? Identity and role perceptions of national officials in EU decision-making' (1999) 6 *Journal of European Public Policy* 456, 470 noting '[b]eing embedded in EU level structures and separated in time and space from their primary institutional affiliations back home, officials tend to develop a sense of allegiance to the supranational level'. But as the author argues loyalty shifts are likely to be 'marginal' (*ibid.*).

SELECT BIBLIOGRAPHY

Alter K., 'Delegation to international courts and the limits of re-contracting political power' in Hawkins D., Lake D., Nielson D. and Tierney M. (eds.), *Delegation and Agency in International Organizations* (Cambridge University Press, 2006) 312

AMF, 'Cartographie 2009 des risques et des tendances sur les marchés financiers et pour l'épargne' (Risques et tendances n° 8, Juine 2009), www.amf-france.org/documents/general/8979_1.pdf

'Décision de l'AMF en matière de reconnaissance des standards américains pour une admission à la négociation sur un marché réglementé' (Communiqué de presse, 1 October 2007), www.amf-france.org/documents/general/7940_1.pdf

'Financial Regulation Newsletter' (Issue No. 8, 4th Quarter 2007), www.amf-france.org/documents/general/7992_1.pdf

'L'Autorité des marchés financiers précise la déclination opérationnelle de son plan stratégique' (Communiqué de presse, Paris, 16 December 2009), www.amf-france.org/documents/general/9251_1.pdf

'Meilleure Régulation: un premier bilan et programme de travail 2008–2009' (25 Apavril 2008), www.amf-france.org/documents/general/8288_1.pdf

Memorandum of Understanding between the Autorité des marchés financiers and the Israel Securities Authority concerning the regulatory equivalence with regards to the cross-listing of securities' (28 January 2008), www.amf-france.org/documents/general/8145_1.pdf.

'Plan stratégique de l'Autorité des marchés financiers' (29 June 2009), www.amf-france.org/documents/general/8983_1.pdf

'Transposition de la directive "prospectus" dans le règlement général de l'AMF: consultation publique jusqu'au 10 juin 2005' (Consultation Document, undated), www.amf-france.org/documents/general/6074_1.pdf

Ammann M. and Seiz R., 'Pricing and hedging mandatory convertible bonds' (2006) 13 *Journal of Derivatives* 30

Ananiadou S. and McNaught J. (eds.), *Text Mining for Biology and Biomedicine* (Artech House, Boston MA, 2006)

Armour J., Deakin S., Lele P. and Siems M., 'How do legal rules evolve? Evidence from a cross-country comparison of shareholder, creditor, and worker protection' (2009) 57 *American Journal of Comparative Law* 579

Armour J., Deakin S., Sarkar P., Siems M. and Singh A., 'Shareholder protection and stock market development: an empirical test of the legal origins hypothesis' (2009) 6 *Journal of Empirical Studies* 343

Arnull A., Dashwood A., Dougan M., Ross M, Spaventa E. and Wyatt D., *European Union Law* (Sweet & Maxwell, London, 2006)

Arons T., '"All roads lead to Rome": Beware of the consequences! The law applicable to prospectus liability claims under the Rome II Regulation' (2008) 4 *Nederlands Internationaal Privaatrecht* 481

Avgouleas E., 'The global financial crisis and the disclosure paradigm in European financial regulation: the case for reform' (2009) 6 *European Company and Financial Law Review* 440

'The global financial crisis, behavioural finance and financial regulation: in search of a new orthodoxy' (2009) 9 *Journal of Corporate Law Studies* 23

Bainbridge S., 'Mandatory disclosure: a behavioral analysis' (2000) 68 *University of Cincinnati Law Review* 1023

Bancel F. and Mittoo U., 'Why do European firms issue convertible debt' (2004) 10 *European Financial Management* 339

Bar-Gill O., 'The law, economics and psychology of subprime mortgage contracts' (2009) 94 *Cornell Law Review* 1073

Barnard C. and Deakin S., 'Market access and regulatory competition' in Barnard C. and Scott J., *The Law of the Single European Market – Unpacking the Premises* (Hart Publishing, Oxford, 2002) 197

Beales III J., 'Licensing and certification systems' in P. Newman (ed.), *The New Palgrave Dictionary of Economics and the Law*, vol. 2 (Palgrave Macmillan, New York, 2002)

Bebchuk L., 'Federalism and the corporation: the desirable limits on state competition in corporate law' (1992) 105 *Harvard Law Review* 1435

Bebchuk L. and Cohen A., 'Firms' decision where to incorporate' (2003) 46 *Journal of Law and Economics* 383

Bebchuk L., Cohen A. and Ferrell A., 'Does the evidence favor state competition in corporate law?' (2002) 90 *California Law Review* 1775

Becht M., Mayer C. and Wagner H., 'Where do firms incorporate? Deregulation and the cost of entry' (2008) 14 *Journal of Corporate Finance* 241

Benedetto G., 'Rapporteurs as legislative entrepreneurs: the dynamics of the codecision procedure in Europe's Parliament' (2005) 12 *Journal of European Public Policy* 67

Benston G., 'Required disclosure and the stock market: an evaluation of the Securities Exchange Act of 1934' (1973) 63 *American Economic Review* 132

'The value of the SEC's accounting disclosure requirements' (1969) 44 *Accounting Review* 515

Bermann G., 'Proportionality and subsidiarity' in Barnard C. and Scott J. (eds.), *The Law of the Single Market – Unpacking the Premises* (Hart Publishing, Oxford, 2002) 75

Bewley T., 'A critique of Tiebout's theory of local public expenditures' (1981) 49 *Econometrica* 713

Bhagwat A., 'Modes of regulatory enforcement and the problem of administrative discretion' (1999) 50 *Hastings Law Journal* 1275

Bonneau T. and Drummond F., *Droit des marchés financiers* (Economica, Paris, 2010)

Börzel T. and Risse T., 'When Europe hits home: Europeanization and domestic change' (2000) 4 *European Integration Online Papers* 1

Bouretz E. and Emery J-L., *Autorité des marchés financiers et Commission bancaire – Pouvoirs de Sanction et Recours* (Revue Banque, Paris, 2008)

Bratton W. and McCahery J., 'The case of corporate law in the United States of America' in Bratton W., McCahery J., Picciotto S. and Scott C. (eds.), *International Regulatory Competition and Coordination: Perspectives on Economic Regulation in Europe and the United States* (Clarendon Press, Oxford, 1996)

'The new economics of jurisdictional competition: devolutionary federalism in a second-best world' (1997) 86 *Georgetown Law Journal* 201

Bratton W., McCahery J., Picciotto S . and Scott C. (eds.), *International Regulatory Competition and Coordination: Perspectives on Economic Regulation in Europe and the United States* (Clarendon Press, Oxford, 1996)

Braun D. and Busch A. (eds.), *Public Policy and Political Ideas* (Edward Elgar, Cheltenham, 1999)

Burn L. and Wells B., 'The pan-European retail market – are we there yet' (2007) 2 *Capital Markets Law Journal* 263

Campbell J., 'Institutional analysis and the role of ideas in political economy' (1998) 27 *Theory and Society* 377

Institutional Change and Globalization (Princeton University Press, Princeton, 2004)

Caporaso J., 'The three worlds of regional integration theory' in Graziano P. and Vink M., *Europeanization – New Research Agendas* (Palgrave Macmillan, Basingstoke, 2008) 23

Casey J. and Lannoo K., *Europe's Hidden Capital Markets – Evolution, Architecture and Regulation of the European Bond Market* (CEPS, Brussels, 2005)

CESR, '6th extract from EECS's database of enforcement decisions' (CESR/09-720 August 2009)

'A proposed evolution of EU securities supervision beyond 2007' (CESR/07-783, November 2007)

'An evaluation of equivalence of supervisory powers in the EU under the Market Abuse Directive and the Prospectus Directive. A report to the Financial Services Committee (FSC)' (CESR/07-334, June 2007)

'Assessment on the equivalence of prospectuses from non-EEA jurisdictions (Article 20.1 Prospectus Directive)' (CESR/08-972 December 2008)

'CESR data on prospectuses approved and passported – July 2009 to December 2009' (CESR/10-282, March 2010)

'CESR mediation mechanism – feedback statement and protocol' (CESR/06-287b, August 2006)

'CESR work to date in relation to the European Commission's measures on the use of third countries' GAAP in the EU' (CESR/07-022b, April 2007)

'CESR's advice on Level 2 implementing measures for the Prospectus Directive' (CESR/03-300, September 2003)

'CESR's advice on Level 2 implementing measures for the Prospectus Directive' (CESR/03-399, December 2003)

'CESR's advice to the European Commission on the work programmes of the Canadian, Japanese and US standard setters, the definition of equivalence and the list of third country GAAPs currently used on the EU capital markets' (CESR/07-138, March 2007)

'CESR's comments on the European Commission's background and consultation document on the review of Directive 2003/71/EC' (CESR/09-240, March 2009)

'CESR's contribution to the discussions on the *de Larosière* report' (CESR/08-289b), published in '3L3 Joint Contribution to the European Commission's consultation on the improvement of supervision for the financial services sector' (CESR/09-356, April 2009)

'CESR's report on the supervisory functioning of the Prospectus Directive and Regulation' (CESR/07-225, June 2007)

'CESR's technical advice on a mechanism for determining the equivalence of the generally accepted accounting principles of third countries' (CESR/07-289, May 2007)

'Charter of the Committee of European Securities Regulators' (CESR/08-375d, September 2008)

'Concept paper on equivalence of certain third country GAAP and on description of certain third countries mechanisms of enforcement of financial information – Feedback statement' (CESR/05-001, January 2005)

'Concept paper on equivalence of certain third country GAAP and on description of certain third countries mechanisms of enforcement of financial information' (CESR/04-509C, February 2005)

'Final report on CESR's peer review of the implementation of Standard No. 2 on financial information – coordination of enforcement activities' (CESR/09-188, July 2009)

'Final report of the review panel concerning the updated self-assessment and peer review of CESR's Standard No. 1 on financial information' (CESR/09-374, September 2009)

'Frequently asked questions regarding prospectuses: common positions agreed by CESR members' (CESR/10-830, 9 July 2010)

'Interim report on the activities of the Committee of European Securities Regulators to the European Commission [...]' (CESR/03-147b, July 2003)

'Multilateral Memorandum of Understanding on the Exchange of Information and Surveillance of Securities Activities' (CESR/05-335, January 1999)

'Preliminary progress report – which supervisory tools for the EU securities markets? An analytical paper by CESR' (CESR/04-333f, October 2004)

'Protocol on mediation mechanism of the Committee of European Securities Regulators' (CESR/06-286b, August 2006)

'Re: The EU Mandate' (CESR/08-210, March 2008)

'Report on CESR Members' powers under the Prospectus Directive and its implementing measures' (CESR/07-383, June 2007)

'Standard No. 1 on financial information – enforcement of standards on financial information in Europe' (CESR/03-073, March 2003)

'Standard No. 2 on financial information – coordination of enforcement activities' (CESR/03-317c, April 2004)

'Summary of the answers to the questionnaire on factual information on the legislation and practices of Member States regarding the treatment of third country issuers with respect to the drawing up and approval of prospectuses (Article 20 of the Prospectus Directive)' (CESR/03-496, December 2003)

'Summary of the answers to the questionnaire on factual information regarding advertisement practices and relevant legislation in the Member States' (CESR/03-494, December 2003)

'Technical advice on equivalence of certain third country GAAP and on description of certain third countries mechanisms of enforcement of financial information' (CESR/05-230b, June 2005)

Choi S. and Guzman A., 'Portable reciprocity: rethinking the international reach of securities regulation' (1998) 71 *Southern California Law Review* 903

Choi S. and Pritchard A., 'Behavioral economics and the SEC' (2003) 56 *Stanford Law Review* 1

Christiansen T., 'The Council of Ministers: facilitating interaction and developing actorness in the EU' in Richardson J. (ed.), *European Union – Power and Policy-Making* (Routledge, Abingdon, 2006) 147

Clerc C., 'La réparation du préjudice subi par un actionnaire du fait de la diffusion de fausses informations' RTDF N° 1 – 2007 p. 31

Coates J. C., 'Private vs. political choice of securities regulation: a political cost/benefit analysis' (2001) 41 *Virginia Journal of International Law* 531

COB, 'Bulletin mensuel d'information de la Commission des opérations de bourse' (n° 352, December 2000) 43, www.amf-france.org/affiche.asp?id=5726

'Bulletin mensuel d'information de la Commission des opérations de bourse' (n° 362, November 2001), www.amf-france.org/affiche.asp?id=5715

'Bulletin mensuel d'information de la Commission des opérations de bourse' (no. 367, April 2002), www.amf-france.org/affiche.asp?id=5709

Coen D. and Thatcher M., 'Network governance and multi-level delegation: European networks of regulatory agencies' (2008) 28 *Journal of Public Policy* 49

Coffee J., *Gatekeepers – The Professions and Corporate Governance* (Oxford University Press, Oxford, 2006)

'Gatekeeper failure and reform: the challenge of fashioning relevant reforms' (2004) 84 *Boston University Law Review* 301

'Law and regulatory competition: can they co-exist?' (2002) 80 *Texas Law Review* 1729

'Law and the market: the impact of enforcement' (2007) 156 *University of Pennsylvania Law Review* 229

'Market failure and the economic case for a mandatory disclosure system' (1984) 70 *Virginia Law Review* 717

'Reforming the securities class action: an essay on deterrence and its implementation' (2006) 106 *Columbia Law Review* 1534

'The future as history: the prospects for global convergence in corporate governance and its implications' (1999) 93 *Northwestern University Law Review* 641

'What went wrong? An initial inquiry into the causes of the 2008 financial crisis' (2009) 9 *Journal of Corporate Law Studies* 1

Coffee J. and Sale H., 'Redesigning the SEC: does the Treasury have a better idea?' (2009) 95 *Virginia Law Review* 707

Cole M., 'The UK FSA: nobody does it better?' (Fordham Law School, New York, 17 October 2006) reprinted in (2007) 2 *Fordham Journal of Corporate and Financial Law* 266

Conac P-H., 'La fusion de la Cob et du CMF' in de Vauplane H. and Daigre J-J. (eds.), *Droit Bancaire et Financier – Mélanges AEDBF-France III* (Revue Banque Editeur, 2002, Paris, 2002) 59

La Régulation des Marchés Financiers par la Commission des Opérations de Bourse (COB) et la Securities and Exchange Commission (SEC) (L.G.D.J., Paris, 2002)

Conrad J. and Schilder F., 'Opinion mining in legal blogs' in *Proceedings of the 11th International Conference on Artificial Intelligence and Law* (ACM Press, New York, 2007) 231

Conrad J., Leidner J., Schilder F. and Kondadadi R., 'Query-based opinion summarization for legal blog entries' in *Proceedings of the 12th International Conference on Artificial Intelligence and Law* (ACM Press, New York, 2009) 167

Council of the European Union (Ecofin), 'Council conclusions on strengthening EU financial supervision' (Luxembourg, 9 June 2009), para. 7, www.consilium.europa.eu/uedocs/cms_Data/docs/pressdata/en/ecofin/108389.pdf

Couret A., Le Nabasque H., Coquelet M-L., Granier T., Poracchia D., Raynouard A., Reygrobellet A. and Robine D., *Droit financier* (Dalloz, Paris, 2008)

CRA International, 'Evaluation of the economic impacts of the Financial Services Action Plan' (Report commissioned by the European Commission, March 2009), http://ec.europa.eu/internal_market/finances/docs/actionplan/index/090707_economic_impact_en.pdf

CSES, 'Study on the impact of the prospectus regime on EU financial markets' (Final Report, July 2008) 53, http://ec.europa.eu/internal_market/securities/docs/prospectus/cses_report_en.pdf

Dashwood A, 'The attribution of external relations competence' in Dashwood A. and Hillion C. (eds.), *The General Law of E.C. External Relations* (Sweet & Maxwell, London, 2000) 115

De Bondt W. and Thaler R., 'Do security analysts overreact?' (1990) 80 *American Economic Review* 52

'Does the stock market overreact?' (1984) 40 *Journal of Finance* 793

De Vauplane H., 'L'Autorité des marchés financiers' in H. de Vauplane and J-J. Daigre (eds.), *La Loi sur la Sécurité Financière* (Revue Banque édition, Paris, 2004) 15

De Vauplane H. and Bornet J., *Droit des Marchés Financiers* (Litec, Paris, 2001)

De Visscher C., Maiscocq O. and Varone F., 'The Lamfalussy reform in the EU securities markets: fiduciary relationships, policy effectiveness and balance of power' (2008) 28 *Journal of Public Policy* 19

Deakin S., 'Legal diversity and regulatory competition: which model for Europe?' (2006) 12 *European Law Journal* 440

'Two types of regulatory competition: competitive federalism versus reflexive harmonisation' (1999) 2 *Cambridge Yearbook of European Legal Studies* 231

Deakin S., Lele P. and Siems M., 'The evolution of labour law: calibrating and comparing regulatory regimes' (2007) 146 *International Labour Review* 133

Djankov S., La Porta R., Lopez-de-Silanes F. and Shleifer A., 'The regulation of entry' (2002) 1 *The Quarterly Journal of Economics* 1

Easterbrook F. and Fischel D., 'Mandatory disclosure and the protection of investors' (1984) 70 *Virginia Law Review* 669

Eberlein B. and Newman A., 'Escaping the international governance dilemma? Incorporated transgovernmental networks in the European Union' (2008) 21 *Governance* 25

Eeckhout P., *External Relations of the European Union – Legal and Constitutional Foundations* (Oxford University Press, 2005)

Egeberg E., 'An organisational approach to European integration: Outline of a complementary perspective' (2004) 43 *European Journal of Political Research* 199

'Transcending intergovernmentalism? Identity and role perceptions of national officials in EU decision-making' (1999) 6 *Journal of European Public Policy* 456

Eising R., 'Policy learning in embedded negotiations: explaining EU electricity liberalization' (2002) 56 *International Organization* 85

Eldredge N. and Gould S., 'Punctuated equilibria: an alternative to phyletic gradualism' in Schopf T. (ed.) *Models in Paleobiology* (Freeman, Cooper & Co., San Francisco, 1972) 82

Enriques L. and Tröger T., 'Issuer choice in Europe' (2008) 67 *Cambridge Law Journal* 521

ESC, 'Draft Summary Record of the 57th Meeting of the European Securities Committee (Members)' (3 December 2007), http://ec.europa.eu/internal_market/securities/esc/index_en.htm

'Draft Summary Record of the 59th Meeting of the European Securities Committee (Alternates)' (21 May 2008), http://ec.europa.eu/internal_market/securities/esc/index_en.htm

'Summary Record of the 62nd Meeting of the European Securities Committee (Members)' (14 November 2008), http://ec.europa.eu/internal_market/securities/esc/index_en.htm

ESME, 'Differences between the definitions of "Qualified investor" in the Prospectus Directive and "Professional Client" and "Eligible Counterparty" in MiFID – is alignment needed?' (November 2008), http://ec.europa.eu/internal_market/securities/docs/esme/report-qualified-investor_en.pdf

'Report on Directive 2003/71/EC of the European Parliament and of the Council on the prospectus to be published when securities are offered to the public or admitted to trading' (Brussels, September 2007)

Esty D. and Gerardin D. (eds.), *Regulatory Competition and Economic Integration – Comparative Perspectives* (Oxford University Press, 2001)

European Commission, '3rd informal meeting on prospectus transposition' (Summary Record, 26 January 2005), http://ec.europa.eu/internal_market/securities/docs/prospectus/summary-note-050126_en.pdf

'4th informal meeting on prospectus transposition' (Summary Record, 8 March 2005), http://ec.europa.eu/internal_market/securities/docs/prospectus/summary-note-050308_en.pdf

'Background Document – Review of Directive 2003/71/EC' (undated), http://ec.europa.eu/internal_market/consultations/docs/2009/prospectus/background_en.pdf

'Call for evidence regarding private placement regimes in the EU' (Brussels, April 2007), http://ec.europa.eu/internal_market/investment/docs/consultations/private_placement_en.pdf

'Communication from the Commission to the European Parliament' (SEC(2003) 396 final, 26 March 2003)

Communication from the Commission to the European Parliament and the Council 'Implementation of Article 290 of the Treaty on the Functioning of the European Union' (COM(2009) 673 final, 9 December 2009)

'Communication from the Commission – the operating framework for the European regulatory agencies' (COM(2002) 718 final, 11 December 2002)

'Financial services: building a framework for action – communication of the Commission' (undated), http://ec.europa.eu/internal_market/finances/docs/actionplan/index/fs_en.pdf

'Proposal for a directive of the European Parliament and of the Council amending Directives 2003/71/EC … and 2004/109/EC …' (COM(2009) 491 final, 23 September 2009)

'Proposal for a directive of the European Parliament and of the Council on the prospectus to be published when securities are offered to the public or admitted to trading' (COM (2001) 280 final, 30 May 2001)

'Proposal for a regulation of the European Parliament and of the Council laying down the rules and general principles concerning mechanisms for control by Member States of the Commission's exercise of implementing powers' (COM(2010) 83 final, 9 March 2010).

'Public consultation paper on amendments to Commission decisions establishing CESR, CEBS & CEIOPS' (23 May 2008), http://ec.europa.eu/internal_market/finances/docs/committees/consultation_en.pdf

European Commission Staff Working Document, 'Impact assessment on the directive on the cross-border transfer of registered office' (Part I, SEC (2007) 1707), http://ec.europa.eu/internal_market/company/docs/shareholders/ia_transfer_122007_part1_en.pdf

Fama E., 'Efficient capital markets: a review of theory and empirical work' (1970) 25 *Journal of Finance* 383

Featherstone K. and Radaelli C. (eds.), *The Politics of Europeanization* (Oxford University Press, 2003)

Feldman R. and Sanger J., *The Text Mining Handbook – Advanced Approaches in Analyzing Unstructured Data* (Cambridge University Press, 2006)

Ferran E., *Building an EU Securities Market* (Cambridge University Press, 2004)

'Cross-border offers of securities in the EU: the standard life flotation' (2007) 4 *European Company and Financial Law Review* 461

'Principles-based, risk-based regulation and effective enforcement' in Tison M., de Wulf H., Van der Elst C. and Steennot R. (eds.), *Perspectives in Company Law and Financial Regulation* (Cambridge University Press, 2009) 427

Ferrarini G., 'Securities regulation and the rise of pan-European securities markets: an overview' in Ferrarini G., Hopt K., Wymeersch E. (eds.), *Capital Markets in the Age of the Euro – Cross-Border Transactions, Listed Companies and Regulation* (Kluwer Law International, The Hague, 2002) 241

Ferrarini G. and Guidici P., 'Financial scandals and the role of private enforcement: the *Parmalat* case' in J. Armour and J. McCahery (eds.), *After Enron: Improving Corporate Law and Modernising Securities Regulation in Europe and the US* (Hart Publishing, Oxford, 2006)

FESCO, 'A "European Passport" for issuers' (FESCO/00138b, 20 December 2000), www.cesr.eu

Fox M., 'Civil liability and mandatory disclosure' (2009) 109 *Columbia Law Review* 237

'Required disclosure and corporate governance' (1999) 62 *Law and Contemporary Problems* 113

'Retaining mandatory securities disclosure: why issuer choice is not investor empowerment' (1999) 85 *Virginia Law Review* 1335

'The issuer choice debate' (2001) 2 *Theoretical Inquiries in Law* 563

'The securities globalization disclosure debate' (2000) 78 *Washington University Law Quarterly* 567

Freshfields Bruckhaus Deringer, 'The Prospectus Directive and its implementation in the UK' (October 2004), www.freshfields.com/publications/pdfs/practices/9790.pdf

FSA, 'A regulatory response to the global banking crisis' (DP09/2, March 2009), www.fsa.gov.uk/pubs/discussion/dp09_02.pdf

'A regulatory response to the global banking crisis – feedback on the Turner review and DP09/2' (Feedback Statement 09/3 September 2009), www.fsa.gov.uk/pubs/discussion/fs09_03.pdf

'A review of the structure of the listing regime' (DP 08/1, January 2008), www.fsa.gov.uk/pubs/discussion/dp08_01.pdf.

'Enforcement financial penalties' (Consultation Paper, 09/19*** July 2009), www.fsa.gov.uk/pubs/cp/cp09_19.pdf;

'Enforcement financial penalties – feedback on CP09/19' (PS 10/4, March 2010), www.fsa.gov.uk/pubs/policy/ps10_04.pdf

'Implementation of the Prospectus Directive' (Policy Statement 05/7, June 2005), www.fsa.gov.uk/pubs/policy/ps05_07.pdf

'Listing regime – FAQs' (Issue 2, June 2010), www.fsa.gov.uk/pages/Doing/UKLA/pdf/listing_regime_faqs.pdf

'Listing regime review – policy statement for CP08/21 and further minor consultation' (CP09/24**, October 2009), www.fsa.gov.uk/pubs/cp/cp09_24.pdf.

'Review of the listing regime' (CP 203, October 2003), www.fsa.gov.uk/pubs/cp/cp203.pdf

'The listing review and implementation of the Prospectus Directive – draft rules and feedback on CP203' (CP 04/16***, October 2004), www.fsa.gov.uk/pubs/cp/cp04_16.pdf

'The Turner review – a regulatory response to the global banking crisis' (March 2009), www.fsa.gov.uk/pubs/other/turner_review.pdf

Fudenberg D., 'Advancing beyond advances in behavioral economics' (2006) 44 *Journal of Economic Literature* 694

Genschel P., 'The dynamics of inertia: institutional persistence and change in telecommunications and health care' (1997) *Governance* 43

'Why no mutual recognition of VAT? Regulation, taxation and the integration of the EU's internal market for goods' (2007) 14 *Journal of European Public Policy* 743

Genschel P. and Plumber T., 'Regulatory competition and international co-operation' (1997) 4 *Journal of European Public Policy* 626

Gewinner D. and Uzan C., 'La transposition de la directive "prospectus" en droit français' (July–August, 2005) *Bulletin Joly Bourse* 375

Gilovich T., Griffin D. and Kahneman D., (eds.), *Heuristics and Biases – The Psychology of Intuitive Judgment* (Cambridge University Press, 2002)

Gilson R. and Kraakman R., 'The mechanisms of market efficiency' (1984) 70 *Virginia Law Review* 549

'The mechanisms of market efficiency twenty years later: the hindsight bias' (2003) 28 *Journal of Corporation Law* 715

Girard O., 'Les méthodes de suppression des frontières au plan mondial dans le domaine bancaire et financier' (2007–2008) 3 *Revue Européenne de droit bancaire & financier* 349

Goldstein J., 'Ideas, institutions, and American trade policy' (1988) 42 *International Organization* 179

Goldstein J. and Keohane R., 'Ideas and Foreign Policy: An Analytical Framework' in Goldstein J. and Keohane R. (eds.), *Ideas and Foreign Policy – Beliefs, Institutions, and Political Change* (Cornell University Press, Ithaca, 1993) 3

Goldstein J. and Keohane R., (eds.), *Ideas and Foreign Policy – Beliefs, Institutions, and Political Change* (Cornell University Press, Ithaca, 1993)

Goshen Z. and Parchomovsky G., 'The essential role of securities regulation' (2006) 55 *Duke Law Journal* 711

Gould S., *The Structure of Evolutionary Theory* (Harvard University Press, Harvard, 2002)

Grant J., 'NYSE Euronext moves swiftly to suspend Satyam listing' (FT online, London, 7 January 2009)

'NYSE set to challenge LSE in Europe' (FT online, 14 April 2008)

Graziano P. and Vink M. (eds.), *Europeanization – New Research Agendas* (Palgrave Macmillan, Basingstoke, 2008)

Griller S. and Orator A., 'Everything under control? The "way forward" for European agencies in the footsteps of the Meroni doctrine' (2010) 35 *European Law Review* 3

Grundfest J., 'Punctuated equilibria in the evolution of United States securities regulation' (2002) 8 *Stanford Journal of Law, Business & Finance* 1

Hall P., *Governing the Economy – The Politics of State Intervention in Britain and France* (Polity Press, Cambridge, 1986)

'Policy paradigms, social learning, and the State – the case of economic policy-making in Britain' (1993) 25 *Comparative Politics* 275

Hall P. and Taylor R. 'Political science and the three new institutionalisms' (1996) 44 *Political Studies* 936

Hayek F., *New Studies in Philosophy, Politics, Economics and the History of Ideas* (Routledge & Kegan Paul, London, 1978)

Hayes-Renshaw F. and Wallace H., 'Executive power in the European Union: the functions and limits of the Council of Ministers' (1995) 2 *Journal of European Public Policy* 559

The Council of Ministers (Palgrave Macmillan, Basingstoke, 2006)

Hearst M., 'Untangling text data mining' in *Proceedings of the 37th Annual Meeting of the Association for Computational Linguistics* (Maryland, US, June 1999)

Heine K. and Kerber W., 'European corporate laws, regulatory competition and path dependence' (2002) 13 *European Journal of Law and Economics* 47

Heisenberg D., 'The institution of "consensus" in the European Union: formal versus informal decision-making in the Council' (2005) 44 *European Journal of Political Research* 65

Héritier A., 'Mutual recognition: comparing policy areas' (2007) 14 *Journal of European Public Policy* 800

Policy-Making and Diversity in Europe – Escape from Deadlock (Cambridge University Press, Cambridge, 1999)

'The accommodation of diversity in European policy-making and its outcomes: regulatory policy as a patchwork' (1996) 3 *Journal of European Public Policy* 149

Hertig G., Kraakman R. and Rock E., 'Issuers and investor protection' in Kraakman R., Davies P., Hansmann H., Hertig G., Hopt K., Kanda H. and Rock E. (eds.), *The Anatomy of Corporate Law – A Comparative and Functional Approach* (Oxford University Press, 2004) 193

Hirschman A., *Exit, Voice, and Loyalty – Responses to Decline in Firms, Organizations and States* (Harvard University Press, Cambridge, MA, 1970)

Hix S., *The Political System of the European Union* (Palgrave Macmillan, Basingstoke, 2005)

HM Treasury, 'A new approach to financial regulation: judgement, focus and stability' (July 2010), www.hm-treasury.gov.uk/d/consult_financial_regulation_condoc.pdf

Hoevers J. and Busch D., 'Dutch securities regulator AFM grants non-EU SEC registered companies fast track access to European equity capital markets' (2007) 22 *Journal of International Banking Law and Regulation* 621

Hopt K. and Voigt H-C., 'Grundsatz- und Reformprobleme der Prospekt- und Kapitalmarktsinformationshaftung' in Hopt K. and Voigt H-C. (eds.), *Prospekt- und Kapitalmarktinformationshaftung – Recht und Reform in der Europäischen Union, der Schweiz und den USA* (Mohr Siebeck, Tübingen, 2005) 9

House of Commons, 'Banking Crisis – Vol. I' (Treasury Committee, 1 April 2009), www.publications.parliament.uk/pa/cm200809/cmselect/cmtreasy/144/144i.pdf

House of Lords European Union Committee, 'The future of EU financial regulation and supervision – Vol. II: Evidence' (14th Report of Session 2008–09), www.publications.parliament.uk/pa/ld200809/ldselect/ldeucom/106/106ii.pdf

Howells G. and Weatherill S., *Consumer Protection Law* (Ashgate, Hants, 2005)

Howlett M. and Cashore B., 'The dependent variable problem in the study of policy change: understanding policy change as a methodological problem' (2009) 11 *Journal of Comparative Policy Analysis* 33

Hudson A., *Securities Law* (Sweet & Maxwell, London, 2008)

ICMA, 'Consultation on the review of the Prospectus Directive' (letter to the European Commission, 10 March 2008), www.icmagroup.org/ICMAGroup/files/54/54d09f97–1137–402b-8cc4-c554e6229908.pdf

IOSCO, 'Principles on point of sale disclosure' (Consultation Report, November 2009), www.iosco.org/library/pubdocs/pdf/IOSCOPD310.pdf

Jackson H., 'The impact of enforcement: a reflection' (2008) 156 *University of Pennsylvania Law Review PENNumbra* 400

'Variation in the intensity of financial regulation: preliminary evidence and potential implications' (2007) 24 *Yale Journal on Regulation* 253

Jackson H. and Pan E., 'Regulatory competition in international securities markets: evidence from Europe in 1999 – Part I' (2001) 56 *Business Lawyer* 653

Jackson H. and Roe M., 'Public and private enforcement of securities laws: resource-based evidence' (2009) 93 *Journal of Financial Economics* 207

Jacobsen J., 'Much ado about ideas: the cognitive factor in economic policy' (1995) 47 *World Politics* 283

Joerges C. and Neyer J., 'From intergovernmental bargaining to deliberative political processes: the constitutionalisation of comitology' (1997) 3 *European Law Journal* 273

'Transforming strategic interaction into deliberative problem-solving: European comitology in the foodstuffs sector (1997) 4 *Journal of European Public Policy* 609

Joerges C. and Vos E. (eds.), *EU Committees: Social Regulation, Law and Politics* (Hart Publishing, Oxford, 1999)

Jolls C., Sunstein C. and Thaler R., 'A behavioral approach to law and economics' (1998) 50 *Stanford Law Review* 1471

Kahan M., 'Securities laws and the social costs of "inaccurate" stock prices' (1992) 41 *Duke Law Journal* 977

Kahneman D. and Tversky A., 'Judgment under uncertainty: heuristics and biases' (1974) 185 *Science* 1124

'Prospect theory: an analysis of decision under risk' (1979) 47 *Econometrica* 263

Kahneman D. and Krueger A., 'Developments in the measurement of subjective well-being' (2006) 20 *Journal of Economic Perspectives* 3

Kindgon J., 'Politicians, self-interest, and ideas' in G. Marcus and R. Hanson (eds.), *Reconsidering the Democratic Public* (Pennsylvania State University Press, University Park PA, 1993)

Kitch E., 'Proposals for Reform of Securities Regulation: An Overview' (2001) 41 *Virginia Journal of International Law* 629

Knill C. and Lehmkuhl D., 'The national impact of European Union regulatory policy: three Europeanization mechanisms' (2002) 41 *European Journal of Political Research* 255

Koutrakos P., *EU International Relations Law* (Hart Publishing, Oxford, 2006)

'Primary law and policy in EU external relations: moving away from the big picture' (2008) 33 *European Law Review* 666

Krasner S., 'Approaches to the State: alternative conceptions and historical dynamics' (1984) 16 *Comparative Politics* 223

La Porta R., Lopez-de-Silanes F. and Shleifer A., 'The economic consequences of legal origins' (2008) 46 *Journal of Economic Literature* 285

'What works in securities laws?' (2006) 61 *Journal of Finance* 1

La Porta R., Lopez-de-Silanes F., Shleifer A. and Vishny R., 'Law and finance' (1998) 106 *Journal of Political Economy* 1113

'Legal determinants of external finance' (1997) 52 *Journal of Finance* 1131

Lamfalussy Committee, 'Final report of the Committee of Wise Men on the regulation of European securities markets' (Brussels, 15 February 2001), http://ec.europa.eu/internal_market/securities/docs/lamfalussy/wisemen/final-report-wise-men_en.pdf

Langevoort D., 'Taming the animal spirits of the stock markets: a behavioral approach to securities regulation' (2002) 97 *Northwestern University Law Review* 135

Lenaerts K., 'Regulating the regulatory process: "delegation of powers" in the European Community' (1993) 18 *European Law Review* 23

Lenschow A., 'Europeanisation of public policy' in Richardson J. (ed.), *European Union – Power and Policy-making* (Routledge, Abingdon, 2006) 55

Levitt S. and List J., 'Homo economicus evolves' (2008) 319 *Science* 909

Lewis C., Rogalski R. and Seward J., 'Understanding the design of convertible debt' (1998) 11 *Journal of Applied Corporate Finance* 45.

Lewis J., 'Informal integration and the supranational construction of the Council' (2003) 10 *Journal of European Public Policy* 996

'Institutional environments and everyday EU decision making: rationalist or constructivist? (2003) 36 *Comparative Political Studies* 97
Lindblom C., 'Still muddling, not yet through' (1979) 39 *Public Administration Review* 517
'The science of 'muddling through' (1959) 19 *Public Administration* 79
Linklaters, 'Amendments to Prospectus Directive published' (10 July 2010), www.linklaters.com/pdfs/publications/PDReview_ClientNote.pdf
Loss L. and Seligman J., *Fundamentals of Securities Regulation* (Aspen, New York, 2004)
Mahoney, P., 'Mandatory disclosure as a solution to agency problems' (1995) 62 *University of Chicago Law Review* 1047
'The exchange as regulator' (1997) 83 *Virginia Law Review* 1453
Mahoney, P. and Majone G., *Dilemmas of European Integration* (Oxford University Press, Oxford, 2009)
'The credibility crisis of Community regulation' (2000) 38 *Journal of Common Market Studies* 273
'The future of regulation in Europe' in G. Majone, (ed.), *Regulating Europe* (Routledge, London, 1996) 265
'The new European agencies: regulation by information' (1997) 4 *Journal of European Public Policy* 262
'The rise of the regulatory state in Europe' (1994) 17 *West European Politics* 77
'Two logics of delegation – agency and fiduciary relations in EU governance' (2001) 2 *European Union Politics* 103
Marini P., 'Rapport fait au nom de la commission des finances, du contrôle budgétaire et des comptes économiques de la Nation (1) sur le projet de loi, adopté part l'Assemblée nationale, après déclaration d'urgence, portant mesures urgentes de réformes à caractère économique et financier' (Rapport n°336, Session Ordinaire de 2000–2001), www.senat.fr/rap/l00-336/l00-3361.pdf
Mazey S. and Richardson J. 'Interest groups and EU policy-making – organisational logic and venue shopping' in Richardson J. (ed.), *European Union – Power and Policy-making* (Routledge, London, 2006) 247
McNamara K., *The Currency of Ideas: Monetary Politics in the European Union* (Cornell University Press, Ithaca, New York, 1998)
Méadal J., *Les Marchés Financiers et l'Ordre Public* (L.G.D.J., Paris, 2007)
Mendales R., 'Collaterized explosive devices: why securities regulation failed to prevent the CDO meltdown, and how to fix it' (2009) 5 *University of Illinois Law Review* 1359
Moloney N., 'Building a retail investment culture through law: the 2004 Markets in Financial Instruments Directive' (2005) 6 *European Business Organization Law Review* 341
EC Securities Regulation (Oxford University Press, 2008)
Moravcsik A., *The Choice for Europe – Social Purpose and State Power from Messina to Maastricht* (UCL Press, London, 1998)

Nahrath S., 'The power of ideas in policy research: a critical assessment' in Braun D. and Busch A. (eds.), *Public Policy and Political Ideas* (Edward Elgar, Cheltenham, 1999) 41

NewGov (J. Almer), 'The reform of comitology and the parallel reform of the European financial services sector' (ref. 7/D07c, December 2006), www.eu-newgov.org

Nicolaïdis K., 'Regulatory cooperation and managed mutual recognition: elements of a strategic model' in Bermann G., Herdegen M. and Lindseth P. (eds.), *Transatlantic Regulatory Cooperation – Legal Problems and Political Prospects* (Oxford University Press, 2000) 571

Nicolaïdis K. and Schmidt S., 'Mutual recognition on "trial": the long road to services liberalization' (2007) 14 *Journal of European Public Policy* 717

Nicolaïdis K. and Shaffer G., 'Transnational mutual recognition regimes: governance without global government' (2005) 68 *Law and Contemporary Problems* 263

NYSE Euronext, 'Fast path listing using SEC filings' (International Listing Guide 2008), www.euronext.com/fic/000/033/111/331110.pdf

'NYSE Euronext welcomes NYSE-listed Satyam Computer Services to its European Market. First issuer to seek cross-listing on NYSE Euronext in Europe using fast-path' (Press Release, 23 January 2008), www.euronext.com/news/press_release/press_release-1731-EN.html?docid=491514

O'Keeffe D., 'Exclusive, concurrent and shared competence' in Dashwood A. and C. Hillion (eds.), *The General Law of E.C. External Relations* (Sweet & Maxwell, London, 2000) 115

Ogus A., *Regulation – Legal Form and Economic Theory* (Hart Publishing, Oxford, 2004)

Ortino O., 'The role and functioning of mutual recognition in the European market of financial services' (2007) 56 *International and Comparative Law Quarterly* 309

Pang B. and Lee L., 'Opinion mining and sentiment analysis' (2008) 2 *Foundations and Trends in Information Retrieval* 1

Peterson J. and Bomberg E., *Decision-making in the European Union* (Macmillan Press, Basingstoke, 1999)

Piao S., Tsuruoka Y. and Ananiadou S., 'Sentiment analysis with knowledge resource and NLP Tools' (2009) 4 *International Journal of Interdisciplinary Social Sciences* 17.

Piris J-C., *The Lisbon Treaty – A Legal and Political Analysis* (Cambridge University Press, 2010)

Pistor K., 'Legal ground rules in coordinated and liberal market economies' in K. Hopt, E. Wymeersch, H. Kanda and H. Baum (eds.), *Corporate Governance in Context – Corporations, States, and Markets in Europe, Japan, and the US* (Oxford University Press, 2005)

Pollack M., 'Representing diffuse interests in EC policy-making' (1997) 4 *Journal of European Public Policy* 572

Ponzano P., '"Executive" and "delegated" acts: the situation after the Lisbon Treaty' in Griller S. and Ziller J. (eds.), *The Lisbon Treaty – EU Constitutionalism without a Constitutional Treaty?* (Springer, Vienna, 2008) 135

Posner R., 'Reply to comments' (2010) 6 *Journal of Institutional Economics* 139

Prentice R., 'The case of the irrational auditor: a behavioral insight into securities fraud litigation' (2000) 95 *Northwestern University Law Review* 133

'Whither securities regulation? Some behavioral observations regarding proposals for its future' (2002) 51 *Duke Law Journal* 1397

Puttfarken H-J. and Schrader, 'Frankreich' in Hopt K. and Voigt H-C. (eds.), *Prospekt- und Kapitalmarktinformationshaftung – Recht und Reform in der Europäischen Union, der Schweiz und den USA* (Mohr Siebeck, Tübingen, 2005)

Quaglia L., 'Financial sector committee governance in the European Union' (2008) 30 *Journal of European Integration* 563

Radaelli C., 'The Europeanization of public policy' in Featherstone K. and Radaelli C. (eds.), *The Politics of Europeanization* (Oxford University Press, 2003) 27

'The puzzle of regulatory competition' (2004) 24 *Journal of Public Policy* 1

Rein M. and Schön D., 'Frame-reflective policy discourse' in Wagner P., Hirschon Weiss C., Wittrock B. and Wollmann H. (eds.), *Social Sciences and Modern States – National Experiences and Theoretical Crossroads* (Cambridge University Press, 1991) 262

Rhinard M., *Ideas, interests, and policy change in the European Union: the mobilization of frames by actors in the agricultural and biotechnical policy sectors* (D.Phil. dissertation, unpublished, Cambridge University, 2002)

Rock E., 'Securities regulation as lobster trap: a credible commitment theory of mandatory disclosure' (2002) 23 *Cardozo Law Review* 675

Romano R., 'Empowering investors: a market approach to securities regulation' (1998) 107 *Yale Law Journal* 2359

The Advantage of Competitive Federalism for Securities Regulation (AEI Press, Washington D.C., 2002)

The Genius of American Corporate Law (AEI Press, Washington D.C., 1993)

Rosamond B., *Theories of European Integration* (Palgrave Macmillan, Basingstoke, 2000)

Rosenfeld E. and Veil J., 'Sanctions administratives, sanction pénales' *Pouvoirs* 2009/1 n° 128, p. 61

Saurugger S. and Radaelli C., 'The Europeanization of public policies: introduction' (2008) 10 *Journal of Comparative Policy Analysis* 213

Schammo P., 'Arbitrage and abuse of rights in the EC legal system' (2008) 14 *European Law Journal* 351

'Comments on abuse of rights' in de la Feria R. and Vogenauer S. (eds.), *Prohibition of Abuse of Law – A New General Principle of EU Law* (Hart Publishing, Oxford, 2010)

'The prospectus approval system' (2006) 7 *European Business Organization Law Review* 501

The Prospectus Directive – new perspectives on issuer's choice and regulatory competition (D.Phil. dissertation, unpublished, Oxford University 2006)

Scharpf F., *Games Real Actors Play – Actor-centered Institutionalism in Policy Research* (Westview Press, Boulder CO, 1997)

Governing in Europe – Effective and Democratic? (Oxford University Press, Oxford, 1999)

'Institutions in comparative policy research' (2000) 33 *Comparative Political Studies* 762

'Legitimate diversity: the new challenge of European integration' in Börzel T. and Chichowski R. (eds.), *The State of the European Union Vol. 6 – Law, Politics, and Society* (Oxford University Press, Oxford, 2003) 79

'The joint-decision trap: lessons from German federalism and European integration' (1988) 66 *Public Administration* 239

'The joint decision trap revisited' (2006) 44 *Journal of Common Market Studies* 845

'What have we learned? Problem solving capacity of the multilevel European polity' (MPIfG Working Paper 01/4, July 2001), www.mpi-fg-koeln.mpg.de/pu/workpap/wp01–4/wp01–4.html

Schmidt V., 'Europeanization and the mechanics of economic policy adjustment' (2002) 9 *Journal of European Public Policy* 894

The Futures of European Capitalism (Oxford University Press, 2002)

Schneider H. and Haag H., 'Retail cascading in Germany – a model for a revision of the PD' (2007) 2 *Capital Markets Law Journal* 370

Schön D. and Rein M., *Frame Reflection – Toward the Resolution of Intractable Policy Controversies* (BasicBooks, New York, 1994)

Schusterschitz G. and Kotz S., 'The comitology reform of 2006' (2007) 3 *European Constitutional Law Review* 68

Schwarcz S., 'Disclosure's failure in the subprime mortgage crisis' (2008) 3 *Utah Law Review* 1109

Schwartz G., 'Reality in the economic analysis of tort law: does tort law really deter?' (1994) 42 *UCLA Law Review* 377

Scott H., 'Internationalization of primary public securities markets' (2000) 63 *Law and Contemporary Problems* 71

Shleifer A., *Inefficient Markets – An Introduction to Behavioral Finance* (Oxford University Press, 2000)

Siems M., 'What does not work in comparing securities laws: a critique on La Porta *et al.*'s methodology' (2005) 16 *International Company and Commercial Law Review* 300

Siems M. and Deakin S., 'Comparative law and finance: past, present and future research' (2010) 166 *Journal of Institutional and Theoretical Economics* 120

Simon H., 'A behavioral model of rational choice' (1955) 69 *Quarterly Journal of Economics* 99

Slot P., 'Harmonisation' (1996) 21 *European Law Review* 378

St Clair Bradley K., 'Halfway house: the 2006 comitology reforms and the European Parliament' (2008) 31 *West European Politics* 837

Stigler G., 'Public regulation of the securities markets' (1964) 37 *Journal of Business* 117

Streit M., 'Comment [on: R. Van den Bergh 'The subsidiarity principle and the EC competition rules: the costs and benefits of decentralisation']' in Schmidtchen D. and Cooter R. (eds.), *Constitutional Law and Economics of the European Union* (Edward Elgar, Cheltenham, 1997) 184

Sun J-M. and Pelkmans J., 'Regulatory competition in the single market' (1995) 33 *Journal of Common Market Studies* 67

Sunstein C., 'Behavioral law and economics: a progress report' (1999) 1 *American Law and Economics Review* 115

Sunstein C. and Thaler R., 'Libertarian paternalism is not an oxymoron' (2003) 70 *University of Chicago Law Review* 1159

Tafara E. and Peterson R., 'A blueprint for cross-border access to U.S. investors: a new international framework' (2007) 48 *Harvard International Law Journal* 31

Thaler R. and Sunstein C., *Nudge – Improving Decisions about Health, Wealth and Happiness* (Penguin Books, London, 2009)

Thatcher M., 'Regulatory agencies, the state and markets: a Franco-British comparison' (2007) 14 *Journal of European Public Policy* 1028

Thatcher M. and Coen D., 'Reshaping European regulatory space: an evolutionary analysis' (2008) 31 *West European Politics* 806

Tiebout C., 'A pure theory of local expenditures' (1956) 64 *Journal of Political Economy* 416

Tison M., 'Financial market integration in the post-FSAP era – In search of overall conceptual consistency in the regulatory framework' in Ferrarini G. and Wymeersch E. (eds.), *Investor Protection in Europe – Corporate Law Making, the MiFID and Beyond* (Oxford University Press, 2006) 443

Tjiong H., 'Breaking the spell of regulatory competition: reframing the problem of regulatory exit' (2002) 66 *Rabels Zeitschrift für ausländisches und internationales Privatrecht* 66

Tung F., 'Lost in translation: from U.S. corporate charter competition to issuer choice in international securities regulation' (2005) 39 *Georgia Law Review* 525.

Van Gerven D., 'General provisions of Community law relating to the prospectus to be published when securities are offered to the public or admitted to trading' in Van Gerven D. (ed.), *Prospectus for the Public Offering of Securities in Europe – Vol. I* (Cambridge University Press, 2008) 3.

Van Gerven D., (ed.), *Prospectus for the Public Offering of Securities in Europe – Vol. I* (Cambridge University Press, 2008)

Vos E., '50 years of European integration, 45 years of comitology' (Maastricht Faculty of Law Working Papers, 2009–3), http://papers.ssrn.com/sol3/papers.cfm?abstract_id=1345729

Vos E., 'The rise of committees' (1997) 3 *European Law Journal* 210

Wagner H. and Limpach M., 'Debt restructurings in connection with Luxembourg listed securities' (2003) 18 *Journal of International Banking Law and Regulation* 453

Weatherill S., 'Beyond preemption? Shared competence and constitutional change in the European Community' in O'Keeffe D. and Twomey P. (eds.), *Legal Issues of the Maastricht Treaty* (Chancery Law Publishing, London, 1994) 13

Cases and Materials on EU Law (Oxford University Press, Oxford, 2010)

'Pre-emption, harmonisation and the distribution of competence to regulate the internal market' in Barnard C. and Scott J. (eds.), *The Law of the Single European Market – Unpacking the Premises* (Hart Publishing, Oxford, 2002) 41

'Why harmonise?' in Tridimas P. and Nebbia P. (eds), *European Union Law for the Twenty-First Century – Rethinking the New Legal Order, Vol. 2* (Hart Publishing, Oxford, 2004) 11

Wei T-b. 'The equivalence approach to securities regulation' (2007) *Northwestern Journal of International Law & Business* 255

Weiler J., 'The transformation of Europe' (1991) 100 *Yale Law Journal* 2403

Wilson T., Wiebe J., and Hoffmann P., 'Recognizing contextual polarity: an exploration of features for phrase-level sentiment analysis' (2009) 35 *Computational Linguistics* 399

'Recognizing contextual polarity in phrase-level sentiment analysis' in *Proceedings of the Conference on Human Language Technology and Empirical Methods in Natural Language Processing* (Vancouver, Canada, October 2005) 347

Wood P., *Law and Practice of International Finance* (Sweet & Maxwell, London, 2008).

Woolcock S., 'Competition among rules in the single European market' in W. Bratton, J. McCahery, S. Picciotto and C. Scott (eds.), *International Regulatory Competition and Coordination: Perspectives on Economic Regulation in Europe and the United States* (Clarendon Press, Oxford, 1996)

Wouters J., Coppens D., and De Meester B., 'The European Union's external relations after the Lisbon Treaty' in Griller S. and Ziller J. (eds.), *The Lisbon Treaty – EU Constitutionalism without a Constitutional Treaty?* (Springer, Vienna, 2008) 143

Wyatt D., 'Community competence to regulate the internal market' in Dougan M. and Currie S. (eds.), *50 Years of the European Treaties: Looking Back and Thinking Forward* (Hart Publishing, Oxford, 2009)

Wymeersch E., 'Preparing for the Future' (CESR/09-203, Speech, 23 February 2009)

'Presentation at the International Conference of the "Giordano Dell'Amore"' (S&C 2010–01, January 2010), www.law.ugent.be/fli/wps/pdf/S&C2010–01.pdf

Yee A., 'The causal effects of ideas on policies' (1996) 50 *International Organization* 69

INDEX

PD denotes Prospectus Directive